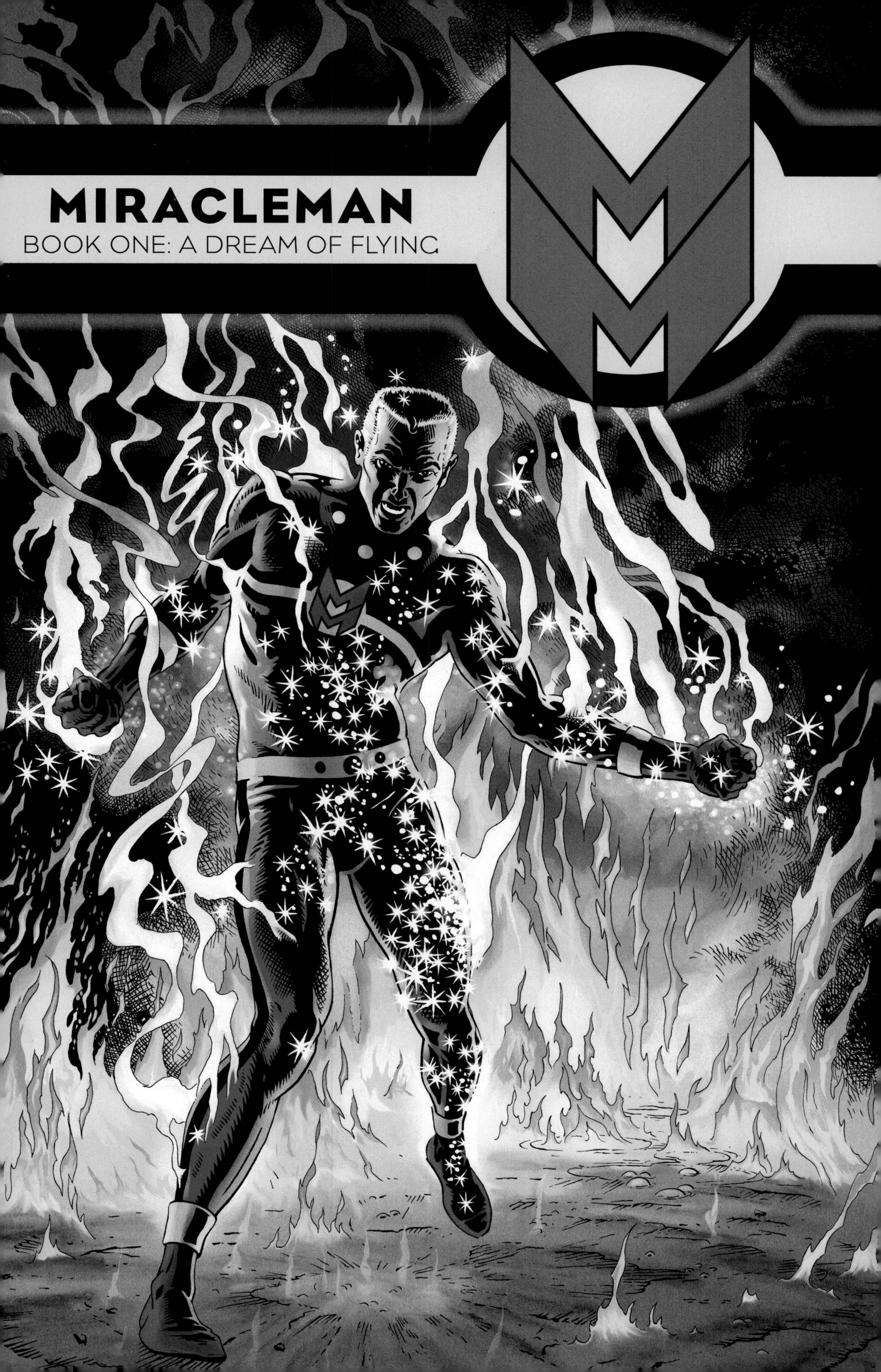
MIRACLEMAN
BOOK ONE: A DREAM OF FLYING

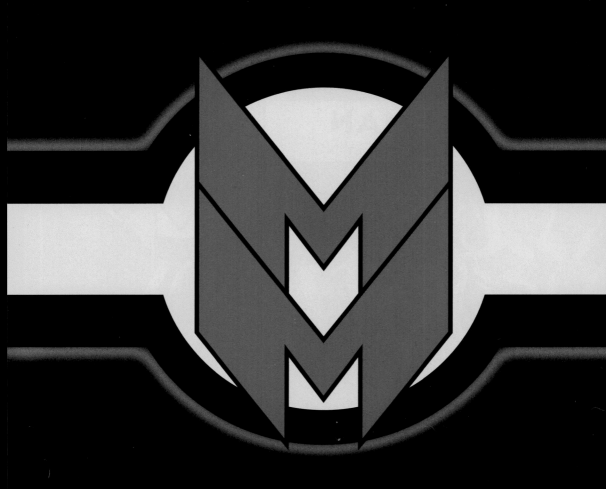

RESTORATION & COLLECTION EDITOR – **CORY SEDLMEIER**

BOOK DESIGN – **JEFF POWELL** · MANAGER, TALENT RELATIONS – **GEORGE BELIARD**

SVP PRINT, SALES & MARKETING – **DAVID GABRIEL** · EDITOR IN CHIEF – **AXEL ALONSO**

CHIEF CREATIVE OFFICER – **JOE QUESADA** · PUBLISHER – **DAN BUCKLEY** · EXECUTIVE PRODUCER – **ALAN FINE**

SPECIAL THANKS TO **ALAN DAVIS** WHOSE COOPERATION HAS MADE THIS PUBLICATION POSSIBLE

SPECIAL THANKS FOR THE CONTRIBUTION OF ORIGINAL ARTWORK –
GARRY LEACH, ALAN DAVIS, DEREK WILSON, DR. SRIHARI NAIDU, VINCENT ZURZOLO, METROPOLIS COLLECTIBLES, FELIX LU, JOHN BUTLER, STEVEN LEE, KEITH VERONESE, ANDREW WILSON, STEVE HAYES, JOHNNY CRESSWELL, COURT GEBEAU, KEVIN HOFFMAN AND GEORGE KHOURY

MIRACLEMAN BOOK 1: A DREAM OF FLYING. Contains material originally published in magazine form as MIRACLEMAN #1-4. First printing 2014. ISBN# 978-0-7851-5462-4. Published by MARVEL WORLDWIDE, INC., a subsidiary of MARVEL ENTERTAINMENT, LLC. OFFICE OF PUBLICATION: 135 West 50th Street, New York, NY 10020. **Printed in the U.S.A.** ALAN FINE, EVP - Office of the President, Marvel Worldwide, Inc. and EVP & CMO Marvel Characters B.V.; DAN BUCKLEY, Publisher & President - Print, Animation & Digital Divisions; JOE QUESADA, Chief Creative Officer; TOM BREVOORT, SVP of Publishing; DAVID BOGART, SVP of Operations & Procurement, Publishing; C.B. CEBULSKI, SVP of Creator & Content Development; DAVID GABRIEL, SVP Print, Sales & Marketing; JIM O'KEEFE, VP of Operations & Logistics; DAN CARR, Executive Director of Publishing Technology; SUSAN CRESPI, Editorial Operations Manager; ALEX MORALES, Publishing Operations Manager; STAN LEE, Chairman Emeritus. For information regarding advertising in Marvel Comics or on Marvel.com, please contact Niza Disla, Director of Marvel Partnerships, at ndisla@marvel.com. For Marvel subscription inquiries, please call 800-217-9158. **Manufactured between 3/21/2014 and 4/28/2014 by WORZALLA PUBLISHING CO., STEVENS POINT, WI, USA.**

10 9 8 7 6 5 4 3 2 1

MIRACLEMAN

BOOK ONE: A DREAM OF FLYING

STORY

THE ORIGINAL WRITER

WITH **MICK ANGLO**

ART

GARRY LEACH & ALAN DAVIS

WITH **DON LAWRENCE, STEVE DILLON & PAUL NEARY**

COLOR ART

STEVE OLIFF

LETTERING

JOE CARAMAGNA
AND **CHRIS ELIOPOULOS**

ART RESTORATION

MICHAEL KELLEHER & KELLUSTRATION
AND **GARRY LEACH**

MIRACLEMAN
BOOK ONE: A DREAM OF FLYING

PROLOGUE, 1956:
"THE INVADERS FROM THE FUTURE".................

CHAPTER ONE:
"...A DREAM OF FLYING"..........................

CHAPTER TWO:
"LEGENDS"......................................

CHAPTER THREE:
"WHEN JOHNNY COMES MARCHING HOME..."........

CHAPTER FOUR:
"DRAGONS"......................................

CHAPTER FIVE:
"FALLEN ANGELS, FORGOTTEN THUNDER.".........

CHAPTER SIX:
"SECRET IDENTITY"..............................

CHAPTER SEVEN:
"BLUE MURDER"..................................

CHAPTER EIGHT:
"OUT OF THE DARK"..............................

CHAPTER NINE:
"INSIDE STORY".................................

CHAPTER TEN:
"ZARATHUSTRA"..................................

CHAPTER ELEVEN:
"SATURDAY MORNING PICTURES"....................

A GLIMPSE INTO THE FUTURE

"THE YESTERDAY GAMBIT"..........................

THE WARPSMITHS

CHAPTERS ONE & TWO:
"COLD WAR, COLD WARRIOR."......................

CHAPTER THREE:
"GHOSTDANCE"...................................

MIRACLEMAN BEHIND THE SCENES....................

PROLOGUE

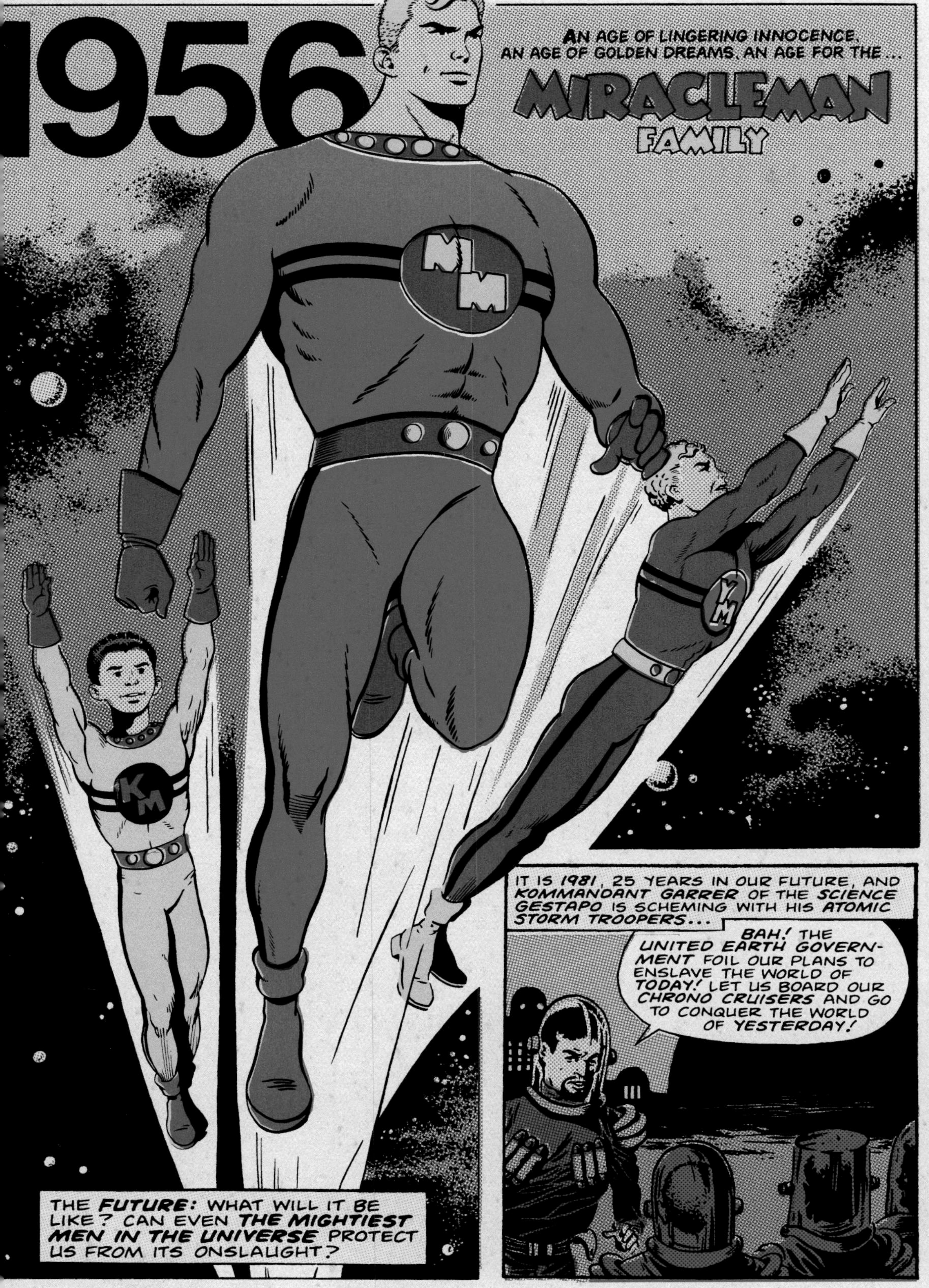

1956
AN AGE OF LINGERING INNOCENCE. AN AGE OF GOLDEN DREAMS. AN AGE FOR THE . . .
MIRACLEMAN FAMILY
THE FUTURE: WHAT WILL IT BE LIKE? CAN EVEN THE MIGHTIEST MEN IN THE UNIVERSE PROTECT US FROM ITS ONSLAUGHT?
IT IS 1981, 25 YEARS IN OUR FUTURE, AND KOMMANDANT GARRER OF THE SCIENCE GESTAPO IS SCHEMING WITH HIS ATOMIC STORM TROOPERS...
BAH! THE UNITED EARTH GOVERNMENT FOIL OUR PLANS TO ENSLAVE THE WORLD OF TODAY! LET US BOARD OUR CHRONO CRUISERS AND GO TO CONQUER THE WORLD OF YESTERDAY!

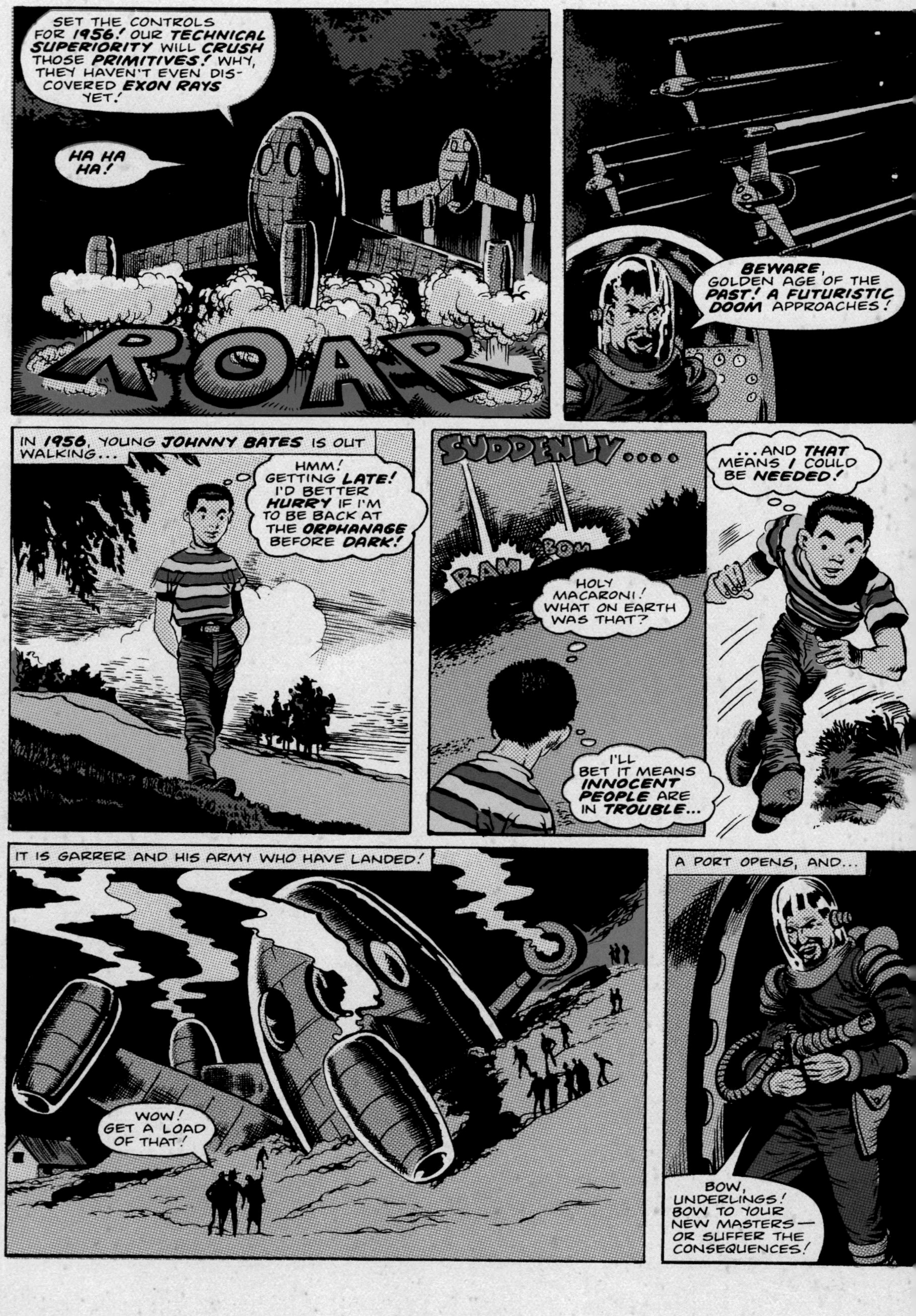
SET THE CONTROLS FOR 1956! OUR TECHNICAL SUPERIORITY WILL CRUSH THOSE PRIMITIVES! WHY, THEY HAVEN'T EVEN DIS-COVERED EXON RAYS YET!
HA HA HA!
ROAR
BEWARE, GOLDEN AGE OF THE PAST! A FUTURISTIC DOOM APPROACHES!
IN 1956, YOUNG JOHNNY BATES IS OUT WALKING...
HMM! GETTING LATE! I'D BETTER HURRY IF I'M TO BE BACK AT THE ORPHANAGE BEFORE DARK!
SUDDENLY....
BAM
BOM
HOLY MACARONI! WHAT ON EARTH WAS THAT?
I'LL BET IT MEANS INNOCENT PEOPLE ARE IN TROUBLE...
...AND THAT MEANS I COULD BE NEEDED!
IT IS GARRER AND HIS ARMY WHO HAVE LANDED!
WOW! GET A LOAD OF THAT!
A PORT OPENS, AND...
BOW, UNDERLINGS! BOW TO YOUR NEW MASTERS— OR SUFFER THE CONSEQUENCES!

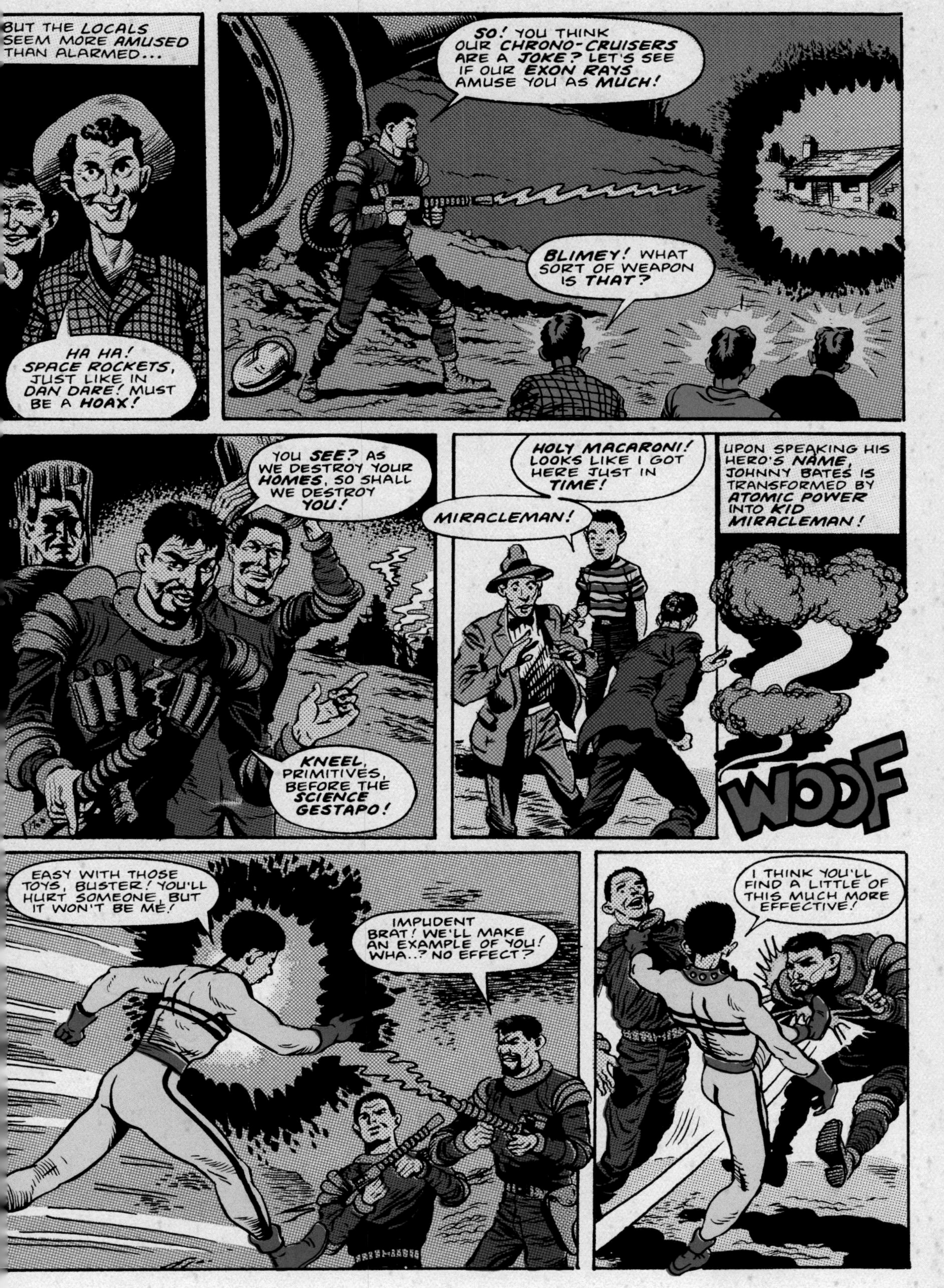

BUT THE LOCALS SEEM MORE AMUSED THAN ALARMED...
HA HA! SPACE ROCKETS, JUST LIKE IN DAN DARE! MUST BE A HOAX!
SO! YOU THINK OUR CHRONO-CRUISERS ARE A JOKE? LET'S SEE IF OUR EXON RAYS AMUSE YOU AS MUCH!
BLIMEY! WHAT SORT OF WEAPON IS THAT?
YOU SEE? AS WE DESTROY YOUR HOMES, SO SHALL WE DESTROY YOU!
KNEEL, PRIMITIVES, BEFORE THE SCIENCE GESTAPO!
HOLY MACARONI! LOOKS LIKE I GOT HERE JUST IN TIME!
MIRACLEMAN!
UPON SPEAKING HIS HERO'S NAME, JOHNNY BATES IS TRANSFORMED BY ATOMIC POWER INTO KID MIRACLEMAN!
WOOF
EASY WITH THOSE TOYS, BUSTER! YOU'LL HURT SOMEONE, BUT IT WON'T BE ME!
IMPUDENT BRAT! WE'LL MAKE AN EXAMPLE OF YOU! WHA..? NO EFFECT?
I THINK YOU'LL FIND A LITTLE OF THIS MUCH MORE EFFECTIVE!

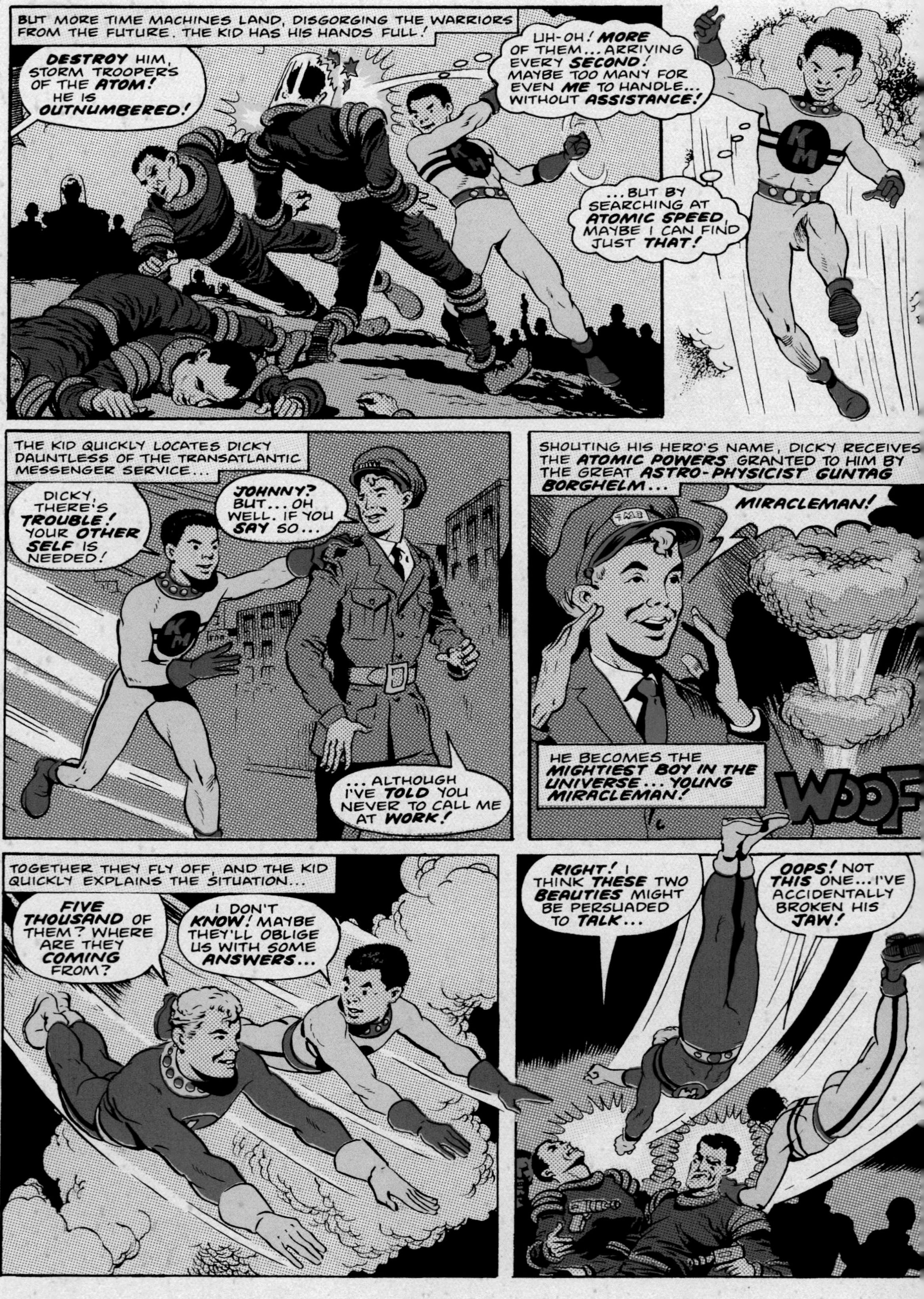

BUT MORE TIME MACHINES LAND, DISGORGING THE WARRIORS FROM THE FUTURE. THE KID HAS HIS HANDS FULL!
DESTROY HIM, STORM TROOPERS OF THE ATOM! HE IS OUTNUMBERED!
UH-OH! MORE OF THEM... ARRIVING EVERY SECOND! MAYBE TOO MANY FOR EVEN ME TO HANDLE... WITHOUT ASSISTANCE!
...BUT BY SEARCHING AT ATOMIC SPEED MAYBE I CAN FIND JUST THAT!
THE KID QUICKLY LOCATES DICKY DAUNTLESS OF THE TRANSATLANTIC MESSENGER SERVICE...
DICKY, THERE'S TROUBLE! YOUR OTHER SELF IS NEEDED!
JOHNNY? BUT... OH WELL. IF YOU SAY SO...
...ALTHOUGH I'VE TOLD YOU NEVER TO CALL ME AT WORK!
SHOUTING HIS HERO'S NAME, DICKY RECEIVES THE ATOMIC POWERS GRANTED TO HIM BY THE GREAT ASTRO-PHYSICIST GUNTAG BORGHELM...
MIRACLEMAN!
HE BECOMES THE MIGHTIEST BOY IN THE UNIVERSE... YOUNG MIRACLEMAN!
WOOF
TOGETHER THEY FLY OFF, AND THE KID QUICKLY EXPLAINS THE SITUATION...
FIVE THOUSAND OF THEM? WHERE ARE THEY COMING FROM?
I DON'T KNOW! MAYBE THEY'LL OBLIGE US WITH SOME ANSWERS...
RIGHT! I THINK THESE TWO BEAUTIES MIGHT BE PERSUADED TO TALK...
OOPS! NOT THIS ONE... I'VE ACCIDENTALLY BROKEN HIS JAW!

BUT NO SOONER DO THE INVADERS HIT THE GROUND THAN THEY RECOVER!

I DON'T GET IT! THEY SHOULD STAY OUT FOR HOURS! I'M NOT PULLING MY PUNCHES!

NOR AM I! WHAT SAY WE GRAB ONE OF THESE CHARACTERS AND ASK SOME QUESTIONS?

GREAT IDEA! THIS GUY WILL DO FOR A START! EASY, PAL!

HOW IS IT THAT YOU'RE ABLE TO WITHSTAND OUR HAMMERING?

TERRIFIED, THE TROOPER EXPLAINS.

WE COME FROM 1981... DECADES IN YOUR FUTURE! WE HAVE WEAPONS THAT CAN TURN WHOLE CITIES TO DUST!

"EVEN NOW OUR LEADER'S ATOMIC STORM TROOPERS ARE ARRIVING IN YOUR WORLD'S OTHER NATIONS. RESISTANCE IS FUTILE!"

PARIS.

PARIS HAS FALLEN TO THE SCIENCE GESTAPO! ON TO WASHINGTON!

SAIGON:

HAH! OUR FUTURISTIC WEAPONS BURN THEIR HOMES AND CROPS! THEY ARE DEFEATED!

IN THE OFFICES OF THE DAILY BUGLE, COPYBOY MICKY MORAN READS THE AWFUL STOP-PRESS NEWS...

LOOKS LIKE MIRACLEMAN IS NEEDED IN A HURRY!

...DAILY BUGLE com! DISASTER!!

KIMOTA!

SPEAKING THE SECRET KEY HARMONIC OF THE UNIVERSE MICKY CHANGES..

WOOF

...INTO THE MIGHTY MIRACLEMAN!

I'LL START BY VISITING CORNWALL, WHERE THE FIRST LANDINGS WERE REPORTED...

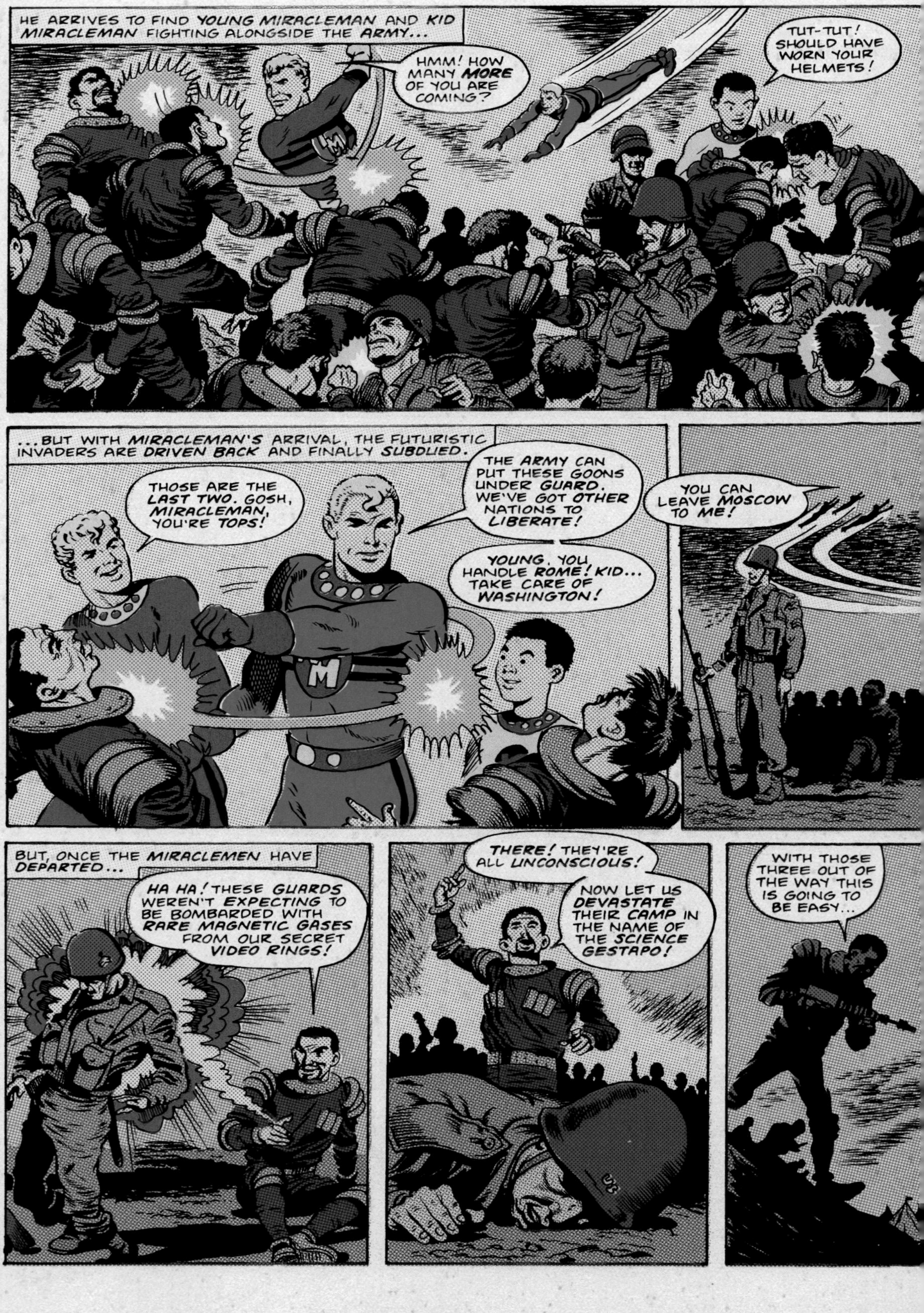
HE ARRIVES TO FIND YOUNG MIRACLEMAN AND KID MIRACLEMAN FIGHTING ALONGSIDE THE ARMY...
HMM! HOW MANY MORE OF YOU ARE COMING?
TUT-TUT! SHOULD HAVE WORN YOUR HELMETS!
...BUT WITH MIRACLEMAN'S ARRIVAL, THE FUTURISTIC INVADERS ARE DRIVEN BACK AND FINALLY SUBDUED.
THOSE ARE THE LAST TWO. GOSH, MIRACLEMAN, YOU'RE TOPS!
THE ARMY CAN PUT THESE GOONS UNDER GUARD. WE'VE GOT OTHER NATIONS TO LIBERATE!
YOUNG, YOU HANDLE ROME! KID... TAKE CARE OF WASHINGTON!
YOU CAN LEAVE MOSCOW TO ME!
BUT, ONCE THE MIRACLEMEN HAVE DEPARTED...
HA HA! THESE GUARDS WEREN'T EXPECTING TO BE BOMBARDED WITH RARE MAGNETIC GASES FROM OUR SECRET VIDEO RINGS!
THERE! THEY'RE ALL UNCONSCIOUS!
NOW LET US DEVASTATE THEIR CAMP IN THE NAME OF THE SCIENCE GESTAPO!
WITH THOSE THREE OUT OF THE WAY THIS IS GOING TO BE EASY...

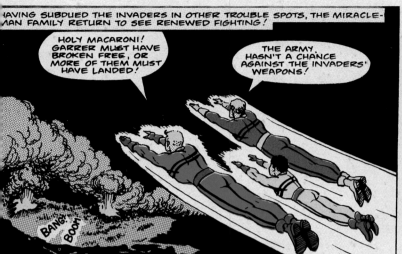

HAVING SUBDUED THE INVADERS IN OTHER TROUBLE SPOTS, THE MIRACLE-MAN FAMILY RETURN TO SEE RENEWED FIGHTING!

HOLY MACARONI! GARRER MUST HAVE BROKEN FREE, OR MORE OF THEM MUST HAVE LANDED!

THE ARMY HASN'T A CHANCE AGAINST THE INVADERS' WEAPONS!

BANG! BOOM!

WE'LL SPLIT UP! YOU TAKE THE LEFT FLANK, THE KID WILL TAKE THE RIGHT...

WITH YOU IN THE CENTRE! MICKY, THAT'S A MARVELLOUS IDEA!

GOOD LUCK, BOYS! WE'LL GIVE THEM A DRUBBING THIS TIME THAT THEY WON'T FORGET IN A HURRY!

WE'LL KNOCK THEM BACK YEARS INTO THE FUTURE!

BUT, AS GARRER SEES MIRACLEMAN APPROACH...

HAH! I'LL OUTSMART HIM YET! BLOW UP OUR CHRONO-CRUISERS!

IMMEDIATELY, ALL THE MACHINES ARE DESTROYED!

BOOM

WHAT'S THE IDEA BEHIND DESTROYING YOUR SHIPS! YOU'LL NEVER GET BACK TO 1981!

EXACTLY! WE ARE STRANDED IN YOUR TIME, AND COMPLETELY INDESTRUCTIBLE! AS MORE AND MORE OF MY MEN ARRIVE, THEY WILL DESTROY THEIR SHIPS, TOO!

JUST THEN THE BOYS ARRIVE FROM THE FLANKS WITH BAD NEWS...

WE'RE UP AGAINST A BRICK WALL! AS FAST AS WE KNOCK THEM DOWN, THEY GET UP!

WHAT CAN WE DO TO PUT THESE GUYS DOWN?

HMM! I'VE AN IDEA. NOW LISTEN TO ME CAREFULLY...

KID, YOU STAY HERE AND DO WHAT YOU CAN, WHILE WE GO FORWARD TO THE FUTURE, TO THEIR POINT OF DEPARTURE!

OKAY, M-M! WHATEVER YOU *SAY!*

WE'LL BE BACK AS SOON AS WE CAN, KID!

GOOD LUCK! I'LL DO WHAT I CAN THIS END!

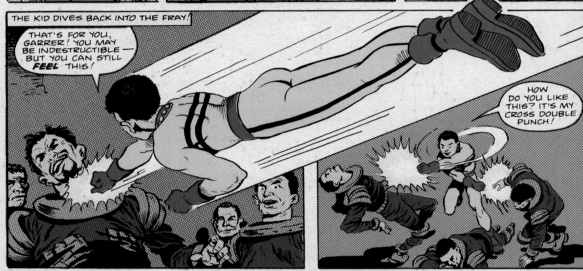

THE KID DIVES BACK INTO THE FRAY!

THAT'S FOR YOU, GARRER! YOU MAY BE INDESTRUCTIBLE — BUT YOU CAN STILL *FEEL* THIS!

HOW DO YOU LIKE THIS? IT'S MY CROSS DOUBLE PUNCH!

MEANWHILE, THE OTHER TWO RACE FORWARD IN TIME AT *ATOMIC SPEED...*

WELL, MICKY? IS THIS THE YEAR WE *WANT?*

YES, IT'S *1981...* LOOK AT THOSE *UGLY* BUILDINGS!

RIGHT! DOWN WE GO!

PLUS, I THINK I SEE GARRER'S *TIME MACHINES* BENEATH US! WE'VE ARRIVED *BEFORE* THEY EMBARKED FOR *1956!*

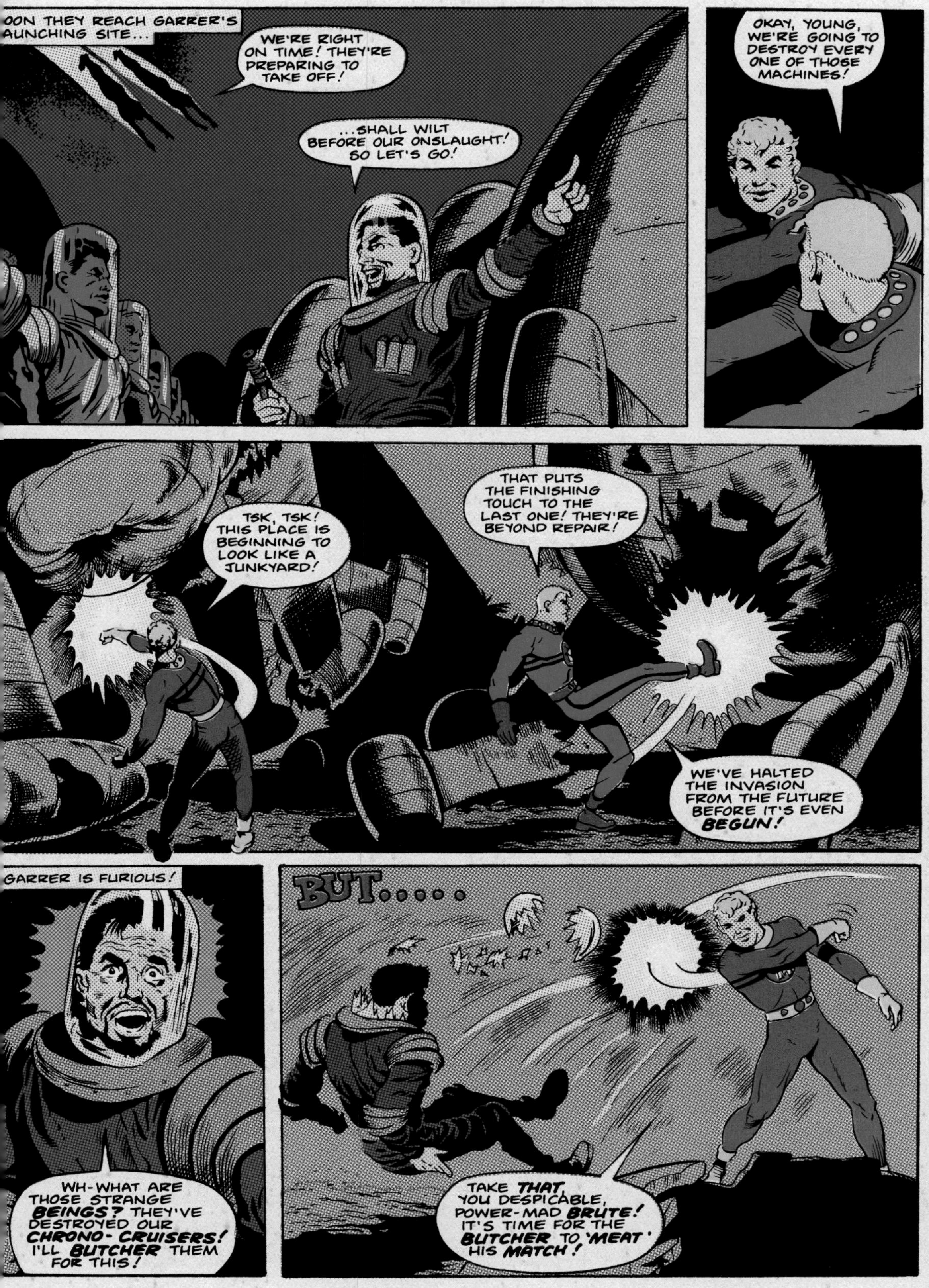
OON THEY REACH GARRER'S AUNCHING SITE...
WE'RE RIGHT ON TIME! THEY'RE PREPARING TO TAKE OFF!
...SHALL WILT BEFORE OUR ONSLAUGHT! SO LET'S GO!
OKAY, YOUNG, WE'RE GOING TO DESTROY EVERY ONE OF THOSE MACHINES!
TSK, TSK! THIS PLACE IS BEGINNING TO LOOK LIKE A JUNKYARD!
THAT PUTS THE FINISHING TOUCH TO THE LAST ONE! THEY'RE BEYOND REPAIR!
WE'VE HALTED THE INVASION FROM THE FUTURE BEFORE IT'S EVEN BEGUN!
GARRER IS FURIOUS!
WH-WHAT ARE THOSE STRANGE BEINGS? THEY'VE DESTROYED OUR CHRONO-CRUISERS! I'LL BUTCHER THEM FOR THIS!
BUT.....
TAKE THAT, YOU DESPICABLE, POWER-MAD BRUTE! IT'S TIME FOR THE BUTCHER TO 'MEAT' HIS MATCH!

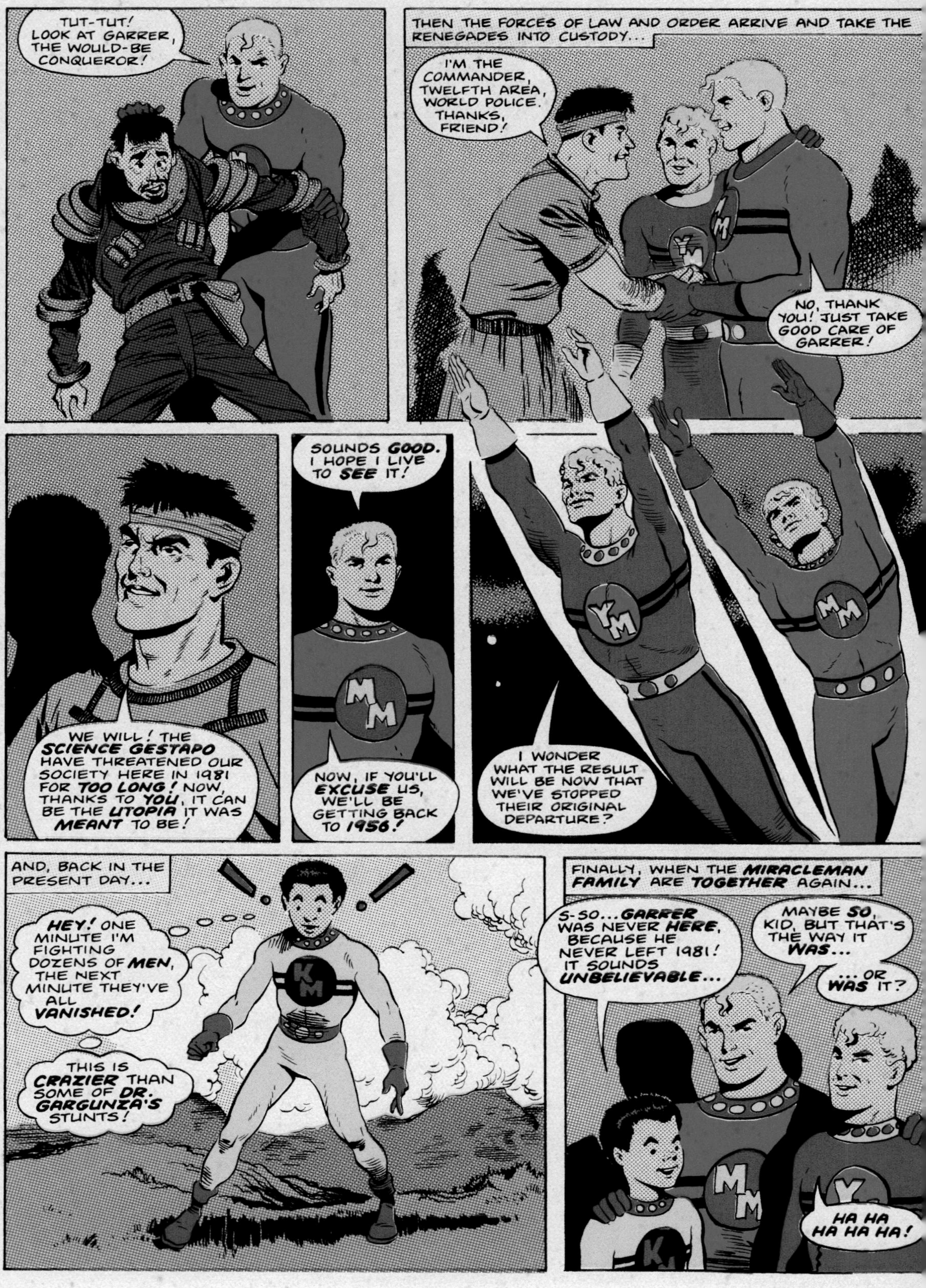

TUT-TUT! LOOK AT GARRER, THE WOULD-BE CONQUEROR!
THEN THE FORCES OF LAW AND ORDER ARRIVE AND TAKE THE RENEGADES INTO CUSTODY...
I'M THE COMMANDER, TWELFTH AREA, WORLD POLICE. THANKS, FRIEND!
NO, THANK YOU! JUST TAKE GOOD CARE OF GARRER!
WE WILL! THE SCIENCE GESTAPO HAVE THREATENED OUR SOCIETY HERE IN 1981 FOR TOO LONG! NOW, THANKS TO YOU, IT CAN BE THE UTOPIA IT WAS MEANT TO BE!
SOUNDS GOOD. I HOPE I LIVE TO SEE IT!
NOW, IF YOU'LL EXCUSE US, WE'LL BE GETTING BACK TO 1956!
I WONDER WHAT THE RESULT WILL BE NOW THAT WE'VE STOPPED THEIR ORIGINAL DEPARTURE?
AND, BACK IN THE PRESENT DAY...
HEY! ONE MINUTE I'M FIGHTING DOZENS OF MEN, THE NEXT MINUTE THEY'VE ALL VANISHED!
THIS IS CRAZIER THAN SOME OF DR. GARGUNZA'S STUNTS!
FINALLY, WHEN THE MIRACLEMAN FAMILY ARE TOGETHER AGAIN...
S-SO... GARRER WAS NEVER HERE, BECAUSE HE NEVER LEFT 1981! IT SOUNDS UNBELIEVABLE...
MAYBE SO, KID, BUT THAT'S THE WAY IT WAS...
...OR WAS IT?
HA HA HA HA HA!

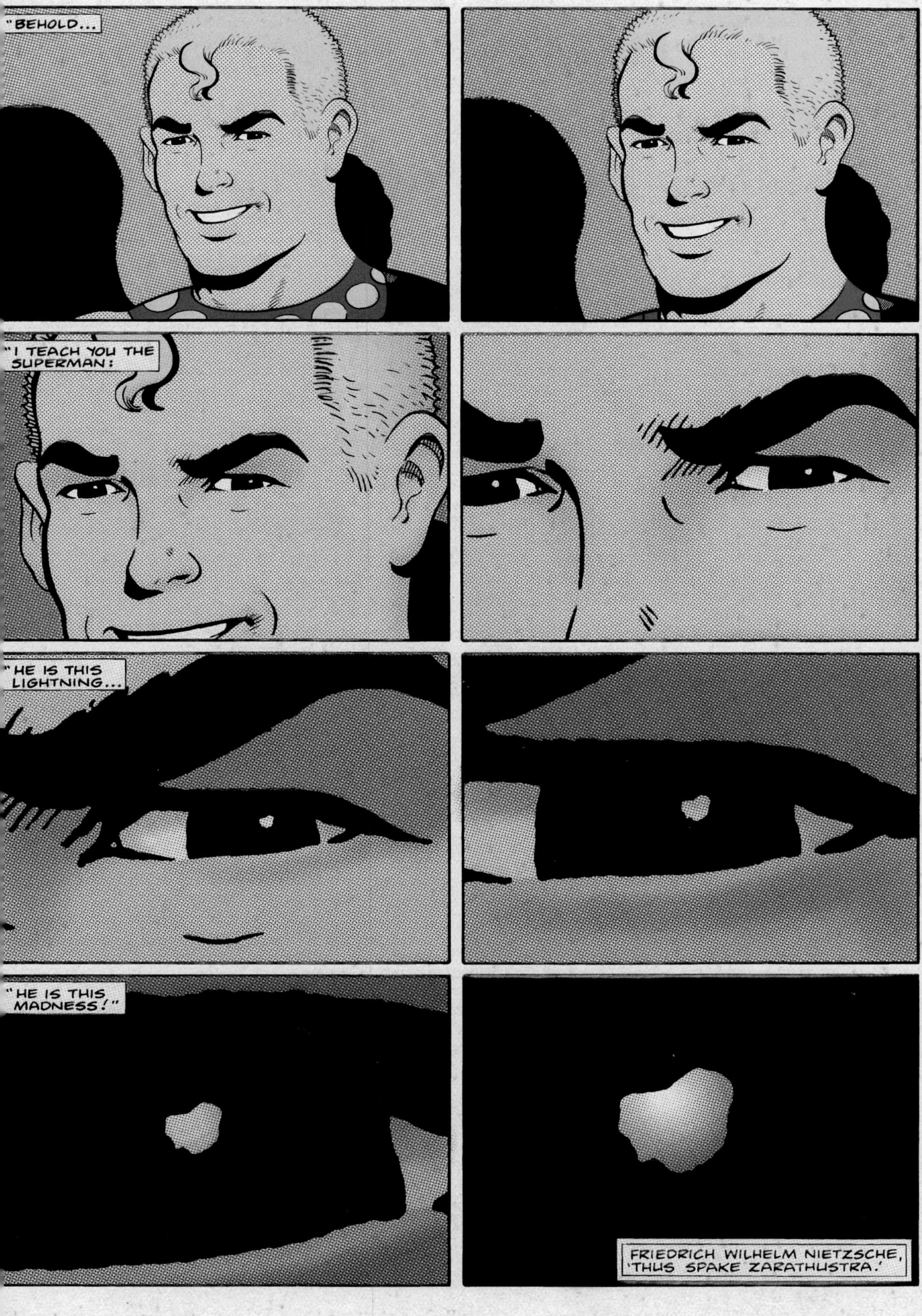
"BEHOLD...
"I TEACH YOU THE SUPERMAN:
"HE IS THIS LIGHTNING...
"HE IS THIS MADNESS!"
FRIEDRICH WILHELM NIETZSCHE, 'THUS SPAKE ZARATHUSTRA.'

1982

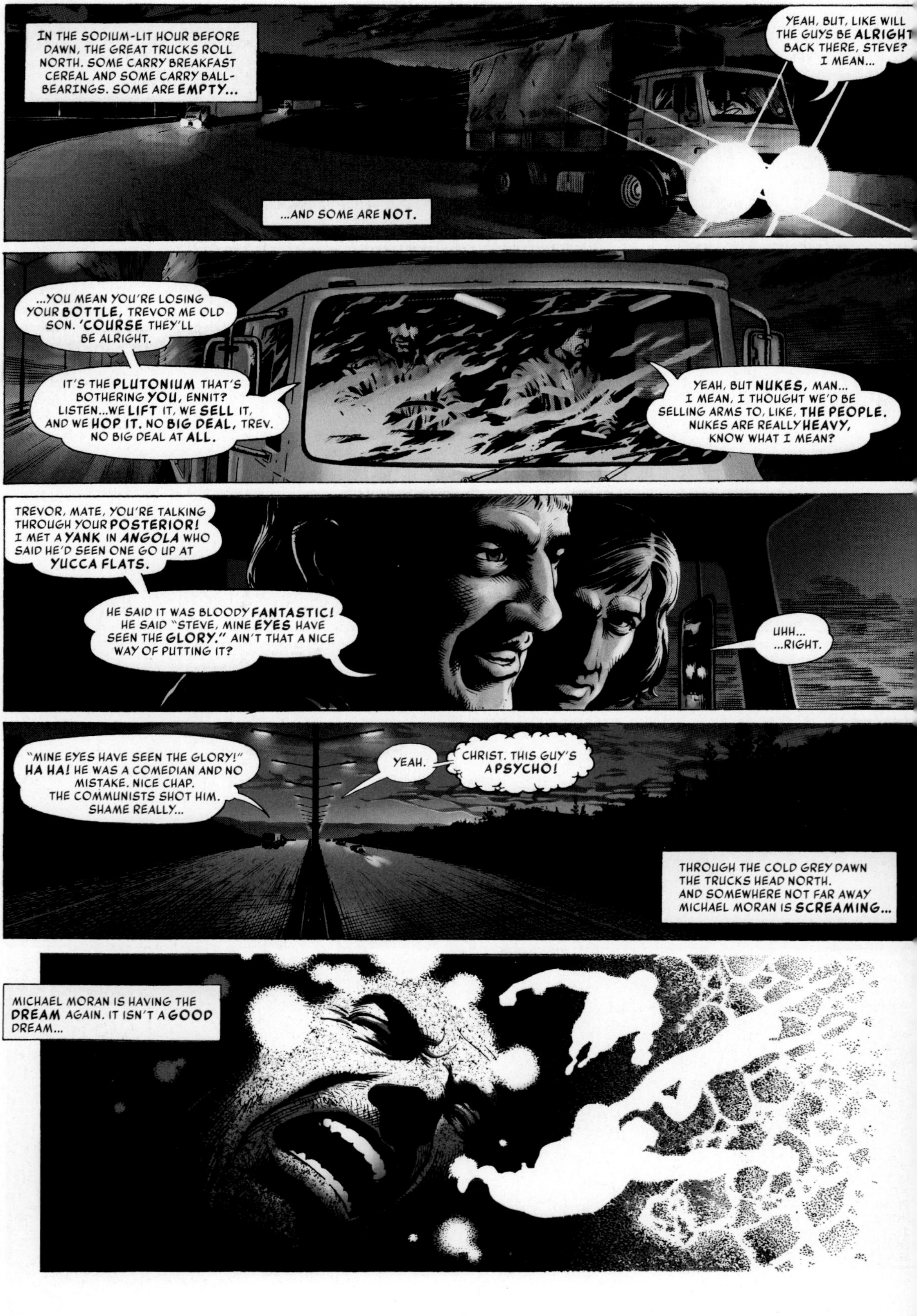

IN THE SODIUM-LIT HOUR BEFORE DAWN, THE GREAT TRUCKS ROLL NORTH. SOME CARRY BREAKFAST CEREAL AND SOME CARRY BALL-BEARINGS. SOME ARE EMPTY...
YEAH, BUT, LIKE WILL THE GUYS BE ALRIGHT BACK THERE, STEVE? I MEAN...
...AND SOME ARE NOT.
...YOU MEAN YOU'RE LOSING YOUR BOTTLE, TREVOR ME OLD SON. 'COURSE THEY'LL BE ALRIGHT.
IT'S THE PLUTONIUM THAT'S BOTHERING YOU, ENNIT? LISTEN...WE LIFT IT, WE SELL IT, AND WE HOP IT. NO BIG DEAL, TREV. NO BIG DEAL AT ALL.
YEAH, BUT NUKES, MAN... I MEAN, I THOUGHT WE'D BE SELLING ARMS TO, LIKE, THE PEOPLE. NUKES ARE REALLY HEAVY, KNOW WHAT I MEAN?
TREVOR, MATE, YOU'RE TALKING THROUGH YOUR POSTERIOR! I MET A YANK IN ANGOLA WHO SAID HE'D SEEN ONE GO UP AT YUCCA FLATS.
HE SAID IT WAS BLOODY FANTASTIC! HE SAID "STEVE, MINE EYES HAVE SEEN THE GLORY." AIN'T THAT A NICE WAY OF PUTTING IT?
UHH... ...RIGHT.
"MINE EYES HAVE SEEN THE GLORY!" HA HA! HE WAS A COMEDIAN AND NO MISTAKE. NICE CHAP. THE COMMUNISTS SHOT HIM. SHAME REALLY...
YEAH.
CHRIST. THIS GUY'S A PSYCHO!
THROUGH THE COLD GREY DAWN THE TRUCKS HEAD NORTH. AND SOMEWHERE NOT FAR AWAY MICHAEL MORAN IS SCREAMING...
MICHAEL MORAN IS HAVING THE DREAM AGAIN. IT ISN'T A GOOD DREAM...

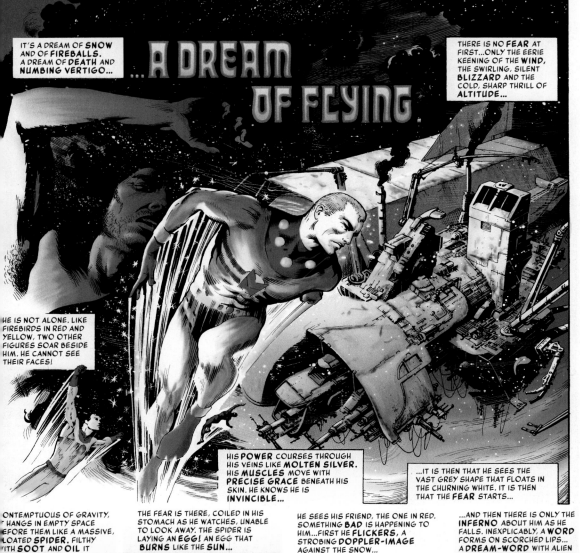

IT'S A DREAM OF **SNOW** AND OF **FIREBALLS**. A DREAM OF **DEATH** AND **NUMBING VERTIGO**...

...A DREAM OF FLYING

THERE IS NO **FEAR** AT FIRST...ONLY THE EERIE **KEENING** OF THE **WIND**, THE SWIRLING, SILENT **BLIZZARD** AND THE COLD, SHARP THRILL OF **ALTITUDE**...

HE IS NOT ALONE. LIKE FIREBIRDS IN RED AND YELLOW, TWO OTHER FIGURES SOAR BESIDE HIM. HE CANNOT SEE THEIR **FACES**!

HIS **POWER** COURSES THROUGH HIS VEINS LIKE **MOLTEN SILVER**. HIS **MUSCLES** MOVE WITH **PRECISE GRACE** BENEATH HIS SKIN. HE KNOWS HE IS **INVINCIBLE**...

...IT IS THEN THAT HE SEES THE VAST GREY SHAPE THAT FLOATS IN THE CHURNING WHITE. IT IS THEN THAT THE **FEAR** STARTS...

[C]ONTEMPTUOUS OF GRAVITY, [I]T HANGS IN EMPTY SPACE [B]EFORE THEM LIKE A MASSIVE, [B]LOATED **SPIDER**. FILTHY [W]ITH **SOOT** AND **OIL** IT [S]TAINS THE AIR...

THE FEAR IS THERE, COILED IN HIS STOMACH AS HE WATCHES, UNABLE TO LOOK AWAY. THE SPIDER IS LAYING AN **EGG**! AN EGG THAT **BURNS** LIKE THE **SUN**...

HE SEES HIS FRIEND, THE ONE IN RED. SOMETHING **BAD** IS HAPPENING TO HIM...FIRST HE **FLICKERS**, A STROBING **DOPPLER-IMAGE** AGAINST THE SNOW...

...AND THEN THERE IS ONLY THE **INFERNO** ABOUT HIM AS HE FALLS. INEXPLICABLY, A **WORD** FORMS ON SCORCHED LIPS... A **DREAM-WORD** WITH ALIEN SYLLABLES...

LIKE GAUDY INCAUTIOUS MOTHS HIS COMPANIONS PLUNGE TOWARDS THE HORROR, LEAVING HIM IN THEIR WAKE. CAN'T THEY **SEE**? DON'T THEY KNOW WHAT HAPPENS **NEXT**?

THE SKY CATCHES FIRE AND HE IS **SCREAMING**! SCREAMING AND BURNING...

...AND THEN HE **EXPLODES**!!

THE LAST THING HE HEARS IS THE SOUND OF **THUNDER**...

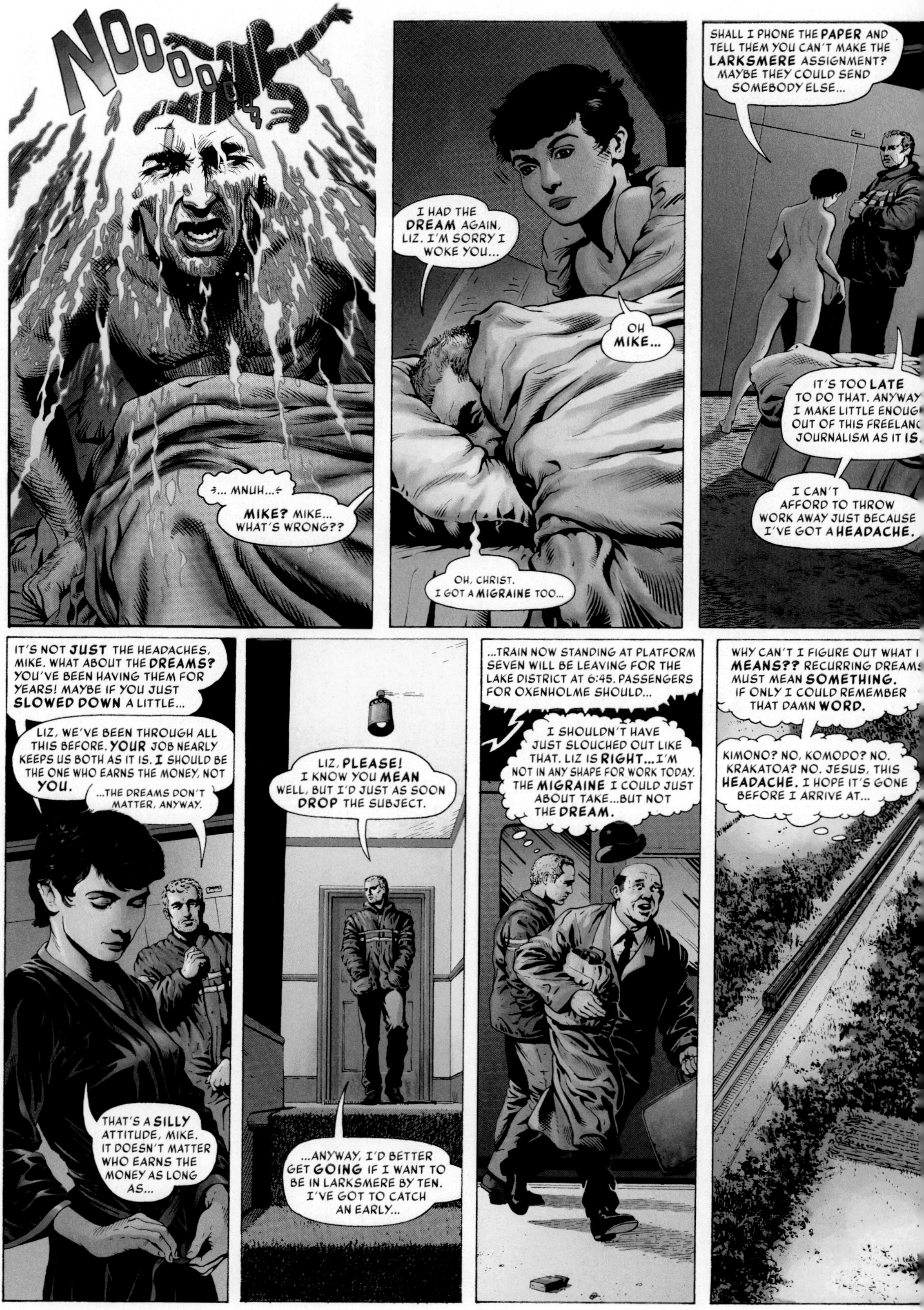
NOOOOOOOO
≈... MNUH...≈
MIKE? MIKE... WHAT'S WRONG??
I HAD THE DREAM AGAIN, LIZ. I'M SORRY I WOKE YOU...
OH MIKE...
OH, CHRIST. I GOT A MIGRAINE TOO...
SHALL I PHONE THE PAPER AND TELL THEM YOU CAN'T MAKE THE LARKSMERE ASSIGNMENT? MAYBE THEY COULD SEND SOMEBODY ELSE...
IT'S TOO LATE TO DO THAT. ANYWAY I MAKE LITTLE ENOUG OUT OF THIS FREELANC JOURNALISM AS IT IS.
I CAN'T AFFORD TO THROW WORK AWAY JUST BECAUSE I'VE GOT A HEADACHE.
IT'S NOT JUST THE HEADACHES, MIKE. WHAT ABOUT THE DREAMS? YOU'VE BEEN HAVING THEM FOR YEARS! MAYBE IF YOU JUST SLOWED DOWN A LITTLE...
LIZ, WE'VE BEEN THROUGH ALL THIS BEFORE. YOUR JOB NEARLY KEEPS US BOTH AS IT IS. I SHOULD BE THE ONE WHO EARNS THE MONEY, NOT YOU.
...THE DREAMS DON'T MATTER, ANYWAY.
THAT'S A SILLY ATTITUDE, MIKE. IT DOESN'T MATTER WHO EARNS THE MONEY AS LONG AS...
LIZ, PLEASE! I KNOW YOU MEAN WELL, BUT I'D JUST AS SOON DROP THE SUBJECT.
...ANYWAY, I'D BETTER GET GOING IF I WANT TO BE IN LARKSMERE BY TEN. I'VE GOT TO CATCH AN EARLY...
...TRAIN NOW STANDING AT PLATFORM SEVEN WILL BE LEAVING FOR THE LAKE DISTRICT AT 6:45. PASSENGERS FOR OXENHOLME SHOULD...
I SHOULDN'T HAVE JUST SLOUCHED OUT LIKE THAT. LIZ IS RIGHT...I'M NOT IN ANY SHAPE FOR WORK TODAY. THE MIGRAINE I COULD JUST ABOUT TAKE...BUT NOT THE DREAM.
WHY CAN'T I FIGURE OUT WHAT I MEANS?? RECURRING DREAMS MUST MEAN SOMETHING. IF ONLY I COULD REMEMBER THAT DAMN WORD.
KIMONO? NO, KOMODO? NO. KRAKATOA? NO. JESUS, THIS HEADACHE. I HOPE IT'S GONE BEFORE I ARRIVE AT...

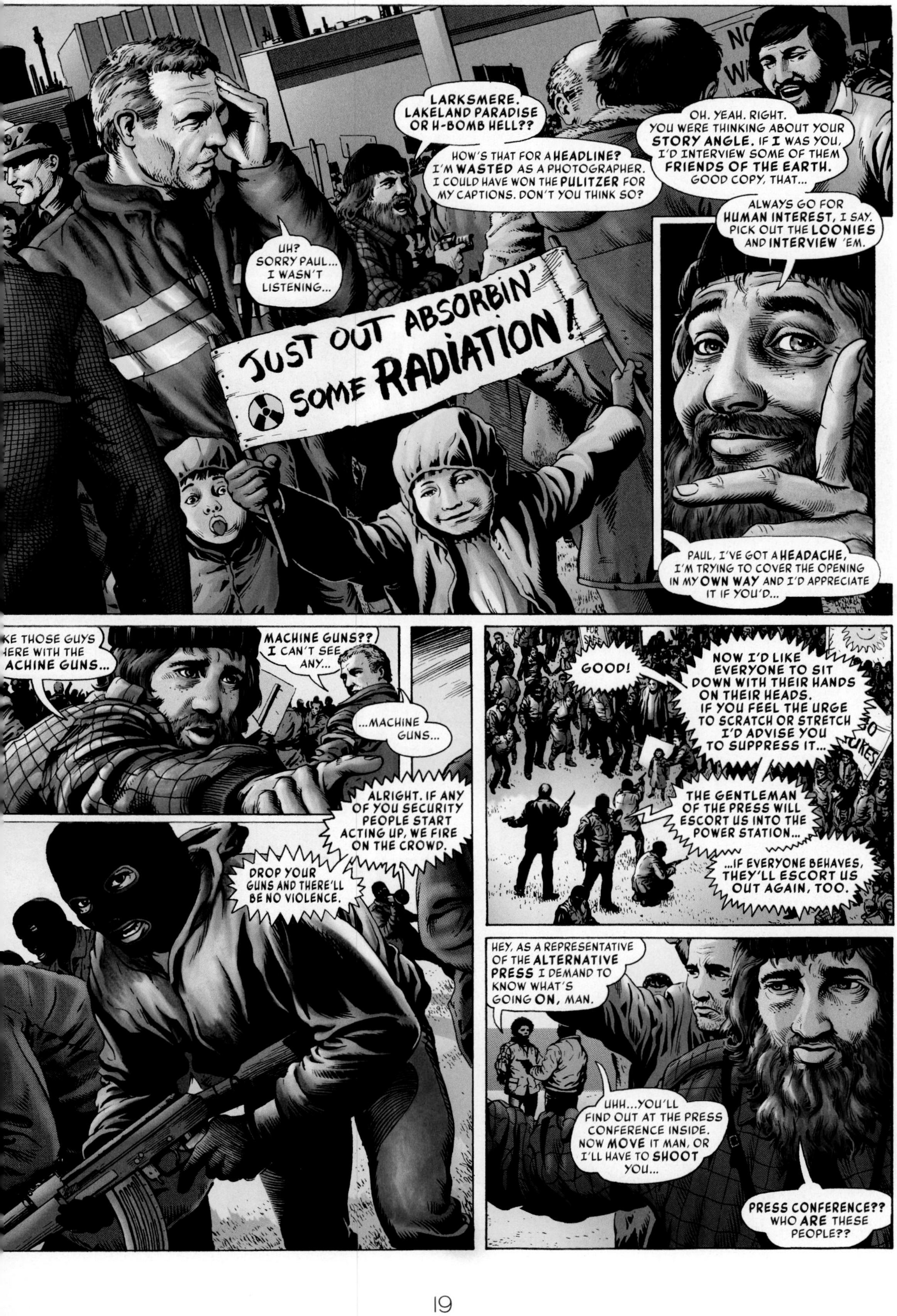
LARKSMERE. LAKELAND PARADISE OR H-BOMB HELL??
HOW'S THAT FOR A HEADLINE? I'M WASTED AS A PHOTOGRAPHER. I COULD HAVE WON THE PULITZER FOR MY CAPTIONS. DON'T YOU THINK SO?
UH? SORRY PAUL... I WASN'T LISTENING...
OH. YEAH. RIGHT. YOU WERE THINKING ABOUT YOUR STORY ANGLE. IF I WAS YOU, I'D INTERVIEW SOME OF THEM FRIENDS OF THE EARTH. GOOD COPY, THAT...
ALWAYS GO FOR HUMAN INTEREST, I SAY. PICK OUT THE LOONIES AND INTERVIEW 'EM.
JUST OUT ABSORBIN' SOME RADIATION!
PAUL, I'VE GOT A HEADACHE, I'M TRYING TO COVER THE OPENING IN MY OWN WAY AND I'D APPRECIATE IT IF YOU'D...
KE THOSE GUYS HERE WITH THE ACHINE GUNS...
MACHINE GUNS?? I CAN'T SEE ANY...
...MACHINE GUNS...
ALRIGHT. IF ANY OF YOU SECURITY PEOPLE START ACTING UP, WE FIRE ON THE CROWD.
DROP YOUR GUNS AND THERE'LL BE NO VIOLENCE.
GOOD!
NOW I'D LIKE EVERYONE TO SIT DOWN WITH THEIR HANDS ON THEIR HEADS. IF YOU FEEL THE URGE TO SCRATCH OR STRETCH I'D ADVISE YOU TO SUPPRESS IT...
THE GENTLEMAN OF THE PRESS WILL ESCORT US INTO THE POWER STATION...
...IF EVERYONE BEHAVES, THEY'LL ESCORT US OUT AGAIN, TOO.
HEY, AS A REPRESENTATIVE OF THE ALTERNATIVE PRESS I DEMAND TO KNOW WHAT'S GOING ON, MAN.
UHH...YOU'LL FIND OUT AT THE PRESS CONFERENCE INSIDE. NOW MOVE IT MAN, OR I'LL HAVE TO SHOOT YOU...
PRESS CONFERENCE?? WHO ARE THESE PEOPLE??

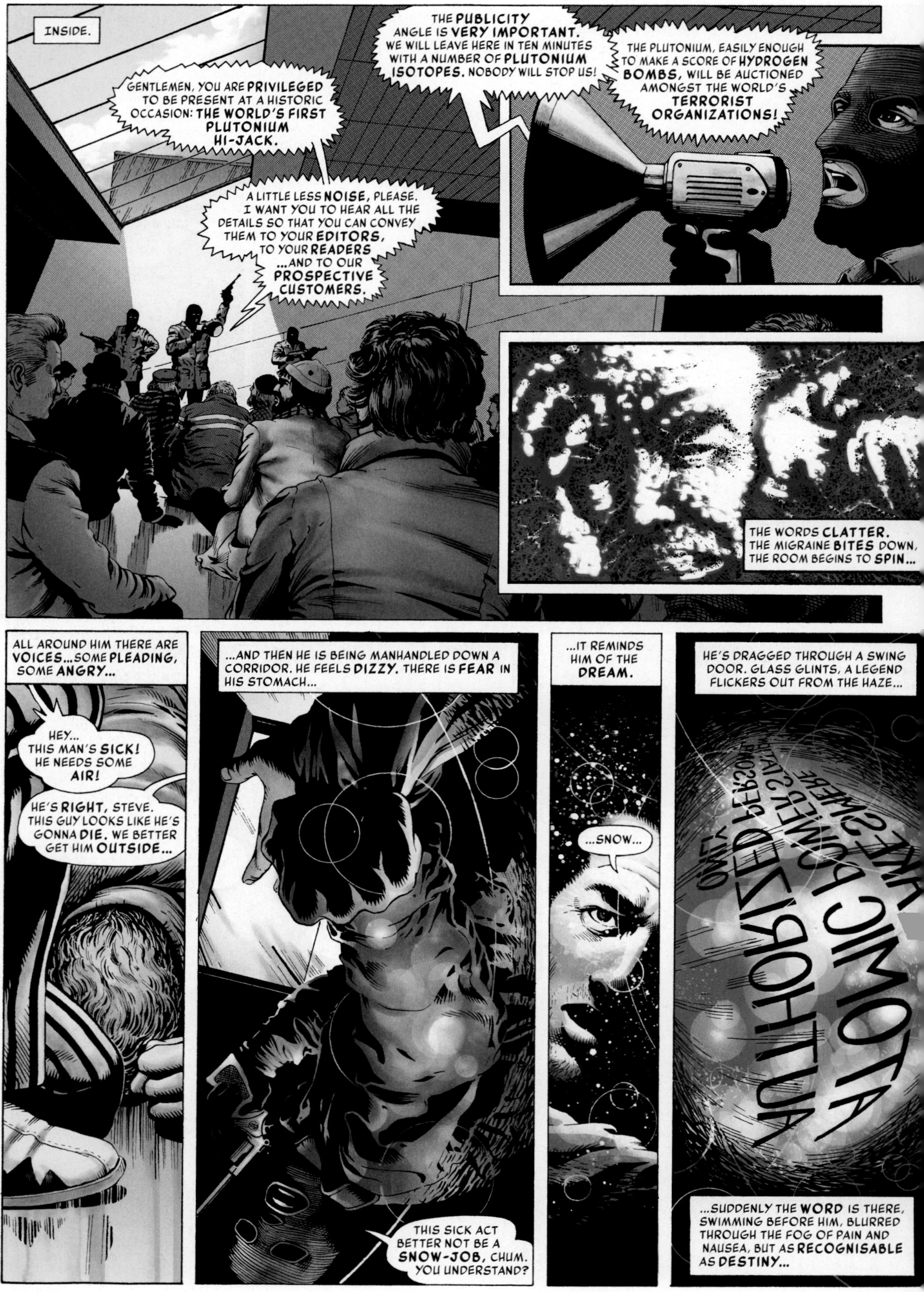
INSIDE.
GENTLEMEN, YOU ARE PRIVILEGED TO BE PRESENT AT A HISTORIC OCCASION: THE WORLD'S FIRST PLUTONIUM HI-JACK.
A LITTLE LESS NOISE, PLEASE. I WANT YOU TO HEAR ALL THE DETAILS SO THAT YOU CAN CONVEY THEM TO YOUR EDITORS, TO YOUR READERS ...AND TO OUR PROSPECTIVE CUSTOMERS.
THE PUBLICITY ANGLE IS VERY IMPORTANT. WE WILL LEAVE HERE IN TEN MINUTES WITH A NUMBER OF PLUTONIUM ISOTOPES. NOBODY WILL STOP US!
THE PLUTONIUM, EASILY ENOUGH TO MAKE A SCORE OF HYDROGEN BOMBS, WILL BE AUCTIONED AMONGST THE WORLD'S TERRORIST ORGANIZATIONS!
THE WORDS CLATTER. THE MIGRAINE BITES DOWN, THE ROOM BEGINS TO SPIN...
ALL AROUND HIM THERE ARE VOICES...SOME PLEADING, SOME ANGRY...
HEY... THIS MAN'S SICK! HE NEEDS SOME AIR!
HE'S RIGHT, STEVE. THIS GUY LOOKS LIKE HE'S GONNA DIE. WE BETTER GET HIM OUTSIDE...
...AND THEN HE IS BEING MANHANDLED DOWN A CORRIDOR. HE FEELS DIZZY. THERE IS FEAR IN HIS STOMACH...
THIS SICK ACT BETTER NOT BE A SNOW-JOB, CHUM. YOU UNDERSTAND?
...IT REMINDS HIM OF THE DREAM.
...SNOW...
HE'S DRAGGED THROUGH A SWING DOOR. GLASS GLINTS, A LEGEND FLICKERS OUT FROM THE HAZE...
...SUDDENLY THE WORD IS THERE, SWIMMING BEFORE HIM, BLURRED THROUGH THE FOG OF PAIN AND NAUSEA, BUT AS RECOGNISABLE AS DESTINY...

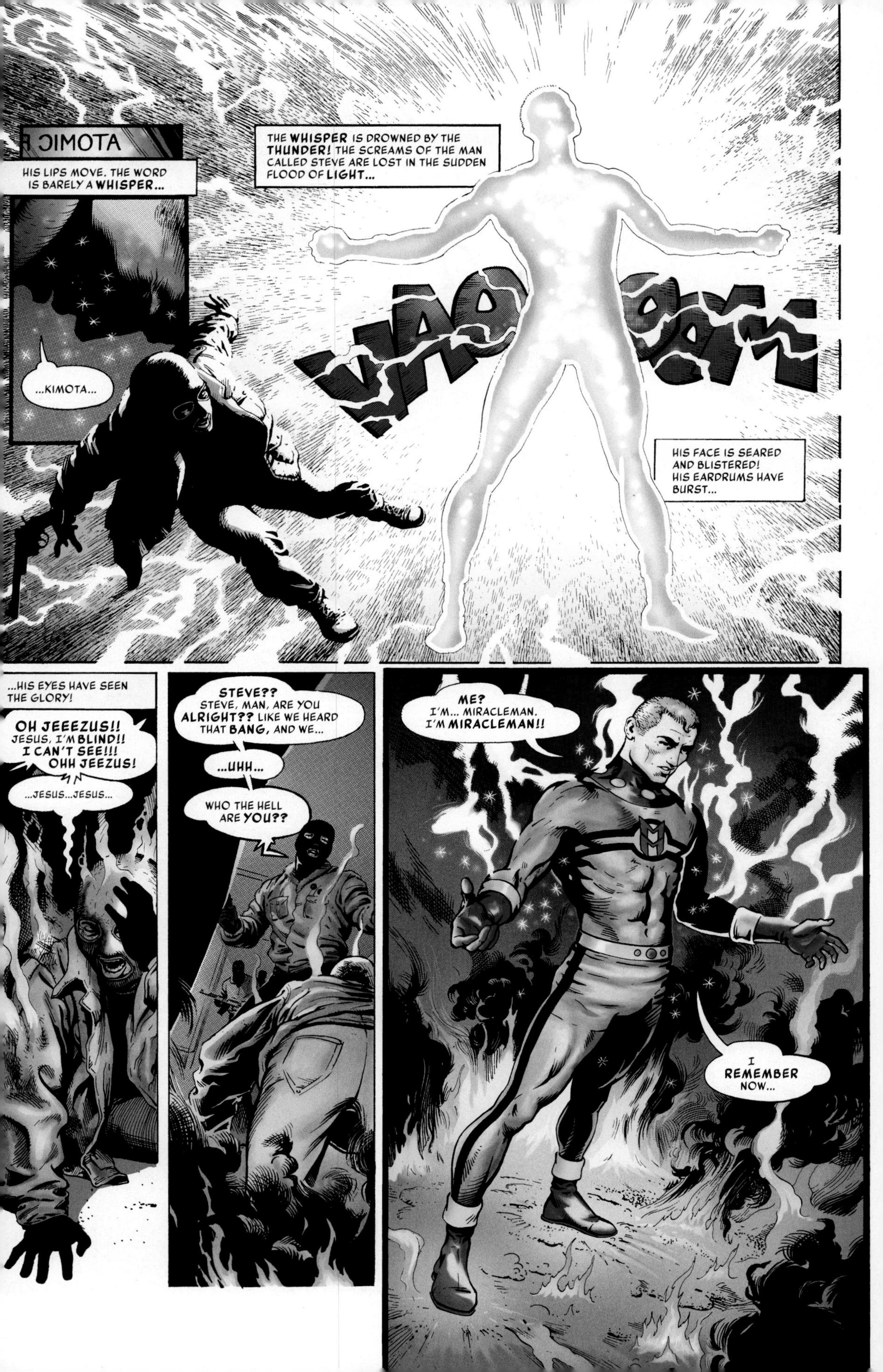
ATOMIC
HIS LIPS MOVE. THE WORD IS BARELY A WHISPER...
...KIMOTA...
THE WHISPER IS DROWNED BY THE THUNDER! THE SCREAMS OF THE MAN CALLED STEVE ARE LOST IN THE SUDDEN FLOOD OF LIGHT...
HIS FACE IS SEARED AND BLISTERED! HIS EARDRUMS HAVE BURST...
...HIS EYES HAVE SEEN THE GLORY!
OH JEEEZUS!! JESUS, I'M BLIND!! I CAN'T SEE!!! OHH JEEZUS!
...JESUS...JESUS...
STEVE?? STEVE, MAN, ARE YOU ALRIGHT?? LIKE WE HEARD THAT BANG, AND WE...
...UHH...
WHO THE HELL ARE YOU??
ME? I'M... MIRACLEMAN. I'M MIRACLEMAN!!
I REMEMBER NOW...

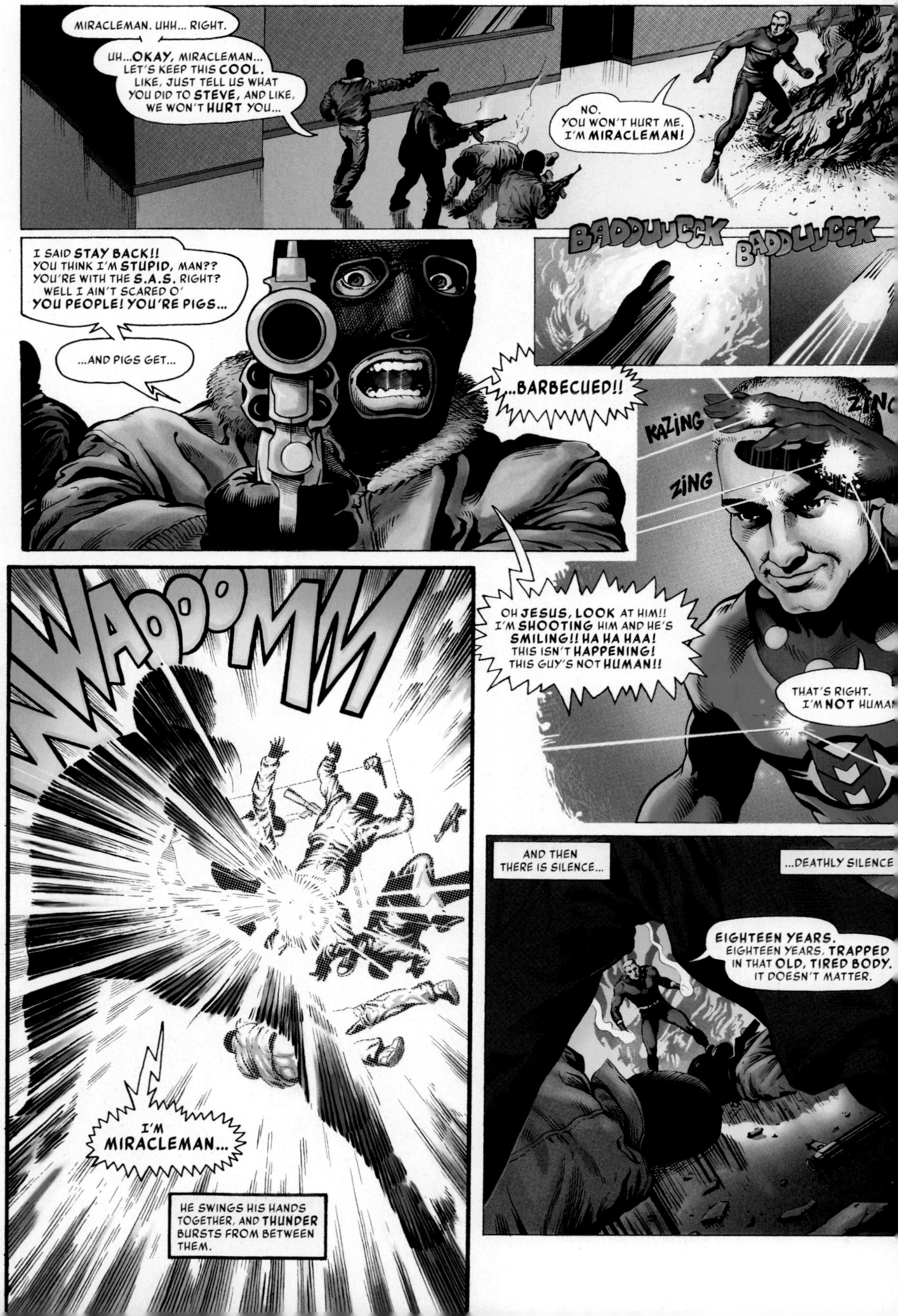
MIRACLEMAN. UHH... RIGHT.
UH...OKAY, MIRACLEMAN... LET'S KEEP THIS COOL. LIKE, JUST TELL US WHAT YOU DID TO STEVE, AND LIKE, WE WON'T HURT YOU...
NO. YOU WON'T HURT ME. I'M MIRACLEMAN!
I SAID STAY BACK!! YOU THINK I'M STUPID, MAN?? YOU'RE WITH THE S.A.S. RIGHT? WELL I AIN'T SCARED O' YOU PEOPLE! YOU'RE PIGS...
...AND PIGS GET...
...BARBECUED!!
BADDUUCCK
BADDUUCCK
KAZING
ZING
ZING
OH JESUS, LOOK AT HIM!! I'M SHOOTING HIM AND HE'S SMILING!! HA HA HAA! THIS ISN'T HAPPENING! THIS GUY'S NOT HUMAN!!
THAT'S RIGHT. I'M NOT HUMAN
WAOOOMM
I'M MIRACLEMAN...
HE SWINGS HIS HANDS TOGETHER, AND THUNDER BURSTS FROM BETWEEN THEM.
AND THEN THERE IS SILENCE...
...DEATHLY SILENCE
EIGHTEEN YEARS. EIGHTEEN YEARS, TRAPPED IN THAT OLD, TIRED BODY. IT DOESN'T MATTER.

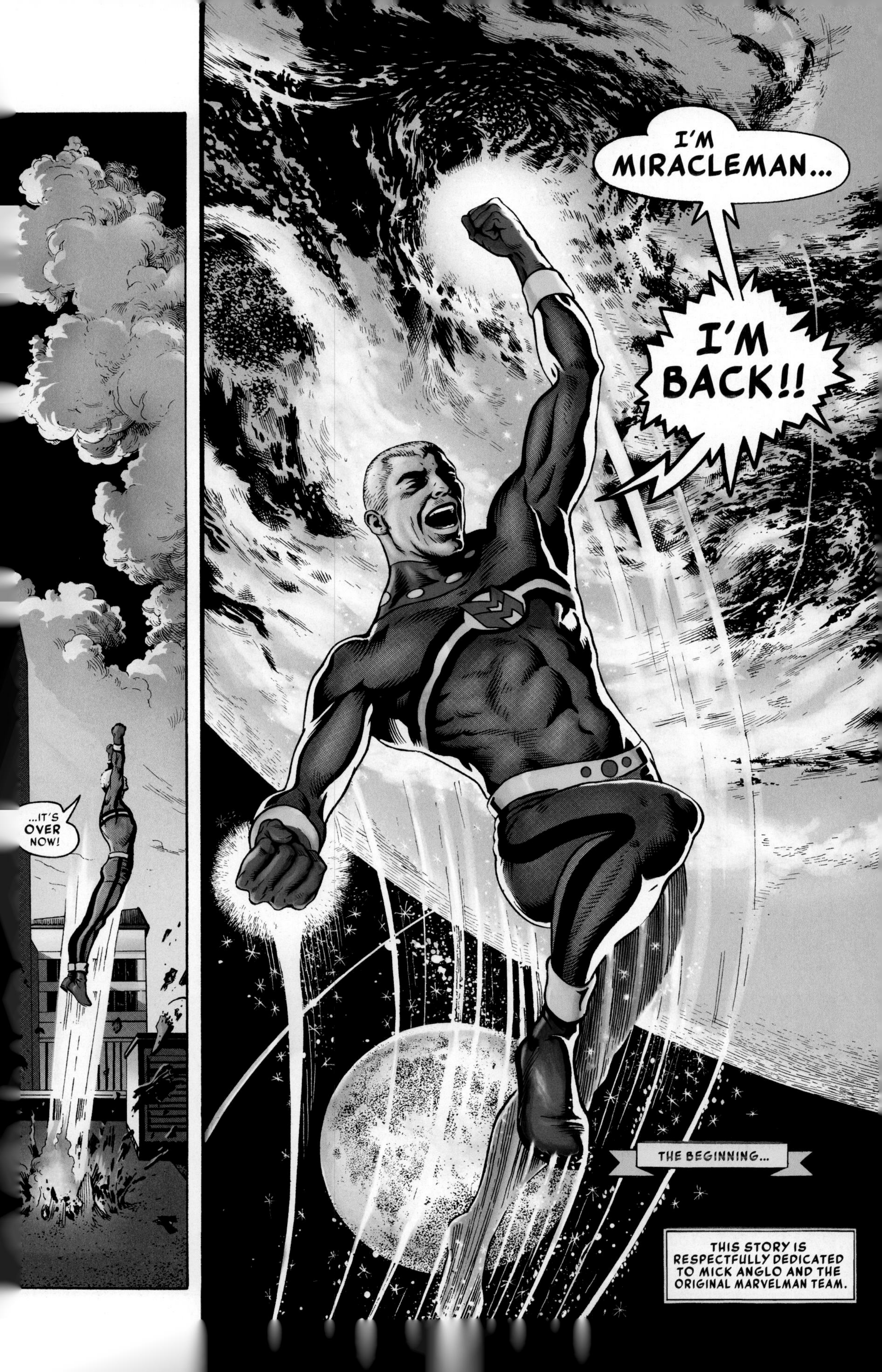
...IT'S OVER NOW!
I'M MIRACLEMAN...
I'M BACK!!
THE BEGINNING...
THIS STORY IS RESPECTFULLY DEDICATED TO MICK ANGLO AND THE ORIGINAL MARVELMAN TEAM.

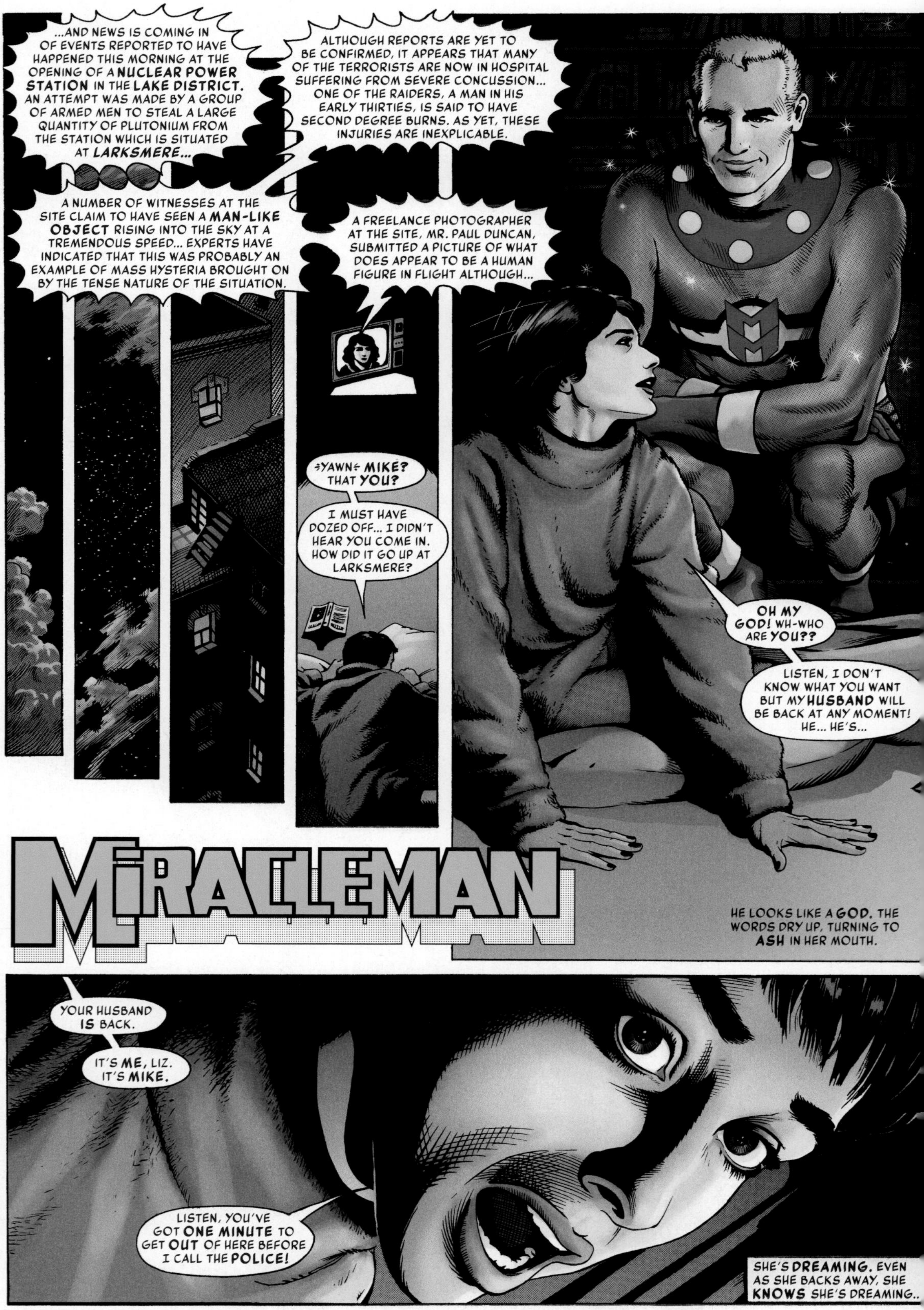
...AND NEWS IS COMING IN OF EVENTS REPORTED TO HAVE HAPPENED THIS MORNING AT THE OPENING OF A NUCLEAR POWER STATION IN THE LAKE DISTRICT. AN ATTEMPT WAS MADE BY A GROUP OF ARMED MEN TO STEAL A LARGE QUANTITY OF PLUTONIUM FROM THE STATION WHICH IS SITUATED AT LARKSMERE...
ALTHOUGH REPORTS ARE YET TO BE CONFIRMED, IT APPEARS THAT MANY OF THE TERRORISTS ARE NOW IN HOSPITAL SUFFERING FROM SEVERE CONCUSSION... ONE OF THE RAIDERS, A MAN IN HIS EARLY THIRTIES, IS SAID TO HAVE SECOND DEGREE BURNS. AS YET, THESE INJURIES ARE INEXPLICABLE.
A NUMBER OF WITNESSES AT THE SITE CLAIM TO HAVE SEEN A MAN-LIKE OBJECT RISING INTO THE SKY AT A TREMENDOUS SPEED... EXPERTS HAVE INDICATED THAT THIS WAS PROBABLY AN EXAMPLE OF MASS HYSTERIA BROUGHT ON BY THE TENSE NATURE OF THE SITUATION.
A FREELANCE PHOTOGRAPHER AT THE SITE, MR. PAUL DUNCAN, SUBMITTED A PICTURE OF WHAT DOES APPEAR TO BE A HUMAN FIGURE IN FLIGHT ALTHOUGH...
=YAWN= MIKE? THAT YOU?
I MUST HAVE DOZED OFF... I DIDN'T HEAR YOU COME IN. HOW DID IT GO UP AT LARKSMERE?
OH MY GOD! WH-WHO ARE YOU??
LISTEN, I DON'T KNOW WHAT YOU WANT BUT MY HUSBAND WILL BE BACK AT ANY MOMENT! HE... HE'S...
MIRACLEMAN
HE LOOKS LIKE A GOD. THE WORDS DRY UP, TURNING TO ASH IN HER MOUTH.
YOUR HUSBAND IS BACK.
IT'S ME, LIZ. IT'S MIKE.
LISTEN, YOU'VE GOT ONE MINUTE TO GET OUT OF HERE BEFORE I CALL THE POLICE!
SHE'S DREAMING. EVEN AS SHE BACKS AWAY, SHE KNOWS SHE'S DREAMING...

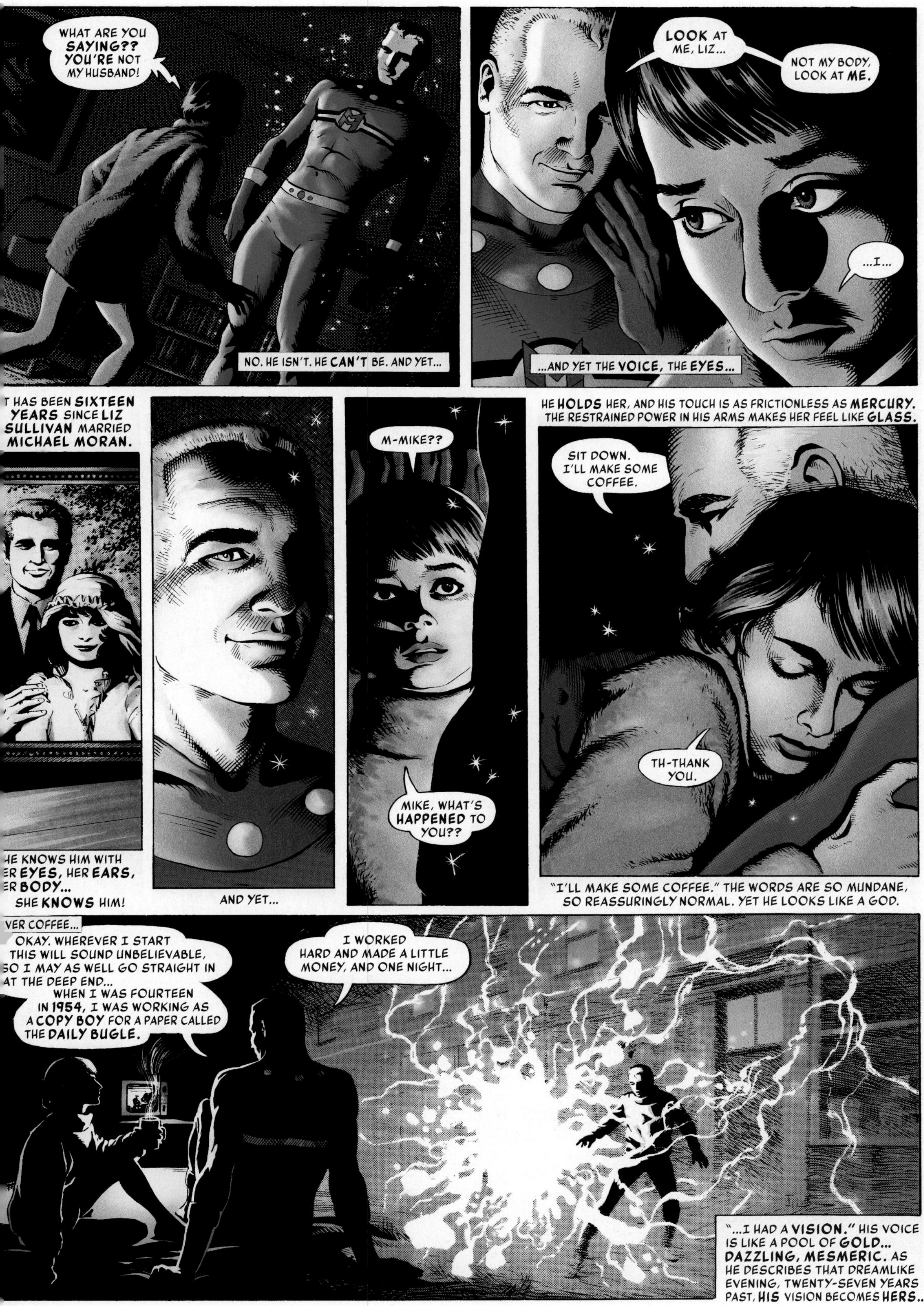

WHAT ARE YOU SAYING?? YOU'RE NOT MY HUSBAND!
NO. HE ISN'T. HE CAN'T BE. AND YET...
LOOK AT ME, LIZ...
NOT MY BODY, LOOK AT ME.
...I...
...AND YET THE VOICE, THE EYES...
T HAS BEEN SIXTEEN YEARS SINCE LIZ SULLIVAN MARRIED MICHAEL MORAN.
HE KNOWS HIM WITH ER EYES, HER EARS, ER BODY... SHE KNOWS HIM!
AND YET...
M-MIKE??
MIKE, WHAT'S HAPPENED TO YOU??
HE HOLDS HER, AND HIS TOUCH IS AS FRICTIONLESS AS MERCURY. THE RESTRAINED POWER IN HIS ARMS MAKES HER FEEL LIKE GLASS.
SIT DOWN. I'LL MAKE SOME COFFEE.
TH-THANK YOU.
"I'LL MAKE SOME COFFEE." THE WORDS ARE SO MUNDANE, SO REASSURINGLY NORMAL. YET HE LOOKS LIKE A GOD.
VER COFFEE...
OKAY. WHEREVER I START THIS WILL SOUND UNBELIEVABLE, SO I MAY AS WELL GO STRAIGHT IN AT THE DEEP END... WHEN I WAS FOURTEEN IN 1954, I WAS WORKING AS A COPY BOY FOR A PAPER CALLED THE DAILY BUGLE.
I WORKED HARD AND MADE A LITTLE MONEY, AND ONE NIGHT...
"...I HAD A VISION." HIS VOICE IS LIKE A POOL OF GOLD... DAZZLING, MESMERIC. AS HE DESCRIBES THAT DREAMLIKE EVENING, TWENTY-SEVEN YEARS PAST, HIS VISION BECOMES HERS...

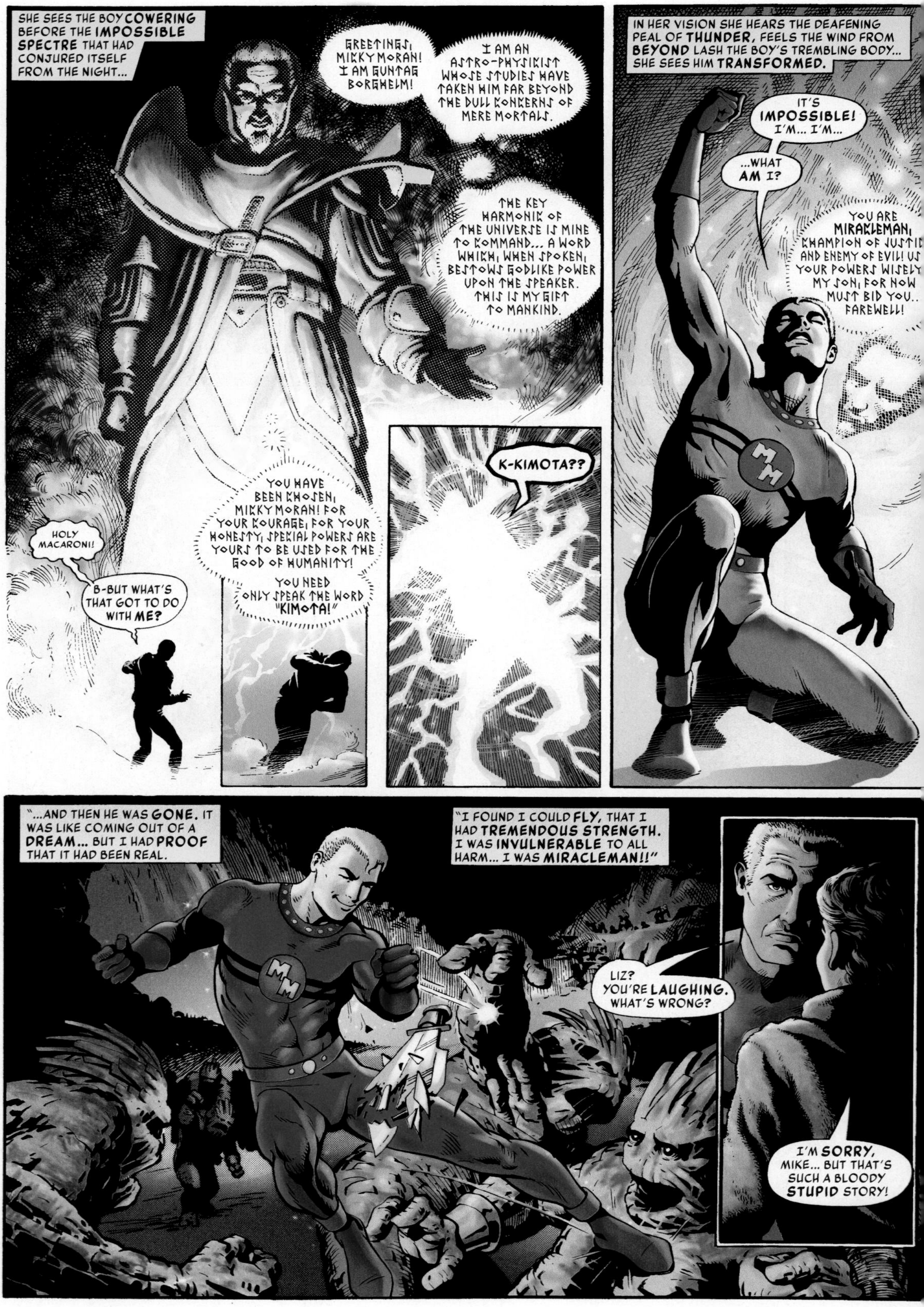

SHE SEES THE BOY COWERING BEFORE THE IMPOSSIBLE SPECTRE THAT HAD CONJURED ITSELF FROM THE NIGHT...
GREETINGS, MICKY MORAN! I AM GUNTAG BORGHELM!
I AM AN ASTRO-PHYSICIST WHOSE STUDIES HAVE TAKEN HIM FAR BEYOND THE DULL CONCERNS OF MERE MORTALS.
THE KEY HARMONIC OF THE UNIVERSE IS MINE TO COMMAND... A WORD WHICH, WHEN SPOKEN, BESTOWS GODLIKE POWER UPON THE SPEAKER. THIS IS MY GIFT TO MANKIND.
HOLY MACARONI!
B-BUT WHAT'S THAT GOT TO DO WITH ME?
YOU HAVE BEEN CHOSEN, MICKY MORAN! FOR YOUR COURAGE, FOR YOUR HONESTY, SPECIAL POWERS ARE YOURS TO BE USED FOR THE GOOD OF HUMANITY!
YOU NEED ONLY SPEAK THE WORD "KIMOTA!"
K-KIMOTA??
IN HER VISION SHE HEARS THE DEAFENING PEAL OF THUNDER, FEELS THE WIND FROM BEYOND LASH THE BOY'S TREMBLING BODY... SHE SEES HIM TRANSFORMED.
IT'S IMPOSSIBLE! I'M... I'M...
...WHAT AM I?
YOU ARE MIRACLEMAN, CHAMPION OF JUSTIC AND ENEMY OF EVIL! US YOUR POWERS WISELY MY SON, FOR NOW MUST BID YOU.. FAREWELL!
"...AND THEN HE WAS GONE. IT WAS LIKE COMING OUT OF A DREAM... BUT I HAD PROOF THAT IT HAD BEEN REAL.
"I FOUND I COULD FLY, THAT I HAD TREMENDOUS STRENGTH. I WAS INVULNERABLE TO ALL HARM... I WAS MIRACLEMAN!!"
LIZ? YOU'RE LAUGHING. WHAT'S WRONG?
I'M SORRY, MIKE... BUT THAT'S SUCH A BLOODY STUPID STORY!

CAN'T YOU **SEE** IT? AN "**ASTRO PHYSICIST**" POPS UP AND TELLS YOU THE "**KEY HARMONIC OF THE UNIVERSE**"... WHICH JUST **HAPPENS** TO TURN YOU INTO A **MUSCLE-MAN** IN A **BLUE LEOTARD**? I'M SORRY, MIKE, I REALLY AM, BUT THAT'S JUST SO **STUPID!**

SUPPOSE YOU'RE RIGHT. ACTUALLY SAYING IT OUT LOUD LIKE THAT, IT DOES SOUND... WELL... PRETTY **UNLIKELY**. I NEVER REALLY THOUGHT ABOUT IT BEFORE. BUT I **HAD** TO BELIEVE IT, DON'T YOU SEE? I WAS **MIRACLEMAN!** I WAS A BEING OF ALMOST UNLIMITED POWER!!

AND I WASN'T THE ONLY ONE. WITHIN A YEAR I WAS JOINED BY ANOTHER YOUNG MAN WITH "**ATOMIC POWERS**" LIKE MINE. HIS NAME WAS **DICKY DAUNTLESS**...

OH, MIKE! DICKY **DAUNTLESS??** THAT WAS HIS **NAME??** COME OFF IT!

YOU'RE LAUGHING AGAIN.

I—I'M SORRY... PLEASE GO ON.

"**DICKY** ONLY HAD TO SAY THE WORD '**MIRACLEMAN**' AND HE BECAME **YOUNG MIRACLEMAN**. HE HAD POWERS LIKE MINE. HE WAS MY **FRIEND.**"

"WE FOUGHT CRIME TOGETHER UNTIL **1956**, WHEN WE WERE JOINED BY..."

MIRACLEDOG?

LIZ, **PLEASE!** THIS MAY, DAMN IT... THIS **DOES** SOUND SILLY IN '82, BUT IN THE FIFTIES IT MADE **PERFECT** SENSE. THIS IS HOW I REMEMBER IT. THIS IS HOW IT **HAPPENED.**

IN 1956 WE WERE JOINED BY **JOHNNY BATES**. HE WAS A LITTLE KID OF MAYBE SEVEN OR EIGHT. WHEN WE SAID MY NAME HE BECAME **KID MIRACLE-MAN**. THEY CALLED US THE **MIRACLEMAN FAMILY.**

"DURING THE YEARS WE WERE TOGETHER WE FOUGHT THE STRANGEST VILLAINS OF ALL TIME..."

"VILLAINS LIKE THE **FIREBUG** AND **YOUNG NASTYMAN**... DON'T SAY A WORD... AND THE MOST TROUBLESOME OF THE LOT, THE FREAKISH DWARF GENIUS CALLED **DOCTOR GARGUNZA**..."

"**TIME** AND **TIME** AGAIN WE THWARTED HIS INSANE PLANS AND JAILED HIM. BUT SOMEHOW HE ALWAYS CAME **BACK**..."

"AND YET HE NEVER DID ANYTHING REALLY **EVIL**..."

"IT WAS ALMOST AS IF WE WERE ALL PLAYING A **GAME**. A GAME WHICH **NEITHER** SIDE TOOK ENTIRELY **SERIOUSLY.**"

27

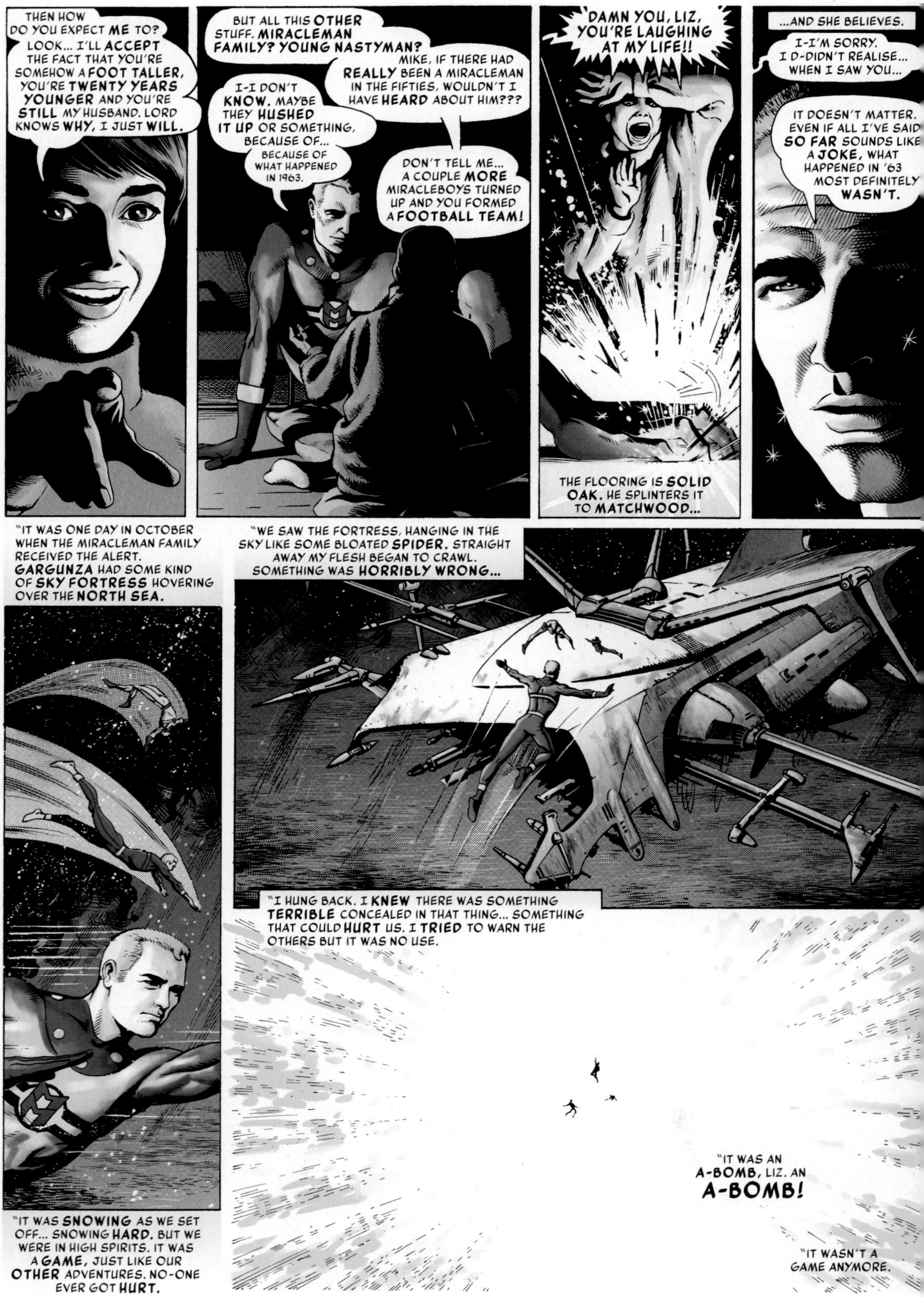
THEN HOW DO YOU EXPECT ME TO? LOOK... I'LL ACCEPT THE FACT THAT YOU'RE SOMEHOW A FOOT TALLER, YOU'RE TWENTY YEARS YOUNGER AND YOU'RE STILL MY HUSBAND. LORD KNOWS WHY, I JUST WILL.
BUT ALL THIS OTHER STUFF. MIRACLEMAN FAMILY? YOUNG NASTYMAN?
I-I DON'T KNOW. MAYBE THEY HUSHED IT UP OR SOMETHING, BECAUSE OF...
MIKE, IF THERE HAD REALLY BEEN A MIRACLEMAN IN THE FIFTIES, WOULDN'T I HAVE HEARD ABOUT HIM???
BECAUSE OF WHAT HAPPENED IN 1963.
DON'T TELL ME... A COUPLE MORE MIRACLEBOYS TURNED UP AND YOU FORMED A FOOTBALL TEAM!
DAMN YOU, LIZ, YOU'RE LAUGHING AT MY LIFE!!
THE FLOORING IS SOLID OAK. HE SPLINTERS IT TO MATCHWOOD...
...AND SHE BELIEVES.
I-I'M SORRY. I D-DIDN'T REALISE... WHEN I SAW YOU...
IT DOESN'T MATTER. EVEN IF ALL I'VE SAID SO FAR SOUNDS LIKE A JOKE, WHAT HAPPENED IN '63 MOST DEFINITELY WASN'T.
"IT WAS ONE DAY IN OCTOBER WHEN THE MIRACLEMAN FAMILY RECEIVED THE ALERT. GARGUNZA HAD SOME KIND OF SKY FORTRESS HOVERING OVER THE NORTH SEA.
"WE SAW THE FORTRESS, HANGING IN THE SKY LIKE SOME BLOATED SPIDER. STRAIGHT AWAY MY FLESH BEGAN TO CRAWL. SOMETHING WAS HORRIBLY WRONG...
"IT WAS SNOWING AS WE SET OFF... SNOWING HARD. BUT WE WERE IN HIGH SPIRITS. IT WAS A GAME, JUST LIKE OUR OTHER ADVENTURES. NO-ONE EVER GOT HURT.
"I HUNG BACK. I KNEW THERE WAS SOMETHING TERRIBLE CONCEALED IN THAT THING... SOMETHING THAT COULD HURT US. I TRIED TO WARN THE OTHERS BUT IT WAS NO USE.
"IT WAS AN A-BOMB, LIZ. AN A-BOMB!
"IT WASN'T A GAME ANYMORE.

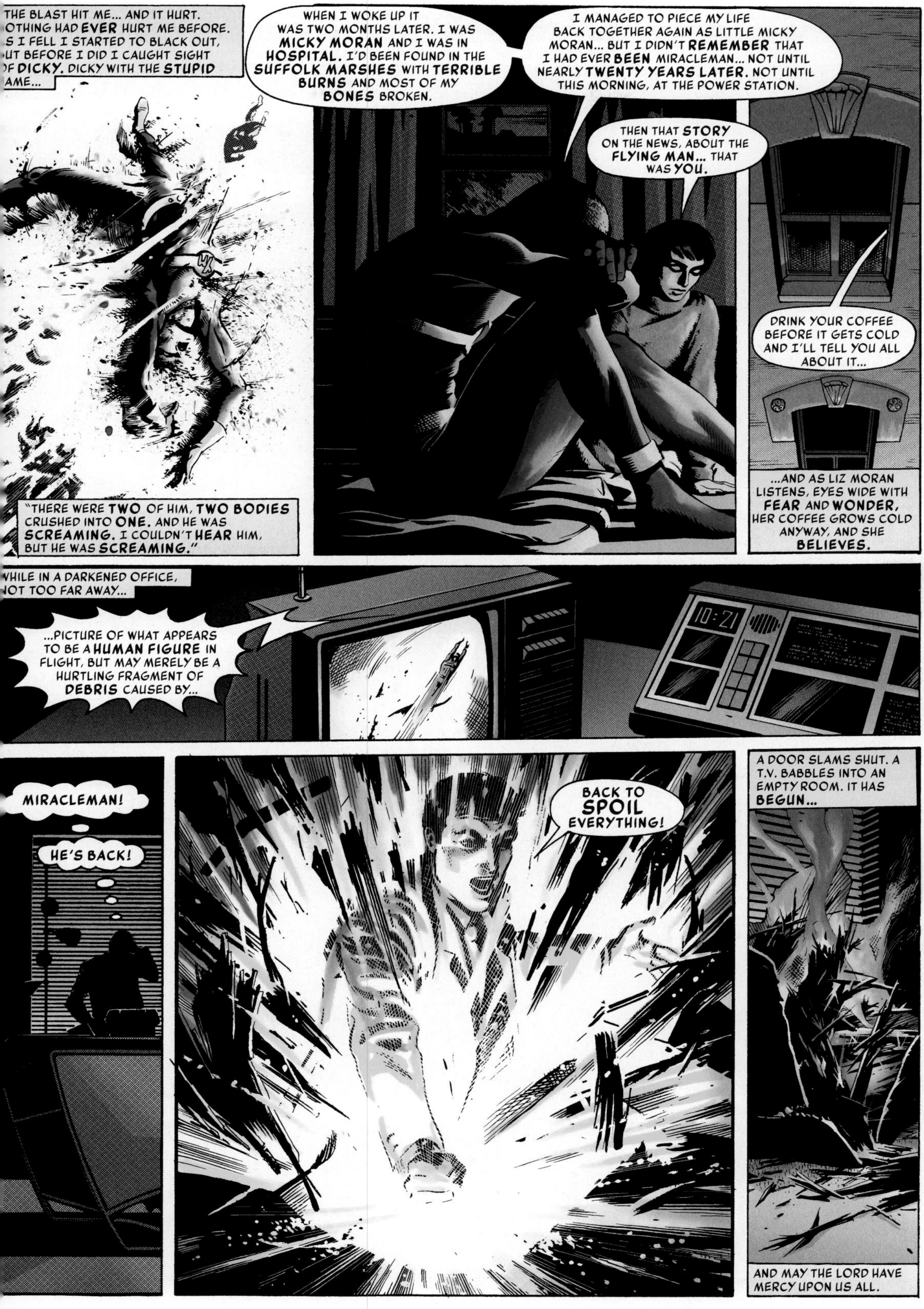
THE BLAST HIT ME... AND IT HURT. OTHING HAD EVER HURT ME BEFORE. S I FELL I STARTED TO BLACK OUT, UT BEFORE I DID I CAUGHT SIGHT OF DICKY. DICKY WITH THE STUPID AME...
"THERE WERE TWO OF HIM, TWO BODIES CRUSHED INTO ONE. AND HE WAS SCREAMING. I COULDN'T HEAR HIM, BUT HE WAS SCREAMING."
WHEN I WOKE UP IT WAS TWO MONTHS LATER. I WAS MICKY MORAN AND I WAS IN HOSPITAL. I'D BEEN FOUND IN THE SUFFOLK MARSHES WITH TERRIBLE BURNS AND MOST OF MY BONES BROKEN.
I MANAGED TO PIECE MY LIFE BACK TOGETHER AGAIN AS LITTLE MICKY MORAN... BUT I DIDN'T REMEMBER THAT I HAD EVER BEEN MIRACLEMAN... NOT UNTIL NEARLY TWENTY YEARS LATER. NOT UNTIL THIS MORNING, AT THE POWER STATION.
THEN THAT STORY ON THE NEWS, ABOUT THE FLYING MAN... THAT WAS YOU.
DRINK YOUR COFFEE BEFORE IT GETS COLD AND I'LL TELL YOU ALL ABOUT IT...
...AND AS LIZ MORAN LISTENS, EYES WIDE WITH FEAR AND WONDER, HER COFFEE GROWS COLD ANYWAY, AND SHE BELIEVES.
WHILE IN A DARKENED OFFICE, NOT TOO FAR AWAY...
...PICTURE OF WHAT APPEARS TO BE A HUMAN FIGURE IN FLIGHT, BUT MAY MERELY BE A HURTLING FRAGMENT OF DEBRIS CAUSED BY...
10:21
MIRACLEMAN!
HE'S BACK!
BACK TO SPOIL EVERYTHING!
A DOOR SLAMS SHUT. A T.V. BABBLES INTO AN EMPTY ROOM. IT HAS BEGUN...
AND MAY THE LORD HAVE MERCY UPON US ALL.

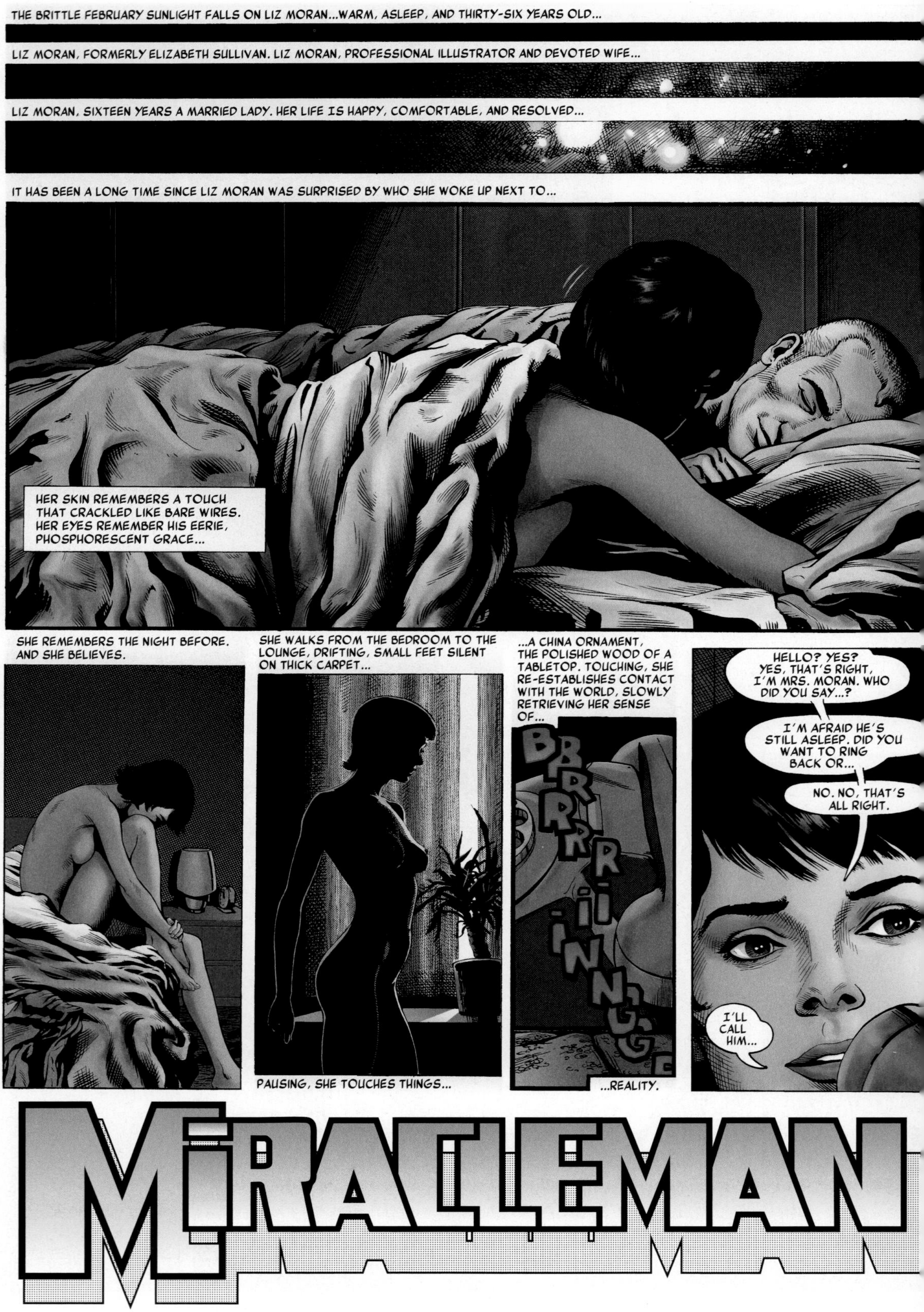
THE BRITTLE FEBRUARY SUNLIGHT FALLS ON LIZ MORAN...WARM, ASLEEP, AND THIRTY-SIX YEARS OLD...
LIZ MORAN, FORMERLY ELIZABETH SULLIVAN. LIZ MORAN, PROFESSIONAL ILLUSTRATOR AND DEVOTED WIFE...
LIZ MORAN, SIXTEEN YEARS A MARRIED LADY. HER LIFE IS HAPPY, COMFORTABLE, AND RESOLVED...
IT HAS BEEN A LONG TIME SINCE LIZ MORAN WAS SURPRISED BY WHO SHE WOKE UP NEXT TO...
HER SKIN REMEMBERS A TOUCH THAT CRACKLED LIKE BARE WIRES. HER EYES REMEMBER HIS EERIE, PHOSPHORESCENT GRACE...
SHE REMEMBERS THE NIGHT BEFORE. AND SHE BELIEVES.
SHE WALKS FROM THE BEDROOM TO THE LOUNGE, DRIFTING, SMALL FEET SILENT ON THICK CARPET...
PAUSING, SHE TOUCHES THINGS...
...A CHINA ORNAMENT, THE POLISHED WOOD OF A TABLETOP. TOUCHING, SHE RE-ESTABLISHES CONTACT WITH THE WORLD, SLOWLY RETRIEVING HER SENSE OF...
BRRRRRR-RIIIINNNGGG
...REALITY.
HELLO? YES? YES, THAT'S RIGHT, I'M MRS. MORAN. WHO DID YOU SAY...?
I'M AFRAID HE'S STILL ASLEEP. DID YOU WANT TO RING BACK OR...
NO. NO, THAT'S ALL RIGHT.
I'LL CALL HIM...
MIRACLEMAN

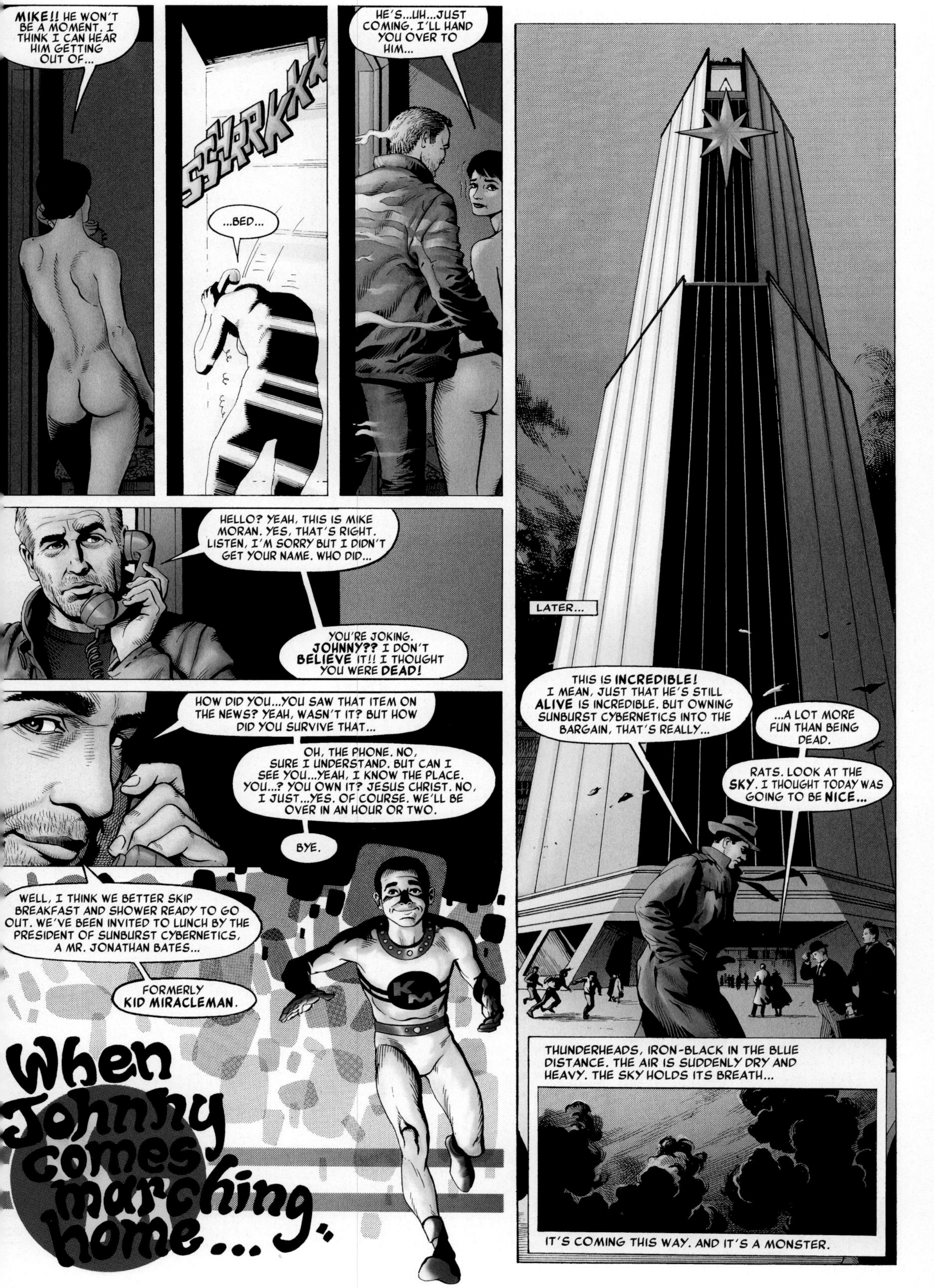

MIKE!! HE WON'T BE A MOMENT. I THINK I CAN HEAR HIM GETTING OUT OF...
SSHRKKK
...BED...
HE'S...UH...JUST COMING. I'LL HAND YOU OVER TO HIM...
HELLO? YEAH, THIS IS MIKE MORAN. YES, THAT'S RIGHT. LISTEN, I'M SORRY BUT I DIDN'T GET YOUR NAME. WHO DID...
YOU'RE JOKING. JOHNNY?? I DON'T BELIEVE IT!! I THOUGHT YOU WERE DEAD!
HOW DID YOU...YOU SAW THAT ITEM ON THE NEWS? YEAH, WASN'T IT? BUT HOW DID YOU SURVIVE THAT...
OH, THE PHONE. NO, SURE I UNDERSTAND. BUT CAN I SEE YOU...YEAH, I KNOW THE PLACE. YOU...? YOU OWN IT? JESUS CHRIST. NO, I JUST...YES. OF COURSE. WE'LL BE OVER IN AN HOUR OR TWO.
BYE.
WELL, I THINK WE BETTER SKIP BREAKFAST AND SHOWER READY TO GO OUT. WE'VE BEEN INVITED TO LUNCH BY THE PRESIDENT OF SUNBURST CYBERNETICS, A MR. JONATHAN BATES...
FORMERLY KID MIRACLEMAN.
KM
When Johnny comes marching home...
LATER...
THIS IS INCREDIBLE! I MEAN, JUST THAT HE'S STILL ALIVE IS INCREDIBLE. BUT OWNING SUNBURST CYBERNETICS INTO THE BARGAIN, THAT'S REALLY...
...A LOT MORE FUN THAN BEING DEAD.
RATS. LOOK AT THE SKY. I THOUGHT TODAY WAS GOING TO BE NICE...
THUNDERHEADS, IRON-BLACK IN THE BLUE DISTANCE. THE AIR IS SUDDENLY DRY AND HEAVY. THE SKY HOLDS ITS BREATH...
IT'S COMING THIS WAY. AND IT'S A MONSTER.

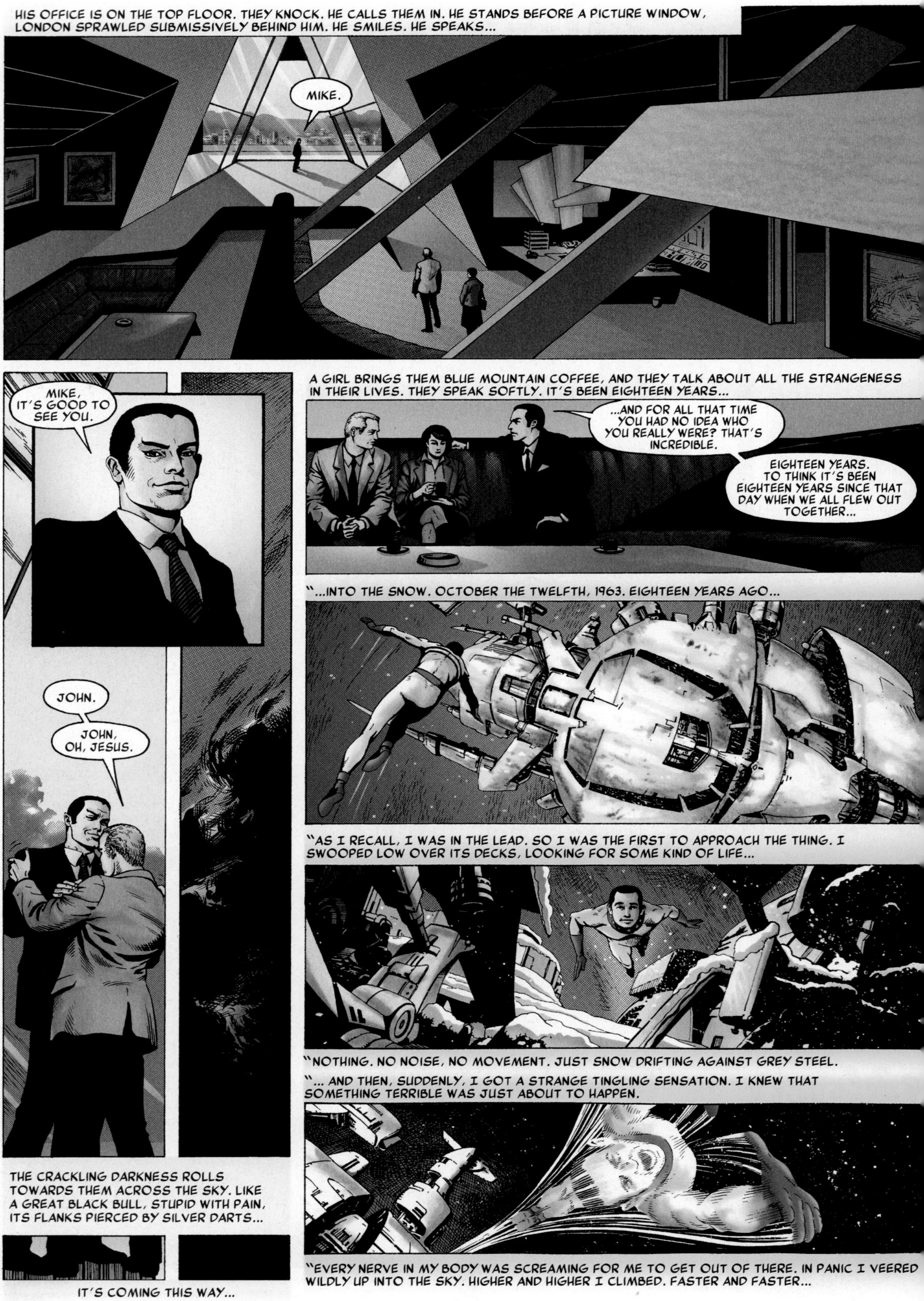
HIS OFFICE IS ON THE TOP FLOOR. THEY KNOCK. HE CALLS THEM IN. HE STANDS BEFORE A PICTURE WINDOW, LONDON SPRAWLED SUBMISSIVELY BEHIND HIM. HE SMILES. HE SPEAKS...
MIKE.
MIKE, IT'S GOOD TO SEE YOU.
JOHN.
JOHN, OH, JESUS.
THE CRACKLING DARKNESS ROLLS TOWARDS THEM ACROSS THE SKY. LIKE A GREAT BLACK BULL, STUPID WITH PAIN, ITS FLANKS PIERCED BY SILVER DARTS...
IT'S COMING THIS WAY...
A GIRL BRINGS THEM BLUE MOUNTAIN COFFEE, AND THEY TALK ABOUT ALL THE STRANGENESS IN THEIR LIVES. THEY SPEAK SOFTLY. IT'S BEEN EIGHTEEN YEARS...
...AND FOR ALL THAT TIME YOU HAD NO IDEA WHO YOU REALLY WERE? THAT'S INCREDIBLE.
EIGHTEEN YEARS. TO THINK IT'S BEEN EIGHTEEN YEARS SINCE THAT DAY WHEN WE ALL FLEW OUT TOGETHER...
"...INTO THE SNOW. OCTOBER THE TWELFTH, 1963. EIGHTEEN YEARS AGO...
"AS I RECALL, I WAS IN THE LEAD. SO I WAS THE FIRST TO APPROACH THE THING. I SWOOPED LOW OVER ITS DECKS, LOOKING FOR SOME KIND OF LIFE...
"NOTHING. NO NOISE, NO MOVEMENT. JUST SNOW DRIFTING AGAINST GREY STEEL.
"... AND THEN, SUDDENLY, I GOT A STRANGE TINGLING SENSATION. I KNEW THAT SOMETHING TERRIBLE WAS JUST ABOUT TO HAPPEN.
"EVERY NERVE IN MY BODY WAS SCREAMING FOR ME TO GET OUT OF THERE. IN PANIC I VEERED WILDLY UP INTO THE SKY. HIGHER AND HIGHER I CLIMBED. FASTER AND FASTER...

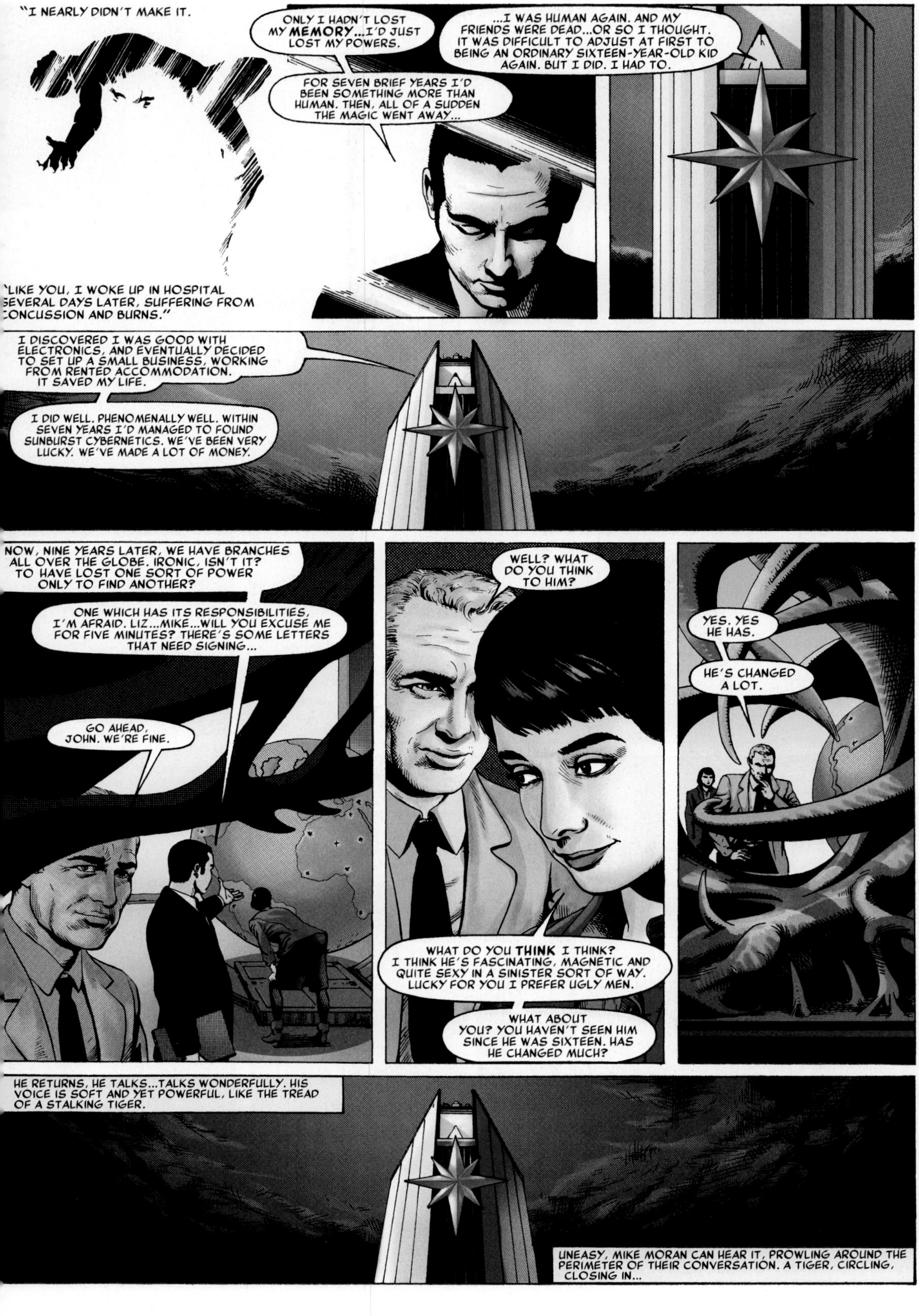
"I NEARLY DIDN'T MAKE IT.
ONLY I HADN'T LOST MY MEMORY...I'D JUST LOST MY POWERS.
FOR SEVEN BRIEF YEARS I'D BEEN SOMETHING MORE THAN HUMAN. THEN, ALL OF A SUDDEN THE MAGIC WENT AWAY...
...I WAS HUMAN AGAIN. AND MY FRIENDS WERE DEAD...OR SO I THOUGHT. IT WAS DIFFICULT TO ADJUST AT FIRST TO BEING AN ORDINARY SIXTEEN-YEAR-OLD KID AGAIN. BUT I DID. I HAD TO.
"LIKE YOU, I WOKE UP IN HOSPITAL SEVERAL DAYS LATER, SUFFERING FROM CONCUSSION AND BURNS."
I DISCOVERED I WAS GOOD WITH ELECTRONICS, AND EVENTUALLY DECIDED TO SET UP A SMALL BUSINESS, WORKING FROM RENTED ACCOMMODATION. IT SAVED MY LIFE.
I DID WELL. PHENOMENALLY WELL. WITHIN SEVEN YEARS I'D MANAGED TO FOUND SUNBURST CYBERNETICS. WE'VE BEEN VERY LUCKY. WE'VE MADE A LOT OF MONEY.
NOW, NINE YEARS LATER, WE HAVE BRANCHES ALL OVER THE GLOBE. IRONIC, ISN'T IT? TO HAVE LOST ONE SORT OF POWER ONLY TO FIND ANOTHER?
ONE WHICH HAS ITS RESPONSIBILITIES, I'M AFRAID. LIZ...MIKE...WILL YOU EXCUSE ME FOR FIVE MINUTES? THERE'S SOME LETTERS THAT NEED SIGNING...
GO AHEAD, JOHN. WE'RE FINE.
WELL? WHAT DO YOU THINK TO HIM?
WHAT DO YOU THINK I THINK? I THINK HE'S FASCINATING, MAGNETIC AND QUITE SEXY IN A SINISTER SORT OF WAY. LUCKY FOR YOU I PREFER UGLY MEN.
WHAT ABOUT YOU? YOU HAVEN'T SEEN HIM SINCE HE WAS SIXTEEN. HAS HE CHANGED MUCH?
YES. YES HE HAS.
HE'S CHANGED A LOT.
HE RETURNS, HE TALKS...TALKS WONDERFULLY. HIS VOICE IS SOFT AND YET POWERFUL, LIKE THE TREAD OF A STALKING TIGER.
UNEASY, MIKE MORAN CAN HEAR IT, PROWLING AROUND THE PERIMETER OF THEIR CONVERSATION. A TIGER, CIRCLING, CLOSING IN...

IT'S COMING THIS WAY. AND IT'S A MONSTER...

ANWAY, ENOUGH ABOUT ME. HOW ABOUT SOME LUNCH?

YEAH, SURE...

UH, LIZ...DO YOU THINK I COULD JUST SPEAK TO JOHN ALONE FOR A MOMENT?

LIZ MORAN NODS, SMILING AS THE TWO MEN STEP OUT ON TO THE BALCONY. SHE WONDERS WHAT MIKE NEEDED TO SAY THAT WAS NOT FOR HER EARS...SUPERHERO TALK.

STORM'S BREWING UP NICELY. IT'S A BEAUTY, ISN'T IT?

JOHN...

JOHN, I LISTENED TO YOUR STORY JUST NOW...RAGS TO RICHES, REDEMPTION THROUGH HONEST TOIL. IT'S A GREAT STORY.

I REALLY WANTED TO BELIEVE IT, JOHN.

"...BUT THEN HALFWAY THROUGH I GOT THIS FUNNY IDEA INTO MY HEAD. I THOUGHT 'WHAT IF HE'S LYING?' I TRIED TO GET RID OF IT. I TRIED. BUT I COULDN'T.

"I THOUGHT 'WHAT IF HE DIDN'T LOSE HIS POWERS? WHAT IF HE SURVIVED THA BLAST THAT TOOK OUT ME AND DICKY AND WAS *STILL* KID MIRACLEMAN??"

I TRIED TO IMAGINE WHAT IT WOULD *FEEL* LIKE...TO BE SIXTEEN YEARS OLD AND THE MOST POWERFUL CREATURE ON THE FACE OF THE PLANET...

...AND TO BE ANSWERABLE TO NO-ONE. YOU COULD DO ANYTHING, JOHN. YOU'D NEVER NEED TO TURN BACK TO DULL, WEAK, HUMAN JOHNNY BATES EVER AGAIN.

OH, SURE, YOU COULD TAKE HIS NAME, HIS IDENTITY...BUT YOU COULD STAY AS KID MIRACLEMAN FOREVER. YOU COULD HAVE IT ALL... MONEY, PRESTIGE, FAME...

YOU COULD SEVER ALL YOUR LINKS WITH HUMANITY. YOU COULD BECOME REMORSELESS, UNSTOPPABLE...

...AND TOTALLY CORRUPT. IS THAT IT, JOHN? IS THAT WHAT HAPPENED? YOU'RE STILL KID MIRACLEMAN, AREN'T YOU?

"I CAN TELL BY YOUR VOICE, BY THE WAY YOU STAND...YOU'RE NOT HUMAN, JOHN. I CAN FEEL IT."

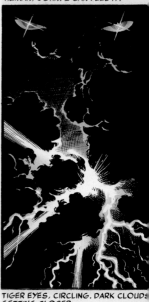

TIGER EYES, CIRCLING. DARK CLOUD: GETTING CLOSER...

34

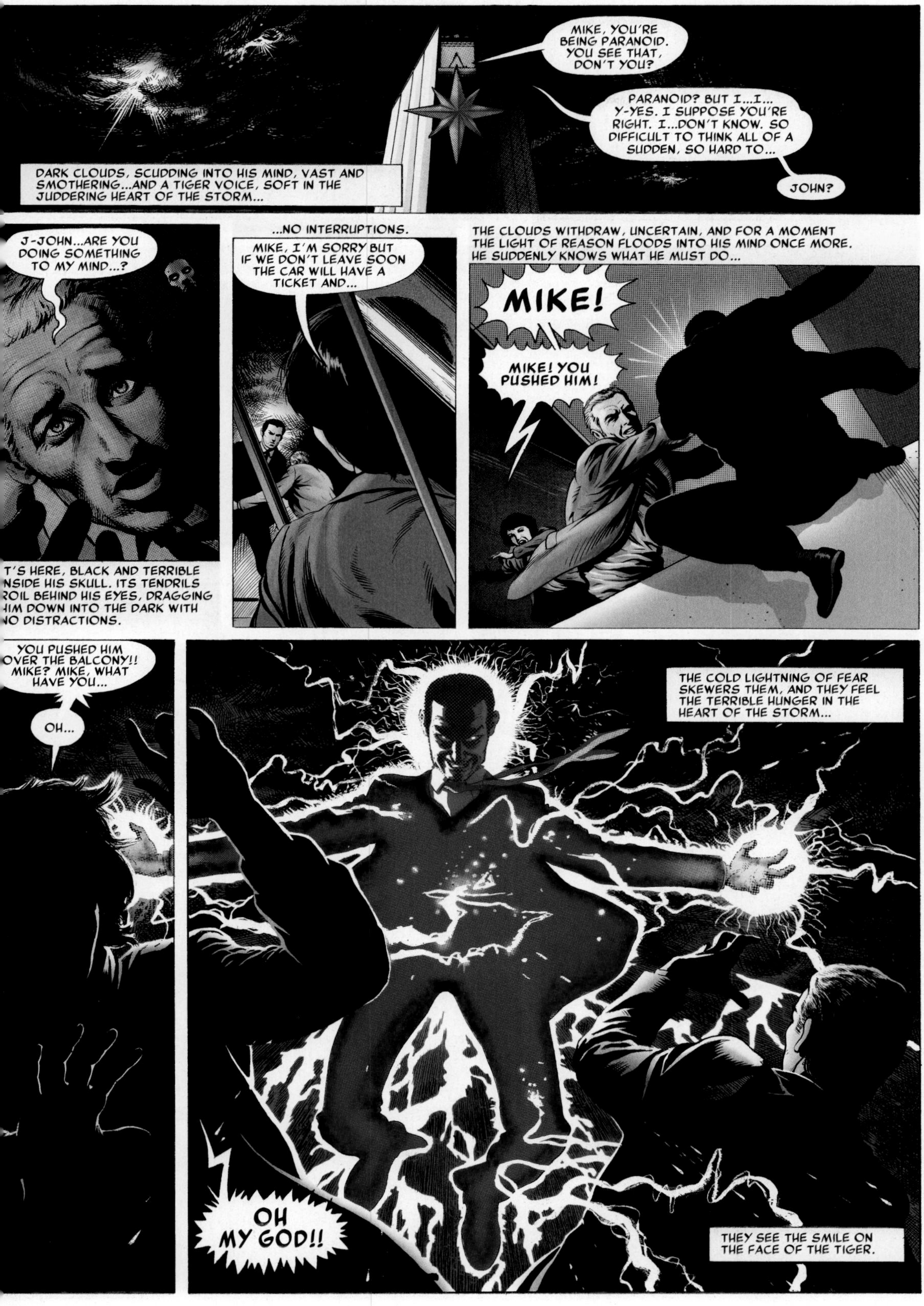
MIKE, YOU'RE BEING PARANOID. YOU SEE THAT, DON'T YOU?
PARANOID? BUT I...I... Y-YES. I SUPPOSE YOU'RE RIGHT. I...DON'T KNOW. SO DIFFICULT TO THINK ALL OF A SUDDEN, SO HARD TO...
DARK CLOUDS, SCUDDING INTO HIS MIND, VAST AND SMOTHERING...AND A TIGER VOICE, SOFT IN THE JUDDERING HEART OF THE STORM...
JOHN?
J-JOHN...ARE YOU DOING SOMETHING TO MY MIND...?
T'S HERE, BLACK AND TERRIBLE NSIDE HIS SKULL. ITS TENDRILS ROIL BEHIND HIS EYES, DRAGGING HIM DOWN INTO THE DARK WITH NO DISTRACTIONS.
...NO INTERRUPTIONS.
MIKE, I'M SORRY BUT IF WE DON'T LEAVE SOON THE CAR WILL HAVE A TICKET AND...
THE CLOUDS WITHDRAW, UNCERTAIN, AND FOR A MOMENT THE LIGHT OF REASON FLOODS INTO HIS MIND ONCE MORE. HE SUDDENLY KNOWS WHAT HE MUST DO...
MIKE!
MIKE! YOU PUSHED HIM!
YOU PUSHED HIM OVER THE BALCONY!! MIKE? MIKE, WHAT HAVE YOU...
OH...
THE COLD LIGHTNING OF FEAR SKEWERS THEM, AND THEY FEEL THE TERRIBLE HUNGER IN THE HEART OF THE STORM...
OH MY GOD!!
THEY SEE THE SMILE ON THE FACE OF THE TIGER.

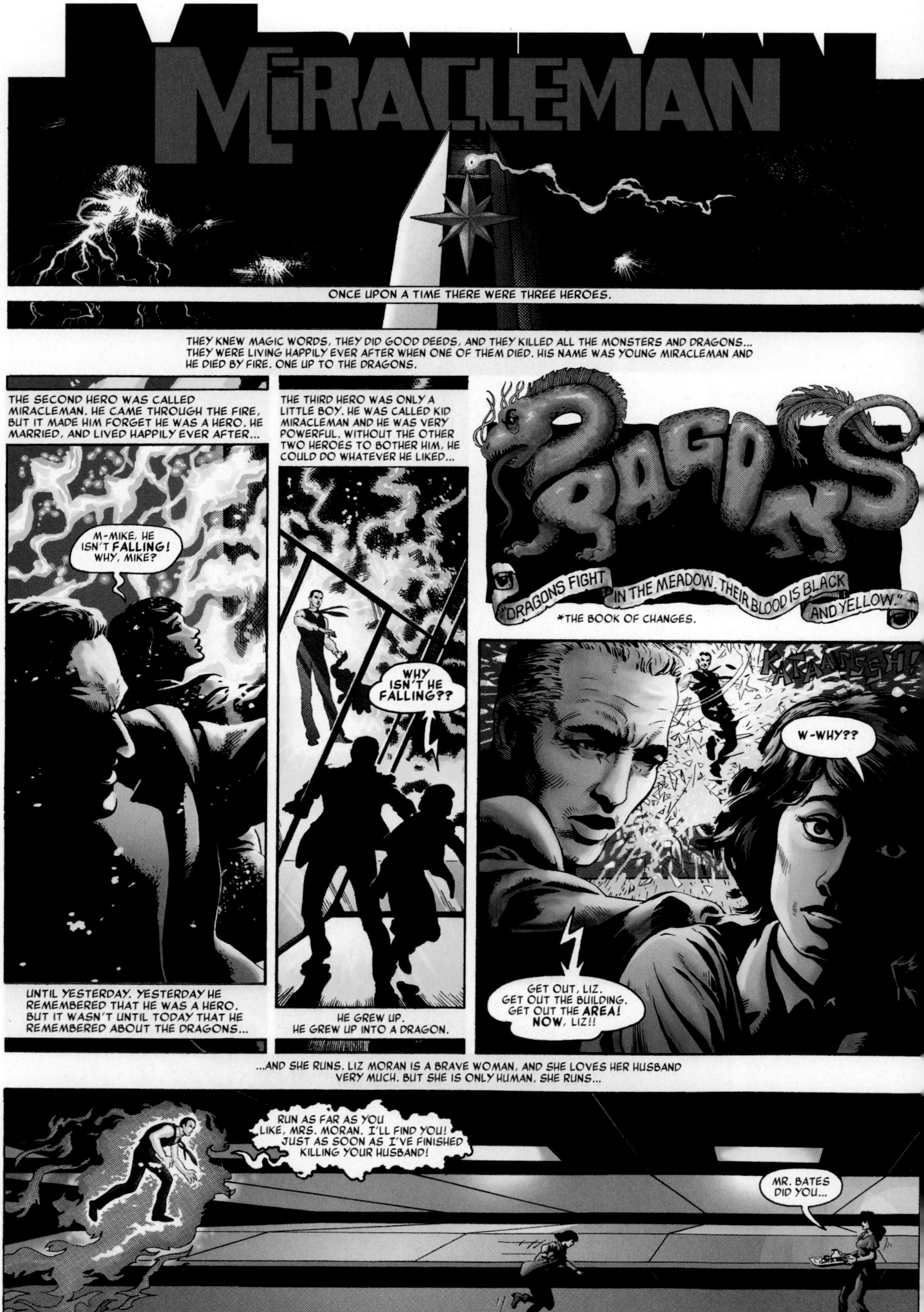
MIRACLEMAN
ONCE UPON A TIME THERE WERE THREE HEROES.
THEY KNEW MAGIC WORDS, THEY DID GOOD DEEDS, AND THEY KILLED ALL THE MONSTERS AND DRAGONS... THEY WERE LIVING HAPPILY EVER AFTER WHEN ONE OF THEM DIED. HIS NAME WAS YOUNG MIRACLEMAN AND HE DIED BY FIRE. ONE UP TO THE DRAGONS.
THE SECOND HERO WAS CALLED MIRACLEMAN. HE CAME THROUGH THE FIRE, BUT IT MADE HIM FORGET HE WAS A HERO. HE MARRIED, AND LIVED HAPPILY EVER AFTER...
M-MIKE, HE ISN'T FALLING! WHY, MIKE?
UNTIL YESTERDAY. YESTERDAY HE REMEMBERED THAT HE WAS A HERO. BUT IT WASN'T UNTIL TODAY THAT HE REMEMBERED ABOUT THE DRAGONS...
THE THIRD HERO WAS ONLY A LITTLE BOY. HE WAS CALLED KID MIRACLEMAN AND HE WAS VERY POWERFUL. WITHOUT THE OTHER TWO HEROES TO BOTHER HIM, HE COULD DO WHATEVER HE LIKED...
WHY ISN'T HE FALLING??
HE GREW UP. HE GREW UP INTO A DRAGON.
DRAGONS
"DRAGONS FIGHT IN THE MEADOW. THEIR BLOOD IS BLACK AND YELLOW."*
*THE BOOK OF CHANGES.
KATAASSSH!
W-WHY??
GET OUT, LIZ. GET OUT THE BUILDING. GET OUT THE AREA! NOW, LIZ!!
...AND SHE RUNS. LIZ MORAN IS A BRAVE WOMAN, AND SHE LOVES HER HUSBAND VERY MUCH. BUT SHE IS ONLY HUMAN. SHE RUNS...
RUN AS FAR AS YOU LIKE, MRS. MORAN. I'LL FIND YOU! JUST AS SOON AS I'VE FINISHED KILLING YOUR HUSBAND!
MR. BATES DID YOU...

FOR TO BE HUMAN IS NOT ENOUGH...

...WANT COFFEE ‡‡
OH...

OH, CHRIST.

WHEN GODS CRY WAR AMIDST THE THUNDER.

YOU DROPPED THE COFFEE, STEPHANIE.

...HUH...HHUH..

HER NAME IS STEPHANIE. SHE LIKES ADAM AND THE ANTS. HER BOYFRIEND'S NAME IS BRIAN. SHE COLLECTS WEDGEWOOD. HER INSIDES HAVE TURNED TO WATER. SHE IS ONLY HUMAN.

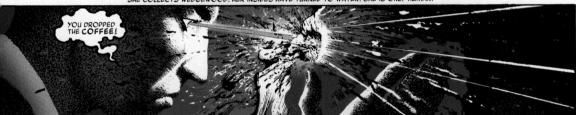

YOU DROPPED THE COFFEE!

HE LOOKS AT THE CHARRED AND PULVERISED THING THAT HAD MET THE GAZE OF A DRAGON. HE WANTS TO VOMIT.

AND HE THINKS, "THAT COULD HAVE BEEN LIZ."

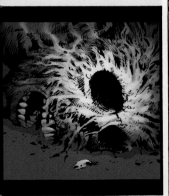

HE LOOKS AT THE TIGER-SMILE AND THE DRAGON EYES OF THE THING THAT HAD ONCE BEEN A BOY CALLED JOHNNY BATES. HE WANTS TO VOMIT.

AND HE THINKS, "THAT COULD HAVE BEEN ME!"

WHY, JOHN? SHE HADN'T DONE ANYTHING...

JESUS CHRIST, WHY?

JUST TO SHOW YOU THAT I DON'T MIND DOING THAT SORT OF THING.

IN FACT, I QUITE ENJOY IT.

THAT'S WHAT I'M GOING TO DO TO YOUR WIFE.

...KIMOTA.

37

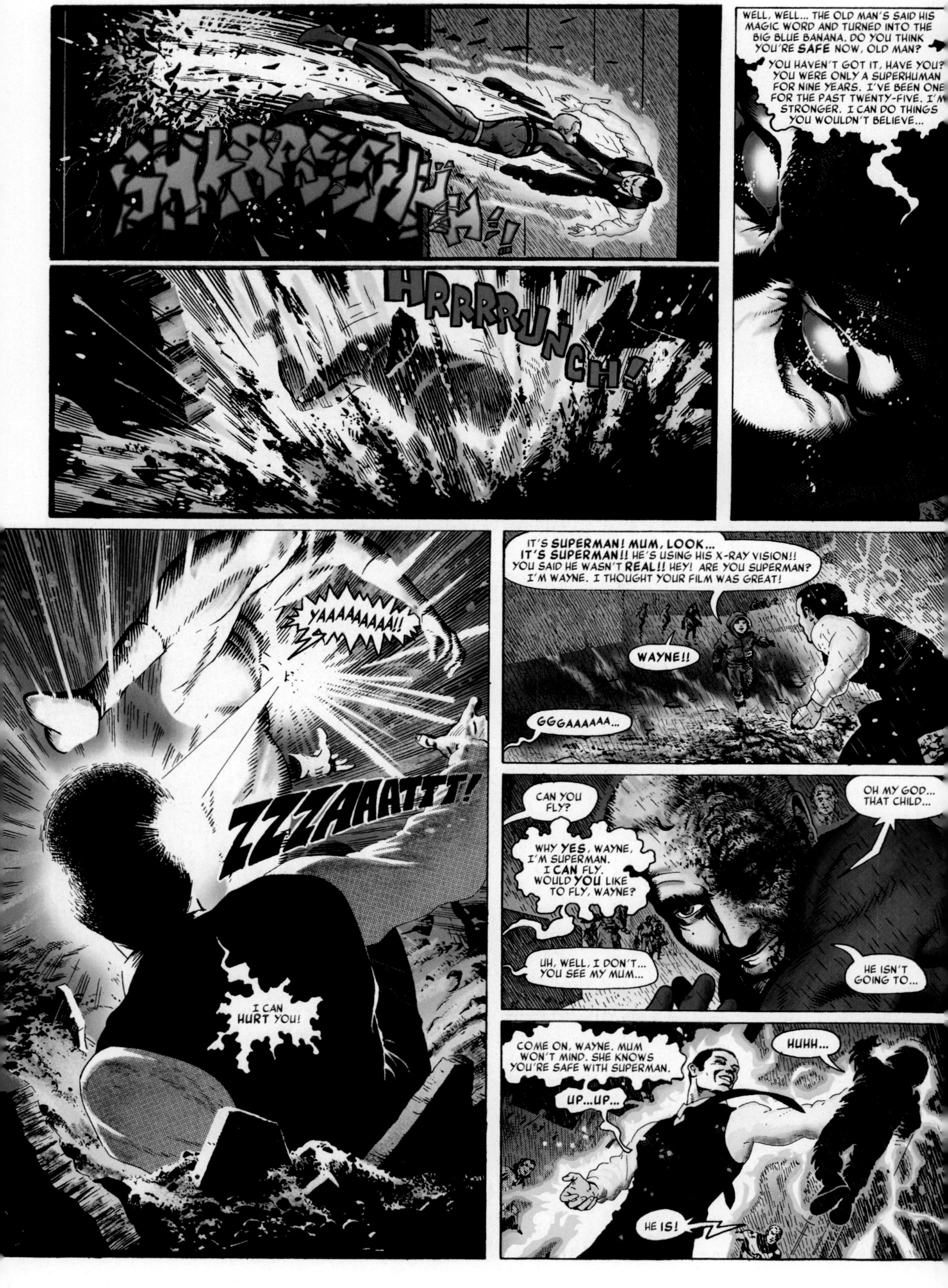
SHHKRASSSHHH!!
WELL, WELL... THE OLD MAN'S SAID HIS MAGIC WORD AND TURNED INTO THE BIG BLUE BANANA. DO YOU THINK YOU'RE SAFE NOW, OLD MAN?
YOU HAVEN'T GOT IT, HAVE YOU? YOU WERE ONLY A SUPERHUMAN FOR NINE YEARS. I'VE BEEN ONE FOR THE PAST TWENTY-FIVE. I'M STRONGER. I CAN DO THINGS YOU WOULDN'T BELIEVE...
HRRRRRUNCH!
YAAAAAAAAA!!
ZZZAAATTT!
I CAN HURT YOU!
IT'S SUPERMAN! MUM, LOOK... IT'S SUPERMAN!! HE'S USING HIS X-RAY VISION!! YOU SAID HE WASN'T REAL!! HEY! ARE YOU SUPERMAN? I'M WAYNE. I THOUGHT YOUR FILM WAS GREAT!
WAYNE!!
GGGAAAAAA...
CAN YOU FLY?
WHY YES, WAYNE, I'M SUPERMAN. I CAN FLY. WOULD YOU LIKE TO FLY, WAYNE?
UH, WELL, I DON'T... YOU SEE MY MUM...
OH MY GOD... THAT CHILD...
HE ISN'T GOING TO...
COME ON, WAYNE. MUM WON'T MIND. SHE KNOWS YOU'RE SAFE WITH SUPERMAN.
UP...UP...
HUHH...
HE IS!

...AND AWAAAAY!!

...WAYNE...

HE'S HEADING TOWARDS THAT WALL! I'VE GOT TO...

DOOFFF!

DONE IT!

HE'S ALRIGHT. I CAUGHT HIM. I THINK I MIGHT HAVE BROKEN A COUPLE OF HIS RIBS... THE SPEED HE WAS TRAVELLING, YOU SEE. I COULDN'T...UH...

...I'M SORRY... I COULDN'T HELP IT... I-IT WAS THE SPEED...

GIVE HIM TO ME, YOU BLOODY MONSTER!!

WAYNE. OH GOD, OH LOVE. WAYNE...

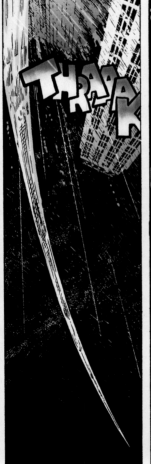

THRAAAK

OH GOD. HE KNOCKED ME INTO THE SKY. HOW DID HE GET TO BE SO STRONG??

WHY IS HE DOING THIS? WHY HAS HE GROWN UP WHILE MIRACLEMAN HASN'T AGED? THIS IS ALL TOO FAST. I NEED TIME TO THINK...

NO GOOD. HE'S COMING AFTER ME!

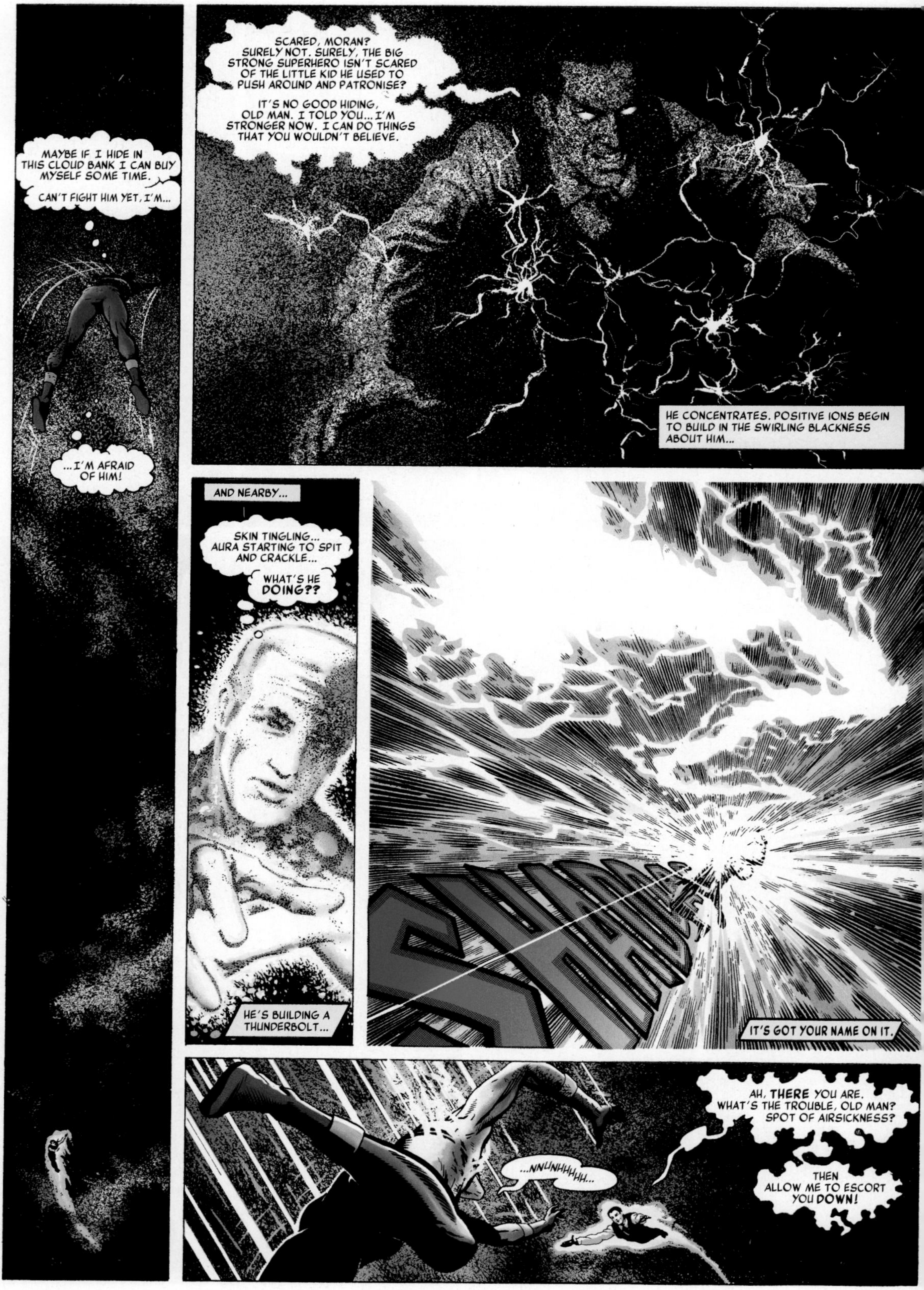

SCARED, MORAN? SURELY NOT. SURELY, THE BIG STRONG SUPERHERO ISN'T SCARED OF THE LITTLE KID HE USED TO PUSH AROUND AND PATRONISE?
IT'S NO GOOD HIDING, OLD MAN. I TOLD YOU... I'M STRONGER NOW. I CAN DO THINGS THAT YOU WOULDN'T BELIEVE.
MAYBE IF I HIDE IN THIS CLOUD BANK I CAN BUY MYSELF SOME TIME.
CAN'T FIGHT HIM YET, I'M...
...I'M AFRAID OF HIM!
HE CONCENTRATES. POSITIVE IONS BEGIN TO BUILD IN THE SWIRLING BLACKNESS ABOUT HIM...
AND NEARBY...
SKIN TINGLING... AURA STARTING TO SPIT AND CRACKLE...
WHAT'S HE DOING??
HE'S BUILDING A THUNDERBOLT...
IT'S GOT YOUR NAME ON IT.
AH, THERE YOU ARE. WHAT'S THE TROUBLE, OLD MAN? SPOT OF AIRSICKNESS?
...NNUNHHHHH...
THEN ALLOW ME TO ESCORT YOU DOWN!

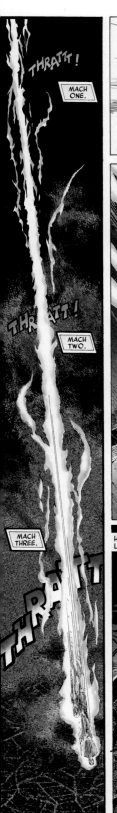

THRATT !

MACH ONE.

THRATT !

MACH TWO.

MACH THREE.

THRATT !

J-JOHNNY...?

DHRUPP!

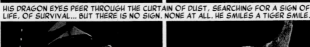

A CROW-BLACK SHAPE DROPS FROM THE SEETHING HELL OF THE SKY, DOWN TO THE RIM OF THE STILL-SMOULDERING CRATER...

HE IS READY TO FIGHT AGAIN.

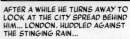

HIS DRAGON EYES PEER THROUGH THE CURTAIN OF DUST, SEARCHING FOR A SIGN OF LIFE, OF SURVIVAL... BUT THERE IS NO SIGN. NONE AT ALL. HE SMILES A TIGER SMILE...

AFTER A WHILE HE TURNS AWAY TO LOOK AT THE CITY SPREAD BEHIND HIM... LONDON, HUDDLED AGAINST THE STINGING RAIN...

HE WONDERS WHAT TO DO NEXT.

41

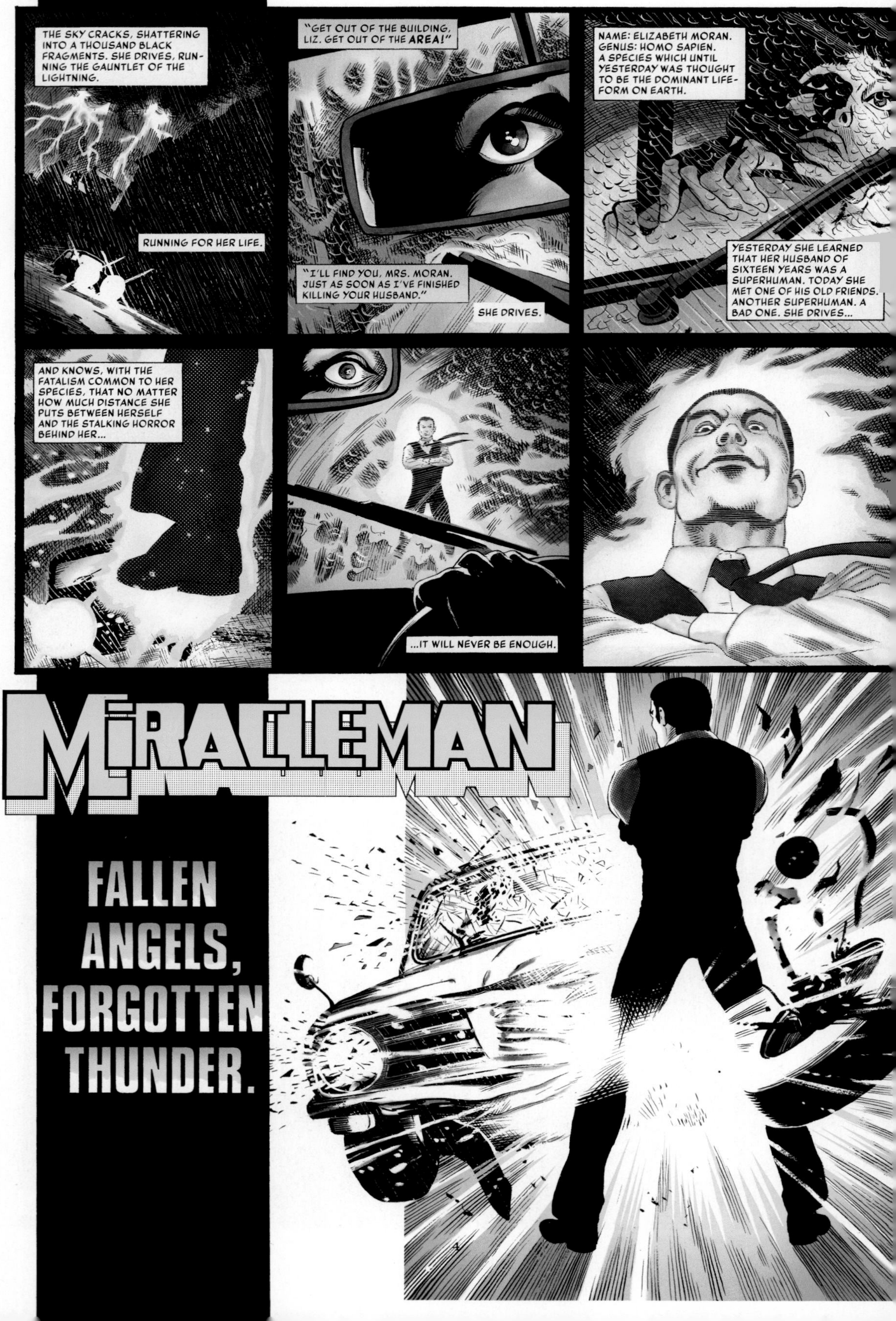
THE SKY CRACKS, SHATTERING INTO A THOUSAND BLACK FRAGMENTS. SHE DRIVES, RUNNING THE GAUNTLET OF THE LIGHTNING.
RUNNING FOR HER LIFE.
"GET OUT OF THE BUILDING, LIZ. GET OUT OF THE AREA!"
"I'LL FIND YOU, MRS. MORAN. JUST AS SOON AS I'VE FINISHED KILLING YOUR HUSBAND."
SHE DRIVES.
NAME: ELIZABETH MORAN. GENUS: HOMO SAPIEN. A SPECIES WHICH UNTIL YESTERDAY WAS THOUGHT TO BE THE DOMINANT LIFE-FORM ON EARTH.
YESTERDAY SHE LEARNED THAT HER HUSBAND OF SIXTEEN YEARS WAS A SUPERHUMAN. TODAY SHE MET ONE OF HIS OLD FRIENDS. ANOTHER SUPERHUMAN. A BAD ONE. SHE DRIVES...
AND KNOWS, WITH THE FATALISM COMMON TO HER SPECIES, THAT NO MATTER HOW MUCH DISTANCE SHE PUTS BETWEEN HERSELF AND THE STALKING HORROR BEHIND HER...
...IT WILL NEVER BE ENOUGH.
MIRACLEMAN
FALLEN ANGELS, FORGOTTEN THUNDER.

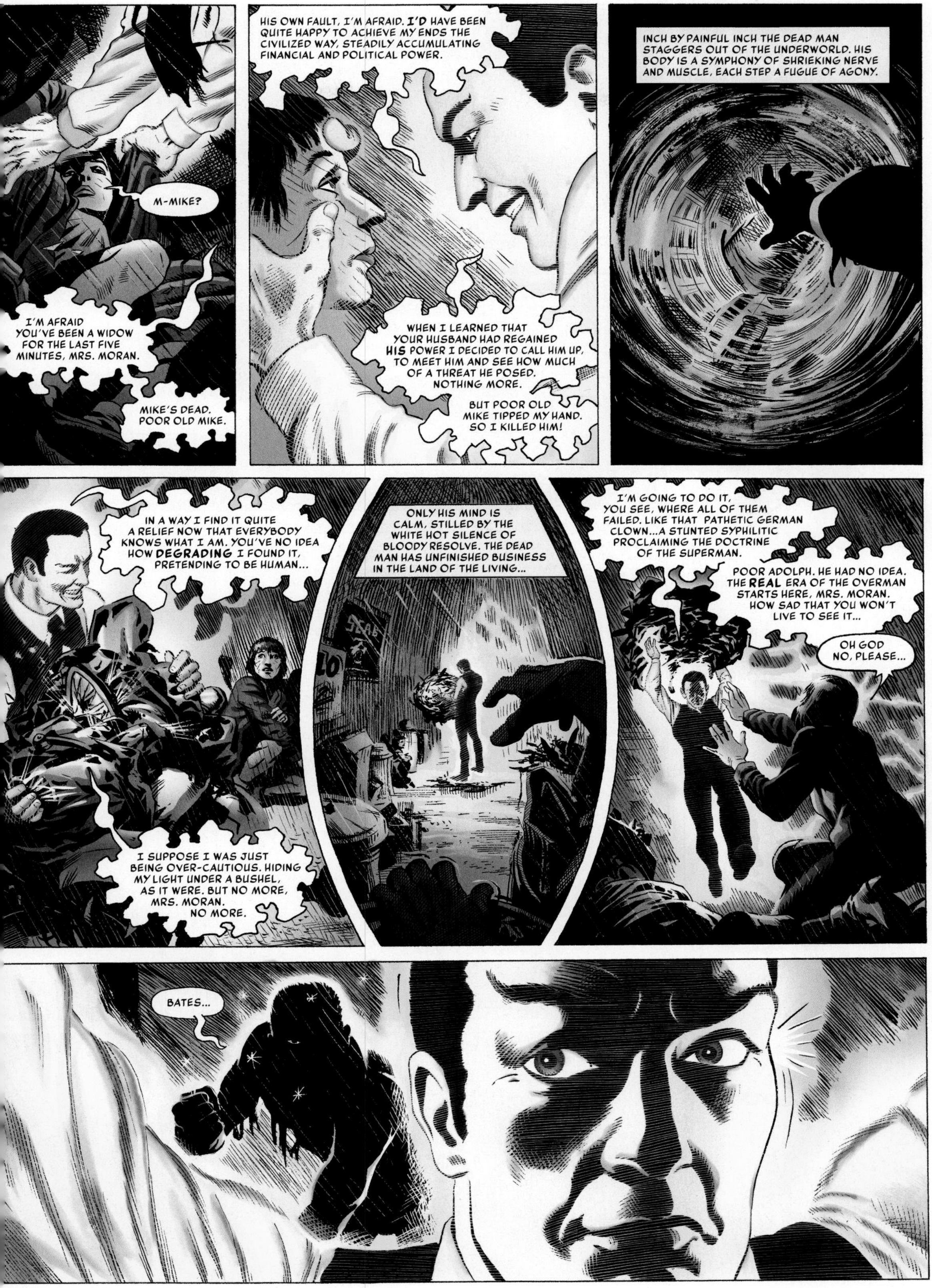
M-MIKE?
I'M AFRAID YOU'VE BEEN A WIDOW FOR THE LAST FIVE MINUTES, MRS. MORAN.
MIKE'S DEAD. POOR OLD MIKE.
HIS OWN FAULT, I'M AFRAID. I'D HAVE BEEN QUITE HAPPY TO ACHIEVE MY ENDS THE CIVILIZED WAY, STEADILY ACCUMULATING FINANCIAL AND POLITICAL POWER.
WHEN I LEARNED THAT YOUR HUSBAND HAD REGAINED HIS POWER I DECIDED TO CALL HIM UP, TO MEET HIM AND SEE HOW MUCH OF A THREAT HE POSED. NOTHING MORE.
BUT POOR OLD MIKE TIPPED MY HAND. SO I KILLED HIM!
INCH BY PAINFUL INCH THE DEAD MAN STAGGERS OUT OF THE UNDERWORLD. HIS BODY IS A SYMPHONY OF SHRIEKING NERVE AND MUSCLE, EACH STEP A FUGUE OF AGONY.
IN A WAY I FIND IT QUITE A RELIEF NOW THAT EVERYBODY KNOWS WHAT I AM. YOU'VE NO IDEA HOW DEGRADING I FOUND IT, PRETENDING TO BE HUMAN...
I SUPPOSE I WAS JUST BEING OVER-CAUTIOUS. HIDING MY LIGHT UNDER A BUSHEL, AS IT WERE. BUT NO MORE, MRS. MORAN. NO MORE.
ONLY HIS MIND IS CALM, STILLED BY THE WHITE HOT SILENCE OF BLOODY RESOLVE. THE DEAD MAN HAS UNFINISHED BUSINESS IN THE LAND OF THE LIVING...
I'M GOING TO DO IT, YOU SEE, WHERE ALL OF THEM FAILED. LIKE THAT PATHETIC GERMAN CLOWN...A STUNTED SYPHILITIC PROCLAIMING THE DOCTRINE OF THE SUPERMAN.
POOR ADOLPH. HE HAD NO IDEA. THE REAL ERA OF THE OVERMAN STARTS HERE, MRS. MORAN. HOW SAD THAT YOU WON'T LIVE TO SEE IT...
OH GOD NO, PLEASE...
BATES...

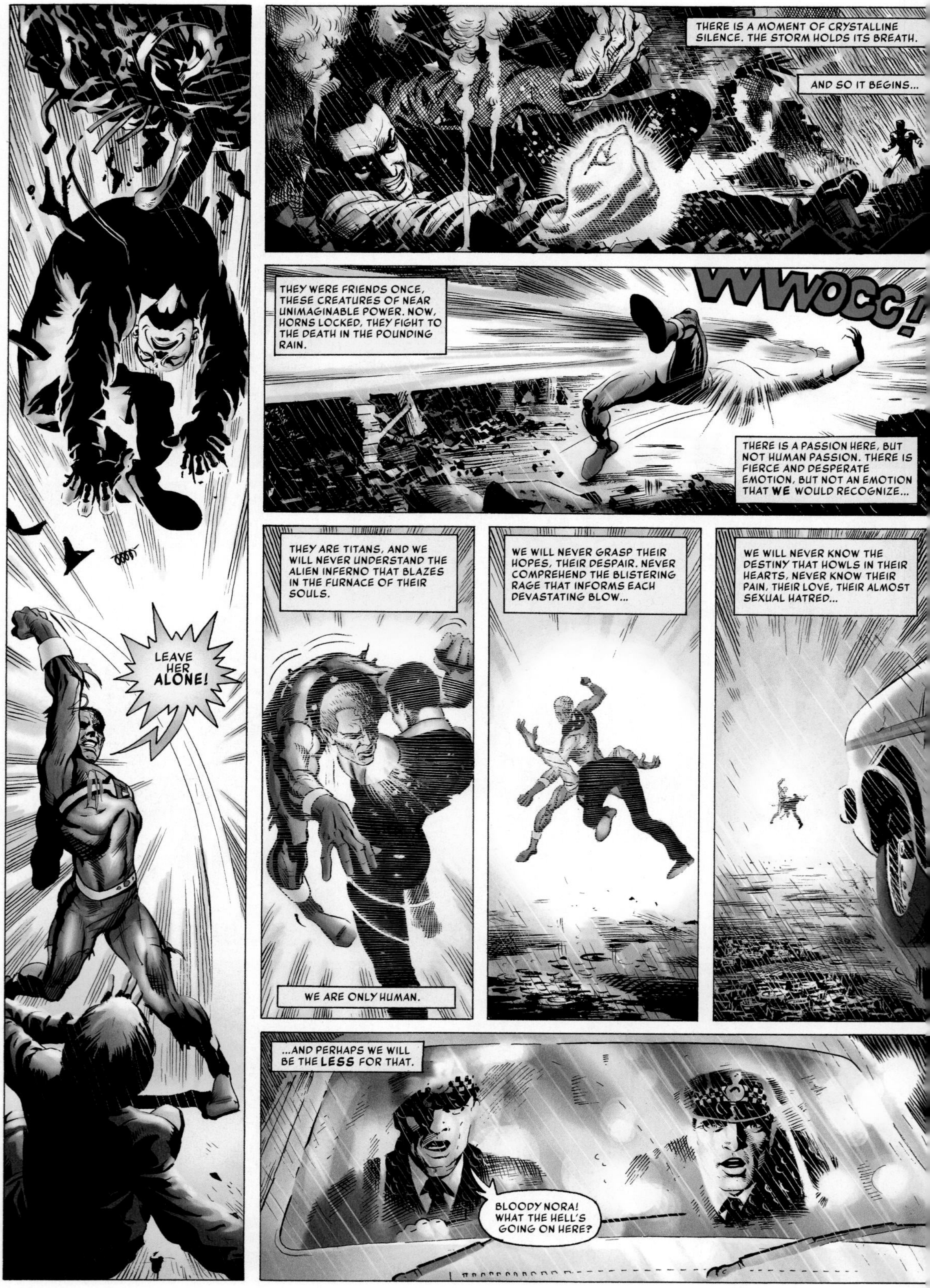
THERE IS A MOMENT OF CRYSTALLINE SILENCE. THE STORM HOLDS ITS BREATH.
AND SO IT BEGINS...
LEAVE HER ALONE!
THEY WERE FRIENDS ONCE, THESE CREATURES OF NEAR UNIMAGINABLE POWER. NOW, HORNS LOCKED, THEY FIGHT TO THE DEATH IN THE POUNDING RAIN.
WWOCC!
THERE IS A PASSION HERE, BUT NOT HUMAN PASSION. THERE IS FIERCE AND DESPERATE EMOTION, BUT NOT AN EMOTION THAT WE WOULD RECOGNIZE...
THEY ARE TITANS, AND WE WILL NEVER UNDERSTAND THE ALIEN INFERNO THAT BLAZES IN THE FURNACE OF THEIR SOULS.
WE ARE ONLY HUMAN.
WE WILL NEVER GRASP THEIR HOPES, THEIR DESPAIR. NEVER COMPREHEND THE BLISTERING RAGE THAT INFORMS EACH DEVASTATING BLOW...
WE WILL NEVER KNOW THE DESTINY THAT HOWLS IN THEIR HEARTS, NEVER KNOW THEIR PAIN, THEIR LOVE, THEIR ALMOST SEXUAL HATRED...
...AND PERHAPS WE WILL BE THE LESS FOR THAT.
BLOODY NORA! WHAT THE HELL'S GOING ON HERE?

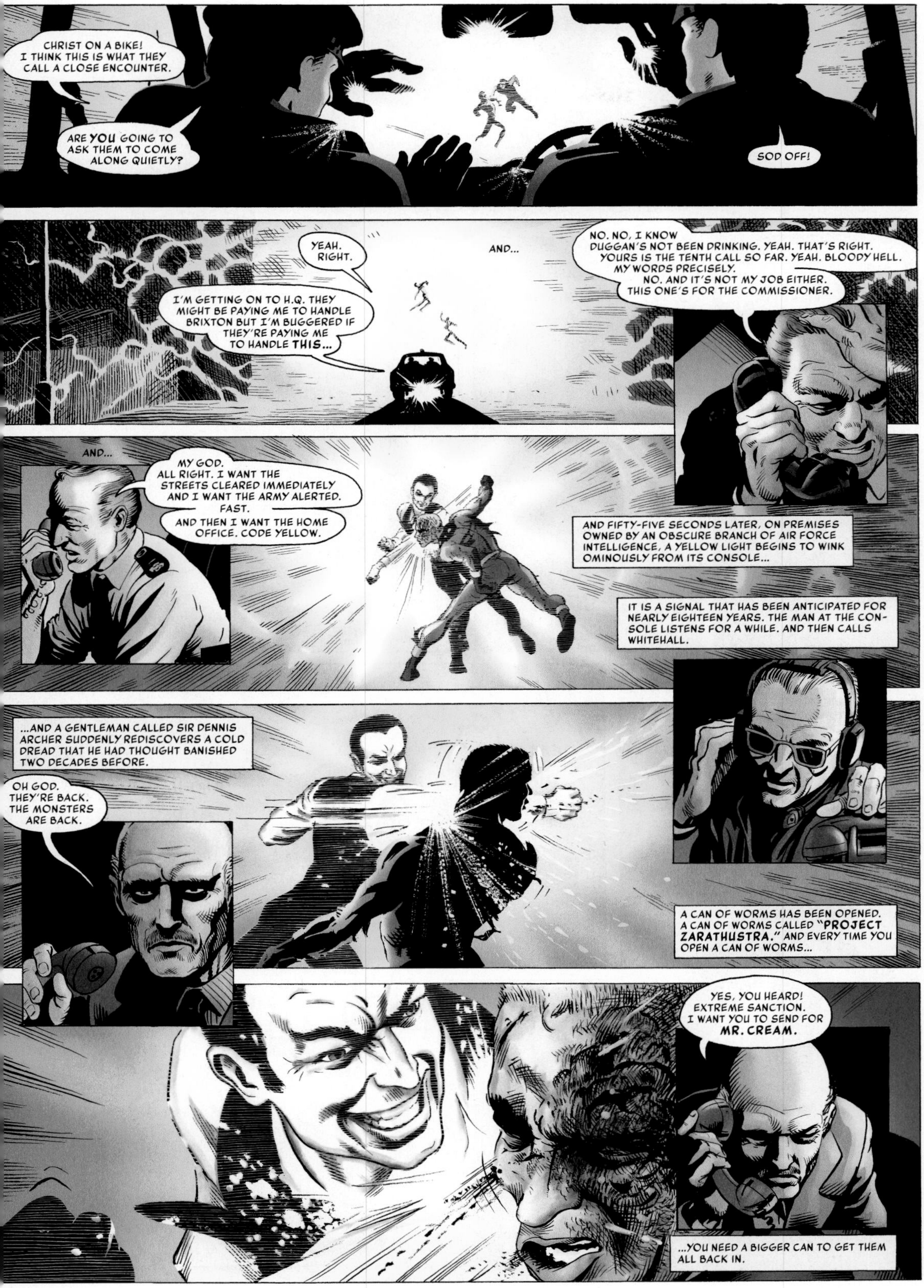
CHRIST ON A BIKE! I THINK THIS IS WHAT THEY CALL A CLOSE ENCOUNTER.
ARE YOU GOING TO ASK THEM TO COME ALONG QUIETLY?
SOD OFF!
YEAH. RIGHT.
I'M GETTING ON TO H.Q. THEY MIGHT BE PAYING ME TO HANDLE BRIXTON BUT I'M BUGGERED IF THEY'RE PAYING ME TO HANDLE THIS...
AND...
NO. NO, I KNOW DUGGAN'S NOT BEEN DRINKING. YEAH. THAT'S RIGHT. YOURS IS THE TENTH CALL SO FAR. YEAH. BLOODY HELL. MY WORDS PRECISELY.
NO. AND IT'S NOT MY JOB EITHER. THIS ONE'S FOR THE COMMISSIONER.
AND...
MY GOD. ALL RIGHT. I WANT THE STREETS CLEARED IMMEDIATELY AND I WANT THE ARMY ALERTED. FAST.
AND THEN I WANT THE HOME OFFICE. CODE YELLOW.
AND FIFTY-FIVE SECONDS LATER, ON PREMISES OWNED BY AN OBSCURE BRANCH OF AIR FORCE INTELLIGENCE, A YELLOW LIGHT BEGINS TO WINK OMINOUSLY FROM ITS CONSOLE...
IT IS A SIGNAL THAT HAS BEEN ANTICIPATED FOR NEARLY EIGHTEEN YEARS. THE MAN AT THE CONSOLE LISTENS FOR A WHILE. AND THEN CALLS WHITEHALL.
...AND A GENTLEMAN CALLED SIR DENNIS ARCHER SUDDENLY REDISCOVERS A COLD DREAD THAT HE HAD THOUGHT BANISHED TWO DECADES BEFORE.
OH GOD. THEY'RE BACK. THE MONSTERS ARE BACK.
A CAN OF WORMS HAS BEEN OPENED. A CAN OF WORMS CALLED "PROJECT ZARATHUSTRA." AND EVERY TIME YOU OPEN A CAN OF WORMS...
YES, YOU HEARD! EXTREME SANCTION. I WANT YOU TO SEND FOR MR. CREAM.
...YOU NEED A BIGGER CAN TO GET THEM ALL BACK IN.

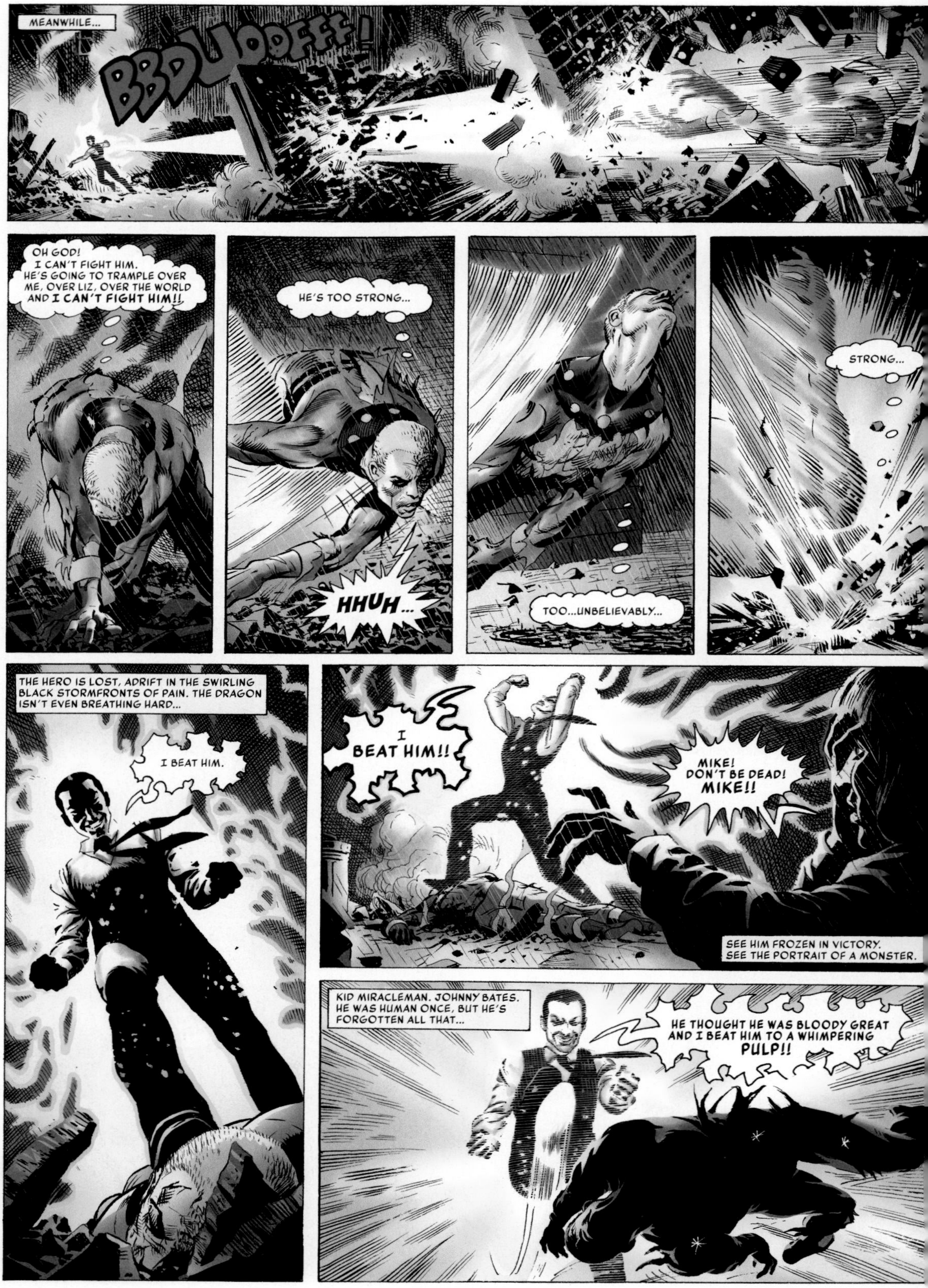
MEANWHILE...
BBDUODFFF!
OH GOD! I CAN'T FIGHT HIM. HE'S GOING TO TRAMPLE OVER ME, OVER LIZ, OVER THE WORLD AND I CAN'T FIGHT HIM!!
HE'S TOO STRONG...
HHUH...
TOO...UNBELIEVABLY...
STRONG...
THE HERO IS LOST, ADRIFT IN THE SWIRLING BLACK STORMFRONTS OF PAIN. THE DRAGON ISN'T EVEN BREATHING HARD...
I BEAT HIM.
I BEAT HIM!!
MIKE! DON'T BE DEAD! MIKE!!
SEE HIM FROZEN IN VICTORY. SEE THE PORTRAIT OF A MONSTER.
KID MIRACLEMAN. JOHNNY BATES. HE WAS HUMAN ONCE, BUT HE'S FORGOTTEN ALL THAT...
HE THOUGHT HE WAS BLOODY GREAT AND I BEAT HIM TO A WHIMPERING PULP!!

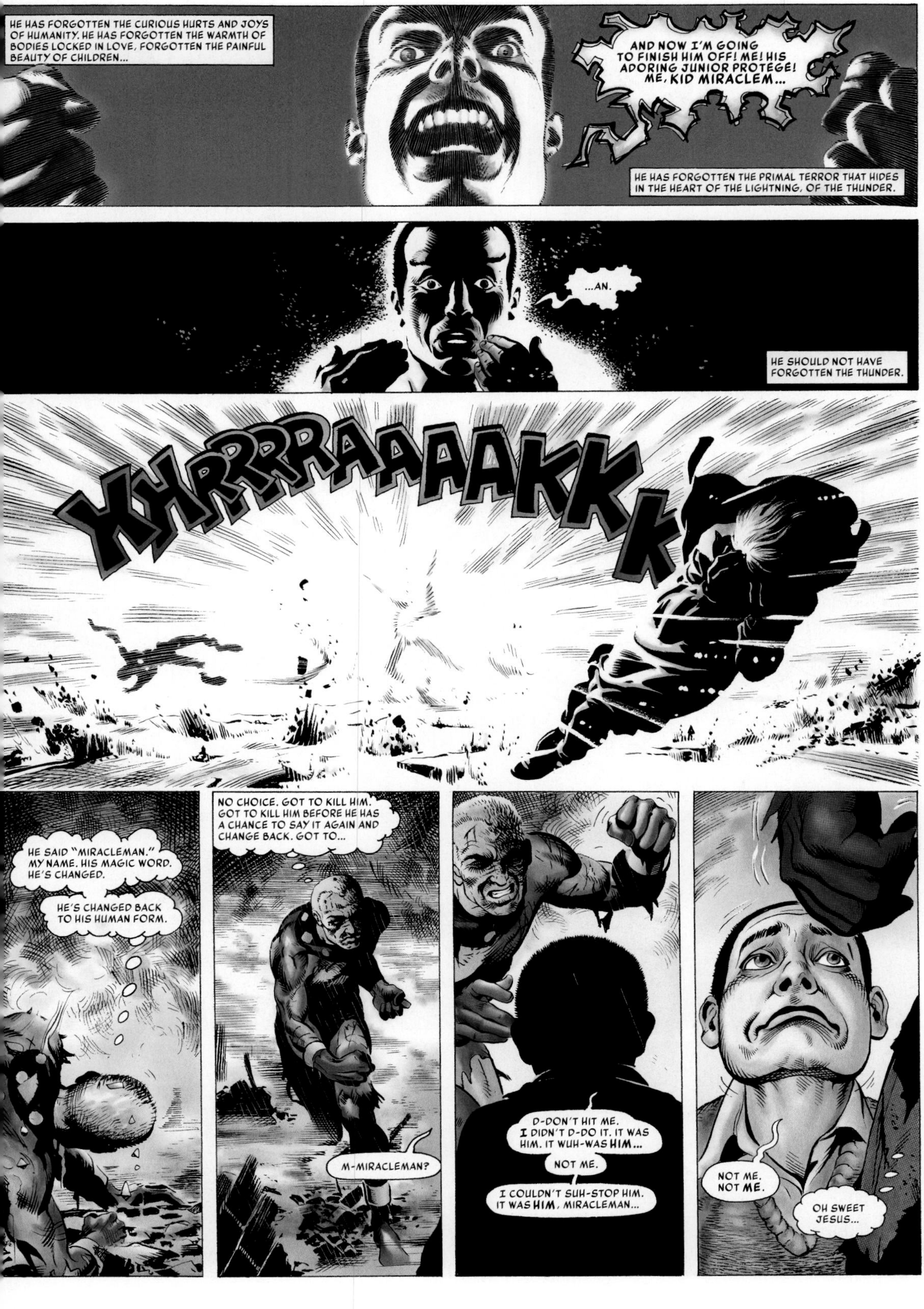
HE HAS FORGOTTEN THE CURIOUS HURTS AND JOYS OF HUMANITY. HE HAS FORGOTTEN THE WARMTH OF BODIES LOCKED IN LOVE, FORGOTTEN THE PAINFUL BEAUTY OF CHILDREN...
AND NOW I'M GOING TO FINISH HIM OFF! ME! HIS ADORING JUNIOR PROTEGE! ME, KID MIRACLEM...
HE HAS FORGOTTEN THE PRIMAL TERROR THAT HIDES IN THE HEART OF THE LIGHTNING, OF THE THUNDER.
...AN.
HE SHOULD NOT HAVE FORGOTTEN THE THUNDER.
XHRRRAAAAKKK
HE SAID "MIRACLEMAN." MY NAME. HIS MAGIC WORD. HE'S CHANGED.
HE'S CHANGED BACK TO HIS HUMAN FORM.
NO CHOICE. GOT TO KILL HIM. GOT TO KILL HIM BEFORE HE HAS A CHANCE TO SAY IT AGAIN AND CHANGE BACK. GOT TO...
M-MIRACLEMAN?
D-DON'T HIT ME. I DIDN'T D-DO IT. IT WAS HIM. IT WUH-WAS HIM...
NOT ME.
I COULDN'T SUH-STOP HIM. IT WAS HIM, MIRACLEMAN...
NOT ME. NOT ME.
OH SWEET JESUS...

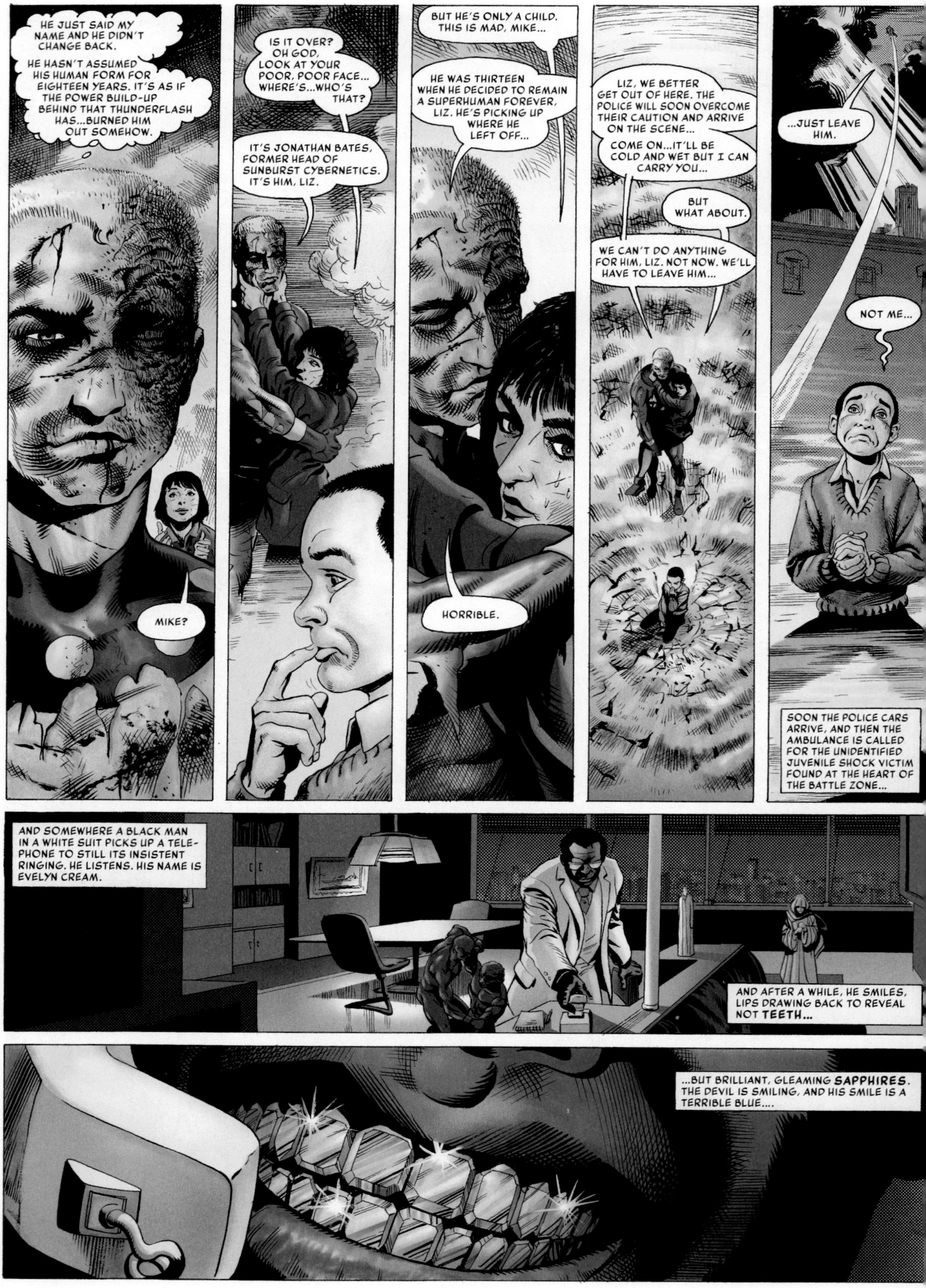
HE JUST SAID MY NAME AND HE DIDN'T CHANGE BACK.
HE HASN'T ASSUMED HIS HUMAN FORM FOR EIGHTEEN YEARS. IT'S AS IF THE POWER BUILD-UP BEHIND THAT THUNDERFLASH HAS...BURNED HIM OUT SOMEHOW.
MIKE?
IS IT OVER? OH GOD, LOOK AT YOUR POOR, POOR FACE... WHERE'S...WHO'S THAT?
IT'S JONATHAN BATES, FORMER HEAD OF SUNBURST CYBERNETICS. IT'S HIM, LIZ.
BUT HE'S ONLY A CHILD. THIS IS MAD, MIKE...
HE WAS THIRTEEN WHEN HE DECIDED TO REMAIN A SUPERHUMAN FOREVER, LIZ. HE'S PICKING UP WHERE HE LEFT OFF...
HORRIBLE.
LIZ, WE BETTER GET OUT OF HERE. THE POLICE WILL SOON OVERCOME THEIR CAUTION AND ARRIVE ON THE SCENE...
COME ON...IT'LL BE COLD AND WET BUT I CAN CARRY YOU...
BUT WHAT ABOUT.
WE CAN'T DO ANYTHING FOR HIM, LIZ. NOT NOW. WE'LL HAVE TO LEAVE HIM...
...JUST LEAVE HIM.
NOT ME...
SOON THE POLICE CARS ARRIVE, AND THEN THE AMBULANCE IS CALLED FOR THE UNIDENTIFIED JUVENILE SHOCK VICTIM FOUND AT THE HEART OF THE BATTLE ZONE...
AND SOMEWHERE A BLACK MAN IN A WHITE SUIT PICKS UP A TELE-PHONE TO STILL ITS INSISTENT RINGING. HE LISTENS. HIS NAME IS EVELYN CREAM.
AND AFTER A WHILE, HE SMILES, LIPS DRAWING BACK TO REVEAL NOT TEETH...
...BUT BRILLIANT, GLEAMING SAPPHIRES. THE DEVIL IS SMILING, AND HIS SMILE IS A TERRIBLE BLUE....

ATTRITION:

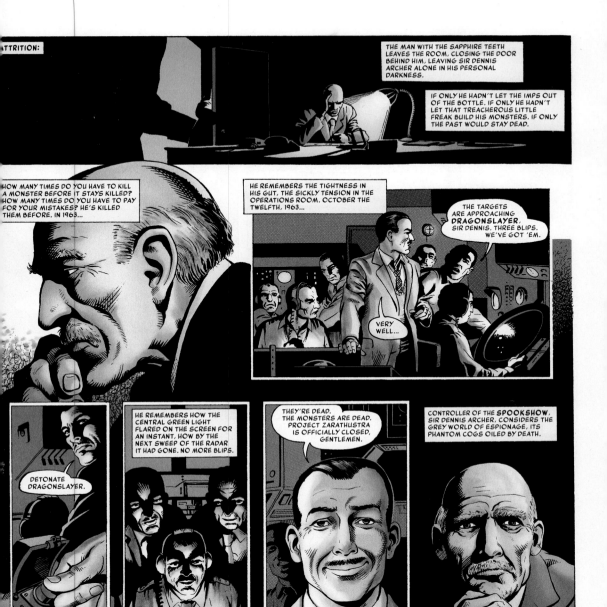

THE MAN WITH THE SAPPHIRE TEETH LEAVES THE ROOM, CLOSING THE DOOR BEHIND HIM, LEAVING SIR DENNIS ARCHER ALONE IN HIS PERSONAL DARKNESS.

IF ONLY HE HADN'T LET THE IMPS OUT OF THE BOTTLE. IF ONLY HE HADN'T LET THAT TREACHEROUS LITTLE FREAK BUILD HIS MONSTERS. IF ONLY THE PAST WOULD STAY DEAD.

HOW MANY TIMES DO YOU HAVE TO KILL A MONSTER BEFORE IT STAYS KILLED? HOW MANY TIMES DO YOU HAVE TO PAY FOR YOUR MISTAKES? HE'S KILLED THEM BEFORE. IN 1963...

HE REMEMBERS THE TIGHTNESS IN HIS GUT, THE SICKLY TENSION IN THE OPERATIONS ROOM. OCTOBER THE TWELFTH, 1963...

THE TARGETS ARE APPROACHING **DRAGONSLAYER**, SIR DENNIS. THREE BLIPS. WE'VE GOT 'EM.

VERY WELL...

DETONATE DRAGONSLAYER.

HE REMEMBERS HOW THE CENTRAL GREEN LIGHT FLARED ON THE SCREEN FOR AN INSTANT, HOW BY THE NEXT SWEEP OF THE RADAR IT HAD GONE. NO MORE BLIPS.

THEY'RE DEAD. THE MONSTERS ARE DEAD. PROJECT ZARATHUSTRA IS OFFICIALLY CLOSED, GENTLEMEN.

CONTROLLER OF THE **SPOOKSHOW**, SIR DENNIS ARCHER, CONSIDERS THE GREY WORLD OF ESPIONAGE, ITS PHANTOM COGS OILED BY DEATH.

HE IS THE MAN WHO TENDS THE MACHINE. BUT IT IS MEN LIKE EVELYN CREAM WHO PROVIDE THE LUBRICATION.

EVELYN CREAM WILL SANCTION THE MONSTER. THE DRAGON WILL BE SLAIN.

AGAIN.

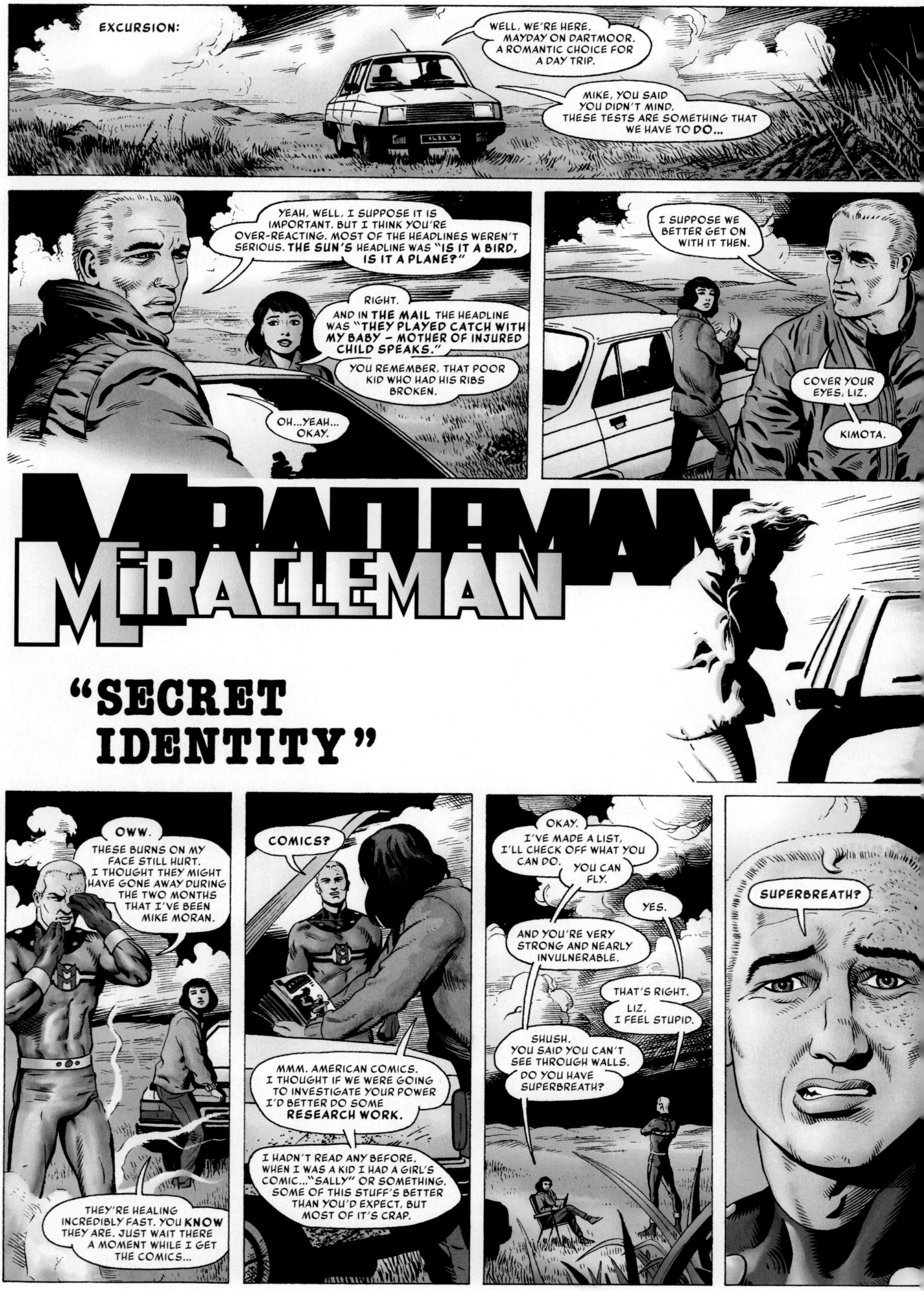
EXCURSION:
WELL, WE'RE HERE. MAYDAY ON DARTMOOR. A ROMANTIC CHOICE FOR A DAY TRIP.
MIKE, YOU SAID YOU DIDN'T MIND. THESE TESTS ARE SOMETHING THAT WE HAVE TO DO...
YEAH, WELL, I SUPPOSE IT IS IMPORTANT. BUT I THINK YOU'RE OVER-REACTING. MOST OF THE HEADLINES WEREN'T SERIOUS. THE SUN'S HEADLINE WAS "IS IT A BIRD, IS IT A PLANE?"
RIGHT. AND IN THE MAIL THE HEADLINE WAS "THEY PLAYED CATCH WITH MY BABY – MOTHER OF INJURED CHILD SPEAKS."
YOU REMEMBER, THAT POOR KID WHO HAD HIS RIBS BROKEN.
OH...YEAH... OKAY.
I SUPPOSE WE BETTER GET ON WITH IT THEN.
COVER YOUR EYES, LIZ.
KIMOTA.
MIRACLEMAN
"SECRET IDENTITY"
OWW.
THESE BURNS ON MY FACE STILL HURT. I THOUGHT THEY MIGHT HAVE GONE AWAY DURING THE TWO MONTHS THAT I'VE BEEN MIKE MORAN.
THEY'RE HEALING INCREDIBLY FAST. YOU KNOW THEY ARE. JUST WAIT THERE A MOMENT WHILE I GET THE COMICS...
COMICS?
MMM. AMERICAN COMICS. I THOUGHT IF WE WERE GOING TO INVESTIGATE YOUR POWER I'D BETTER DO SOME RESEARCH WORK.
I HADN'T READ ANY BEFORE. WHEN I WAS A KID I HAD A GIRL'S COMIC..."SALLY" OR SOMETHING. SOME OF THIS STUFF'S BETTER THAN YOU'D EXPECT, BUT MOST OF IT'S CRAP.
OKAY. I'VE MADE A LIST, I'LL CHECK OFF WHAT YOU CAN DO.
YOU CAN FLY.
YES.
AND YOU'RE VERY STRONG AND NEARLY INVULNERABLE.
THAT'S RIGHT.
LIZ, I FEEL STUPID.
SHUSH. YOU SAID YOU CAN'T SEE THROUGH WALLS. DO YOU HAVE SUPERBREATH?
SUPERBREATH?

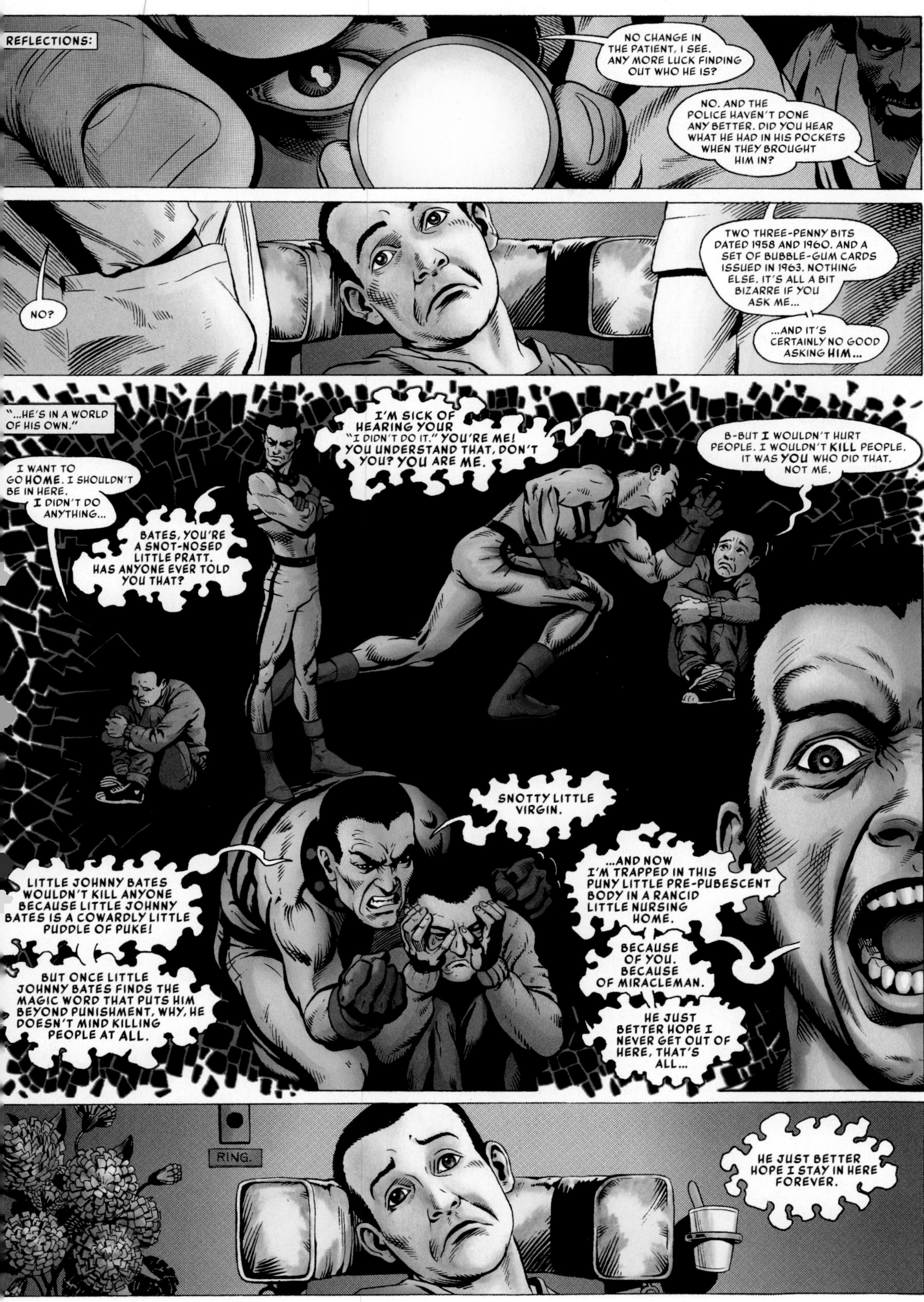

REFLECTIONS:
NO CHANGE IN THE PATIENT, I SEE. ANY MORE LUCK FINDING OUT WHO HE IS?
NO. AND THE POLICE HAVEN'T DONE ANY BETTER. DID YOU HEAR WHAT HE HAD IN HIS POCKETS WHEN THEY BROUGHT HIM IN?
NO?
TWO THREE-PENNY BITS DATED 1958 AND 1960, AND A SET OF BUBBLE-GUM CARDS ISSUED IN 1963. NOTHING ELSE. IT'S ALL A BIT BIZARRE IF YOU ASK ME...
...AND IT'S CERTAINLY NO GOOD ASKING HIM...
"...HE'S IN A WORLD OF HIS OWN."
I WANT TO GO HOME. I SHOULDN'T BE IN HERE. I DIDN'T DO ANYTHING...
BATES, YOU'RE A SNOT-NOSED LITTLE PRATT. HAS ANYONE EVER TOLD YOU THAT?
I'M SICK OF HEARING YOUR "I DIDN'T DO IT." YOU'RE ME! YOU UNDERSTAND THAT, DON'T YOU? YOU ARE ME.
B-BUT I WOULDN'T HURT PEOPLE. I WOULDN'T KILL PEOPLE. IT WAS YOU WHO DID THAT. NOT ME.
SNOTTY LITTLE VIRGIN.
LITTLE JOHNNY BATES WOULDN'T KILL ANYONE BECAUSE LITTLE JOHNNY BATES IS A COWARDLY LITTLE PUDDLE OF PUKE!
BUT ONCE LITTLE JOHNNY BATES FINDS THE MAGIC WORD THAT PUTS HIM BEYOND PUNISHMENT, WHY, HE DOESN'T MIND KILLING PEOPLE AT ALL.
...AND NOW I'M TRAPPED IN THIS PUNY LITTLE PRE-PUBESCENT BODY IN A RANCID LITTLE NURSING HOME.
BECAUSE OF YOU. BECAUSE OF MIRACLEMAN.
HE JUST BETTER HOPE I NEVER GET OUT OF HERE, THAT'S ALL...
RING.
HE JUST BETTER HOPE I STAY IN HERE FOREVER.

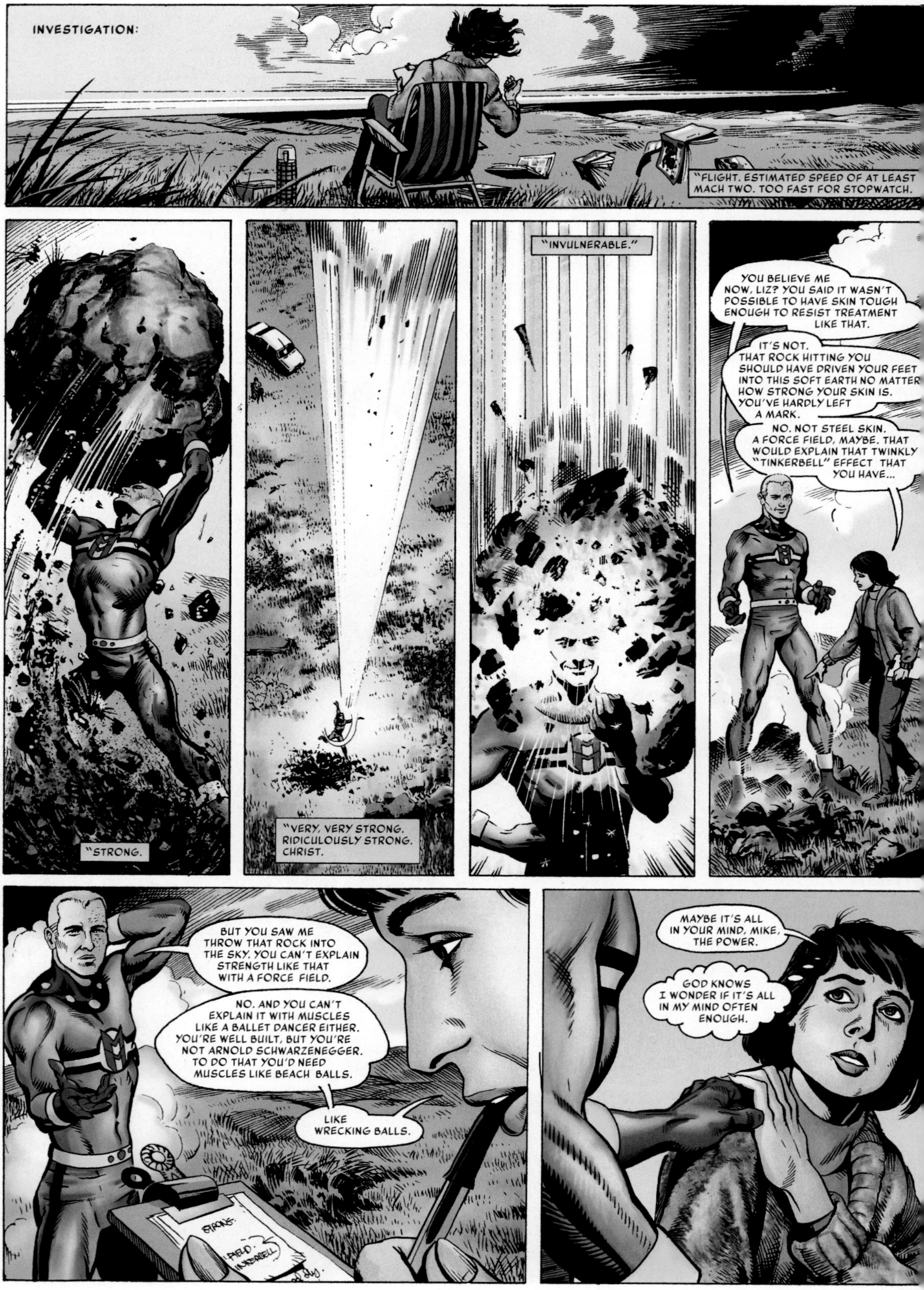
INVESTIGATION:
"FLIGHT. ESTIMATED SPEED OF AT LEAST MACH TWO. TOO FAST FOR STOPWATCH.
"STRONG.
"VERY, VERY STRONG. RIDICULOUSLY STRONG. CHRIST.
"INVULNERABLE."
YOU BELIEVE ME NOW, LIZ? YOU SAID IT WASN'T POSSIBLE TO HAVE SKIN TOUGH ENOUGH TO RESIST TREATMENT LIKE THAT.
IT'S NOT. THAT ROCK HITTING YOU SHOULD HAVE DRIVEN YOUR FEET INTO THIS SOFT EARTH NO MATTER HOW STRONG YOUR SKIN IS. YOU'VE HARDLY LEFT A MARK.
NO. NOT STEEL SKIN. A FORCE FIELD, MAYBE. THAT WOULD EXPLAIN THAT TWINKLY "TINKERBELL" EFFECT THAT YOU HAVE...
BUT YOU SAW ME THROW THAT ROCK INTO THE SKY. YOU CAN'T EXPLAIN STRENGTH LIKE THAT WITH A FORCE FIELD.
NO. AND YOU CAN'T EXPLAIN IT WITH MUSCLES LIKE A BALLET DANCER EITHER. YOU'RE WELL BUILT, BUT YOU'RE NOT ARNOLD SCHWARZENEGGER. TO DO THAT YOU'D NEED MUSCLES LIKE BEACH BALLS.
LIKE WRECKING BALLS.
MAYBE IT'S ALL IN YOUR MIND, MIKE. THE POWER.
GOD KNOWS I WONDER IF IT'S ALL IN MY MIND OFTEN ENOUGH.

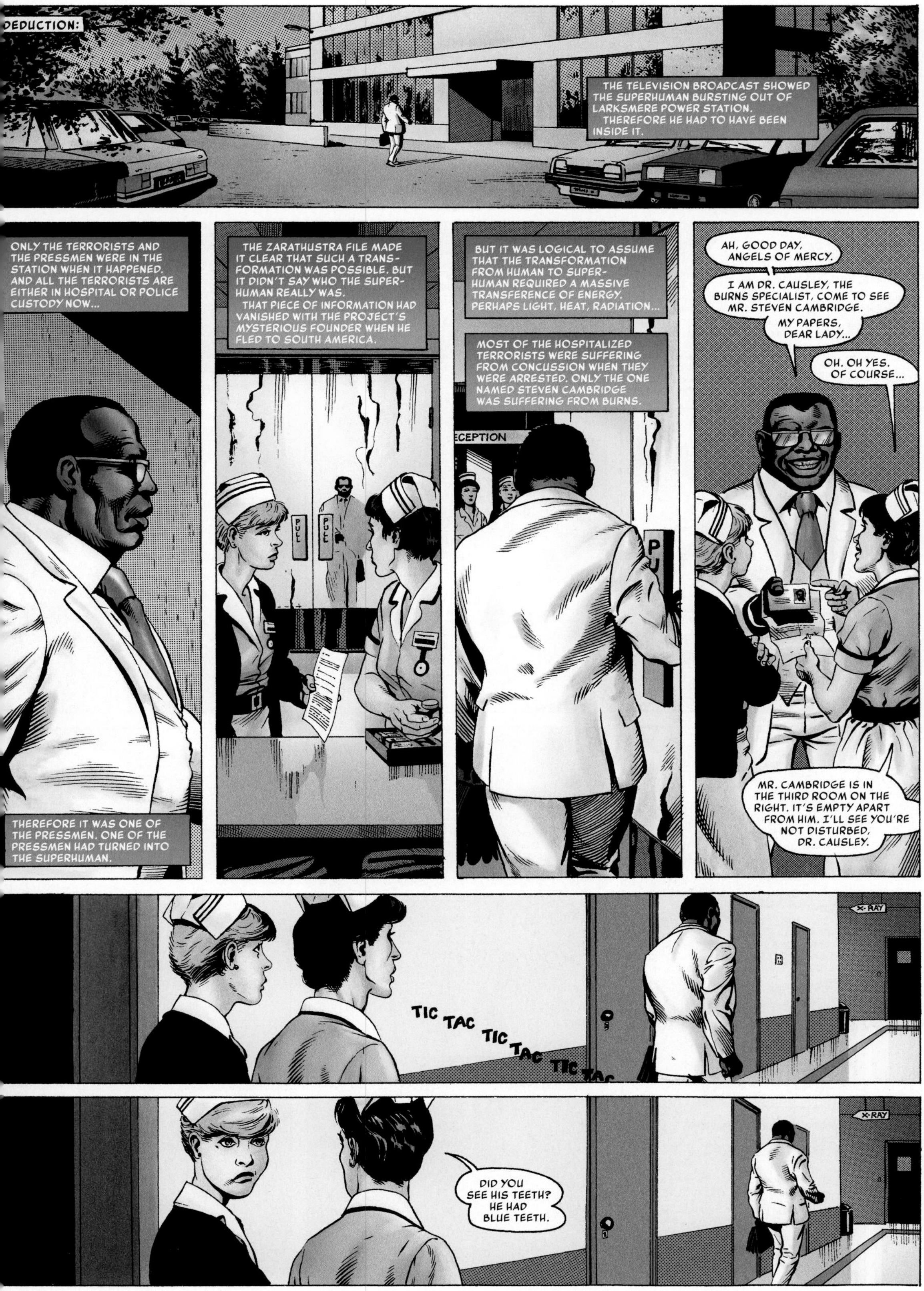
DEDUCTION:
THE TELEVISION BROADCAST SHOWED THE SUPERHUMAN BURSTING OUT OF LARKSMERE POWER STATION. THEREFORE HE HAD TO HAVE BEEN INSIDE IT.
ONLY THE TERRORISTS AND THE PRESSMEN WERE IN THE STATION WHEN IT HAPPENED. AND ALL THE TERRORISTS ARE EITHER IN HOSPITAL OR POLICE CUSTODY NOW...
THEREFORE IT WAS ONE OF THE PRESSMEN. ONE OF THE PRESSMEN HAD TURNED INTO THE SUPERHUMAN.
THE ZARATHUSTRA FILE MADE IT CLEAR THAT SUCH A TRANSFORMATION WAS POSSIBLE. BUT IT DIDN'T SAY WHO THE SUPERHUMAN REALLY WAS.
THAT PIECE OF INFORMATION HAD VANISHED WITH THE PROJECT'S MYSTERIOUS FOUNDER WHEN HE FLED TO SOUTH AMERICA.
BUT IT WAS LOGICAL TO ASSUME THAT THE TRANSFORMATION FROM HUMAN TO SUPERHUMAN REQUIRED A MASSIVE TRANSFERENCE OF ENERGY. PERHAPS LIGHT, HEAT, RADIATION...
MOST OF THE HOSPITALIZED TERRORISTS WERE SUFFERING FROM CONCUSSION WHEN THEY WERE ARRESTED. ONLY THE ONE NAMED STEVEN CAMBRIDGE WAS SUFFERING FROM BURNS.
ECEPTION
AH, GOOD DAY, ANGELS OF MERCY.
I AM DR. CAUSLEY, THE BURNS SPECIALIST, COME TO SEE MR. STEVEN CAMBRIDGE.
MY PAPERS, DEAR LADY...
OH. OH YES. OF COURSE...
MR. CAMBRIDGE IS IN THE THIRD ROOM ON THE RIGHT. IT'S EMPTY APART FROM HIM. I'LL SEE YOU'RE NOT DISTURBED, DR. CAUSLEY.
X-RAY
TIC TAC TIC TAC TIC TAC
X-RAY
DID YOU SEE HIS TEETH? HE HAD BLUE TEETH.

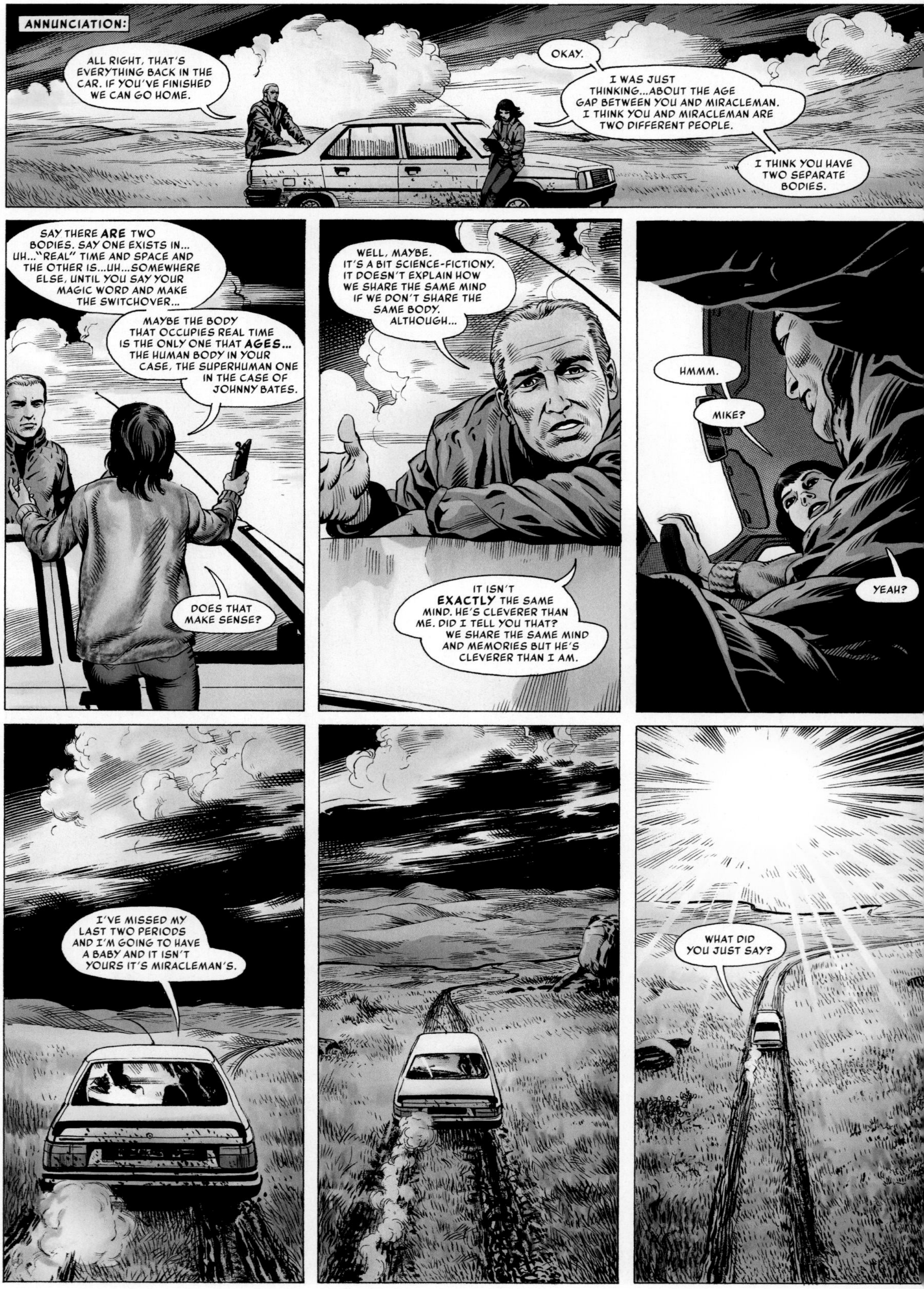
ANNUNCIATION:
ALL RIGHT, THAT'S EVERYTHING BACK IN THE CAR. IF YOU'VE FINISHED WE CAN GO HOME.
OKAY.
I WAS JUST THINKING...ABOUT THE AGE GAP BETWEEN YOU AND MIRACLEMAN. I THINK YOU AND MIRACLEMAN ARE TWO DIFFERENT PEOPLE.
I THINK YOU HAVE TWO SEPARATE BODIES.
SAY THERE ARE TWO BODIES. SAY ONE EXISTS IN... UH..."REAL" TIME AND SPACE AND THE OTHER IS...UH...SOMEWHERE ELSE, UNTIL YOU SAY YOUR MAGIC WORD AND MAKE THE SWITCHOVER...
MAYBE THE BODY THAT OCCUPIES REAL TIME IS THE ONLY ONE THAT AGES... THE HUMAN BODY IN YOUR CASE, THE SUPERHUMAN ONE IN THE CASE OF JOHNNY BATES.
DOES THAT MAKE SENSE?
WELL, MAYBE. IT'S A BIT SCIENCE-FICTIONY. IT DOESN'T EXPLAIN HOW WE SHARE THE SAME MIND IF WE DON'T SHARE THE SAME BODY. ALTHOUGH...
IT ISN'T EXACTLY THE SAME MIND. HE'S CLEVERER THAN ME. DID I TELL YOU THAT? WE SHARE THE SAME MIND AND MEMORIES BUT HE'S CLEVERER THAN I AM.
HMMM.
MIKE?
YEAH?
I'VE MISSED MY LAST TWO PERIODS AND I'M GOING TO HAVE A BABY AND IT ISN'T YOURS IT'S MIRACLEMAN'S.
WHAT DID YOU JUST SAY?

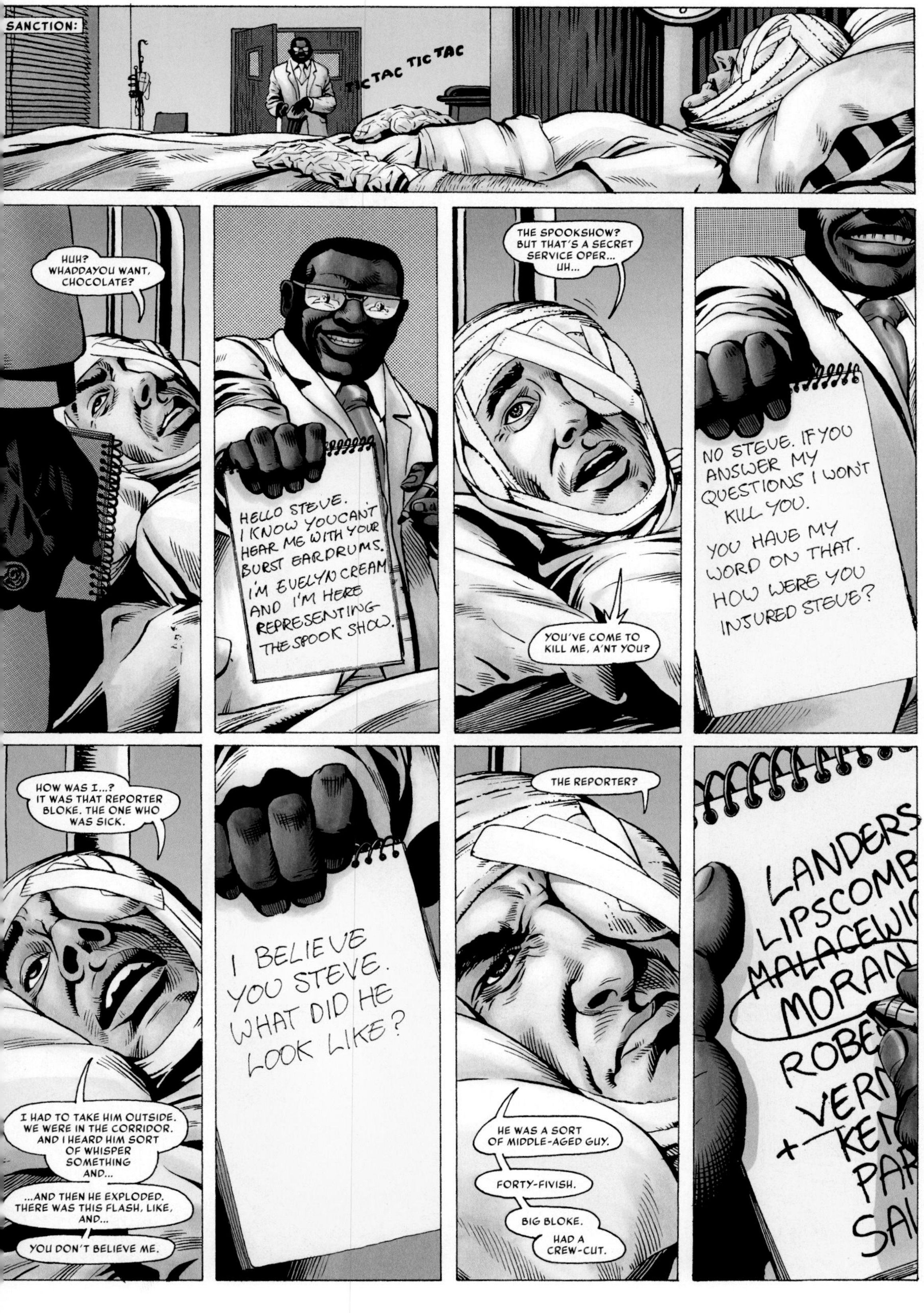
SANCTION:
TIC TAC TIC TAC
HUH? WHADDAYOU WANT, CHOCOLATE?
HELLO STEVE. I KNOW YOUCANT HEAR ME WITH YOUR BURST EARDRUMS. I'M EVELYN CREAM AND I'M HERE REPRESENTING THE SPOOK SHOW.
THE SPOOKSHOW? BUT THAT'S A SECRET SERVICE OPER... UH...
YOU'VE COME TO KILL ME, A'NT YOU?
NO STEVE. IF YOU ANSWER MY QUESTIONS I WONT KILL YOU.
YOU HAVE MY WORD ON THAT.
HOW WERE YOU INJURED STEVE?
HOW WAS I...? IT WAS THAT REPORTER BLOKE. THE ONE WHO WAS SICK.
I HAD TO TAKE HIM OUTSIDE. WE WERE IN THE CORRIDOR. AND I HEARD HIM SORT OF WHISPER SOMETHING AND...
...AND THEN HE EXPLODED. THERE WAS THIS FLASH, LIKE, AND...
YOU DON'T BELIEVE ME.
I BELIEVE YOU STEVE. WHAT DID HE LOOK LIKE?
THE REPORTER?
HE WAS A SORT OF MIDDLE-AGED GUY.
FORTY-FIVISH.
BIG BLOKE.
HAD A CREW-CUT.
LANDERS
LIPSCOMB
MALACEWIC
MORAN
ROBE
VER
KEN
PA
SA

THANK YOU STEVE YOU'VE BEEN TERRIBLY HELPFUL OH... AND YOU REMEMBER HOW I PROMISED NOT TO KILL YOU?

YEAH?

I WAS LYING STEVE

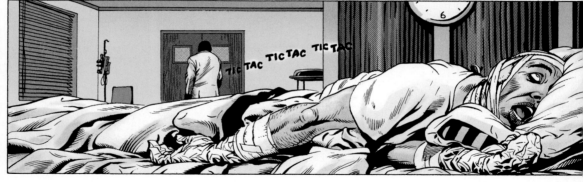

TIC TAC TIC TAC TIC TAC

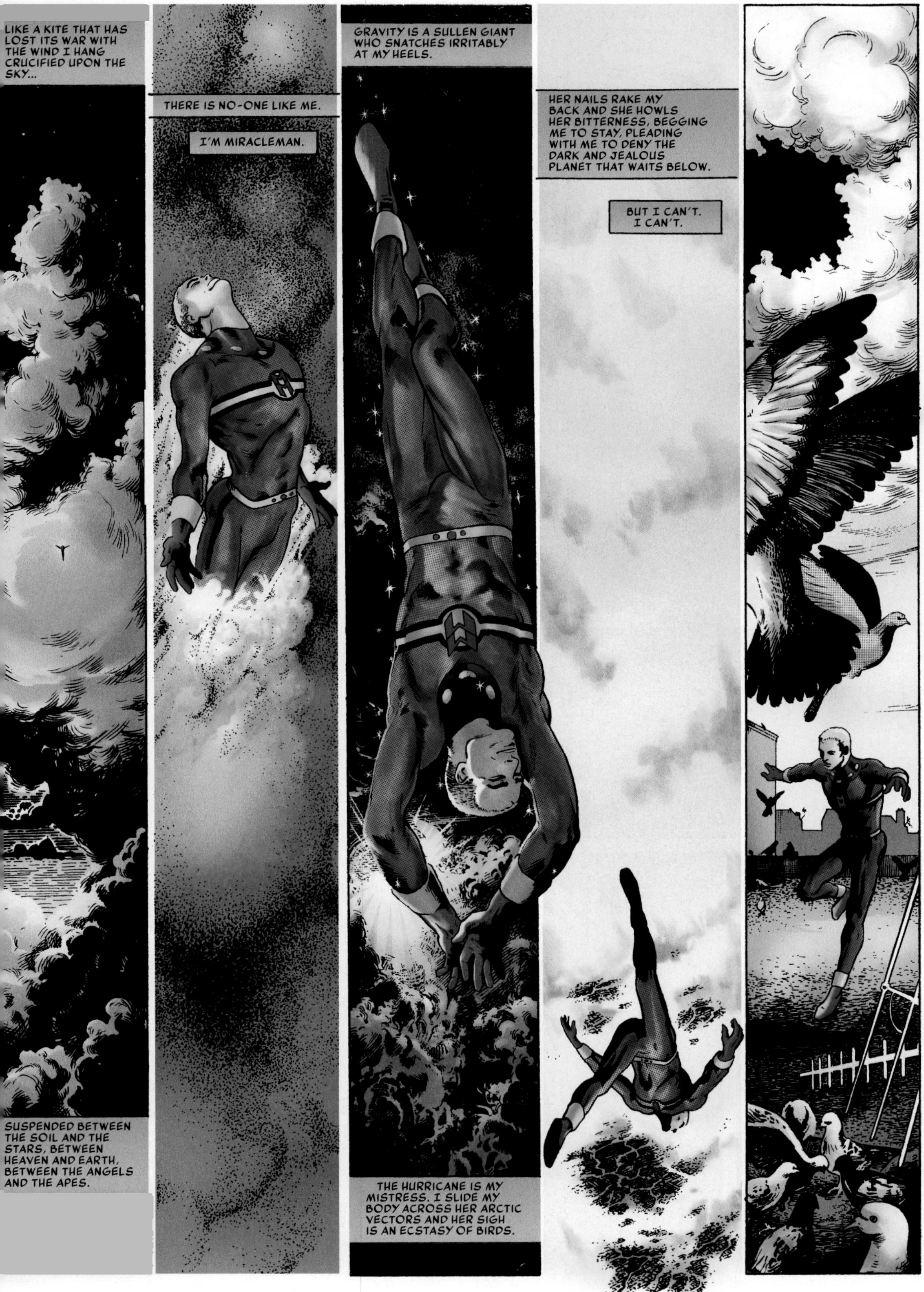
LIKE A KITE THAT HAS LOST ITS WAR WITH THE WIND I HANG CRUCIFIED UPON THE SKY...
SUSPENDED BETWEEN THE SOIL AND THE STARS, BETWEEN HEAVEN AND EARTH, BETWEEN THE ANGELS AND THE APES.
THERE IS NO-ONE LIKE ME.
I'M MIRACLEMAN.
GRAVITY IS A SULLEN GIANT WHO SNATCHES IRRITABLY AT MY HEELS.
THE HURRICANE IS MY MISTRESS. I SLIDE MY BODY ACROSS HER ARCTIC VECTORS AND HER SIGH IS AN ECSTASY OF BIRDS.
HER NAILS RAKE MY BACK AND SHE HOWLS HER BITTERNESS, BEGGING ME TO STAY, PLEADING WITH ME TO DENY THE DARK AND JEALOUS PLANET THAT WAITS BELOW.
BUT I CAN'T. I CAN'T.

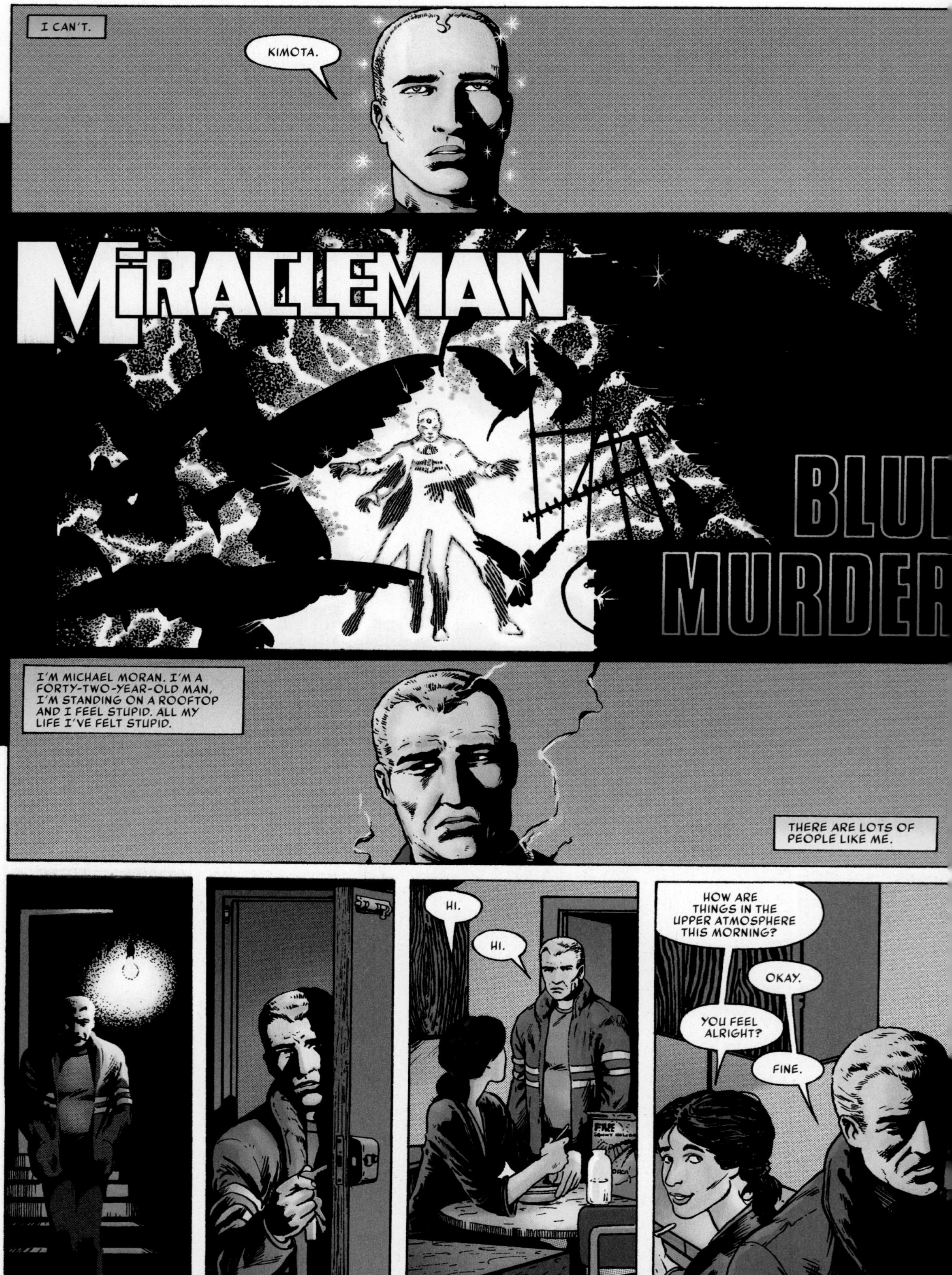
I CAN'T.
KIMOTA.
MIRACLEMAN
BLUE MURDER
I'M MICHAEL MORAN. I'M A FORTY-TWO-YEAR-OLD MAN, I'M STANDING ON A ROOFTOP AND I FEEL STUPID. ALL MY LIFE I'VE FELT STUPID.
THERE ARE LOTS OF PEOPLE LIKE ME.
HI.
HI.
HOW ARE THINGS IN THE UPPER ATMOSPHERE THIS MORNING?
OKAY.
YOU FEEL ALRIGHT?
FINE.

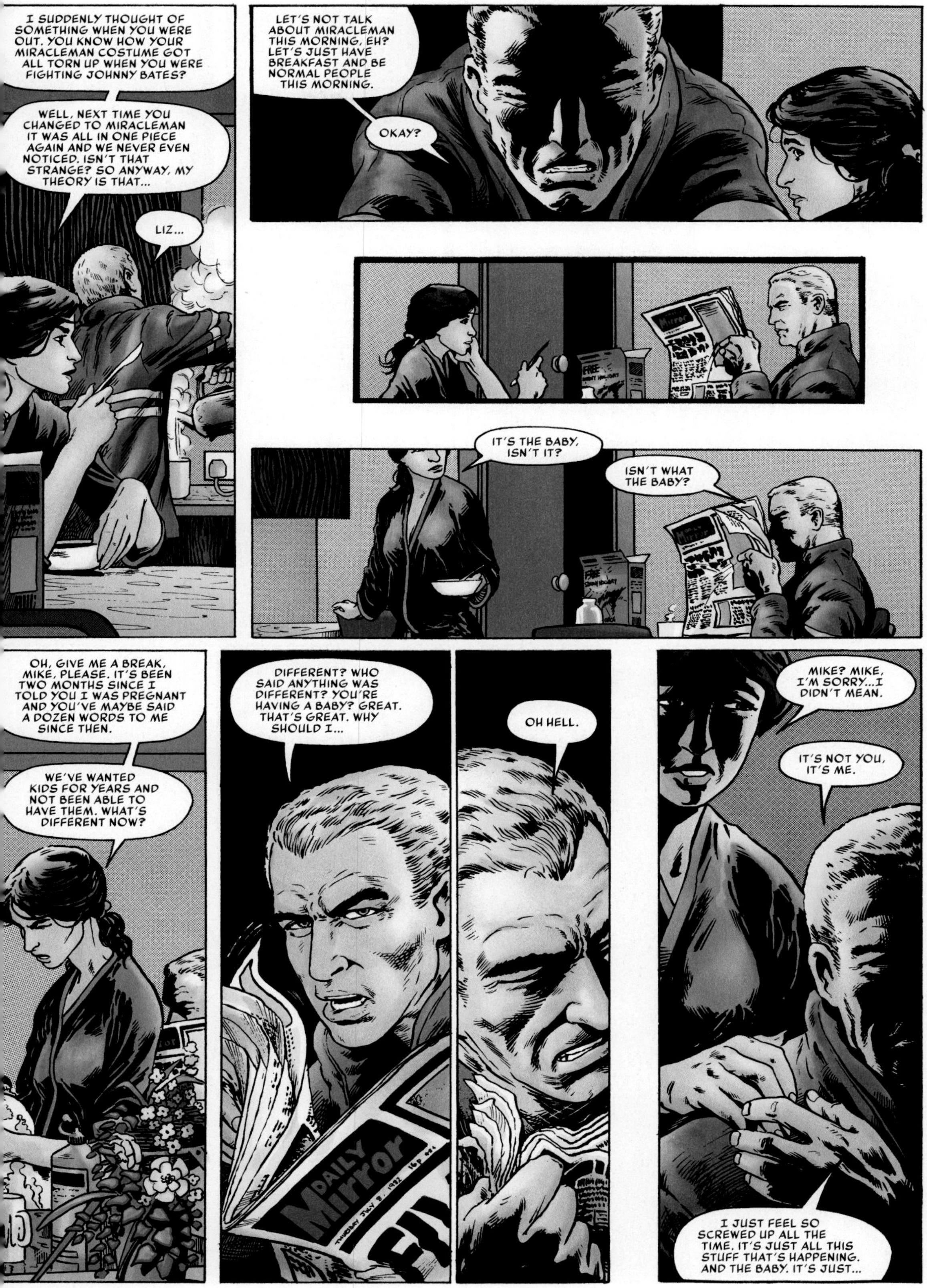
I SUDDENLY THOUGHT OF SOMETHING WHEN YOU WERE OUT. YOU KNOW HOW YOUR MIRACLEMAN COSTUME GOT ALL TORN UP WHEN YOU WERE FIGHTING JOHNNY BATES?
WELL, NEXT TIME YOU CHANGED TO MIRACLEMAN IT WAS ALL IN ONE PIECE AGAIN AND WE NEVER EVEN NOTICED. ISN'T THAT STRANGE? SO ANYWAY, MY THEORY IS THAT...
LIZ...
LET'S NOT TALK ABOUT MIRACLEMAN THIS MORNING, EH? LET'S JUST HAVE BREAKFAST AND BE NORMAL PEOPLE THIS MORNING.
OKAY?
IT'S THE BABY, ISN'T IT?
ISN'T WHAT THE BABY?
OH, GIVE ME A BREAK, MIKE, PLEASE. IT'S BEEN TWO MONTHS SINCE I TOLD YOU I WAS PREGNANT AND YOU'VE MAYBE SAID A DOZEN WORDS TO ME SINCE THEN.
WE'VE WANTED KIDS FOR YEARS AND NOT BEEN ABLE TO HAVE THEM. WHAT'S DIFFERENT NOW?
DIFFERENT? WHO SAID ANYTHING WAS DIFFERENT? YOU'RE HAVING A BABY? GREAT. THAT'S GREAT. WHY SHOULD I...
DAILY Mirror
OH HELL.
MIKE? MIKE, I'M SORRY...I DIDN'T MEAN.
IT'S NOT YOU, IT'S ME.
I JUST FEEL SO SCREWED UP ALL THE TIME. IT'S JUST ALL THIS STUFF THAT'S HAPPENING. AND THE BABY. IT'S JUST...

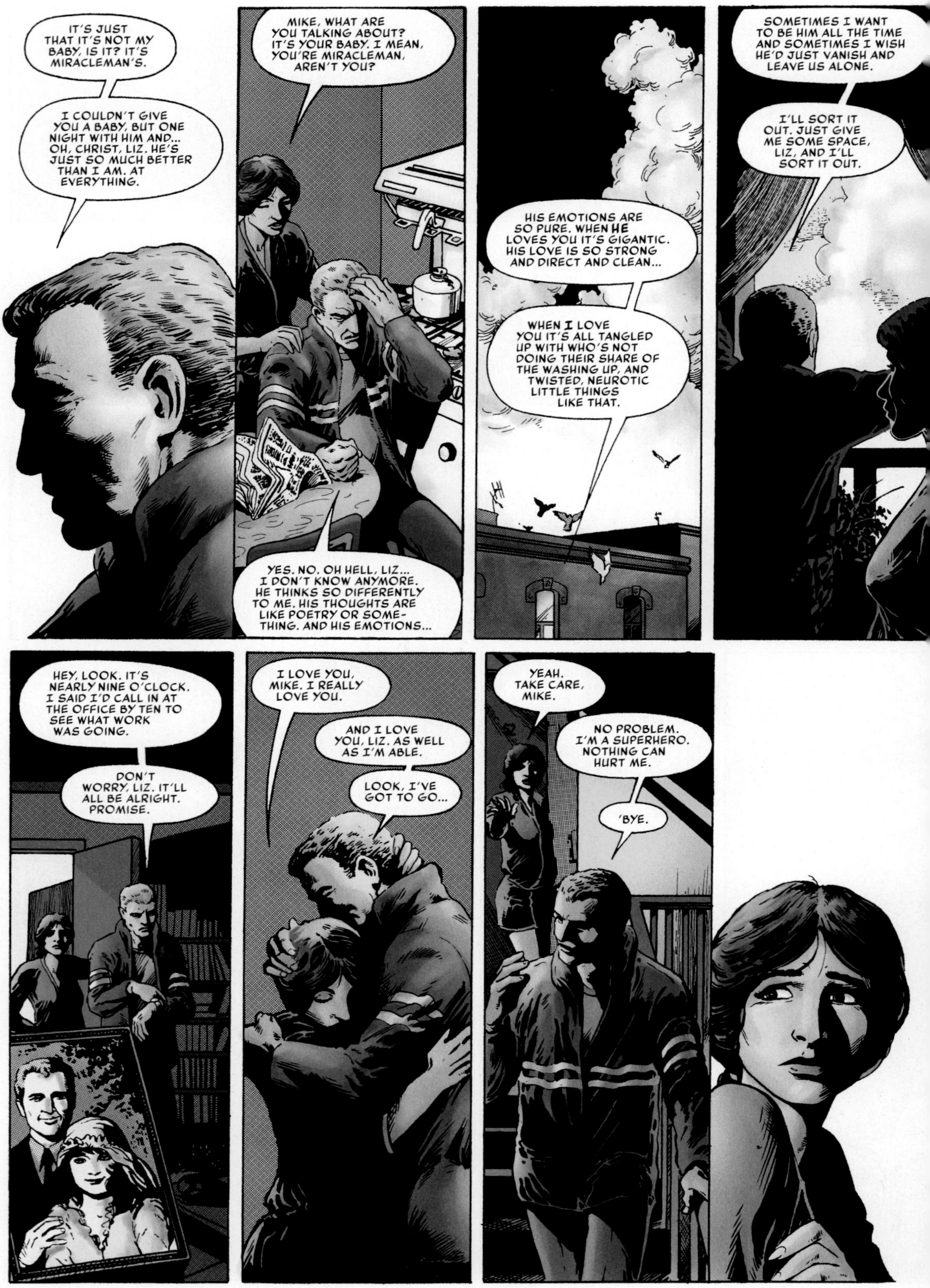
IT'S JUST THAT IT'S NOT MY BABY, IS IT? IT'S MIRACLEMAN'S.
I COULDN'T GIVE YOU A BABY, BUT ONE NIGHT WITH HIM AND... OH, CHRIST, LIZ. HE'S JUST SO MUCH BETTER THAN I AM. AT EVERYTHING.
MIKE, WHAT ARE YOU TALKING ABOUT? IT'S YOUR BABY. I MEAN, YOU'RE MIRACLEMAN, AREN'T YOU?
YES. NO. OH HELL, LIZ... I DON'T KNOW ANYMORE. HE THINKS SO DIFFERENTLY TO ME. HIS THOUGHTS ARE LIKE POETRY OR SOMETHING. AND HIS EMOTIONS...
HIS EMOTIONS ARE SO PURE. WHEN HE LOVES YOU IT'S GIGANTIC. HIS LOVE IS SO STRONG AND DIRECT AND CLEAN...
WHEN I LOVE YOU IT'S ALL TANGLED UP WITH WHO'S NOT DOING THEIR SHARE OF THE WASHING UP, AND TWISTED, NEUROTIC LITTLE THINGS LIKE THAT.
SOMETIMES I WANT TO BE HIM ALL THE TIME AND SOMETIMES I WISH HE'D JUST VANISH AND LEAVE US ALONE.
I'LL SORT IT OUT. JUST GIVE ME SOME SPACE, LIZ, AND I'LL SORT IT OUT.
HEY, LOOK. IT'S NEARLY NINE O'CLOCK. I SAID I'D CALL IN AT THE OFFICE BY TEN TO SEE WHAT WORK WAS GOING.
DON'T WORRY, LIZ. IT'LL ALL BE ALRIGHT. PROMISE.
I LOVE YOU, MIKE. I REALLY LOVE YOU.
AND I LOVE YOU, LIZ. AS WELL AS I'M ABLE.
LOOK, I'VE GOT TO GO...
YEAH. TAKE CARE, MIKE.
NO PROBLEM. I'M A SUPERHERO. NOTHING CAN HURT ME.
'BYE.

FIVE TO TEN.

AILY RECORD

MORNING, MICK.

JULIE.

A WHAT? A D-NOTICE? OH, THAT'S BLOODY GREAT. THAT'S JUST WHAT I NEED.

NO, I KNOW IT'S NOT YOUR FAULT. OKAY, BRIAN. THANKS.

'BYE.

FEATURES EDITOR

HOW DO, MICK. TAKE A SEAT.

THANKS. WHAT WAS THAT ABOUT A D-NOTICE? SOMETHING ELSE ON THE FALKLANDS OR WHAT?

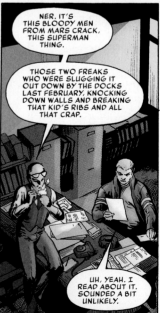

NER. IT'S THIS BLOODY MEN FROM MARS CRACK, THIS SUPERMAN THING.

THOSE TWO FREAKS WHO WERE SLUGGING IT OUT DOWN BY THE DOCKS LAST FEBRUARY, KNOCKING DOWN WALLS AND BREAKING THAT KID'S RIBS AND ALL THAT CRAP.

UH, YEAH. I READ ABOUT IT. SOUNDED A BIT UNLIKELY.

61

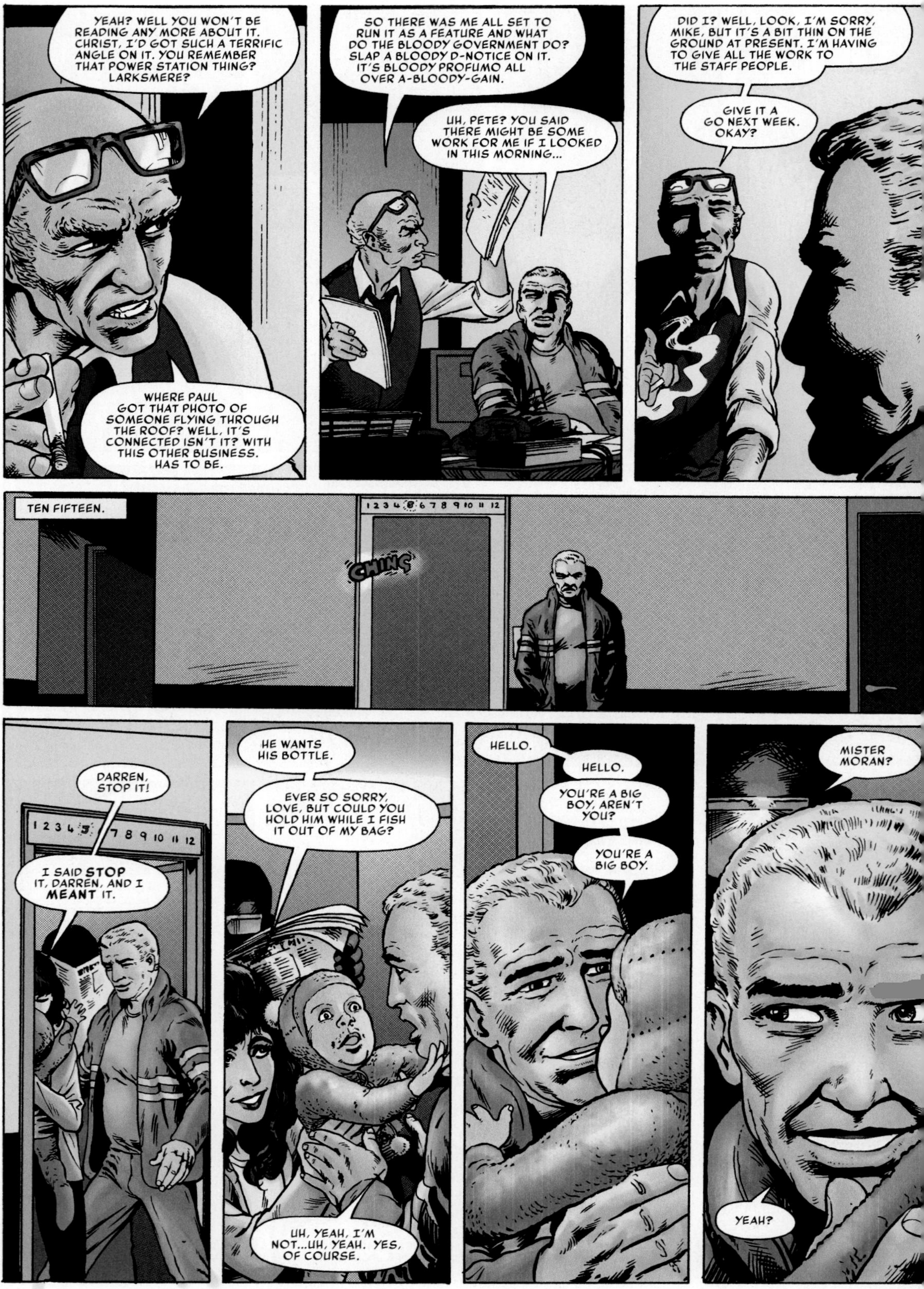
YEAH? WELL YOU WON'T BE READING ANY MORE ABOUT IT. CHRIST, I'D GOT SUCH A TERRIFIC ANGLE ON IT. YOU REMEMBER THAT POWER STATION THING? LARKSMERE?
WHERE PAUL GOT THAT PHOTO OF SOMEONE FLYING THROUGH THE ROOF? WELL, IT'S CONNECTED ISN'T IT? WITH THIS OTHER BUSINESS. HAS TO BE.
SO THERE WAS ME ALL SET TO RUN IT AS A FEATURE AND WHAT DO THE BLOODY GOVERNMENT DO? SLAP A BLOODY D-NOTICE ON IT. IT'S BLOODY PROFUMO ALL OVER A-BLOODY-GAIN.
UH, PETE? YOU SAID THERE MIGHT BE SOME WORK FOR ME IF I LOOKED IN THIS MORNING...
DID I? WELL, LOOK, I'M SORRY, MIKE, BUT IT'S A BIT THIN ON THE GROUND AT PRESENT. I'M HAVING TO GIVE ALL THE WORK TO THE STAFF PEOPLE.
GIVE IT A GO NEXT WEEK. OKAY?
TEN FIFTEEN.
1 2 3 4 5 6 7 8 9 10 11 12
CHING
DARREN, STOP IT!
1 2 3 4 5 7 8 9 10 11 12
I SAID STOP IT, DARREN, AND I MEANT IT.
HE WANTS HIS BOTTLE.
EVER SO SORRY, LOVE, BUT COULD YOU HOLD HIM WHILE I FISH IT OUT OF MY BAG?
UH, YEAH, I'M NOT...UH, YEAH. YES, OF COURSE.
HELLO.
HELLO.
YOU'RE A BIG BOY, AREN'T YOU?
YOU'RE A BIG BOY.
MISTER MORAN?
YEAH?

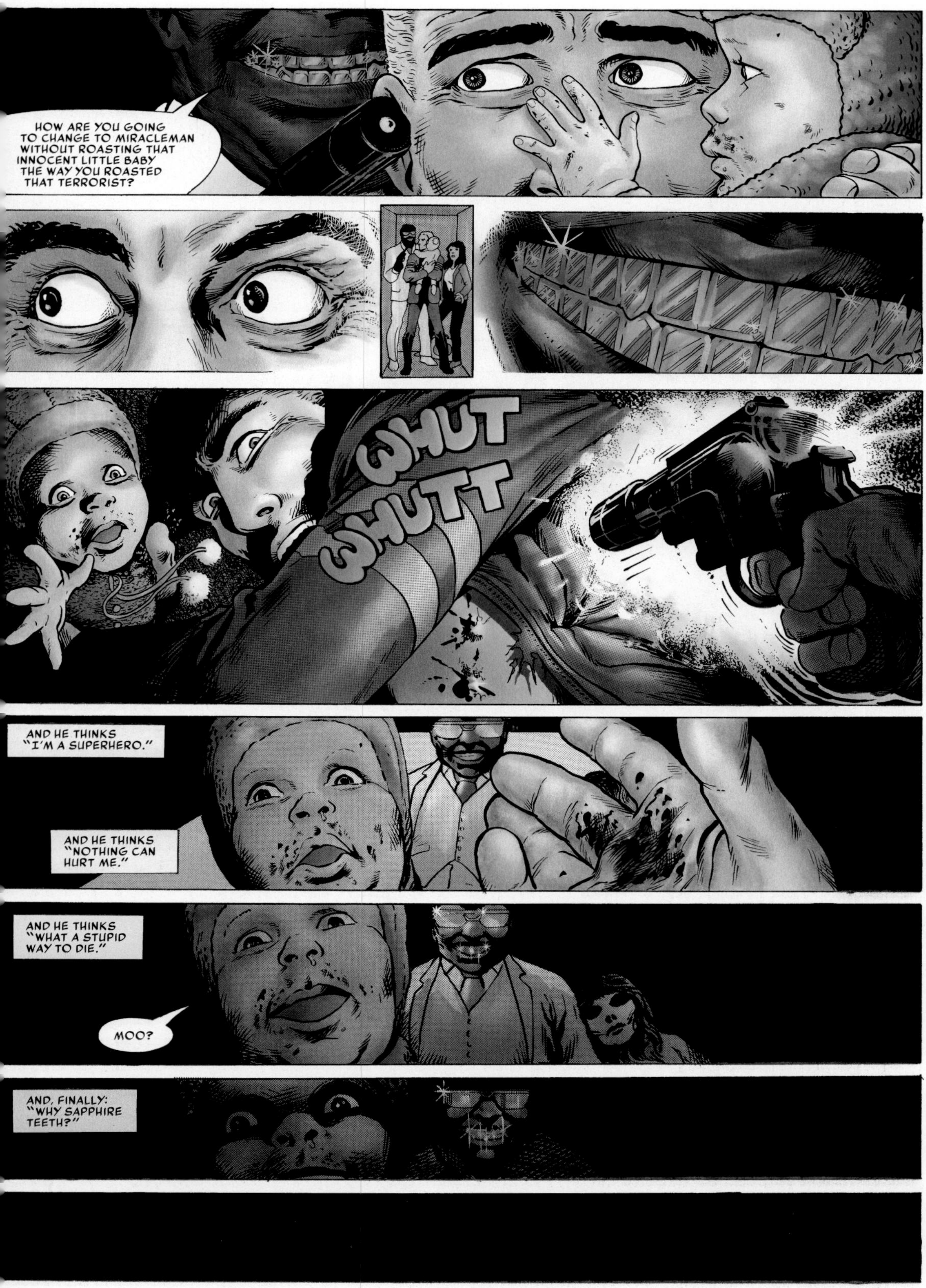
HOW ARE YOU GOING TO CHANGE TO MIRACLEMAN WITHOUT ROASTING THAT INNOCENT LITTLE BABY THE WAY YOU ROASTED THAT TERRORIST?
WHUT
WHUTT
AND HE THINKS "I'M A SUPERHERO."
AND HE THINKS "NOTHING CAN HURT ME."
AND HE THINKS "WHAT A STUPID WAY TO DIE."
MOO?
AND, FINALLY: "WHY SAPPHIRE TEETH?"

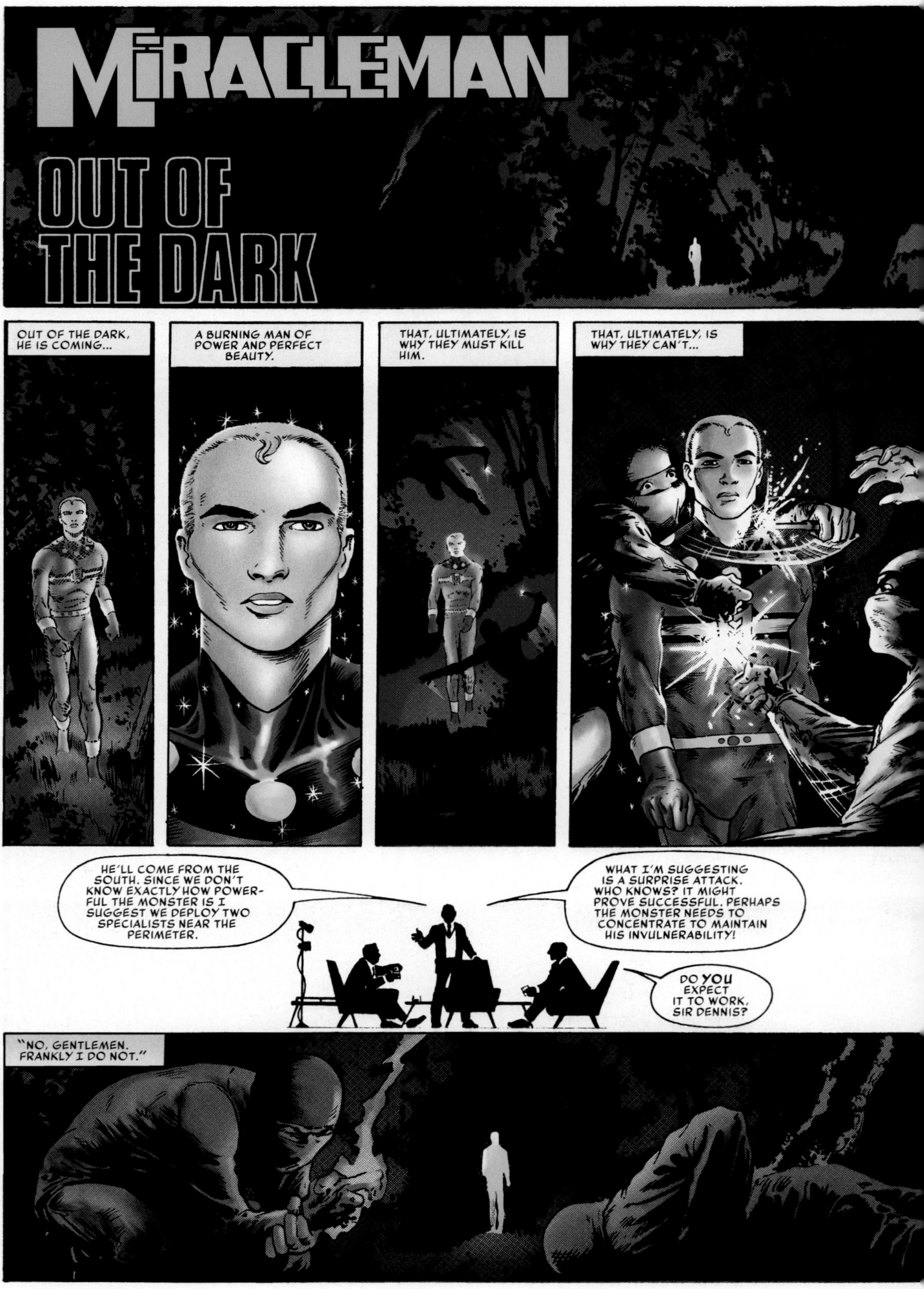
MIRACLEMAN
OUT OF THE DARK
OUT OF THE DARK, HE IS COMING...
A BURNING MAN OF POWER AND PERFECT BEAUTY.
THAT, ULTIMATELY, IS WHY THEY MUST KILL HIM.
THAT, ULTIMATELY, IS WHY THEY CAN'T...
HE'LL COME FROM THE SOUTH. SINCE WE DON'T KNOW EXACTLY HOW POWERFUL THE MONSTER IS I SUGGEST WE DEPLOY TWO SPECIALISTS NEAR THE PERIMETER.
WHAT I'M SUGGESTING IS A SURPRISE ATTACK. WHO KNOWS? IT MIGHT PROVE SUCCESSFUL. PERHAPS THE MONSTER NEEDS TO CONCENTRATE TO MAINTAIN HIS INVULNERABILITY!
DO YOU EXPECT IT TO WORK, SIR DENNIS?
"NO, GENTLEMEN. FRANKLY I DO NOT."

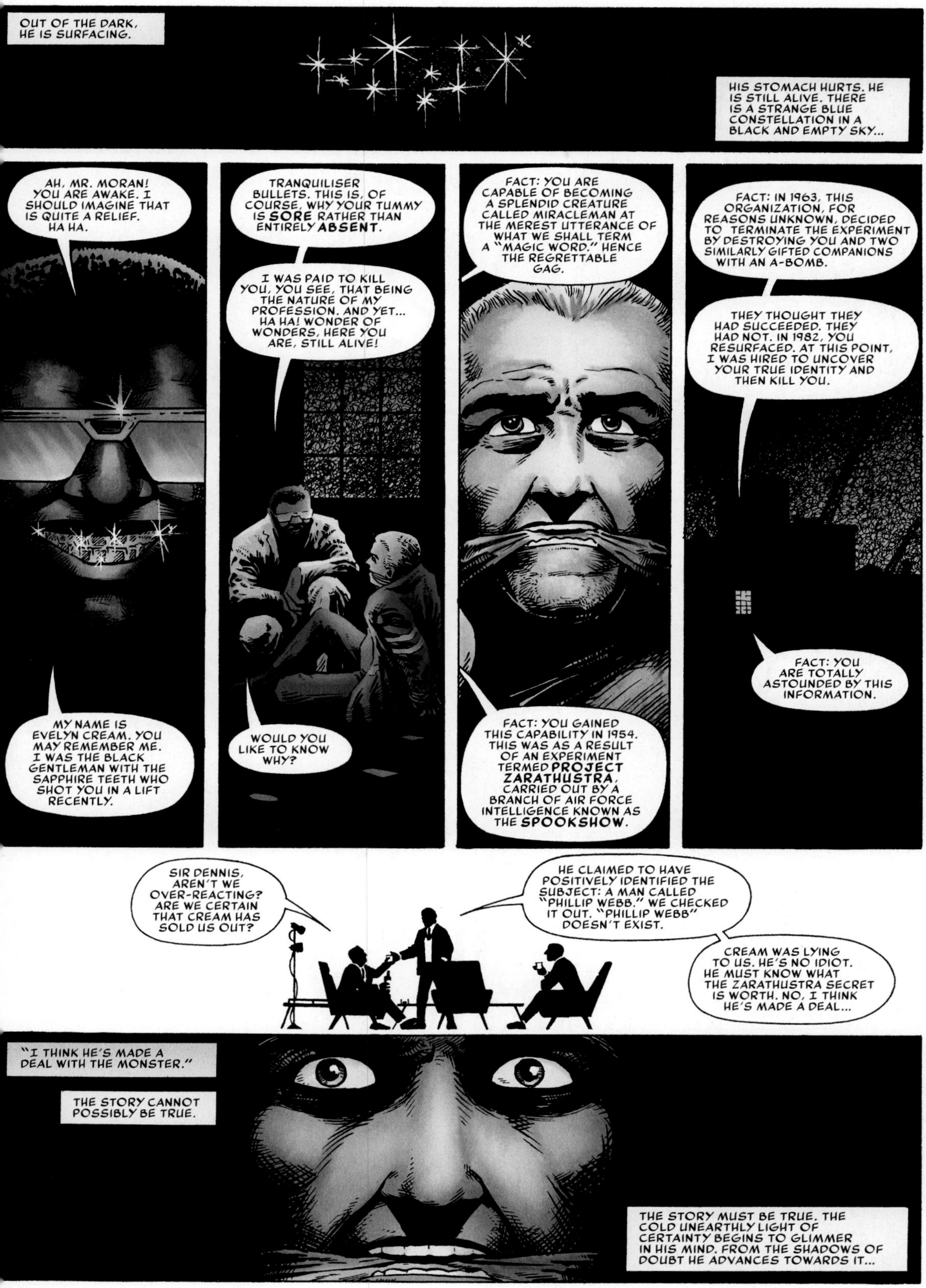

OUT OF THE DARK, HE IS SURFACING.
HIS STOMACH HURTS. HE IS STILL ALIVE. THERE IS A STRANGE BLUE CONSTELLATION IN A BLACK AND EMPTY SKY...
AH, MR. MORAN! YOU ARE AWAKE. I SHOULD IMAGINE THAT IS QUITE A RELIEF. HA HA.
MY NAME IS EVELYN CREAM. YOU MAY REMEMBER ME. I WAS THE BLACK GENTLEMAN WITH THE SAPPHIRE TEETH WHO SHOT YOU IN A LIFT RECENTLY.
TRANQUILISER BULLETS. THIS IS, OF COURSE, WHY YOUR TUMMY IS SORE RATHER THAN ENTIRELY ABSENT.
I WAS PAID TO KILL YOU, YOU SEE, THAT BEING THE NATURE OF MY PROFESSION. AND YET... HA HA! WONDER OF WONDERS, HERE YOU ARE, STILL ALIVE!
WOULD YOU LIKE TO KNOW WHY?
FACT: YOU ARE CAPABLE OF BECOMING A SPLENDID CREATURE CALLED MIRACLEMAN AT THE MEREST UTTERANCE OF WHAT WE SHALL TERM A "MAGIC WORD." HENCE THE REGRETTABLE GAG.
FACT: YOU GAINED THIS CAPABILITY IN 1954. THIS WAS AS A RESULT OF AN EXPERIMENT TERMED PROJECT ZARATHUSTRA, CARRIED OUT BY A BRANCH OF AIR FORCE INTELLIGENCE KNOWN AS THE SPOOKSHOW.
FACT: IN 1963, THIS ORGANIZATION, FOR REASONS UNKNOWN, DECIDED TO TERMINATE THE EXPERIMENT BY DESTROYING YOU AND TWO SIMILARLY GIFTED COMPANIONS WITH AN A-BOMB.
THEY THOUGHT THEY HAD SUCCEEDED. THEY HAD NOT. IN 1982, YOU RESURFACED. AT THIS POINT, I WAS HIRED TO UNCOVER YOUR TRUE IDENTITY AND THEN KILL YOU.
FACT: YOU ARE TOTALLY ASTOUNDED BY THIS INFORMATION.
SIR DENNIS, AREN'T WE OVER-REACTING? ARE WE CERTAIN THAT CREAM HAS SOLD US OUT?
HE CLAIMED TO HAVE POSITIVELY IDENTIFIED THE SUBJECT: A MAN CALLED "PHILLIP WEBB." WE CHECKED IT OUT. "PHILLIP WEBB" DOESN'T EXIST.
CREAM WAS LYING TO US. HE'S NO IDIOT. HE MUST KNOW WHAT THE ZARATHUSTRA SECRET IS WORTH. NO, I THINK HE'S MADE A DEAL...
"I THINK HE'S MADE A DEAL WITH THE MONSTER."
THE STORY CANNOT POSSIBLY BE TRUE.
THE STORY MUST BE TRUE. THE COLD UNEARTHLY LIGHT OF CERTAINTY BEGINS TO GLIMMER IN HIS MIND. FROM THE SHADOWS OF DOUBT HE ADVANCES TOWARDS IT...

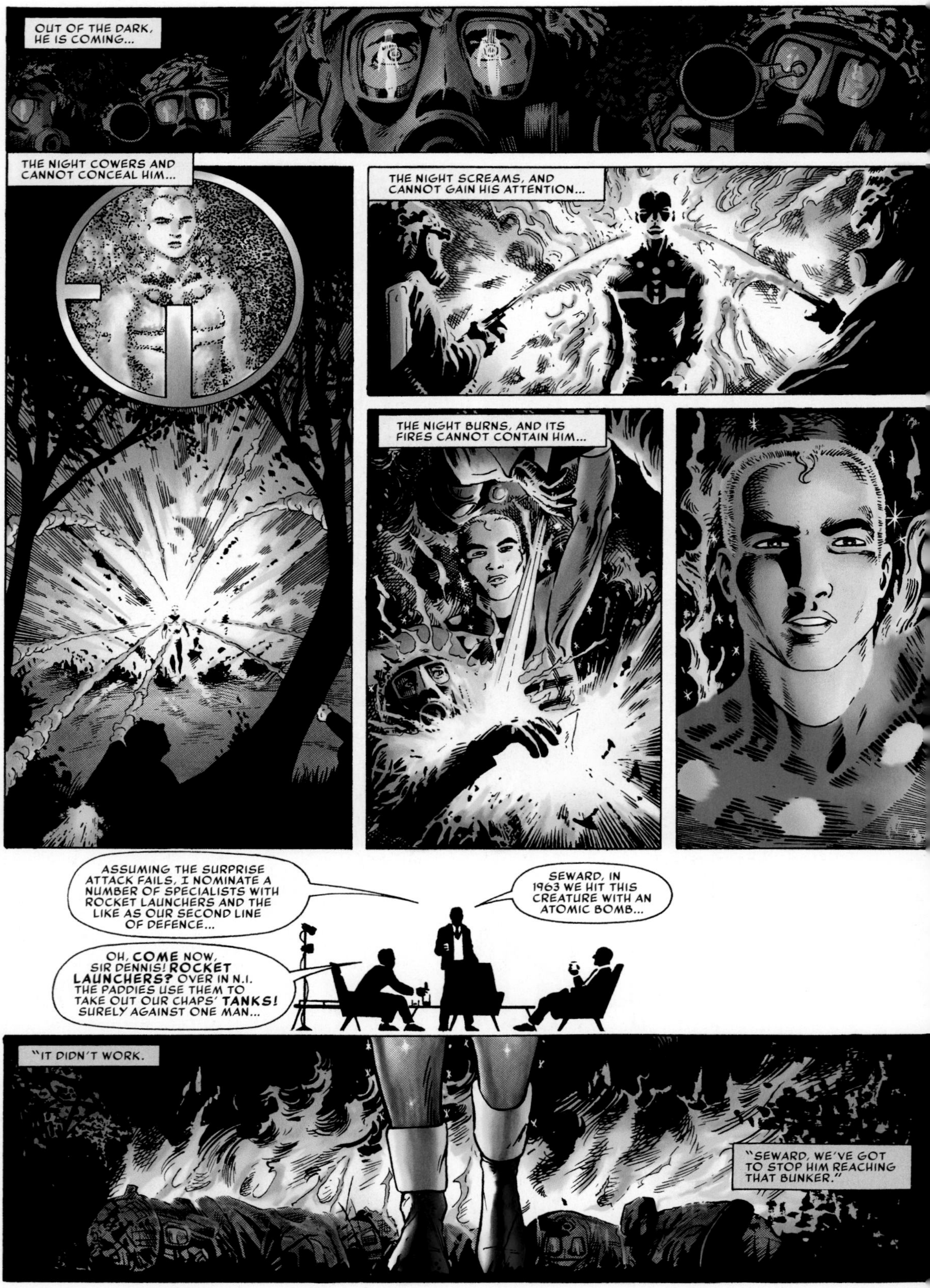
OUT OF THE DARK, HE IS COMING...
THE NIGHT COWERS AND CANNOT CONCEAL HIM...
THE NIGHT SCREAMS, AND CANNOT GAIN HIS ATTENTION...
THE NIGHT BURNS, AND ITS FIRES CANNOT CONTAIN HIM...
ASSUMING THE SURPRISE ATTACK FAILS, I NOMINATE A NUMBER OF SPECIALISTS WITH ROCKET LAUNCHERS AND THE LIKE AS OUR SECOND LINE OF DEFENCE...
SEWARD, IN 1963 WE HIT THIS CREATURE WITH AN ATOMIC BOMB...
OH, COME NOW, SIR DENNIS! ROCKET LAUNCHERS? OVER IN N.I. THE PADDIES USE THEM TO TAKE OUT OUR CHAPS' TANKS! SURELY AGAINST ONE MAN...
"IT DIDN'T WORK.
"SEWARD, WE'VE GOT TO STOP HIM REACHING THAT BUNKER."

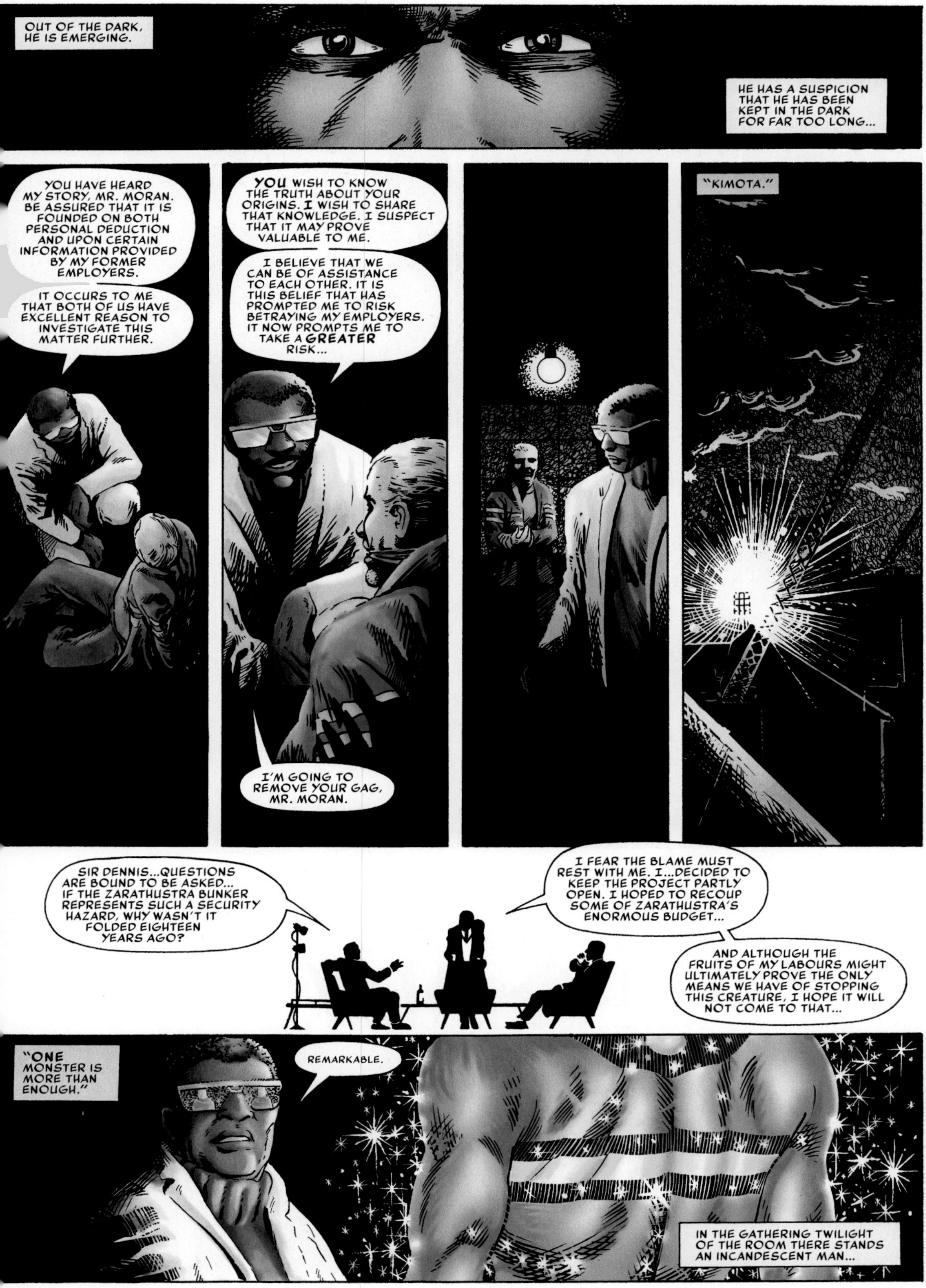
OUT OF THE DARK, HE IS EMERGING.
HE HAS A SUSPICION THAT HE HAS BEEN KEPT IN THE DARK FOR FAR TOO LONG...
YOU HAVE HEARD MY STORY, MR. MORAN. BE ASSURED THAT IT IS FOUNDED ON BOTH PERSONAL DEDUCTION AND UPON CERTAIN INFORMATION PROVIDED BY MY FORMER EMPLOYERS.
IT OCCURS TO ME THAT BOTH OF US HAVE EXCELLENT REASON TO INVESTIGATE THIS MATTER FURTHER.
YOU WISH TO KNOW THE TRUTH ABOUT YOUR ORIGINS. I WISH TO SHARE THAT KNOWLEDGE. I SUSPECT THAT IT MAY PROVE VALUABLE TO ME.
I BELIEVE THAT WE CAN BE OF ASSISTANCE TO EACH OTHER. IT IS THIS BELIEF THAT HAS PROMPTED ME TO RISK BETRAYING MY EMPLOYERS. IT NOW PROMPTS ME TO TAKE A GREATER RISK...
I'M GOING TO REMOVE YOUR GAG, MR. MORAN.
"KIMOTA."
SIR DENNIS...QUESTIONS ARE BOUND TO BE ASKED... IF THE ZARATHUSTRA BUNKER REPRESENTS SUCH A SECURITY HAZARD, WHY WASN'T IT FOLDED EIGHTEEN YEARS AGO?
I FEAR THE BLAME MUST REST WITH ME. I...DECIDED TO KEEP THE PROJECT PARTLY OPEN. I HOPED TO RECOUP SOME OF ZARATHUSTRA'S ENORMOUS BUDGET...
AND ALTHOUGH THE FRUITS OF MY LABOURS MIGHT ULTIMATELY PROVE THE ONLY MEANS WE HAVE OF STOPPING THIS CREATURE, I HOPE IT WILL NOT COME TO THAT...
"ONE MONSTER IS MORE THAN ENOUGH."
REMARKABLE.
IN THE GATHERING TWILIGHT OF THE ROOM THERE STANDS AN INCANDESCENT MAN...

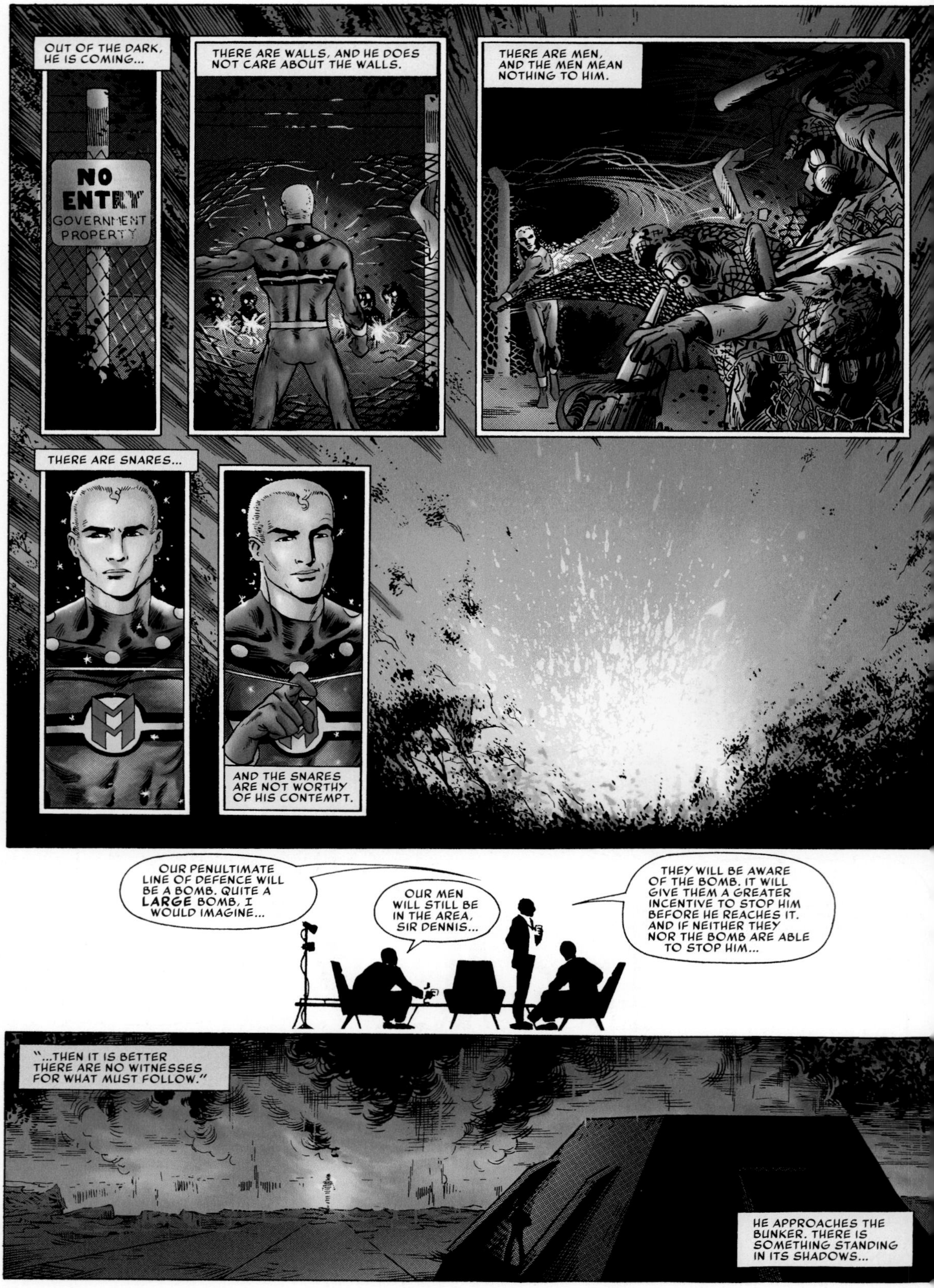
OUT OF THE DARK, HE IS COMING...
NO ENTRY GOVERNMENT PROPERTY
THERE ARE WALLS, AND HE DOES NOT CARE ABOUT THE WALLS.
THERE ARE MEN, AND THE MEN MEAN NOTHING TO HIM.
THERE ARE SNARES...
AND THE SNARES ARE NOT WORTHY OF HIS CONTEMPT.
OUR PENULTIMATE LINE OF DEFENCE WILL BE A BOMB. QUITE A LARGE BOMB, I WOULD IMAGINE...
OUR MEN WILL STILL BE IN THE AREA, SIR DENNIS...
THEY WILL BE AWARE OF THE BOMB. IT WILL GIVE THEM A GREATER INCENTIVE TO STOP HIM BEFORE HE REACHES IT. AND IF NEITHER THEY NOR THE BOMB ARE ABLE TO STOP HIM...
"...THEN IT IS BETTER THERE ARE NO WITNESSES FOR WHAT MUST FOLLOW."
HE APPROACHES THE BUNKER. THERE IS SOMETHING STANDING IN ITS SHADOWS...

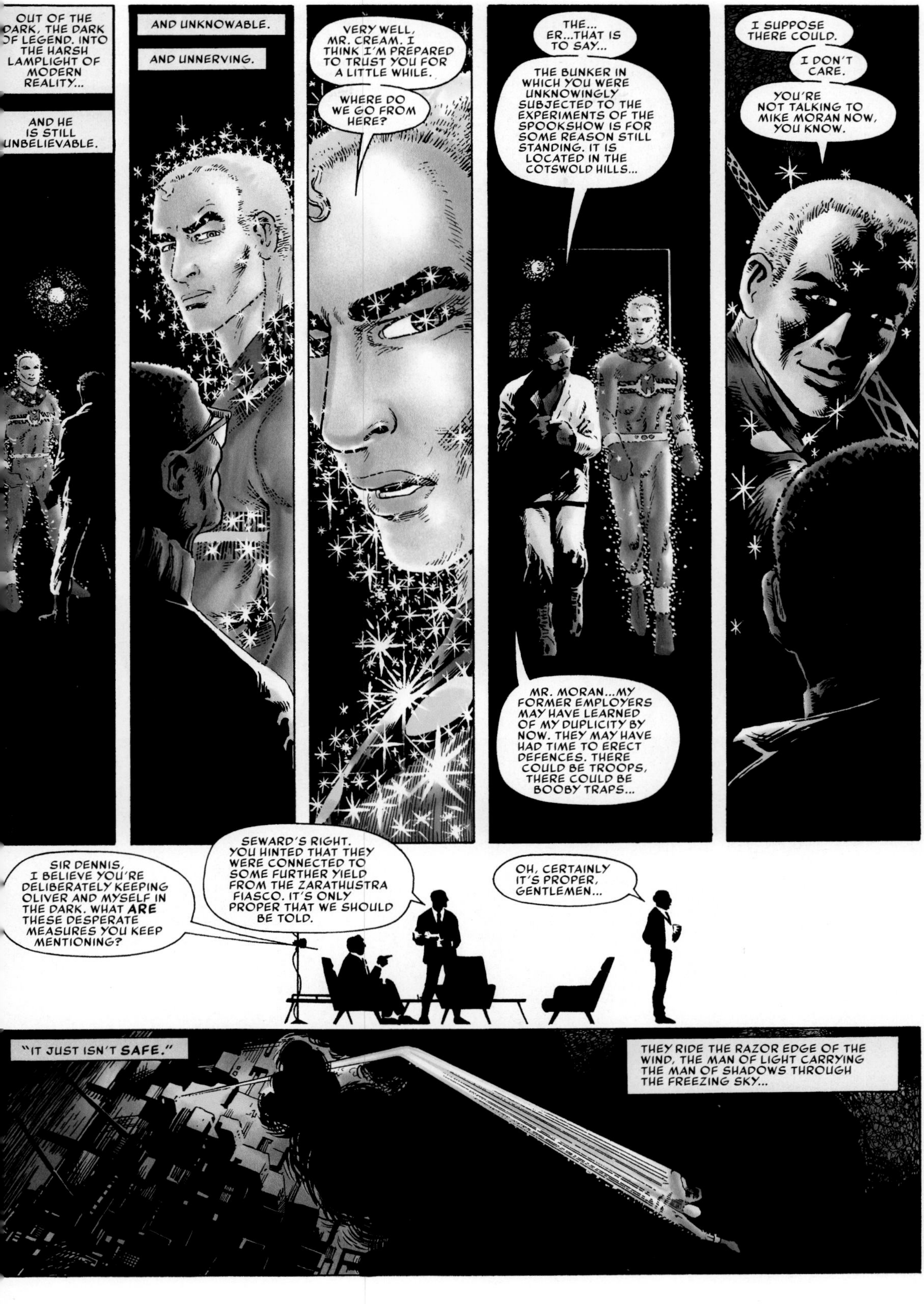
OUT OF THE DARK, THE DARK OF LEGEND. INTO THE HARSH LAMPLIGHT OF MODERN REALITY...
AND HE IS STILL UNBELIEVABLE.
AND UNKNOWABLE.
AND UNNERVING.
VERY WELL, MR. CREAM. I THINK I'M PREPARED TO TRUST YOU FOR A LITTLE WHILE.
WHERE DO WE GO FROM HERE?
THE... ER...THAT IS TO SAY...
THE BUNKER IN WHICH YOU WERE UNKNOWINGLY SUBJECTED TO THE EXPERIMENTS OF THE SPOOKSHOW IS FOR SOME REASON STILL STANDING. IT IS LOCATED IN THE COTSWOLD HILLS...
MR. MORAN...MY FORMER EMPLOYERS MAY HAVE LEARNED OF MY DUPLICITY BY NOW. THEY MAY HAVE HAD TIME TO ERECT DEFENCES. THERE COULD BE TROOPS, THERE COULD BE BOOBY TRAPS...
I SUPPOSE THERE COULD.
I DON'T CARE.
YOU'RE NOT TALKING TO MIKE MORAN NOW, YOU KNOW.
SIR DENNIS, I BELIEVE YOU'RE DELIBERATELY KEEPING OLIVER AND MYSELF IN THE DARK. WHAT **ARE** THESE DESPERATE MEASURES YOU KEEP MENTIONING?
SEWARD'S RIGHT. YOU HINTED THAT THEY WERE CONNECTED TO SOME FURTHER YIELD FROM THE ZARATHUSTRA FIASCO. IT'S ONLY PROPER THAT WE SHOULD BE TOLD.
OH, CERTAINLY IT'S PROPER, GENTLEMEN...
"IT JUST ISN'T **SAFE**."
THEY RIDE THE RAZOR EDGE OF THE WIND, THE MAN OF LIGHT CARRYING THE MAN OF SHADOWS THROUGH THE FREEZING SKY...

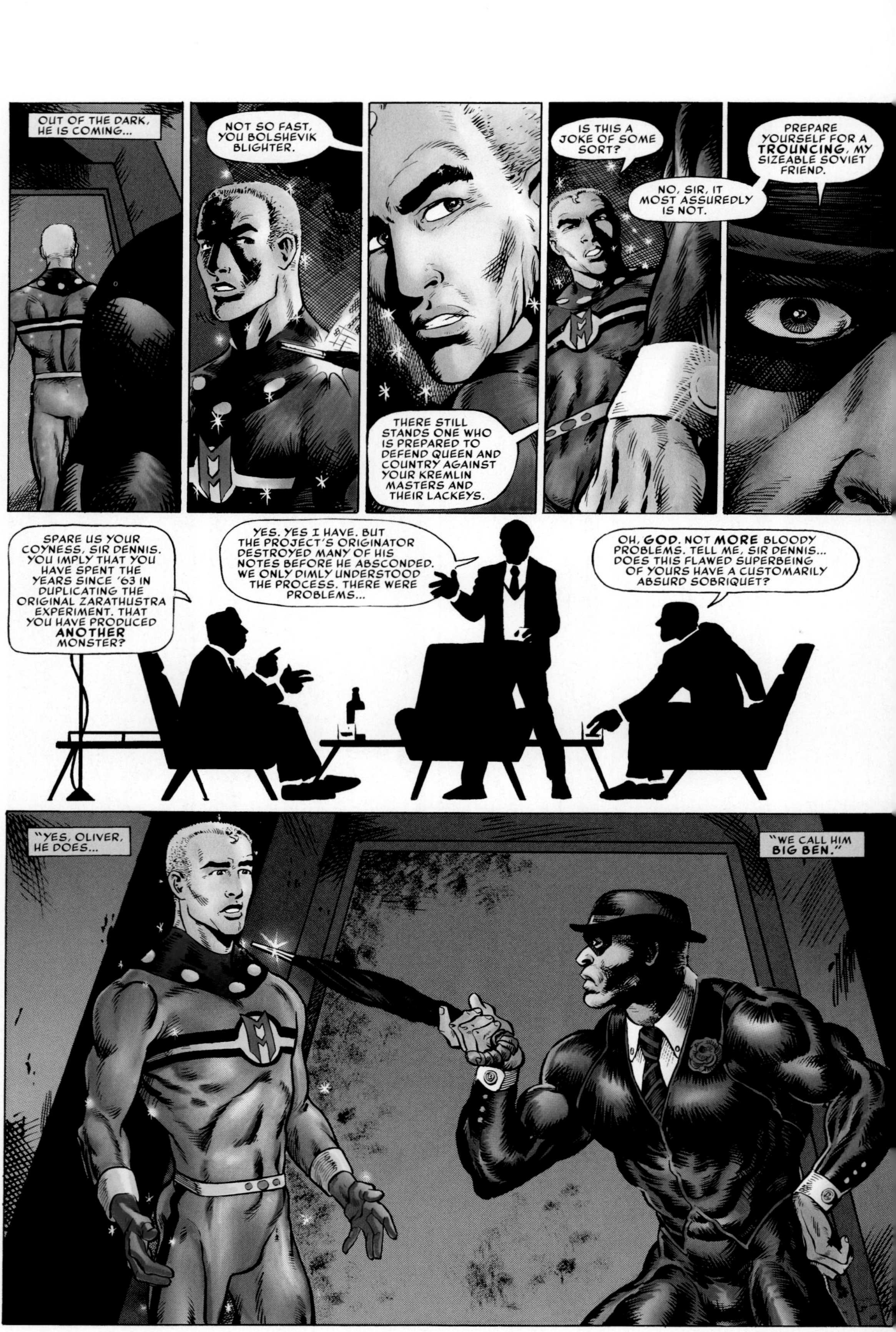

OUT OF THE DARK, HE IS COMING...
NOT SO FAST, YOU BOLSHEVIK BLIGHTER.
THERE STILL STANDS ONE WHO IS PREPARED TO DEFEND QUEEN AND COUNTRY AGAINST YOUR KREMLIN MASTERS AND THEIR LACKEYS.
IS THIS A JOKE OF SOME SORT?
NO, SIR, IT MOST ASSUREDLY IS NOT.
PREPARE YOURSELF FOR A **TROUNCING**, MY SIZEABLE SOVIET FRIEND.
SPARE US YOUR COYNESS, SIR DENNIS. YOU IMPLY THAT YOU HAVE SPENT THE YEARS SINCE '63 IN DUPLICATING THE ORIGINAL ZARATHUSTRA EXPERIMENT. THAT YOU HAVE PRODUCED **ANOTHER** MONSTER?
YES. YES I HAVE. BUT THE PROJECT'S ORIGINATOR DESTROYED MANY OF HIS NOTES BEFORE HE ABSCONDED. WE ONLY DIMLY UNDERSTOOD THE PROCESS. THERE WERE PROBLEMS...
OH, **GOD**. NOT **MORE** BLOODY PROBLEMS. TELL ME, SIR DENNIS... DOES THIS FLAWED SUPERBEING OF YOURS HAVE A CUSTOMARILY ABSURD SOBRIQUET?
"YES, OLIVER, HE DOES...
"WE CALL HIM **BIG BEN**."

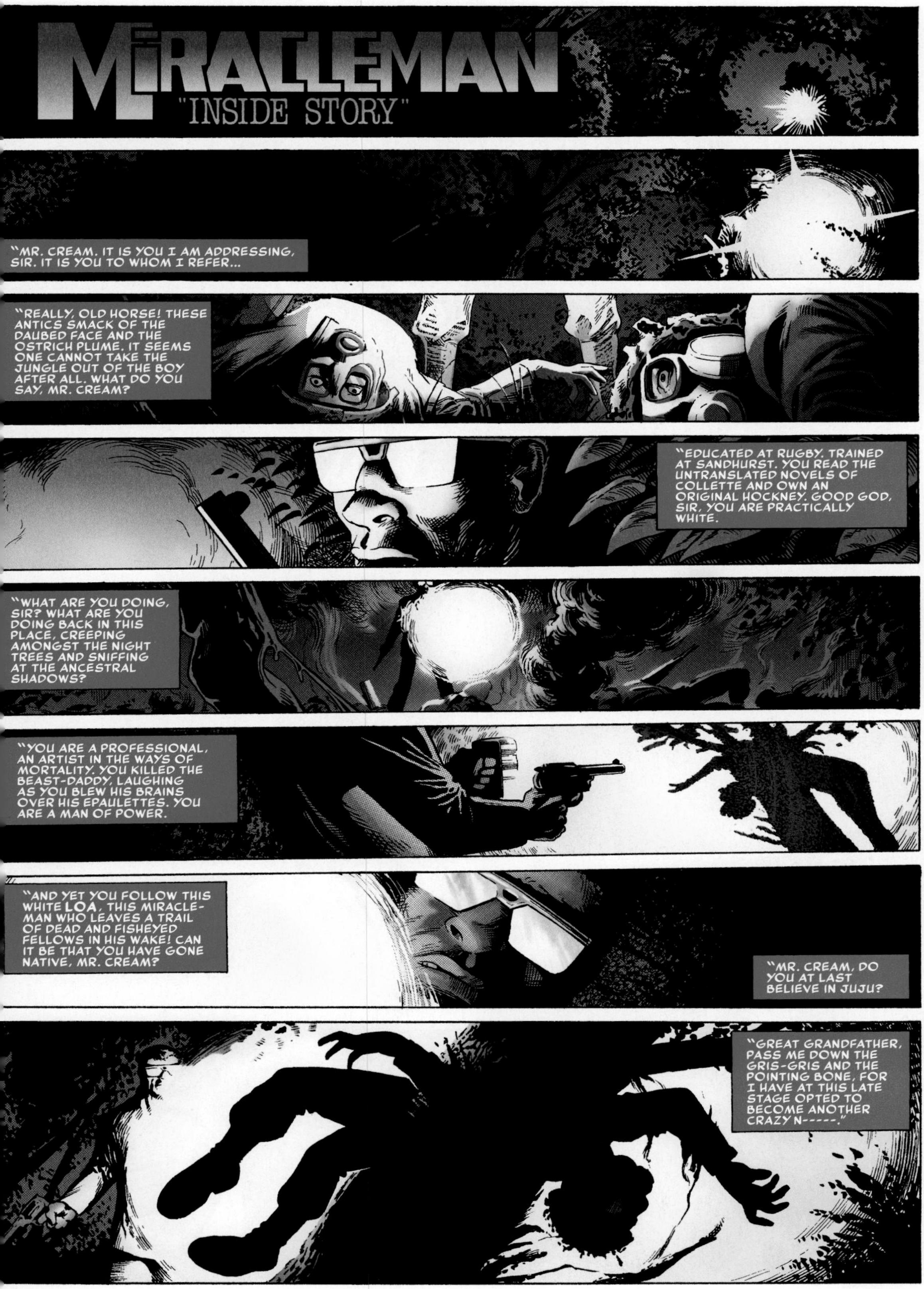

MIRACLEMAN
"INSIDE STORY"
"MR. CREAM. IT IS YOU I AM ADDRESSING, SIR. IT IS YOU TO WHOM I REFER...
"REALLY, OLD HORSE! THESE ANTICS SMACK OF THE DAUBED FACE AND THE OSTRICH PLUME. IT SEEMS ONE CANNOT TAKE THE JUNGLE OUT OF THE BOY AFTER ALL. WHAT DO YOU SAY, MR. CREAM?
"EDUCATED AT RUGBY. TRAINED AT SANDHURST. YOU READ THE UNTRANSLATED NOVELS OF COLLETTE AND OWN AN ORIGINAL HOCKNEY. GOOD GOD, SIR, YOU ARE PRACTICALLY WHITE.
"WHAT ARE YOU DOING, SIR? WHAT ARE YOU DOING BACK IN THIS PLACE, CREEPING AMONGST THE NIGHT TREES AND SNIFFING AT THE ANCESTRAL SHADOWS?
"YOU ARE A PROFESSIONAL, AN ARTIST IN THE WAYS OF MORTALITY. YOU KILLED THE BEAST-DADDY, LAUGHING AS YOU BLEW HIS BRAINS OVER HIS EPAULETTES. YOU ARE A MAN OF POWER.
"AND YET YOU FOLLOW THIS WHITE LOA, THIS MIRACLEMAN WHO LEAVES A TRAIL OF DEAD AND FISHEYED FELLOWS IN HIS WAKE! CAN IT BE THAT YOU HAVE GONE NATIVE, MR. CREAM?
"MR. CREAM, DO YOU AT LAST BELIEVE IN JUJU?
"GREAT GRANDFATHER, PASS ME DOWN THE GRIS-GRIS AND THE POINTING BONE, FOR I HAVE AT THIS LATE STAGE OPTED TO BECOME ANOTHER CRAZY N-----."

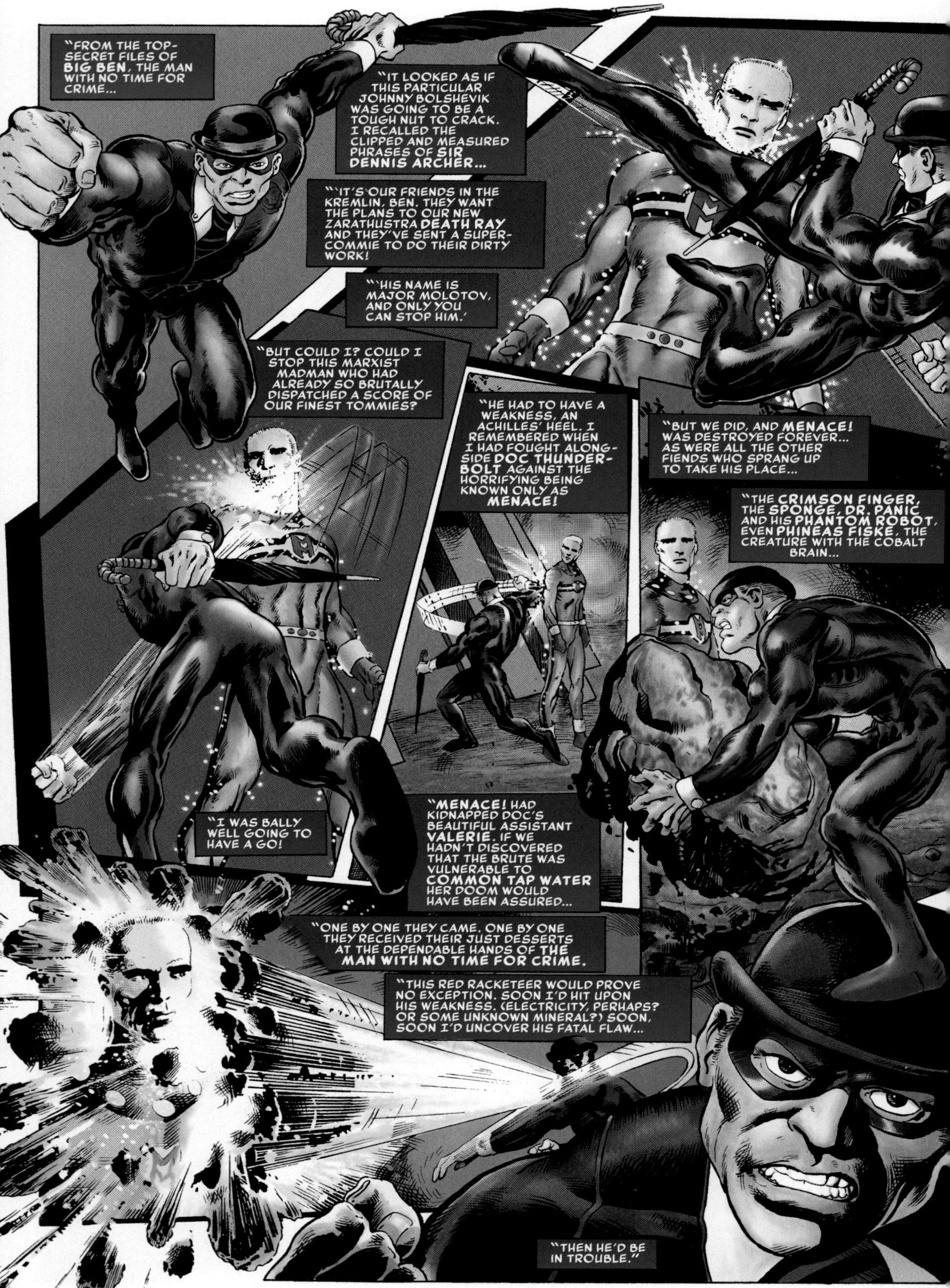
"FROM THE TOP-SECRET FILES OF BIG BEN, THE MAN WITH NO TIME FOR CRIME...
"IT LOOKED AS IF THIS PARTICULAR JOHNNY BOLSHEVIK WAS GOING TO BE A TOUGH NUT TO CRACK. I RECALLED THE CLIPPED AND MEASURED PHRASES OF SIR DENNIS ARCHER...
"'IT'S OUR FRIENDS IN THE KREMLIN, BEN. THEY WANT THE PLANS TO OUR NEW ZARATHUSTRA DEATH RAY AND THEY'VE SENT A SUPER-COMMIE TO DO THEIR DIRTY WORK!
"'HIS NAME IS MAJOR MOLOTOV, AND ONLY YOU CAN STOP HIM.'
"BUT COULD I? COULD I STOP THIS MARXIST MADMAN WHO HAD ALREADY SO BRUTALLY DISPATCHED A SCORE OF OUR FINEST TOMMIES?
"I WAS BALLY WELL GOING TO HAVE A GO!
"HE HAD TO HAVE A WEAKNESS, AN ACHILLES' HEEL. I REMEMBERED WHEN I HAD FOUGHT ALONGSIDE DOC THUNDERBOLT AGAINST THE HORRIFYING BEING KNOWN ONLY AS MENACE!
"MENACE! HAD KIDNAPPED DOC'S BEAUTIFUL ASSISTANT VALERIE. IF WE HADN'T DISCOVERED THAT THE BRUTE WAS VULNERABLE TO COMMON TAP WATER HER DOOM WOULD HAVE BEEN ASSURED...
"BUT WE DID, AND MENACE! WAS DESTROYED FOREVER... AS WERE ALL THE OTHER FIENDS WHO SPRANG UP TO TAKE HIS PLACE...
"THE CRIMSON FINGER, THE SPONGE, DR. PANIC AND HIS PHANTOM ROBOT, EVEN PHINEAS FISKE, THE CREATURE WITH THE COBALT BRAIN...
"ONE BY ONE THEY CAME. ONE BY ONE THEY RECEIVED THEIR JUST DESSERTS AT THE DEPENDABLE HANDS OF THE MAN WITH NO TIME FOR CRIME.
"THIS RED RACKETEER WOULD PROVE NO EXCEPTION. SOON I'D HIT UPON HIS WEAKNESS. (ELECTRICITY, PERHAPS? OR SOME UNKNOWN MINERAL?) SOON, SOON I'D UNCOVER HIS FATAL FLAW...
"THEN HE'D BE IN TROUBLE."

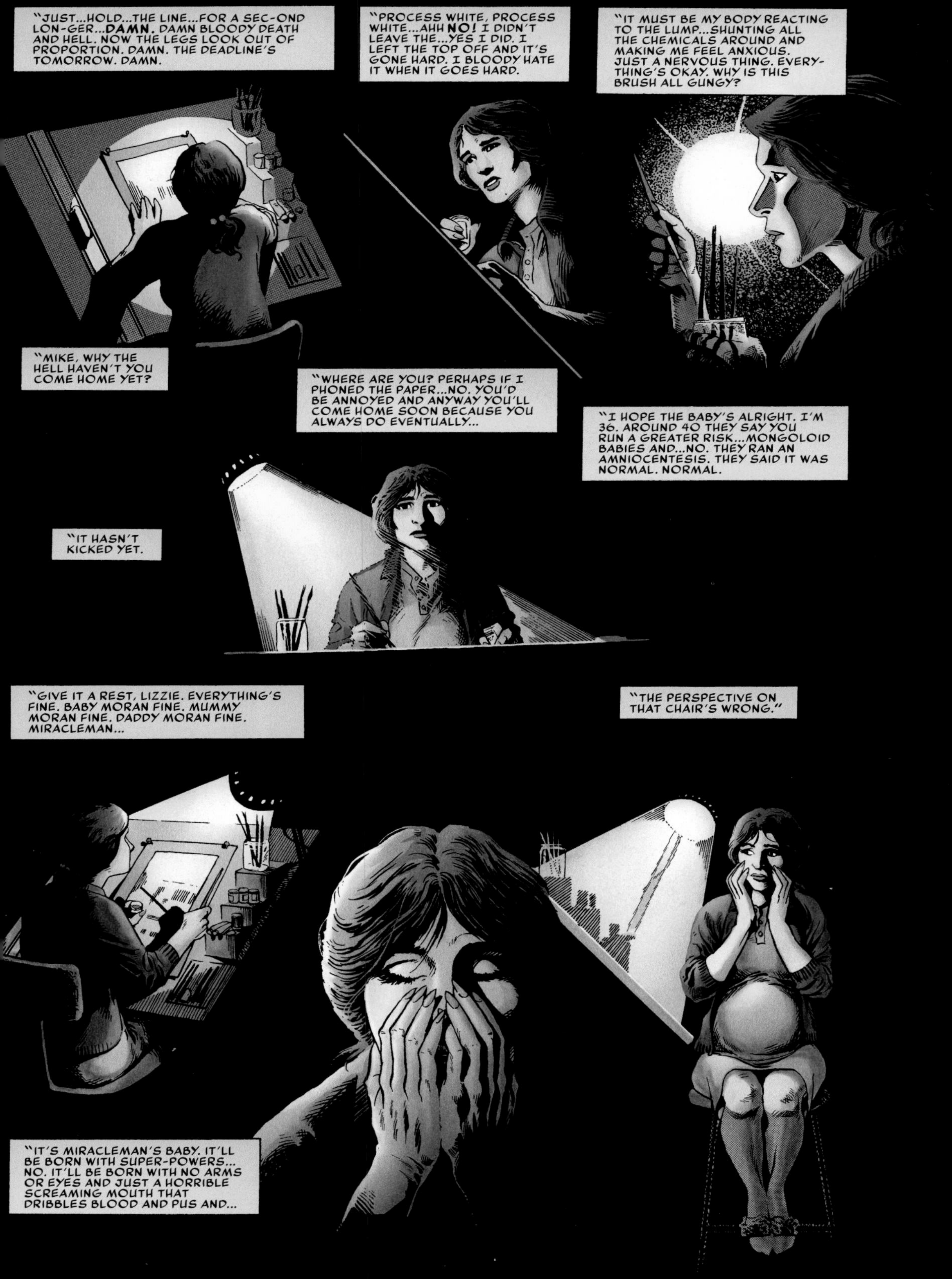
"JUST...HOLD...THE LINE...FOR A SEC-OND LON-GER...DAMN. DAMN BLOODY DEATH AND HELL. NOW THE LEGS LOOK OUT OF PROPORTION. DAMN. THE DEADLINE'S TOMORROW. DAMN.
"PROCESS WHITE, PROCESS WHITE...AHH NO! I DIDN'T LEAVE THE...YES I DID. I LEFT THE TOP OFF AND IT'S GONE HARD. I BLOODY HATE IT WHEN IT GOES HARD.
"IT MUST BE MY BODY REACTING TO THE LUMP...SHUNTING ALL THE CHEMICALS AROUND AND MAKING ME FEEL ANXIOUS. JUST A NERVOUS THING. EVERY-THING'S OKAY. WHY IS THIS BRUSH ALL GUNGY?
"MIKE, WHY THE HELL HAVEN'T YOU COME HOME YET?
"WHERE ARE YOU? PERHAPS IF I PHONED THE PAPER...NO. YOU'D BE ANNOYED AND ANYWAY YOU'LL COME HOME SOON BECAUSE YOU ALWAYS DO EVENTUALLY...
"I HOPE THE BABY'S ALRIGHT. I'M 36. AROUND 40 THEY SAY YOU RUN A GREATER RISK...MONGOLOID BABIES AND...NO. THEY RAN AN AMNIOCENTESIS. THEY SAID IT WAS NORMAL. NORMAL.
"IT HASN'T KICKED YET.
"GIVE IT A REST, LIZZIE. EVERYTHING'S FINE. BABY MORAN FINE. MUMMY MORAN FINE. DADDY MORAN FINE. MIRACLEMAN...
"THE PERSPECTIVE ON THAT CHAIR'S WRONG."
"IT'S MIRACLEMAN'S BABY. IT'LL BE BORN WITH SUPER-POWERS... NO. IT'LL BE BORN WITH NO ARMS OR EYES AND JUST A HORRIBLE SCREAMING MOUTH THAT DRIBBLES BLOOD AND PUS AND...

"I WISH I KNEW WHO HE WAS."

"I WISH HE'D STOP HITTING ME."

"I DON'T WANT TO HURT HIM. HE ISN'T AS POWERFUL AS I AM AND I THINK THERE'S SOMETHING WRONG WITH HIS MIND."

"FLAWLESS CHINA BLUE EYES THAT NEVER BLINK AND GLITTER LIKE MARBLES. HE'S A PSYCHOPATH."

"...AND HE'S A SUPERHUMAN. BUT WHERE DID HE COME FROM? FIRST A HIRED KILLER CHANGES SIDES AND TELLS ME OF A GOVERNMENT PLOT TO MURDER ME...

"THEN HE LEADS ME TO A BUNKER UP HERE IN THE COTSWOLDS WHERE HE ASSURES ME I'LL FIND EVIDENCE CONCERNING MY TRUE ORIGINS AS MIRACLEMAN. HE TELLS ME TO GO ON AHEAD..."

"SOME SOLDIERS TRY TO CUT MY THROAT. SOME MORE SOLDIERS FIRE ROCKETS AND FLAME-THROWERS AT ME. A BOMB IS EXPLODED UNDERNEATH MY FEET.

"FINALLY I'M ATTACKED BY A SUPERHUMAN LUNATIC IN A BOWLER HAT WHO THINKS I'M A COMMUNIST."

"I COULD GET TIRED OF THIS."

SURRENDER, BUTCHER OF LENINGRAD! SURRENDER OR FIGHT LIKE A MAN, DAMN YOUR EYES!

"ALL RIGHT."

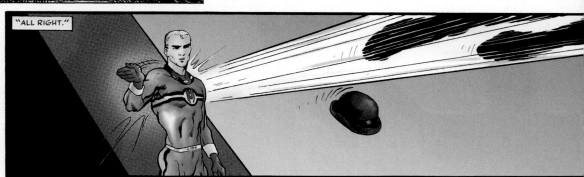

"ALL RIGHT."

74

CCKRIKK BRRTCHHH
SHRITCH
KKRRAAATCCHH
SCHITTRANKK

"WHITE MAN'S MAGIC..."

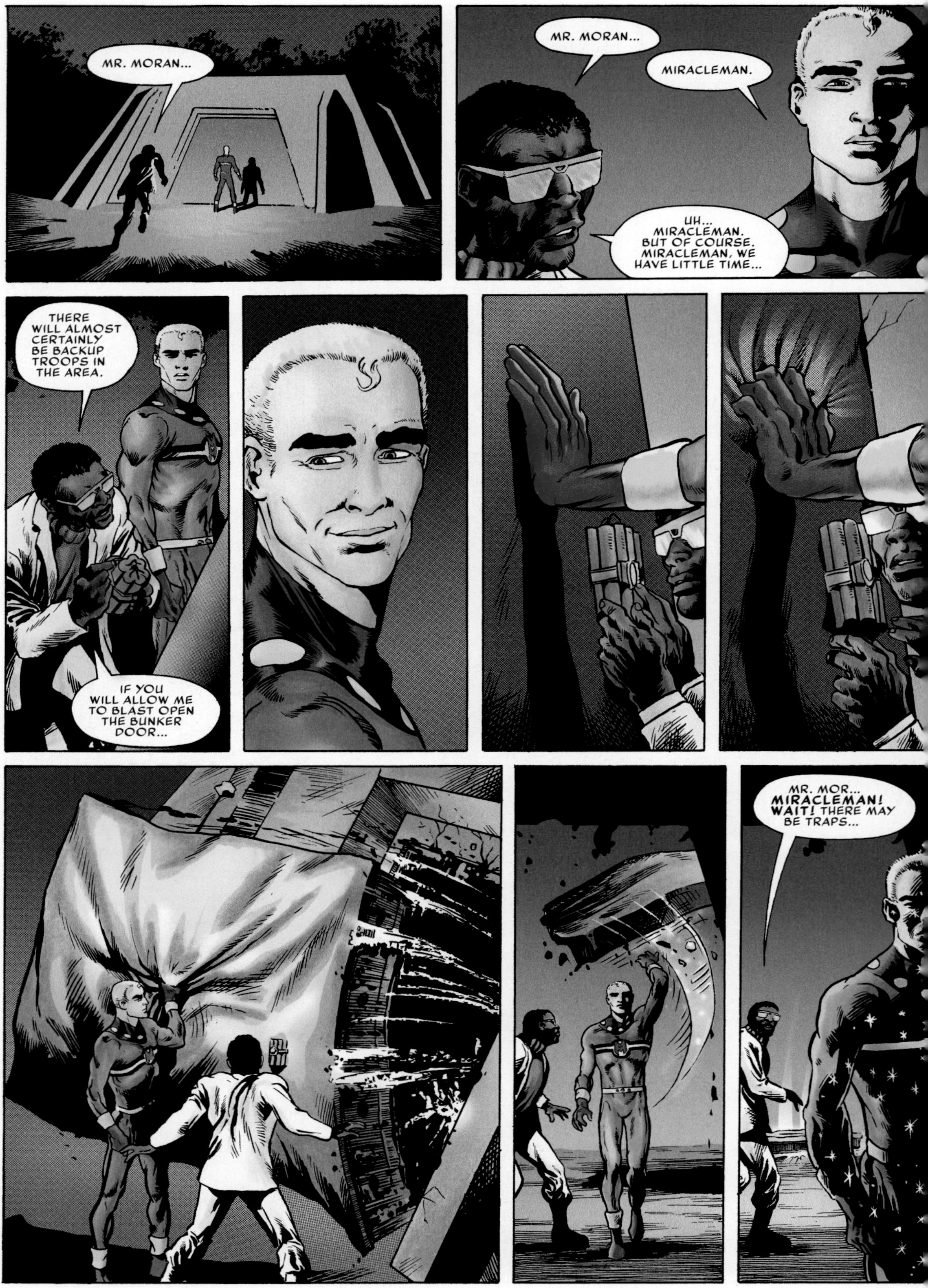
MR. MORAN...
MR. MORAN...
MIRACLEMAN.
UH... MIRACLEMAN. BUT OF COURSE. MIRACLEMAN, WE HAVE LITTLE TIME...
THERE WILL ALMOST CERTAINLY BE BACKUP TROOPS IN THE AREA.
IF YOU WILL ALLOW ME TO BLAST OPEN THE BUNKER DOOR...
MR. MOR... MIRACLEMAN! WAIT! THERE MAY BE TRAPS...

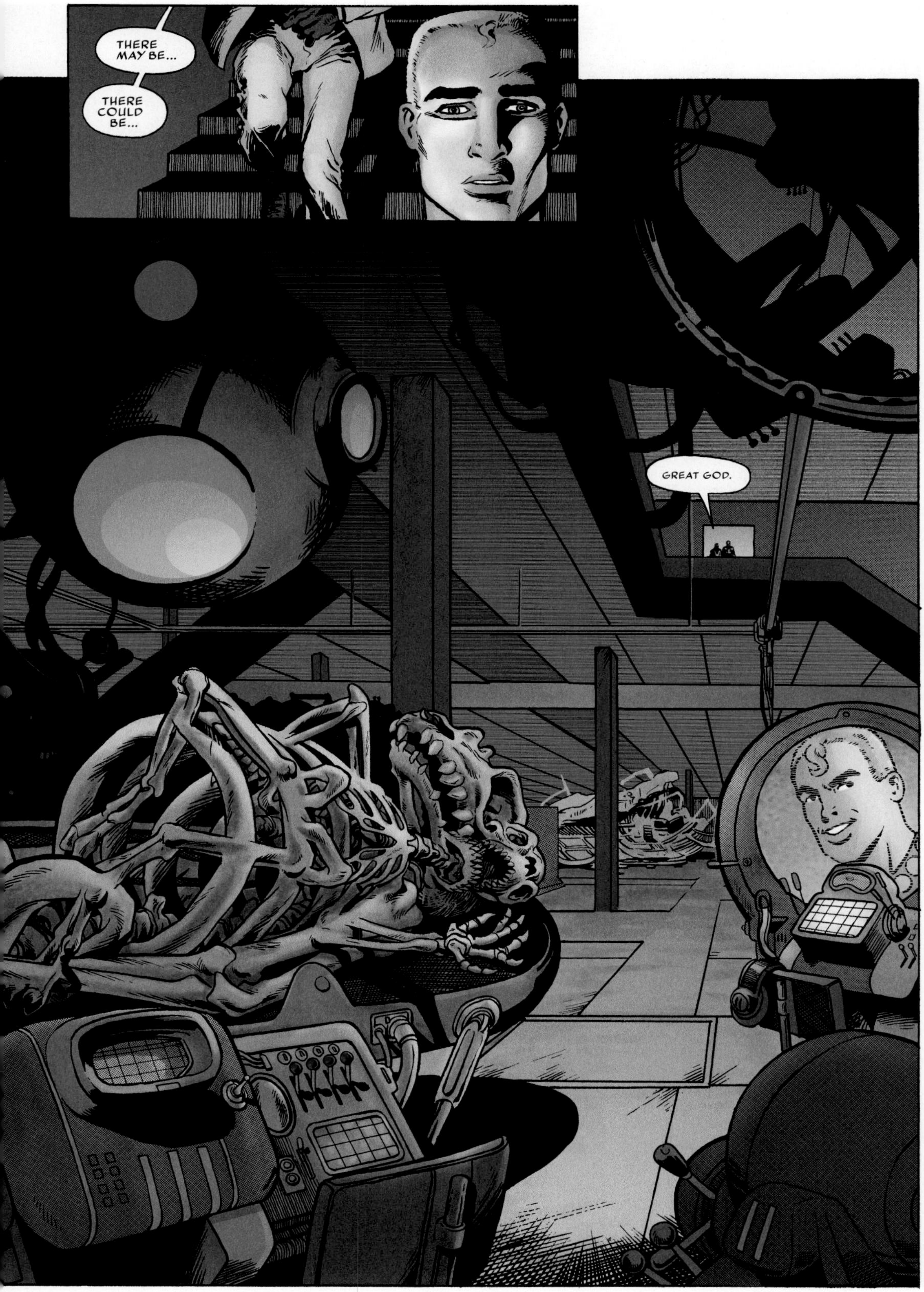
THERE MAY BE...
THERE COULD BE...
GREAT GOD.

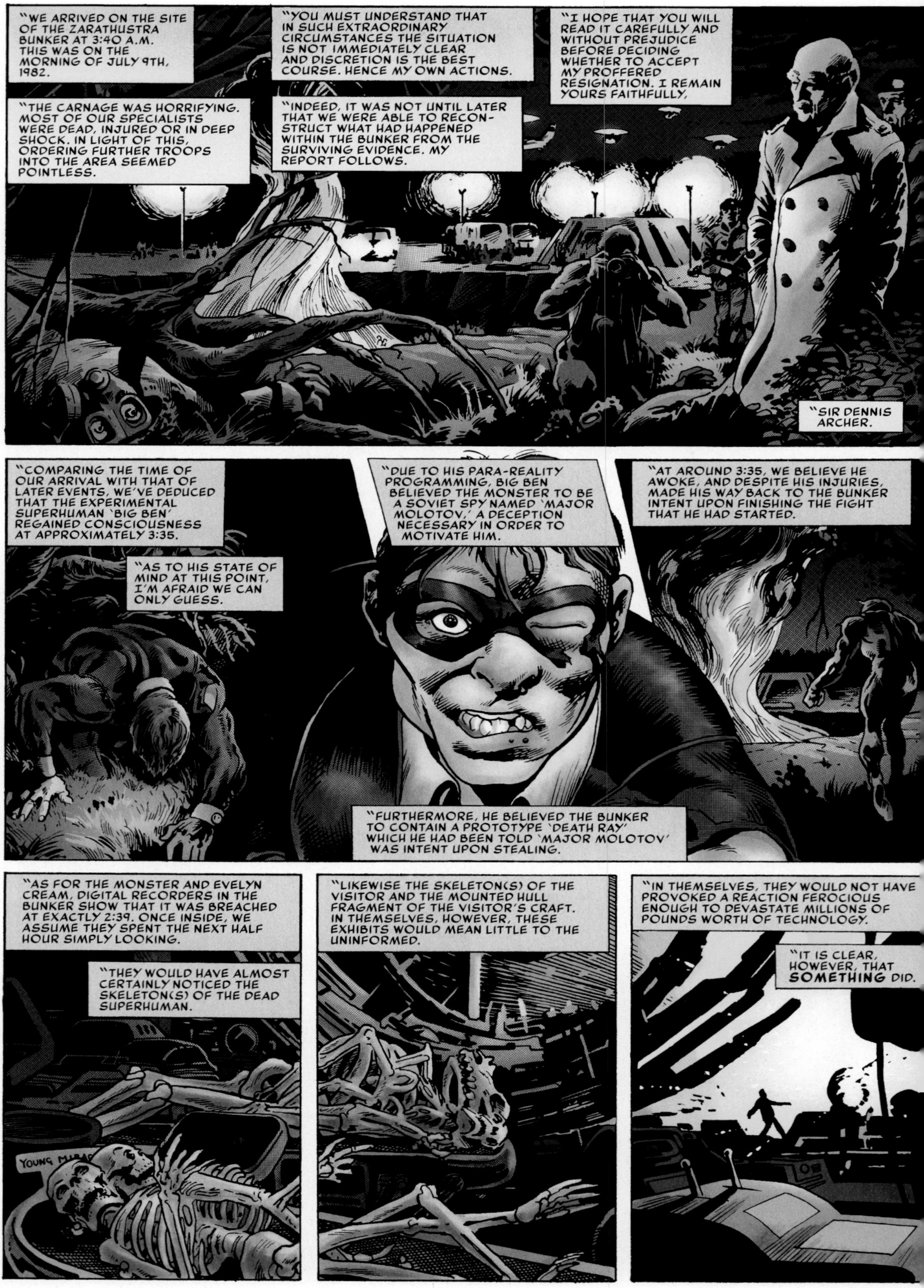
"WE ARRIVED ON THE SITE OF THE ZARATHUSTRA BUNKER AT 3:40 A.M. THIS WAS ON THE MORNING OF JULY 9TH, 1982.
"THE CARNAGE WAS HORRIFYING. MOST OF OUR SPECIALISTS WERE DEAD, INJURED OR IN DEEP SHOCK. IN LIGHT OF THIS, ORDERING FURTHER TROOPS INTO THE AREA SEEMED POINTLESS.
"YOU MUST UNDERSTAND THAT IN SUCH EXTRAORDINARY CIRCUMSTANCES THE SITUATION IS NOT IMMEDIATELY CLEAR AND DISCRETION IS THE BEST COURSE. HENCE MY OWN ACTIONS.
"INDEED, IT WAS NOT UNTIL LATER THAT WE WERE ABLE TO RECONSTRUCT WHAT HAD HAPPENED WITHIN THE BUNKER FROM THE SURVIVING EVIDENCE. MY REPORT FOLLOWS.
"I HOPE THAT YOU WILL READ IT CAREFULLY AND WITHOUT PREJUDICE BEFORE DECIDING WHETHER TO ACCEPT MY PROFFERED RESIGNATION. I REMAIN YOURS FAITHFULLY,
"SIR DENNIS ARCHER.
"COMPARING THE TIME OF OUR ARRIVAL WITH THAT OF LATER EVENTS, WE'VE DEDUCED THAT THE EXPERIMENTAL SUPERHUMAN 'BIG BEN' REGAINED CONSCIOUSNESS AT APPROXIMATELY 3:35.
"AS TO HIS STATE OF MIND AT THIS POINT, I'M AFRAID WE CAN ONLY GUESS.
"DUE TO HIS PARA-REALITY PROGRAMMING, BIG BEN BELIEVED THE MONSTER TO BE A SOVIET SPY NAMED 'MAJOR MOLOTOV,' A DECEPTION NECESSARY IN ORDER TO MOTIVATE HIM.
"FURTHERMORE, HE BELIEVED THE BUNKER TO CONTAIN A PROTOTYPE 'DEATH RAY' WHICH HE HAD BEEN TOLD 'MAJOR MOLOTOV' WAS INTENT UPON STEALING.
"AT AROUND 3:35, WE BELIEVE HE AWOKE, AND DESPITE HIS INJURIES, MADE HIS WAY BACK TO THE BUNKER INTENT UPON FINISHING THE FIGHT THAT HE HAD STARTED.
"AS FOR THE MONSTER AND EVELYN CREAM, DIGITAL RECORDERS IN THE BUNKER SHOW THAT IT WAS BREACHED AT EXACTLY 2:39. ONCE INSIDE, WE ASSUME THEY SPENT THE NEXT HALF HOUR SIMPLY LOOKING.
"THEY WOULD HAVE ALMOST CERTAINLY NOTICED THE SKELETON(S) OF THE DEAD SUPERHUMAN.
"LIKEWISE THE SKELETON(S) OF THE VISITOR AND THE MOUNTED HULL FRAGMENT OF THE VISITOR'S CRAFT. IN THEMSELVES, HOWEVER, THESE EXHIBITS WOULD MEAN LITTLE TO THE UNINFORMED.
"IN THEMSELVES, THEY WOULD NOT HAVE PROVOKED A REACTION FEROCIOUS ENOUGH TO DEVASTATE MILLIONS OF POUNDS WORTH OF TECHNOLOGY.
"IT IS CLEAR, HOWEVER, THAT **SOMETHING** DID.

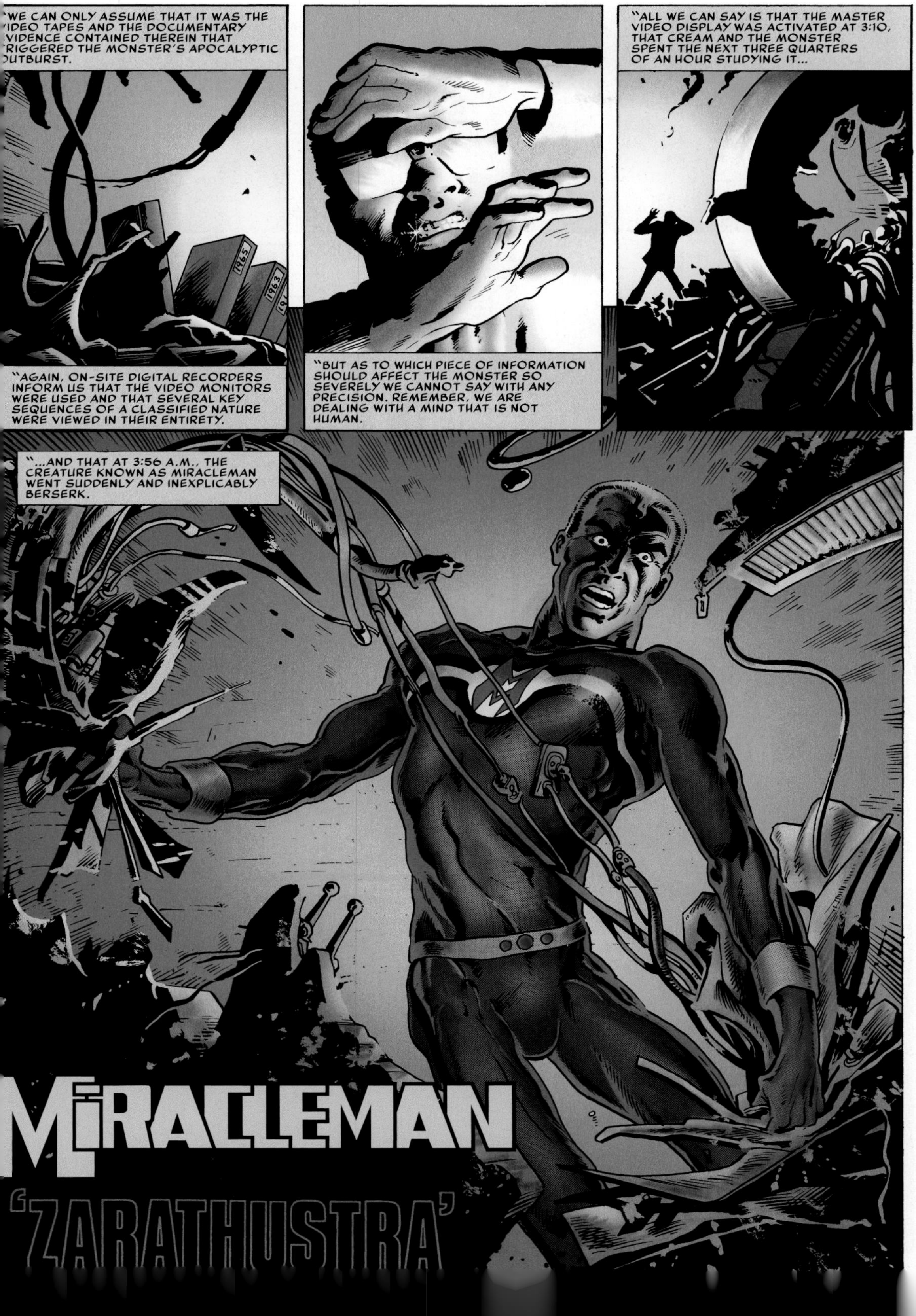
"WE CAN ONLY ASSUME THAT IT WAS THE VIDEO TAPES AND THE DOCUMENTARY EVIDENCE CONTAINED THEREIN THAT TRIGGERED THE MONSTER'S APOCALYPTIC OUTBURST.
1965
1963
"AGAIN, ON-SITE DIGITAL RECORDERS INFORM US THAT THE VIDEO MONITORS WERE USED AND THAT SEVERAL KEY SEQUENCES OF A CLASSIFIED NATURE WERE VIEWED IN THEIR ENTIRETY.
"BUT AS TO WHICH PIECE OF INFORMATION SHOULD AFFECT THE MONSTER SO SEVERELY WE CANNOT SAY WITH ANY PRECISION. REMEMBER, WE ARE DEALING WITH A MIND THAT IS NOT HUMAN.
"ALL WE CAN SAY IS THAT THE MASTER VIDEO DISPLAY WAS ACTIVATED AT 3:10, THAT CREAM AND THE MONSTER SPENT THE NEXT THREE QUARTERS OF AN HOUR STUDYING IT...
"...AND THAT AT 3:56 A.M., THE CREATURE KNOWN AS MIRACLEMAN WENT SUDDENLY AND INEXPLICABLY BERSERK.
MIRACLEMAN
'ZARATHUSTRA'

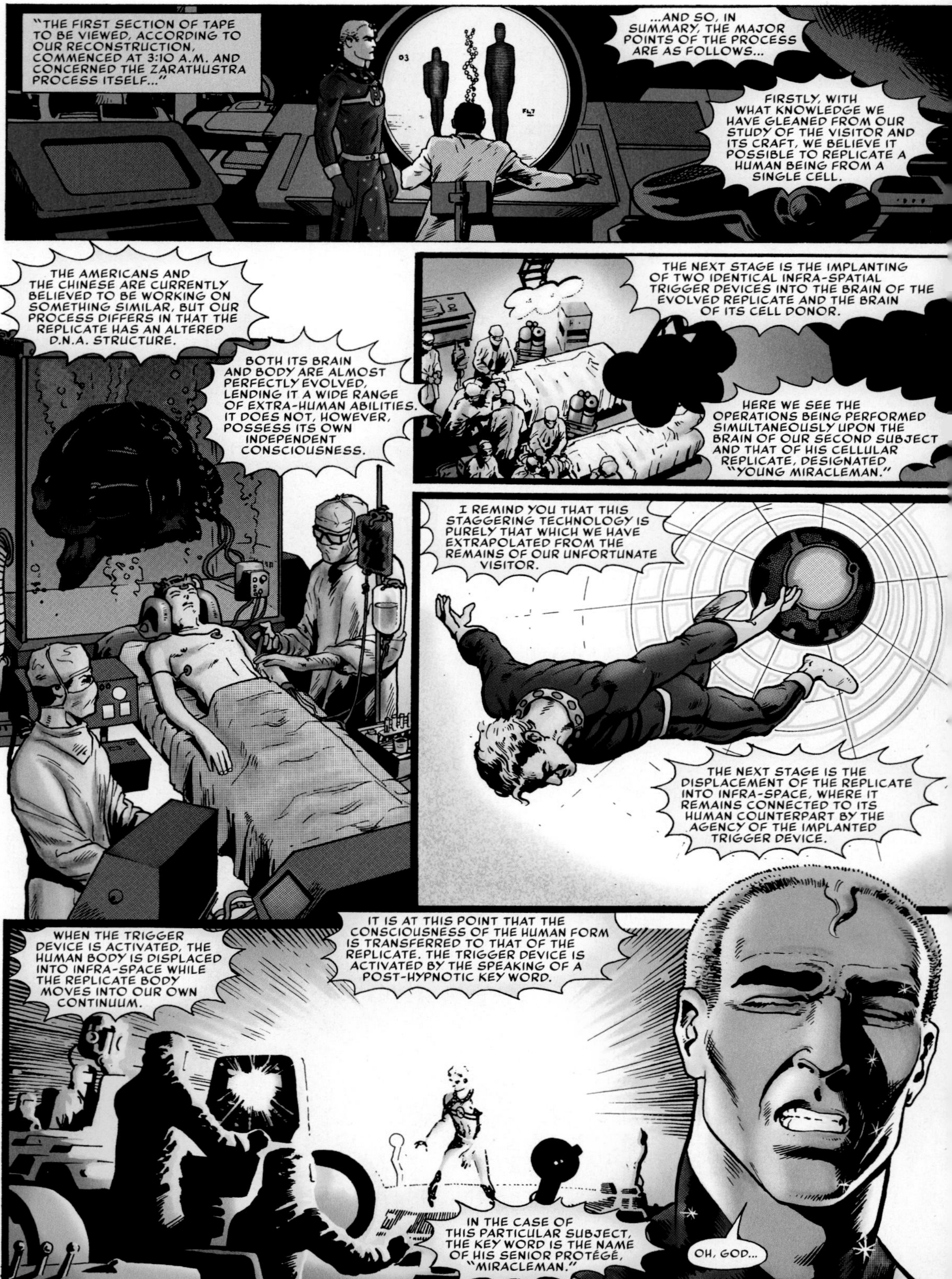
"THE FIRST SECTION OF TAPE TO BE VIEWED, ACCORDING TO OUR RECONSTRUCTION, COMMENCED AT 3:10 A.M. AND CONCERNED THE ZARATHUSTRA PROCESS ITSELF..."
...AND SO, IN SUMMARY, THE MAJOR POINTS OF THE PROCESS ARE AS FOLLOWS...
FIRSTLY, WITH WHAT KNOWLEDGE WE HAVE GLEANED FROM OUR STUDY OF THE VISITOR AND ITS CRAFT, WE BELIEVE IT POSSIBLE TO REPLICATE A HUMAN BEING FROM A SINGLE CELL.
THE AMERICANS AND THE CHINESE ARE CURRENTLY BELIEVED TO BE WORKING ON SOMETHING SIMILAR, BUT OUR PROCESS DIFFERS IN THAT THE REPLICATE HAS AN ALTERED D.N.A. STRUCTURE.
BOTH ITS BRAIN AND BODY ARE ALMOST PERFECTLY EVOLVED, LENDING IT A WIDE RANGE OF EXTRA-HUMAN ABILITIES. IT DOES NOT, HOWEVER, POSSESS ITS OWN INDEPENDENT CONSCIOUSNESS.
THE NEXT STAGE IS THE IMPLANTING OF TWO IDENTICAL INFRA-SPATIAL TRIGGER DEVICES INTO THE BRAIN OF THE EVOLVED REPLICATE AND THE BRAIN OF ITS CELL DONOR.
HERE WE SEE THE OPERATIONS BEING PERFORMED SIMULTANEOUSLY UPON THE BRAIN OF OUR SECOND SUBJECT AND THAT OF HIS CELLULAR REPLICATE, DESIGNATED "YOUNG MIRACLEMAN."
I REMIND YOU THAT THIS STAGGERING TECHNOLOGY IS PURELY THAT WHICH WE HAVE EXTRAPOLATED FROM THE REMAINS OF OUR UNFORTUNATE VISITOR.
THE NEXT STAGE IS THE DISPLACEMENT OF THE REPLICATE INTO INFRA-SPACE, WHERE IT REMAINS CONNECTED TO ITS HUMAN COUNTERPART BY THE AGENCY OF THE IMPLANTED TRIGGER DEVICE.
WHEN THE TRIGGER DEVICE IS ACTIVATED, THE HUMAN BODY IS DISPLACED INTO INFRA-SPACE WHILE THE REPLICATE BODY MOVES INTO OUR OWN CONTINUUM.
IT IS AT THIS POINT THAT THE CONSCIOUSNESS OF THE HUMAN FORM IS TRANSFERRED TO THAT OF THE REPLICATE. THE TRIGGER DEVICE IS ACTIVATED BY THE SPEAKING OF A POST-HYPNOTIC KEY WORD.
IN THE CASE OF THIS PARTICULAR SUBJECT, THE KEY WORD IS THE NAME OF HIS SENIOR PROTÉGÉ, "MIRACLEMAN."
OH, GOD...

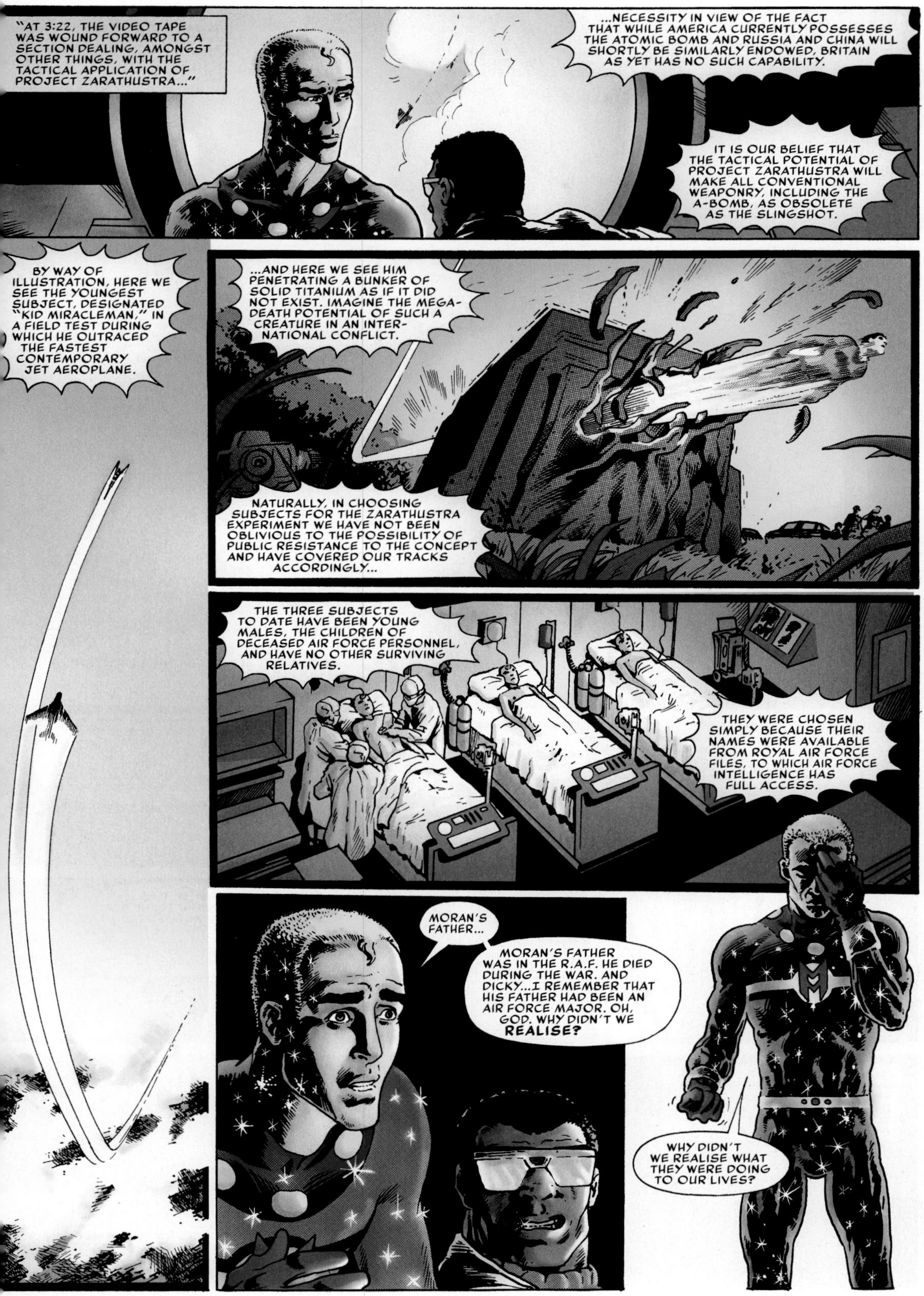
"AT 3:22, THE VIDEO TAPE WAS WOUND FORWARD TO A SECTION DEALING, AMONGST OTHER THINGS, WITH THE TACTICAL APPLICATION OF PROJECT ZARATHUSTRA..."
...NECESSITY IN VIEW OF THE FACT THAT WHILE AMERICA CURRENTLY POSSESSES THE ATOMIC BOMB AND RUSSIA AND CHINA WILL SHORTLY BE SIMILARLY ENDOWED, BRITAIN AS YET HAS NO SUCH CAPABILITY.
IT IS OUR BELIEF THAT THE TACTICAL POTENTIAL OF PROJECT ZARATHUSTRA WILL MAKE ALL CONVENTIONAL WEAPONRY, INCLUDING THE A-BOMB, AS OBSOLETE AS THE SLINGSHOT.
BY WAY OF ILLUSTRATION, HERE WE SEE THE YOUNGEST SUBJECT, DESIGNATED "KID MIRACLEMAN," IN A FIELD TEST DURING WHICH HE OUTRACED THE FASTEST CONTEMPORARY JET AEROPLANE.
...AND HERE WE SEE HIM PENETRATING A BUNKER OF SOLID TITANIUM AS IF IT DID NOT EXIST. IMAGINE THE MEGA-DEATH POTENTIAL OF SUCH A CREATURE IN AN INTER-NATIONAL CONFLICT.
NATURALLY, IN CHOOSING SUBJECTS FOR THE ZARATHUSTRA EXPERIMENT WE HAVE NOT BEEN OBLIVIOUS TO THE POSSIBILITY OF PUBLIC RESISTANCE TO THE CONCEPT AND HAVE COVERED OUR TRACKS ACCORDINGLY...
THE THREE SUBJECTS TO DATE HAVE BEEN YOUNG MALES, THE CHILDREN OF DECEASED AIR FORCE PERSONNEL, AND HAVE NO OTHER SURVIVING RELATIVES.
THEY WERE CHOSEN SIMPLY BECAUSE THEIR NAMES WERE AVAILABLE FROM ROYAL AIR FORCE FILES, TO WHICH AIR FORCE INTELLIGENCE HAS FULL ACCESS.
MORAN'S FATHER...
MORAN'S FATHER WAS IN THE R.A.F. HE DIED DURING THE WAR. AND DICKY...I REMEMBER THAT HIS FATHER HAD BEEN AN AIR FORCE MAJOR. OH, GOD. WHY DIDN'T WE REALISE?
WHY DIDN'T WE REALISE WHAT THEY WERE DOING TO OUR LIVES?

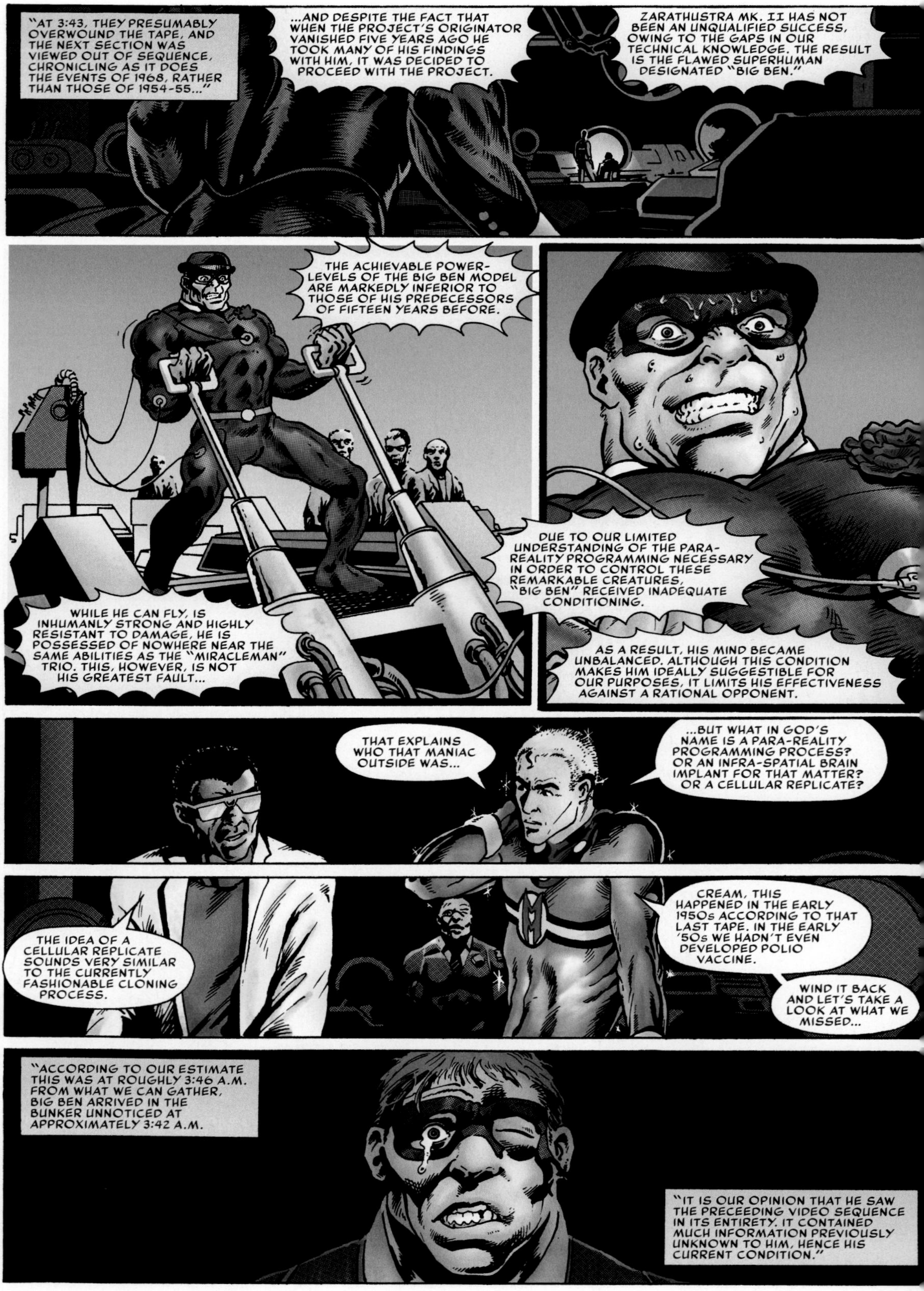
"AT 3:43, THEY PRESUMABLY OVERWOUND THE TAPE, AND THE NEXT SECTION WAS VIEWED OUT OF SEQUENCE, CHRONICLING AS IT DOES THE EVENTS OF 1968, RATHER THAN THOSE OF 1954-55..."
...AND DESPITE THE FACT THAT WHEN THE PROJECT'S ORIGINATOR VANISHED FIVE YEARS AGO HE TOOK MANY OF HIS FINDINGS WITH HIM, IT WAS DECIDED TO PROCEED WITH THE PROJECT.
ZARATHUSTRA MK. II HAS NOT BEEN AN UNQUALIFIED SUCCESS, OWING TO THE GAPS IN OUR TECHNICAL KNOWLEDGE. THE RESULT IS THE FLAWED SUPERHUMAN DESIGNATED "BIG BEN."
THE ACHIEVABLE POWER-LEVELS OF THE BIG BEN MODEL ARE MARKEDLY INFERIOR TO THOSE OF HIS PREDECESSORS OF FIFTEEN YEARS BEFORE.
WHILE HE CAN FLY, IS INHUMANLY STRONG AND HIGHLY RESISTANT TO DAMAGE, HE IS POSSESSED OF NOWHERE NEAR THE SAME ABILITIES AS THE "MIRACLEMAN" TRIO. THIS, HOWEVER, IS NOT HIS GREATEST FAULT...
DUE TO OUR LIMITED UNDERSTANDING OF THE PARA-REALITY PROGRAMMING NECESSARY IN ORDER TO CONTROL THESE REMARKABLE CREATURES, "BIG BEN" RECEIVED INADEQUATE CONDITIONING.
AS A RESULT, HIS MIND BECAME UNBALANCED. ALTHOUGH THIS CONDITION MAKES HIM IDEALLY SUGGESTIBLE FOR OUR PURPOSES, IT LIMITS HIS EFFECTIVENESS AGAINST A RATIONAL OPPONENT.
THAT EXPLAINS WHO THAT MANIAC OUTSIDE WAS...
...BUT WHAT IN GOD'S NAME IS A PARA-REALITY PROGRAMMING PROCESS? OR AN INFRA-SPATIAL BRAIN IMPLANT FOR THAT MATTER? OR A CELLULAR REPLICATE?
THE IDEA OF A CELLULAR REPLICATE SOUNDS VERY SIMILAR TO THE CURRENTLY FASHIONABLE CLONING PROCESS.
CREAM, THIS HAPPENED IN THE EARLY 1950s ACCORDING TO THAT LAST TAPE. IN THE EARLY '50s WE HADN'T EVEN DEVELOPED POLIO VACCINE.
WIND IT BACK AND LET'S TAKE A LOOK AT WHAT WE MISSED...
"ACCORDING TO OUR ESTIMATE THIS WAS AT ROUGHLY 3:46 A.M. FROM WHAT WE CAN GATHER BIG BEN ARRIVED IN THE BUNKER UNNOTICED AT APPROXIMATELY 3:42 A.M.
"IT IS OUR OPINION THAT HE SAW THE PRECEEDING VIDEO SEQUENCE IN ITS ENTIRETY. IT CONTAINED MUCH INFORMATION PREVIOUSLY UNKNOWN TO HIM, HENCE HIS CURRENT CONDITION."

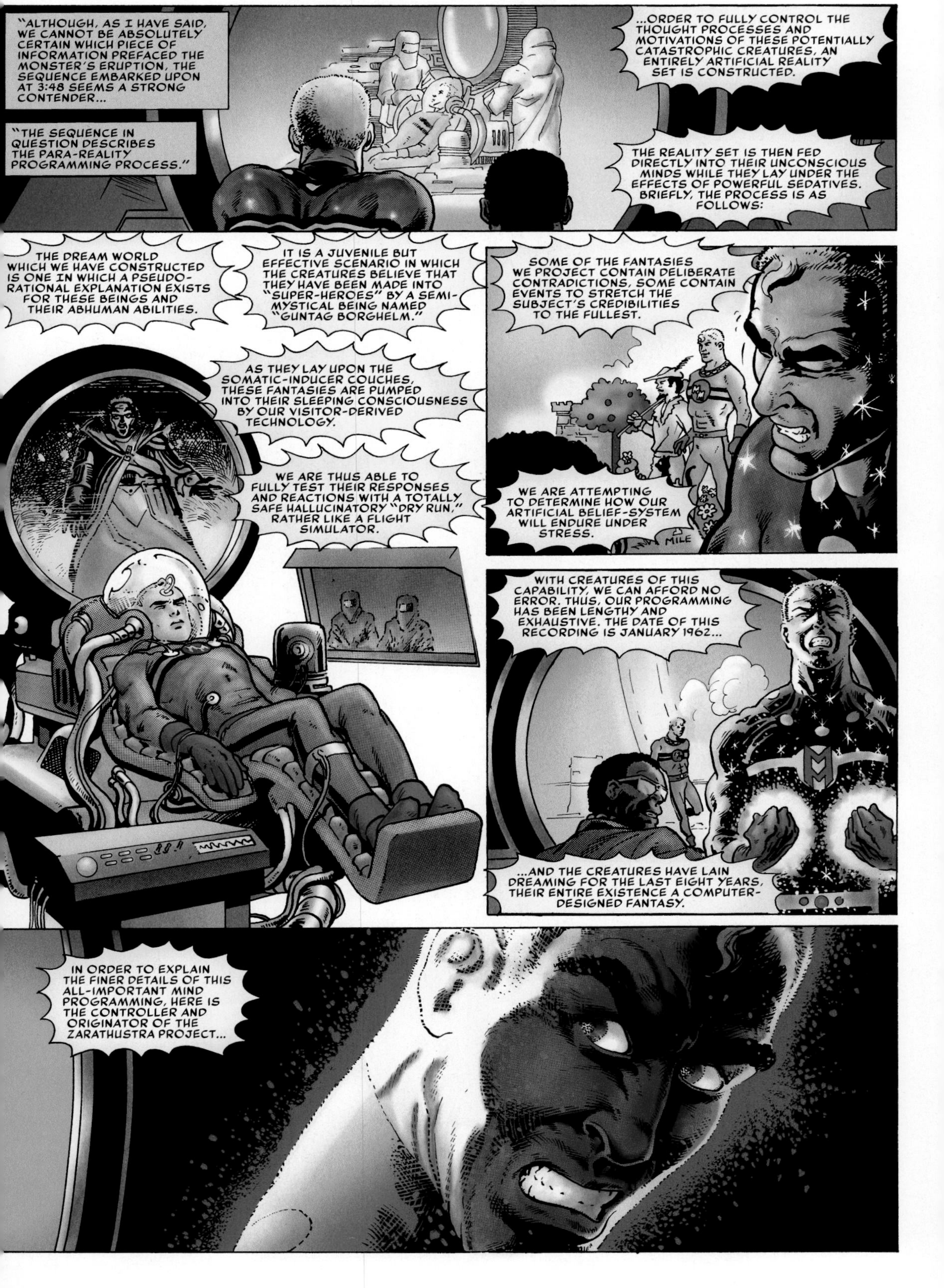
"ALTHOUGH, AS I HAVE SAID, WE CANNOT BE ABSOLUTELY CERTAIN WHICH PIECE OF INFORMATION PREFACED THE MONSTER'S ERUPTION, THE SEQUENCE EMBARKED UPON AT 3:48 SEEMS A STRONG CONTENDER...
"THE SEQUENCE IN QUESTION DESCRIBES THE PARA-REALITY PROGRAMMING PROCESS."
...ORDER TO FULLY CONTROL THE THOUGHT PROCESSES AND MOTIVATIONS OF THESE POTENTIALLY CATASTROPHIC CREATURES, AN ENTIRELY ARTIFICIAL REALITY SET IS CONSTRUCTED.
THE REALITY SET IS THEN FED DIRECTLY INTO THEIR UNCONSCIOUS MINDS WHILE THEY LAY UNDER THE EFFECTS OF POWERFUL SEDATIVES. BRIEFLY, THE PROCESS IS AS FOLLOWS:
THE DREAM WORLD WHICH WE HAVE CONSTRUCTED IS ONE IN WHICH A PSEUDO-RATIONAL EXPLANATION EXISTS FOR THESE BEINGS AND THEIR ABHUMAN ABILITIES.
IT IS A JUVENILE BUT EFFECTIVE SCENARIO IN WHICH THE CREATURES BELIEVE THAT THEY HAVE BEEN MADE INTO "SUPER-HEROES" BY A SEMI-MYSTICAL BEING NAMED "GUNTAG BORGHELM."
AS THEY LAY UPON THE SOMATIC-INDUCER COUCHES, THESE FANTASIES ARE PUMPED INTO THEIR SLEEPING CONSCIOUSNESS BY OUR VISITOR-DERIVED TECHNOLOGY.
WE ARE THUS ABLE TO FULLY TEST THEIR RESPONSES AND REACTIONS WITH A TOTALLY SAFE HALLUCINATORY "DRY RUN," RATHER LIKE A FLIGHT SIMULATOR.
SOME OF THE FANTASIES WE PROJECT CONTAIN DELIBERATE CONTRADICTIONS, SOME CONTAIN EVENTS TO STRETCH THE SUBJECT'S CREDIBILITIES TO THE FULLEST.
WE ARE ATTEMPTING TO DETERMINE HOW OUR ARTIFICIAL BELIEF-SYSTEM WILL ENDURE UNDER STRESS.
MILE
WITH CREATURES OF THIS CAPABILITY, WE CAN AFFORD NO ERROR. THUS, OUR PROGRAMMING HAS BEEN LENGTHY AND EXHAUSTIVE. THE DATE OF THIS RECORDING IS JANUARY 1962...
...AND THE CREATURES HAVE LAIN DREAMING FOR THE LAST EIGHT YEARS, THEIR ENTIRE EXISTENCE A COMPUTER-DESIGNED FANTASY.
IN ORDER TO EXPLAIN THE FINER DETAILS OF THIS ALL-IMPORTANT MIND PROGRAMMING, HERE IS THE CONTROLLER AND ORIGINATOR OF THE ZARATHUSTRA PROJECT...

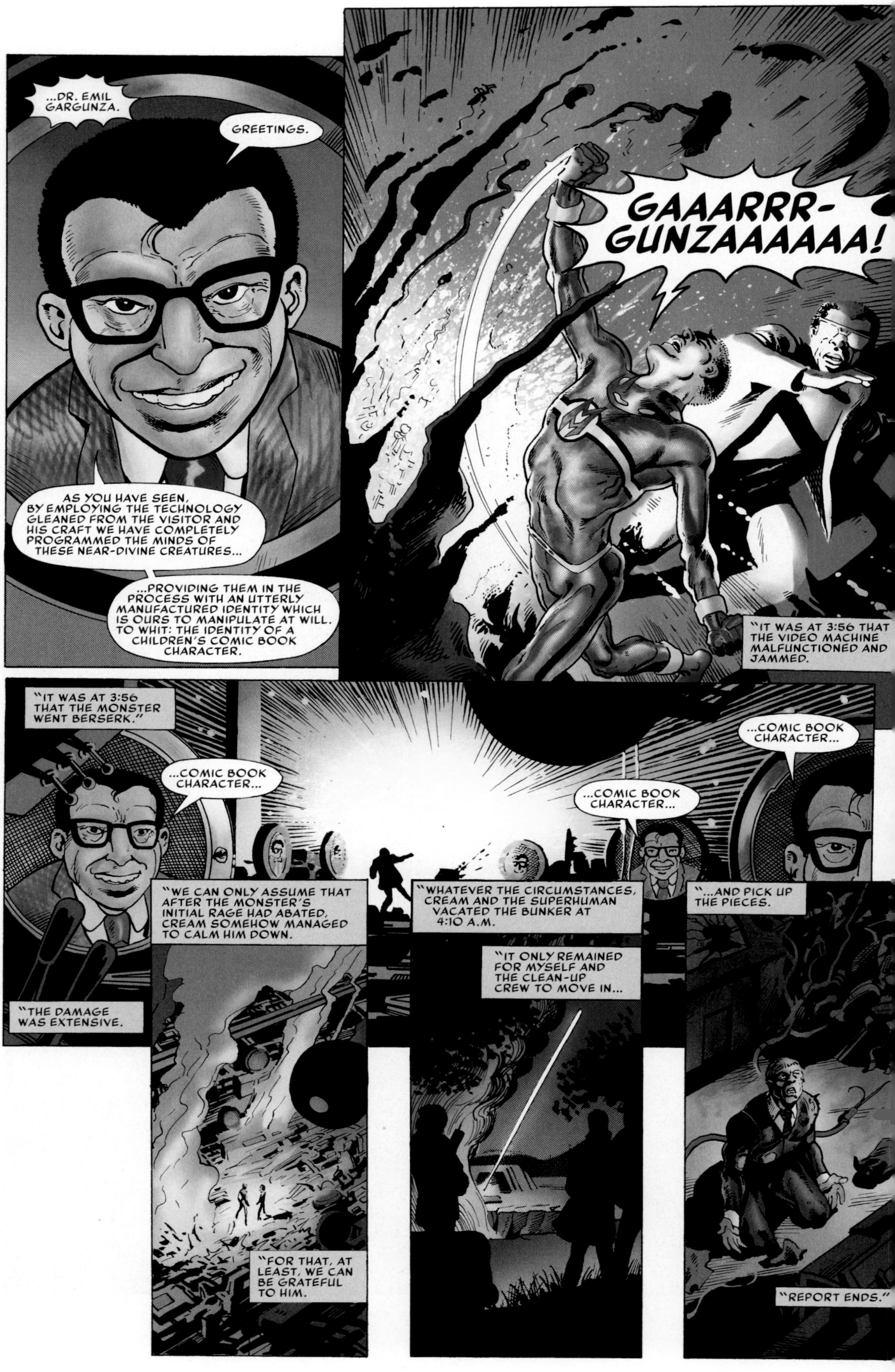
...DR. EMIL GARGUNZA.
GREETINGS.
AS YOU HAVE SEEN, BY EMPLOYING THE TECHNOLOGY GLEANED FROM THE VISITOR AND HIS CRAFT WE HAVE COMPLETELY PROGRAMMED THE MINDS OF THESE NEAR-DIVINE CREATURES...
...PROVIDING THEM IN THE PROCESS WITH AN UTTERLY MANUFACTURED IDENTITY WHICH IS OURS TO MANIPULATE AT WILL. TO WHIT: THE IDENTITY OF A CHILDREN'S COMIC BOOK CHARACTER.
GAAARRR-GUNZAAAAAA!
"IT WAS AT 3:56 THAT THE VIDEO MACHINE MALFUNCTIONED AND JAMMED.
"IT WAS AT 3:56 THAT THE MONSTER WENT BERSERK."
...COMIC BOOK CHARACTER...
...COMIC BOOK CHARACTER...
...COMIC BOOK CHARACTER...
"THE DAMAGE WAS EXTENSIVE.
"WE CAN ONLY ASSUME THAT AFTER THE MONSTER'S INITIAL RAGE HAD ABATED, CREAM SOMEHOW MANAGED TO CALM HIM DOWN.
"FOR THAT, AT LEAST, WE CAN BE GRATEFUL TO HIM.
"WHATEVER THE CIRCUMSTANCES, CREAM AND THE SUPERHUMAN VACATED THE BUNKER AT 4:10 A.M.
"IT ONLY REMAINED FOR MYSELF AND THE CLEAN-UP CREW TO MOVE IN...
"...AND PICK UP THE PIECES.
"REPORT ENDS."

EPILOGUE:

FROM THE TOP-SECRET FILES OF BIG BEN, THE MAN WITH NO TIME FOR CRIME...

"FOR A MOMENT, MAJOR MOLOTOV HAD ALMOST HAD ME FOOLED WITH HIS DEVILISH RED PROPAGANDA. LUCKILY, **JACK KETCH** AND **OWLWOMAN**, MY COLLEAGUES FROM THE **BULLDOG BRIGADE**, ARRIVED JUST IN TIME..."

OKAY, FIONA... THERE HE IS. APPROACH HIM CAREFULLY.

REMEMBER, HE'S DANGEROUS...

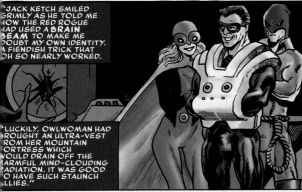

"JACK KETCH SMILED GRIMLY AS HE TOLD ME HOW THE RED ROGUE HAD USED A **BRAIN BEAM** TO MAKE ME DOUBT MY OWN IDENTITY. A FIENDISH TRICK THAT OH SO NEARLY WORKED.

"LUCKILY, OWLWOMAN HAD BROUGHT AN ULTRA-VEST FROM HER MOUNTAIN FORTRESS WHICH WOULD DRAIN OFF THE HARMFUL MIND-CLOUDING RADIATION. IT WAS GOOD TO HAVE SUCH STAUNCH ALLIES."

THERE'S A DOUBLE LOCK ON THE CLASP. MAKE SURE IT'S PROPERLY FASTENED. WE DON'T WANT THIS BLOODY LUNATIC BURSTING LOOSE HALFWAY DOWN THE M-WAY...

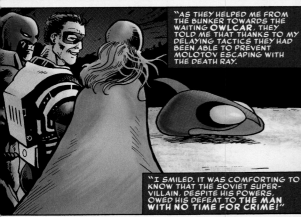

"AS THEY HELPED ME FROM THE BUNKER TOWARDS THE WAITING **OWLCAR**, THEY TOLD ME THAT THANKS TO MY DELAYING TACTICS THEY HAD BEEN ABLE TO PREVENT MOLOTOV ESCAPING WITH THE DEATH RAY.

"I SMILED. IT WAS COMFORTING TO KNOW THAT THE SOVIET SUPER-VILLAIN, DESPITE HIS POWERS, OWED HIS DEFEAT TO **THE MAN WITH NO TIME FOR CRIME!**"

OKAY. EASY DOES IT. EASY...

COME ON. LET'S GET HIM FASTENED IN AND THEN LET'S TAKE THE POOR BASTARD HOME.

4:38: IN THE SODIUM LIT HOUR BEFORE DAWN THE GREAT TRUCKS ROLL SOUTH. SOME CARRY BREAKFAST CEREAL AND SOME CARRY BALLBEARINGS. SOME ARE **EMPTY**...

...AND SOME ARE **NOT**.

END EPILOGUE

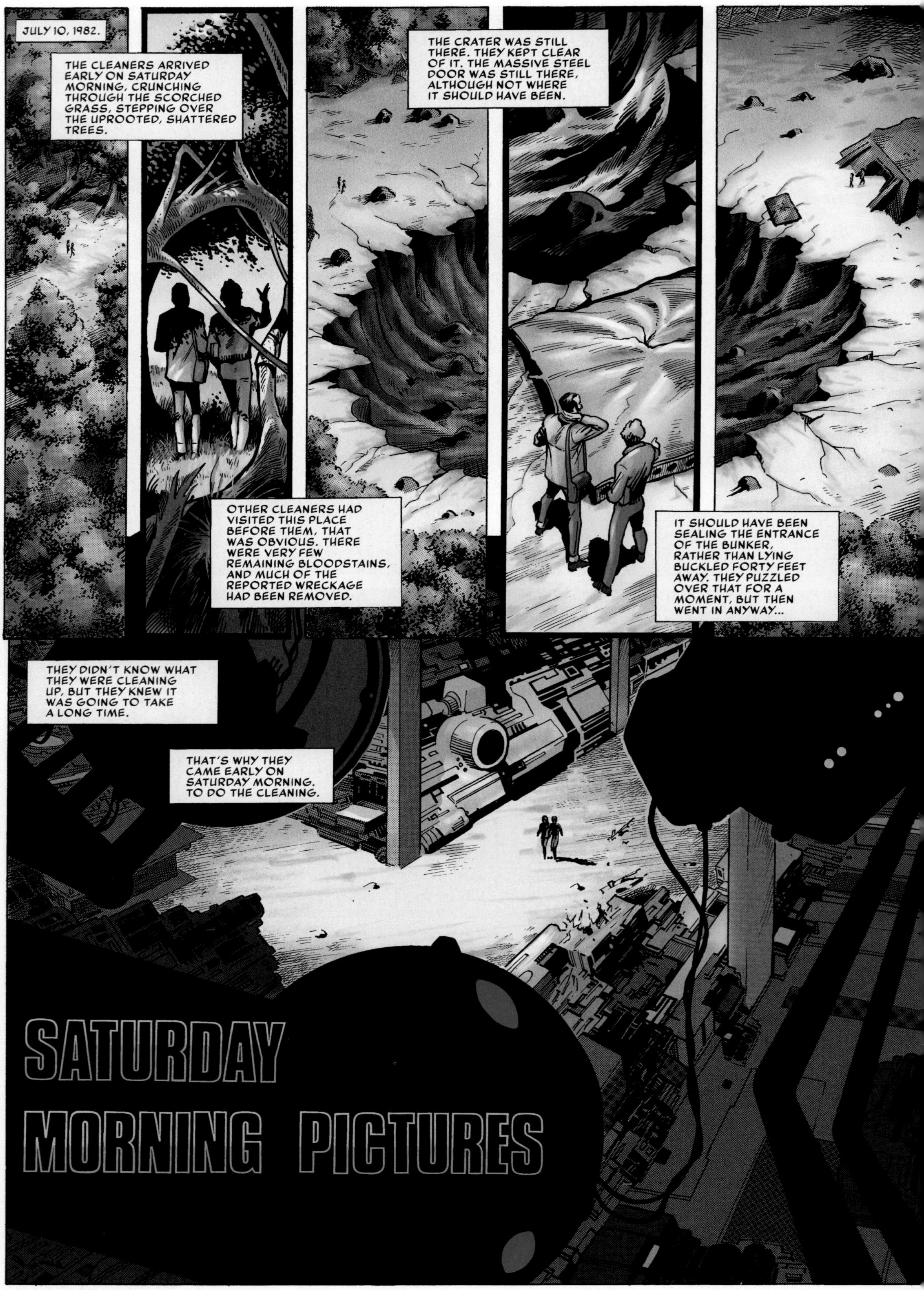
JULY 10, 1982.
THE CLEANERS ARRIVED EARLY ON SATURDAY MORNING, CRUNCHING THROUGH THE SCORCHED GRASS, STEPPING OVER THE UPROOTED, SHATTERED TREES.
OTHER CLEANERS HAD VISITED THIS PLACE BEFORE THEM, THAT WAS OBVIOUS. THERE WERE VERY FEW REMAINING BLOODSTAINS, AND MUCH OF THE REPORTED WRECKAGE HAD BEEN REMOVED.
THE CRATER WAS STILL THERE. THEY KEPT CLEAR OF IT. THE MASSIVE STEEL DOOR WAS STILL THERE, ALTHOUGH NOT WHERE IT SHOULD HAVE BEEN.
IT SHOULD HAVE BEEN SEALING THE ENTRANCE OF THE BUNKER, RATHER THAN LYING BUCKLED FORTY FEET AWAY. THEY PUZZLED OVER THAT FOR A MOMENT, BUT THEN WENT IN ANYWAY...
THEY DIDN'T KNOW WHAT THEY WERE CLEANING UP, BUT THEY KNEW IT WAS GOING TO TAKE A LONG TIME.
THAT'S WHY THEY CAME EARLY ON SATURDAY MORNING. TO DO THE CLEANING.
SATURDAY MORNING PICTURES

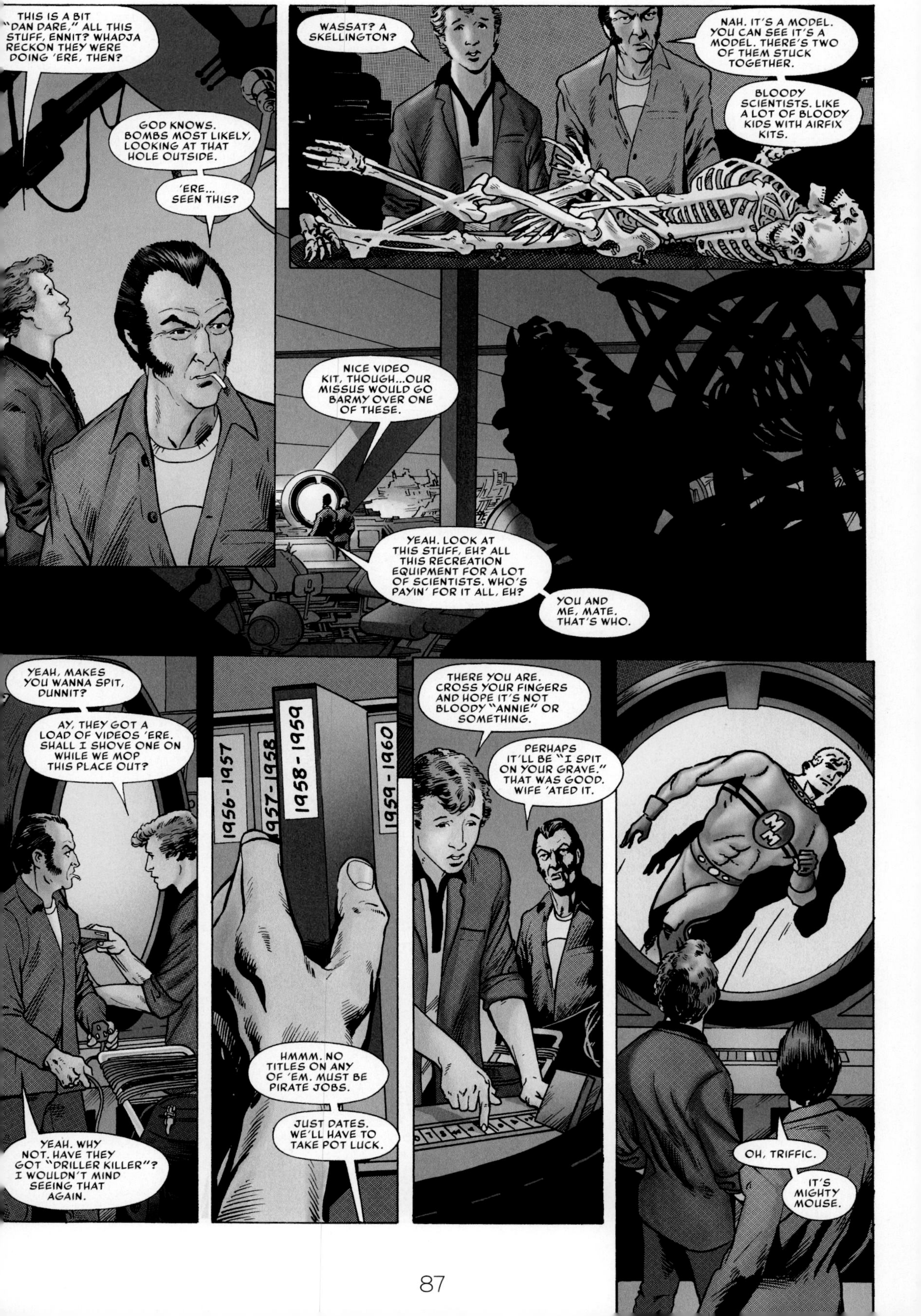
THIS IS A BIT "DAN DARE," ALL THIS STUFF, ENNIT? WHADJA RECKON THEY WERE DOING 'ERE, THEN?
GOD KNOWS. BOMBS MOST LIKELY, LOOKING AT THAT HOLE OUTSIDE.
'ERE... SEEN THIS?
WASSAT? A SKELLINGTON?
NAH. IT'S A MODEL. YOU CAN SEE IT'S A MODEL. THERE'S TWO OF THEM STUCK TOGETHER.
BLOODY SCIENTISTS. LIKE A LOT OF BLOODY KIDS WITH AIRFIX KITS.
NICE VIDEO KIT, THOUGH...OUR MISSUS WOULD GO BARMY OVER ONE OF THESE.
YEAH. LOOK AT THIS STUFF, EH? ALL THIS RECREATION EQUIPMENT FOR A LOT OF SCIENTISTS. WHO'S PAYIN' FOR IT ALL, EH?
YOU AND ME, MATE. THAT'S WHO.
YEAH, MAKES YOU WANNA SPIT, DUNNIT?
AY, THEY GOT A LOAD OF VIDEOS 'ERE. SHALL I SHOVE ONE ON WHILE WE MOP THIS PLACE OUT?
YEAH. WHY NOT. HAVE THEY GOT "DRILLER KILLER"? I WOULDN'T MIND SEEING THAT AGAIN.
1956-1957
1957-1958
1958-1959
1959-1960
HMMM. NO TITLES ON ANY OF 'EM. MUST BE PIRATE JOBS.
JUST DATES. WE'LL HAVE TO TAKE POT LUCK.
THERE YOU ARE. CROSS YOUR FINGERS AND HOPE IT'S NOT BLOODY "ANNIE" OR SOMETHING.
PERHAPS IT'LL BE "I SPIT ON YOUR GRAVE." THAT WAS GOOD. WIFE 'ATED IT.
OH, TRIFFIC.
IT'S MIGHTY MOUSE.

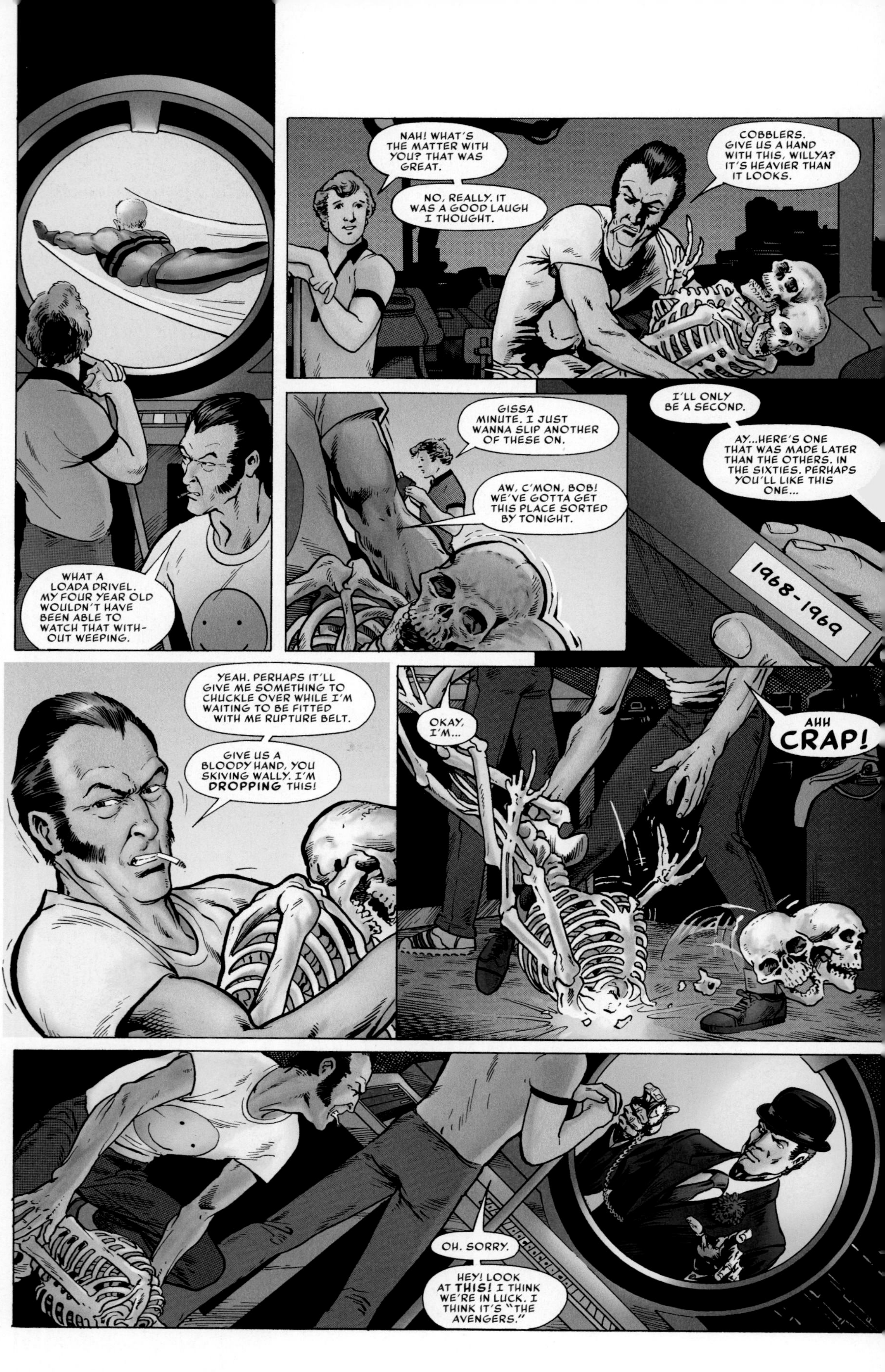

NAH! WHAT'S THE MATTER WITH YOU? THAT WAS GREAT.
NO, REALLY. IT WAS A GOOD LAUGH I THOUGHT.
COBBLERS. GIVE US A HAND WITH THIS, WILLYA? IT'S HEAVIER THAN IT LOOKS.
WHAT A LOADA DRIVEL. MY FOUR YEAR OLD WOULDN'T HAVE BEEN ABLE TO WATCH THAT WITH-OUT WEEPING.
GISSA MINUTE. I JUST WANNA SLIP ANOTHER OF THESE ON.
AW, C'MON, BOB! WE'VE GOTTA GET THIS PLACE SORTED BY TONIGHT.
I'LL ONLY BE A SECOND.
AY...HERE'S ONE THAT WAS MADE LATER THAN THE OTHERS. IN THE SIXTIES. PERHAPS YOU'LL LIKE THIS ONE...
1968-1969
YEAH. PERHAPS IT'LL GIVE ME SOMETHING TO CHUCKLE OVER WHILE I'M WAITING TO BE FITTED WITH ME RUPTURE BELT.
GIVE US A BLOODY HAND, YOU SKIVING WALLY. I'M DROPPING THIS!
OKAY, I'M...
AHH CRAP!
OH. SORRY.
HEY! LOOK AT THIS! I THINK WE'RE IN LUCK. I THINK IT'S "THE AVENGERS."

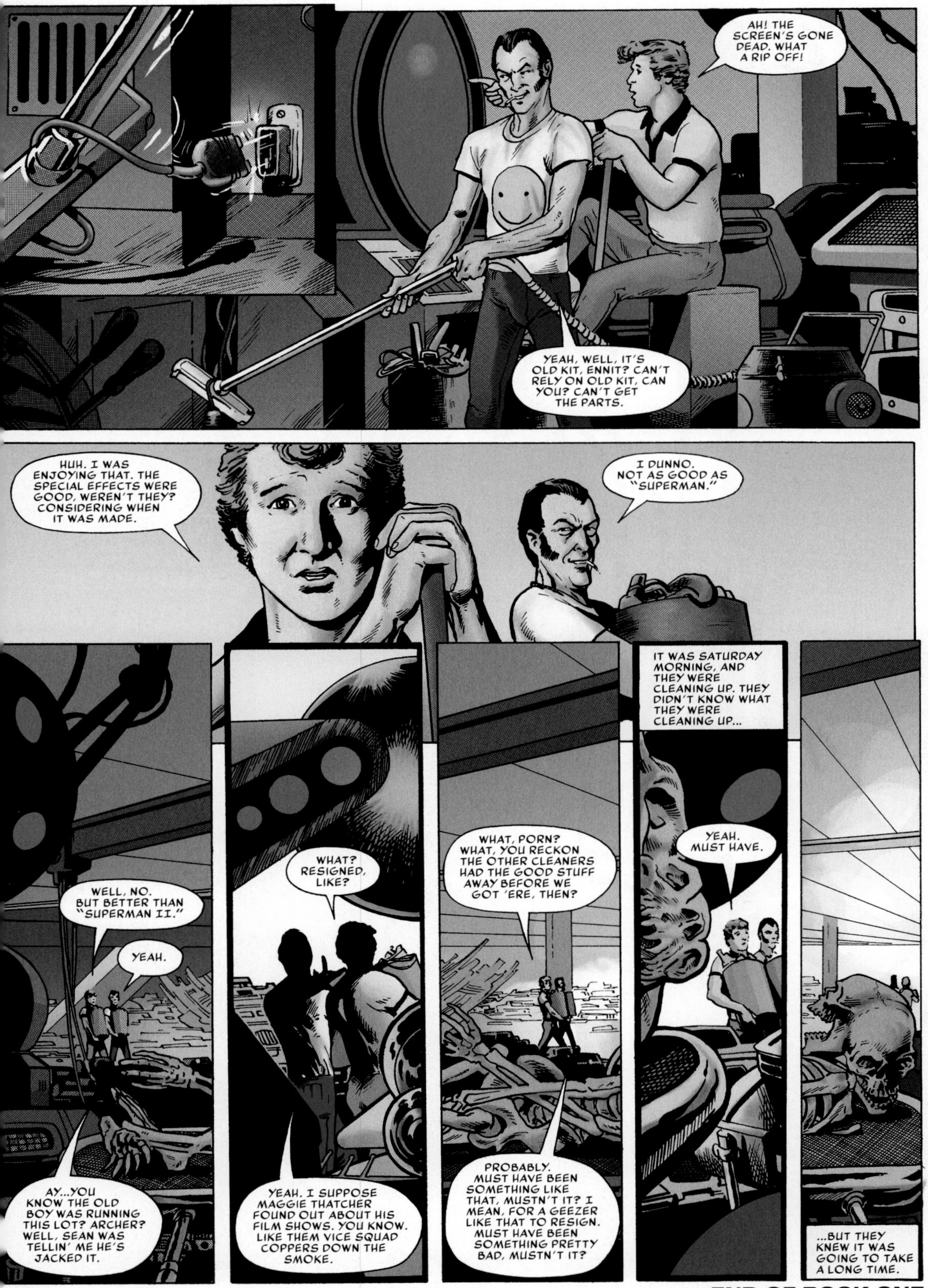
AH! THE SCREEN'S GONE DEAD. WHAT A RIP OFF!
YEAH, WELL, IT'S OLD KIT, ENNIT? CAN'T RELY ON OLD KIT, CAN YOU? CAN'T GET THE PARTS.
HUH. I WAS ENJOYING THAT. THE SPECIAL EFFECTS WERE GOOD, WEREN'T THEY? CONSIDERING WHEN IT WAS MADE.
I DUNNO. NOT AS GOOD AS "SUPERMAN."
WELL, NO. BUT BETTER THAN "SUPERMAN II."
YEAH.
AY...YOU KNOW THE OLD BOY WAS RUNNING THIS LOT? ARCHER? WELL, SEAN WAS TELLIN' ME HE'S JACKED IT.
WHAT? RESIGNED, LIKE?
YEAH. I SUPPOSE MAGGIE THATCHER FOUND OUT ABOUT HIS FILM SHOWS. YOU KNOW. LIKE THEM VICE SQUAD COPPERS DOWN THE SMOKE.
WHAT, PORN? WHAT, YOU RECKON THE OTHER CLEANERS HAD THE GOOD STUFF AWAY BEFORE WE GOT 'ERE, THEN?
PROBABLY. MUST HAVE BEEN SOMETHING LIKE THAT, MUSTN'T IT? I MEAN, FOR A GEEZER LIKE THAT TO RESIGN. MUST HAVE BEEN SOMETHING PRETTY BAD, MUSTN'T IT?
IT WAS SATURDAY MORNING, AND THEY WERE CLEANING UP. THEY DIDN'T KNOW WHAT THEY WERE CLEANING UP...
YEAH. MUST HAVE.
...BUT THEY KNEW IT WAS GOING TO TAKE A LONG TIME.

END OF BOOK ONE

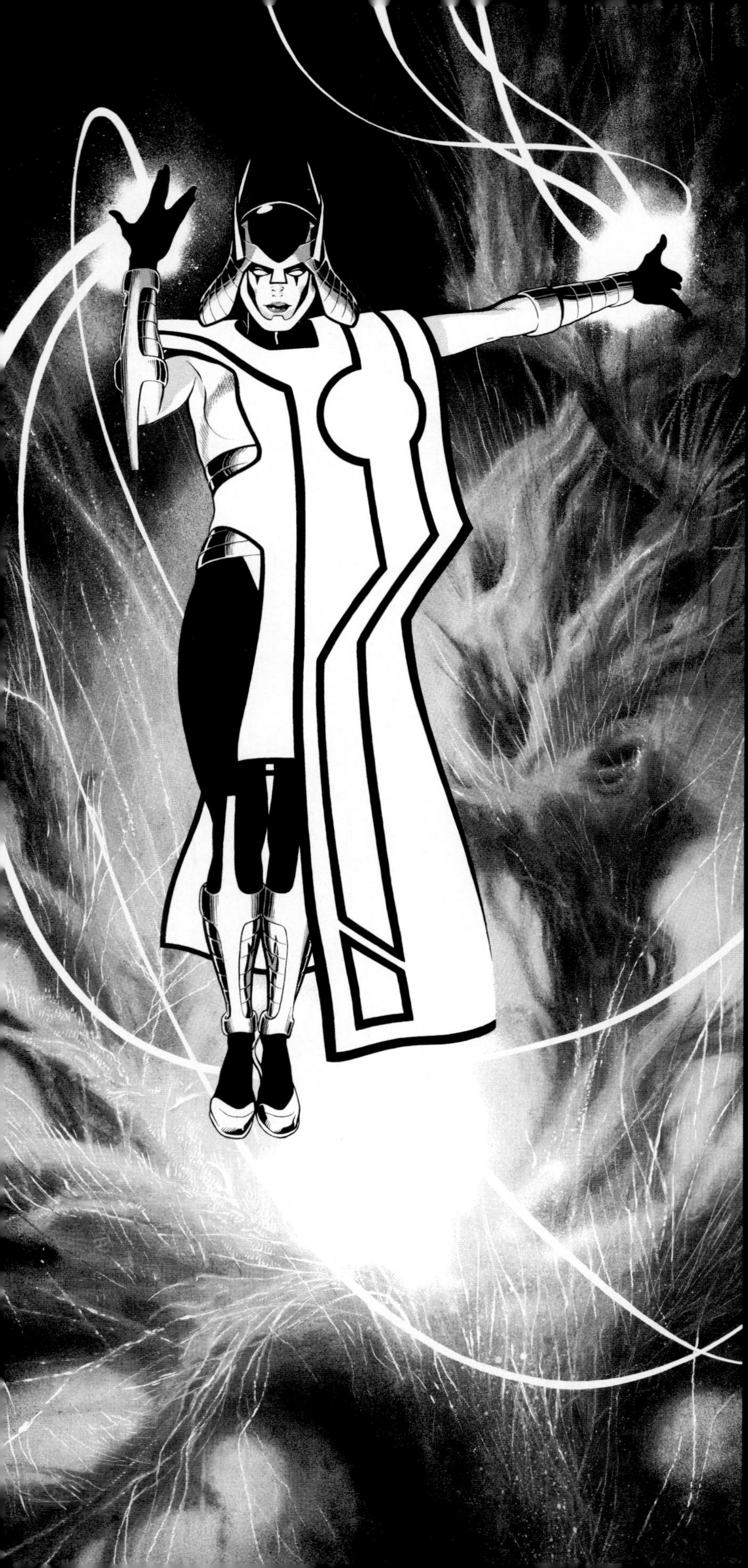

THE YESTERDAY GAMBIT:

STORY – **THE ORIGINAL WRITER**

ART – **STEVE DILLON**, **PAUL NEARY** & **ALAN DAVIS**

Released in *Warrior* #4 (August 1982) between regular installments of Miracleman's ongoing serial, "The Yesterday Gambit" leapt forward telling a story of Miracleman's possible future.

THE WARPSMITHS:

STORY – **THE ORIGINAL WRITER**

ART – **GARRY LEACH**

To a Warpsmith, distance is an abstract concept. With a mere gesture, they can step from here to the edge of infinity. Fiercely dedicated and serving under a strict code of conduct, they guard the Gulf Worlds from the Qys Imperium.

LEFT: Garry Leach illustration promoting the Warpsmiths' appearance in *A1* #1 (1989).

COMPLETE IN THIS SPECIAL -- A STUNNING GLIMPSE INTO THE MIRACLEMAN LEGEND!*

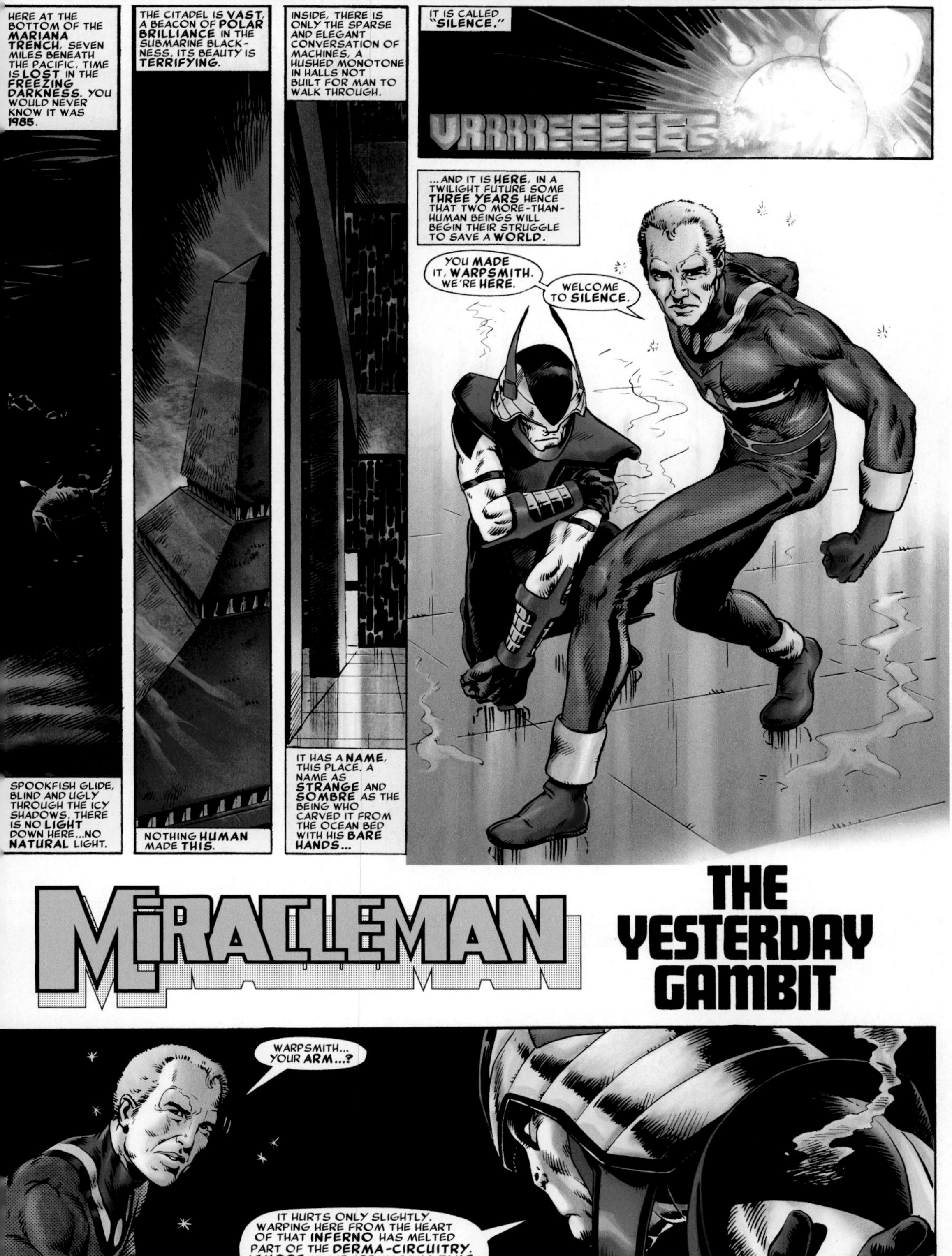
HERE AT THE BOTTOM OF THE MARIANA TRENCH, SEVEN MILES BENEATH THE PACIFIC, TIME IS LOST IN THE FREEZING DARKNESS. YOU WOULD NEVER KNOW IT WAS 1985.
SPOOKFISH GLIDE, BLIND AND UGLY THROUGH THE ICY SHADOWS. THERE IS NO LIGHT DOWN HERE...NO NATURAL LIGHT.
THE CITADEL IS VAST, A BEACON OF POLAR BRILLIANCE IN THE SUBMARINE BLACKNESS. ITS BEAUTY IS TERRIFYING.
NOTHING HUMAN MADE THIS.
INSIDE, THERE IS ONLY THE SPARSE AND ELEGANT CONVERSATION OF MACHINES, A HUSHED MONOTONE IN HALLS NOT BUILT FOR MAN TO WALK THROUGH.
IT HAS A NAME, THIS PLACE. A NAME AS STRANGE AND SOMBRE AS THE BEING WHO CARVED IT FROM THE OCEAN BED WITH HIS BARE HANDS...
IT IS CALLED "SILENCE."
VRRRREEEEEE
...AND IT IS HERE, IN A TWILIGHT FUTURE SOME THREE YEARS HENCE THAT TWO MORE-THAN-HUMAN BEINGS WILL BEGIN THEIR STRUGGLE TO SAVE A WORLD.
YOU MADE IT, WARPSMITH. WE'RE HERE.
WELCOME TO SILENCE.
MIRACLEMAN
THE YESTERDAY GAMBIT
WARPSMITH... YOUR ARM...?
IT HURTS ONLY SLIGHTLY. WARPING HERE FROM THE HEART OF THAT INFERNO HAS MELTED PART OF THE DERMA-CIRCUITRY. IGNORE IT. WE ARE WASTING TIME.

* PROVIDING A DRAMATIC PAUSE IN OUR REGULAR SERIAL, UNTIL NEXT MONTH

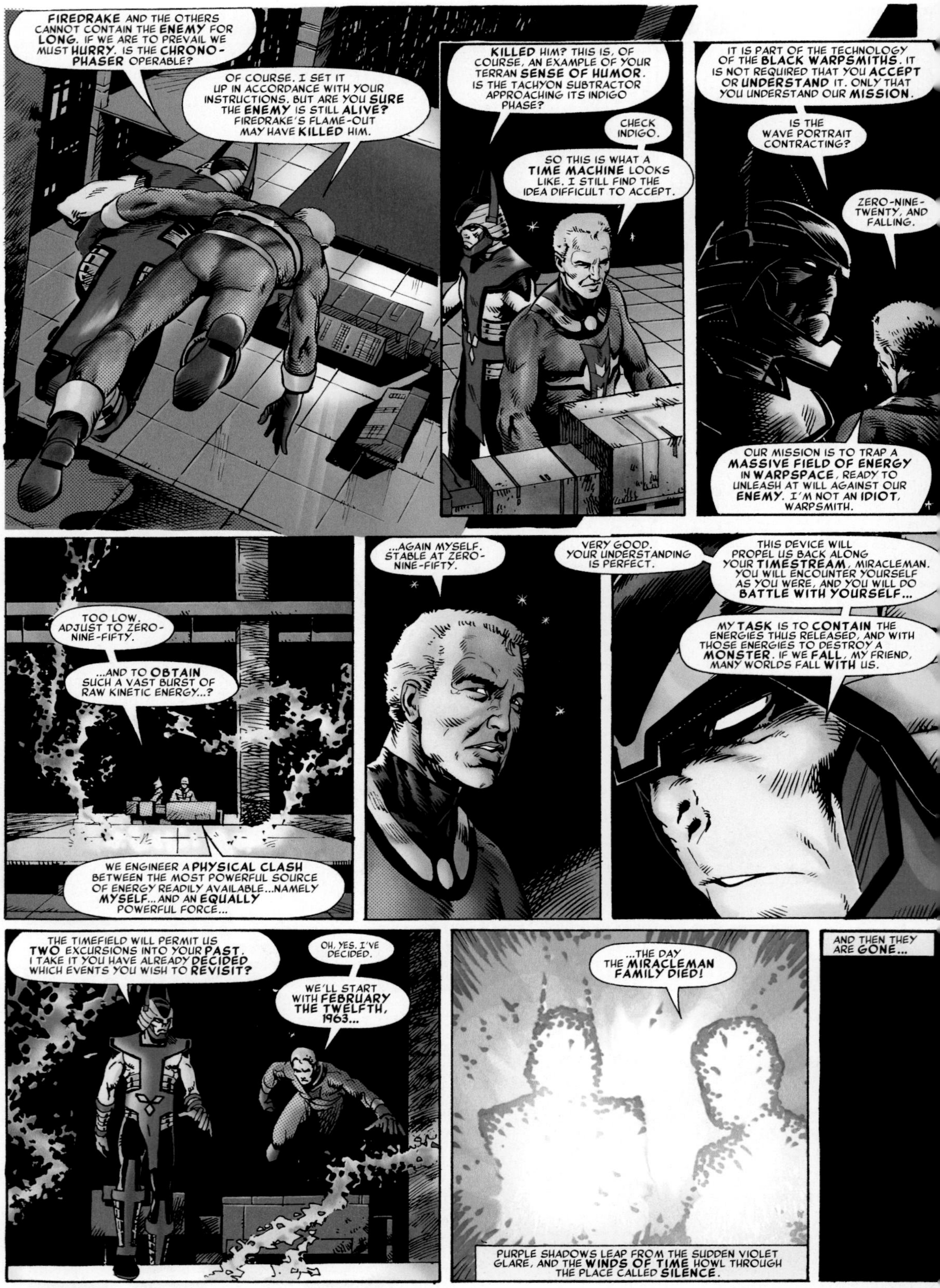
FIREDRAKE AND THE OTHERS CANNOT CONTAIN THE ENEMY FOR LONG. IF WE ARE TO PREVAIL WE MUST HURRY. IS THE CHRONO-PHASER OPERABLE?
OF COURSE. I SET IT UP IN ACCORDANCE WITH YOUR INSTRUCTIONS. BUT ARE YOU SURE THE ENEMY IS STILL ALIVE? FIREDRAKE'S FLAME-OUT MAY HAVE KILLED HIM.
KILLED HIM? THIS IS, OF COURSE, AN EXAMPLE OF YOUR TERRAN SENSE OF HUMOR. IS THE TACHYON SUBTRACTOR APPROACHING ITS INDIGO PHASE?
CHECK INDIGO.
SO THIS IS WHAT A TIME MACHINE LOOKS LIKE. I STILL FIND THE IDEA DIFFICULT TO ACCEPT.
IT IS PART OF THE TECHNOLOGY OF THE BLACK WARPSMITHS. IT IS NOT REQUIRED THAT YOU ACCEPT OR UNDERSTAND IT. ONLY THAT YOU UNDERSTAND OUR MISSION.
IS THE WAVE PORTRAIT CONTRACTING?
ZERO-NINE-TWENTY, AND FALLING.
OUR MISSION IS TO TRAP A MASSIVE FIELD OF ENERGY IN WARPSPACE, READY TO UNLEASH AT WILL AGAINST OUR ENEMY. I'M NOT AN IDIOT, WARPSMITH.
TOO LOW. ADJUST TO ZERO-NINE-FIFTY.
...AND TO OBTAIN SUCH A VAST BURST OF RAW KINETIC ENERGY...?
WE ENGINEER A PHYSICAL CLASH BETWEEN THE MOST POWERFUL SOURCE OF ENERGY READILY AVAILABLE...NAMELY MYSELF...AND AN EQUALLY POWERFUL FORCE...
...AGAIN MYSELF. STABLE AT ZERO-NINE-FIFTY.
VERY GOOD. YOUR UNDERSTANDING IS PERFECT.
THIS DEVICE WILL PROPEL US BACK ALONG YOUR TIMESTREAM, MIRACLEMAN. YOU WILL ENCOUNTER YOURSELF AS YOU WERE, AND YOU WILL DO BATTLE WITH YOURSELF...
MY TASK IS TO CONTAIN THE ENERGIES THUS RELEASED, AND WITH THOSE ENERGIES TO DESTROY A MONSTER. IF WE FALL, MY FRIEND, MANY WORLDS FALL WITH US.
THE TIMEFIELD WILL PERMIT US TWO EXCURSIONS INTO YOUR PAST. I TAKE IT YOU HAVE ALREADY DECIDED WHICH EVENTS YOU WISH TO REVISIT?
OH, YES. I'VE DECIDED.
WE'LL START WITH FEBRUARY THE TWELFTH, 1963...
...THE DAY THE MIRACLEMAN FAMILY DIED!
PURPLE SHADOWS LEAP FROM THE SUDDEN VIOLET GLARE, AND THE WINDS OF TIME HOWL THROUGH THE PLACE CALLED SILENCE.
AND THEN THEY ARE GONE...

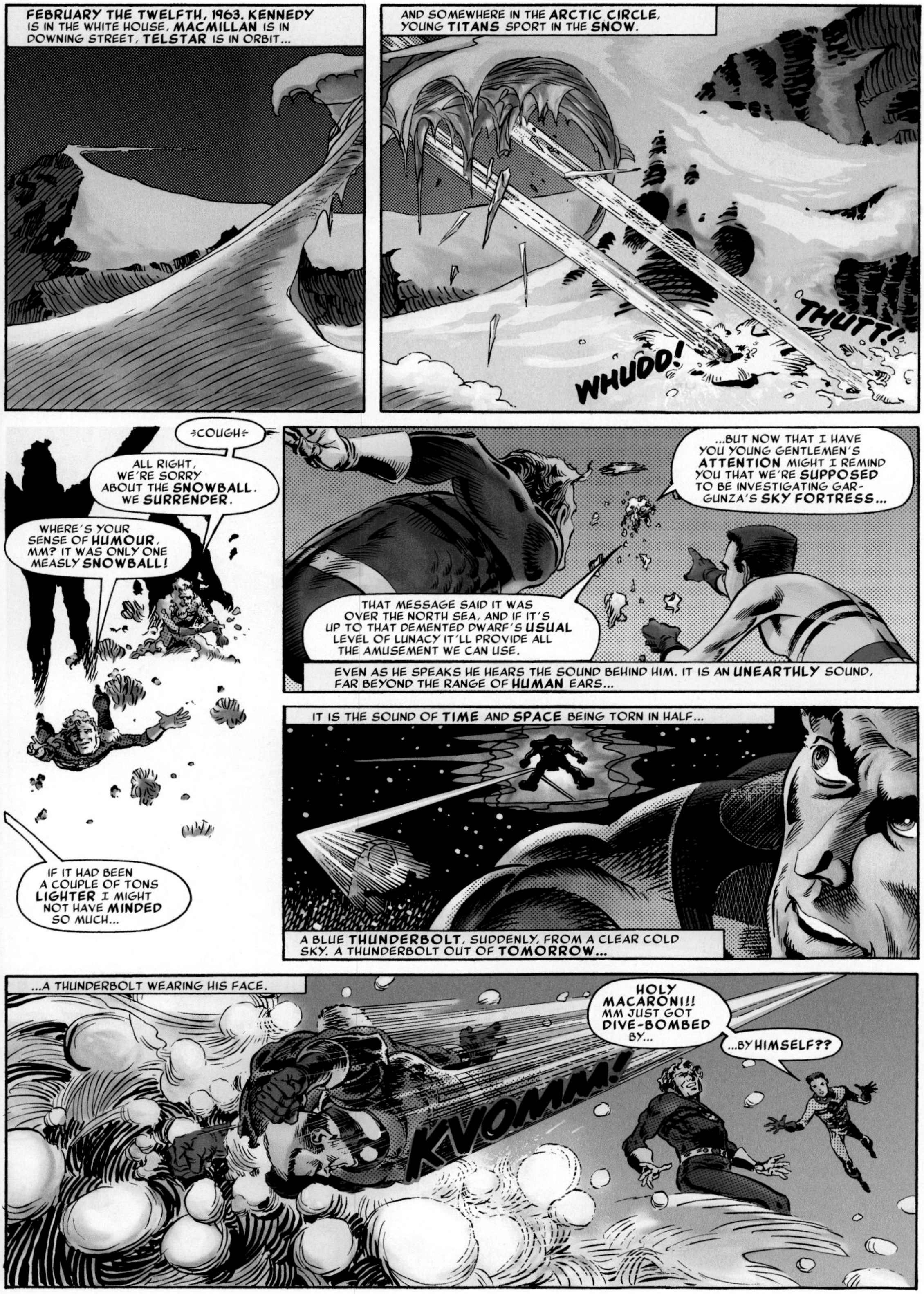
FEBRUARY THE TWELFTH, 1963. KENNEDY IS IN THE WHITE HOUSE, MACMILLAN IS IN DOWNING STREET, TELSTAR IS IN ORBIT...
AND SOMEWHERE IN THE ARCTIC CIRCLE, YOUNG TITANS SPORT IN THE SNOW.
THUTT!
WHUDD!
COUGH
ALL RIGHT, WE'RE SORRY ABOUT THE SNOWBALL. WE SURRENDER.
WHERE'S YOUR SENSE OF HUMOUR, MM? IT WAS ONLY ONE MEASLY SNOWBALL!
IF IT HAD BEEN A COUPLE OF TONS LIGHTER I MIGHT NOT HAVE MINDED SO MUCH...
...BUT NOW THAT I HAVE YOU YOUNG GENTLEMEN'S ATTENTION MIGHT I REMIND YOU THAT WE'RE SUPPOSED TO BE INVESTIGATING GAR-GUNZA'S SKY FORTRESS...
THAT MESSAGE SAID IT WAS OVER THE NORTH SEA, AND IF IT'S UP TO THAT DEMENTED DWARF'S USUAL LEVEL OF LUNACY IT'LL PROVIDE ALL THE AMUSEMENT WE CAN USE.
EVEN AS HE SPEAKS HE HEARS THE SOUND BEHIND HIM. IT IS AN UNEARTHLY SOUND, FAR BEYOND THE RANGE OF HUMAN EARS...
IT IS THE SOUND OF TIME AND SPACE BEING TORN IN HALF...
A BLUE THUNDERBOLT, SUDDENLY, FROM A CLEAR COLD SKY. A THUNDERBOLT OUT OF TOMORROW...
...A THUNDERBOLT WEARING HIS FACE.
HOLY MACARONI!!! MM JUST GOT DIVE-BOMBED BY...
...BY HIMSELF??
KVOMMM!

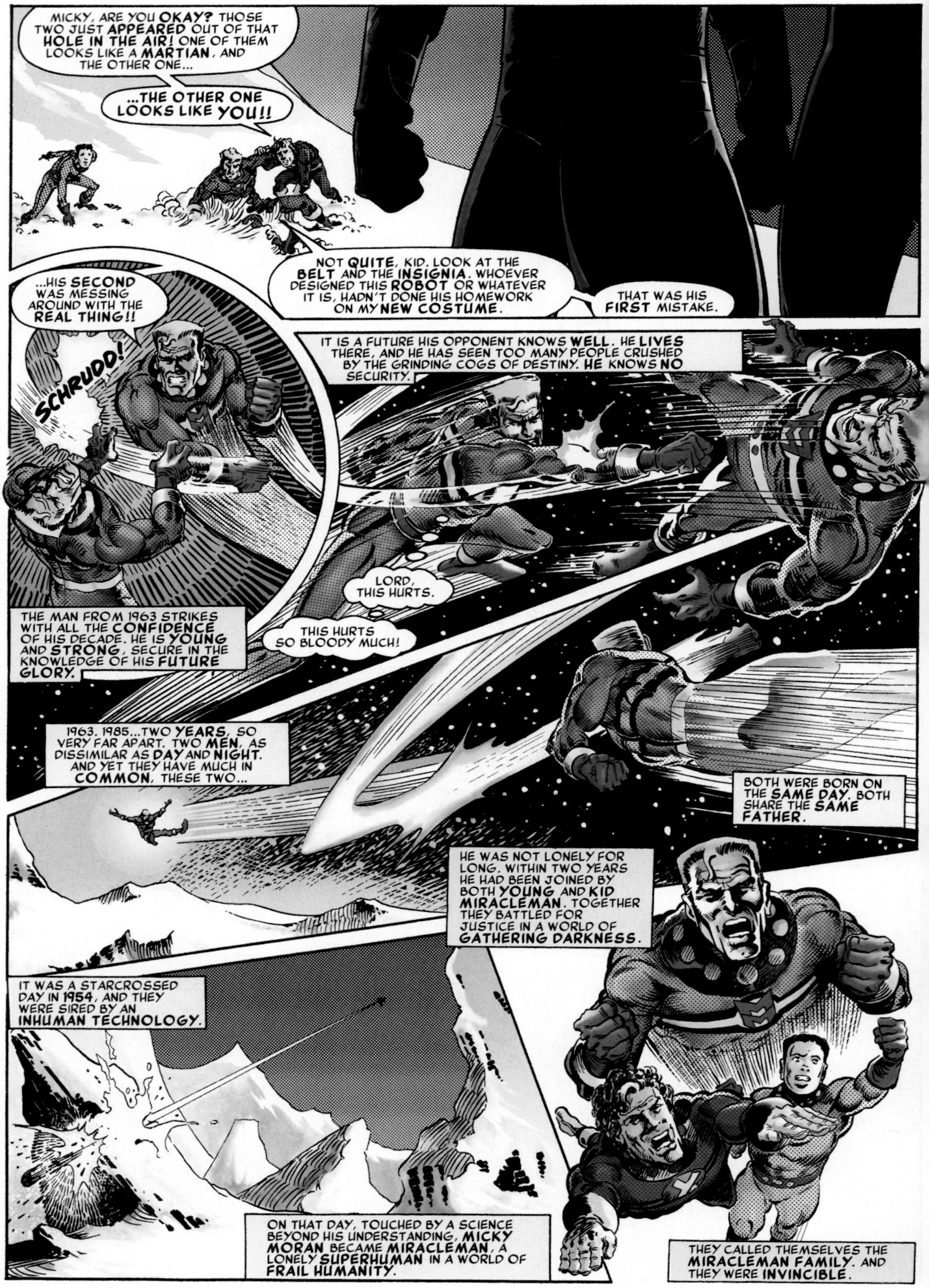
MICKY, ARE YOU OKAY? THOSE TWO JUST APPEARED OUT OF THAT HOLE IN THE AIR! ONE OF THEM LOOKS LIKE A MARTIAN, AND THE OTHER ONE...
...THE OTHER ONE LOOKS LIKE YOU!!
NOT QUITE, KID. LOOK AT THE BELT AND THE INSIGNIA. WHOEVER DESIGNED THIS ROBOT OR WHATEVER IT IS, HADN'T DONE HIS HOMEWORK ON MY NEW COSTUME.
THAT WAS HIS FIRST MISTAKE.
...HIS SECOND WAS MESSING AROUND WITH THE REAL THING!!
SCHRUDD!
IT IS A FUTURE HIS OPPONENT KNOWS WELL. HE LIVES THERE, AND HE HAS SEEN TOO MANY PEOPLE CRUSHED BY THE GRINDING COGS OF DESTINY. HE KNOWS NO SECURITY.
LORD, THIS HURTS.
THIS HURTS SO BLOODY MUCH!
THE MAN FROM 1963 STRIKES WITH ALL THE CONFIDENCE OF HIS DECADE. HE IS YOUNG AND STRONG, SECURE IN THE KNOWLEDGE OF HIS FUTURE GLORY.
1963. 1985...TWO YEARS, SO VERY FAR APART. TWO MEN, AS DISSIMILAR AS DAY AND NIGHT. AND YET THEY HAVE MUCH IN COMMON, THESE TWO...
BOTH WERE BORN ON THE SAME DAY. BOTH SHARE THE SAME FATHER.
IT WAS A STARCROSSED DAY IN 1954, AND THEY WERE SIRED BY AN INHUMAN TECHNOLOGY.
ON THAT DAY, TOUCHED BY A SCIENCE BEYOND HIS UNDERSTANDING, MICKY MORAN BECAME MIRACLEMAN, A LONELY SUPERHUMAN IN A WORLD OF FRAIL HUMANITY.
HE WAS NOT LONELY FOR LONG. WITHIN TWO YEARS HE HAD BEEN JOINED BY BOTH YOUNG AND KID MIRACLEMAN. TOGETHER THEY BATTLED FOR JUSTICE IN A WORLD OF GATHERING DARKNESS.
THEY CALLED THEMSELVES THE MIRACLEMAN FAMILY. AND THEY WERE INVINCIBLE.

BUT ONE DAY THEY FLEW OUT TOGETHER IN THE SNOW TO INVESTIGATE A MYSTERIOUS FLYING WARSHIP. THEY NEVER CAME BACK.

ONE DIED.

ONE BECAME A THING OF **UNUTTERABLE EVIL.**

ONE SURVIVED TO BE REBORN MANY YEARS LATER WITH ALL BUT HIS **HEART** INTACT.

ALL ON THAT DAY, **FEBRUARY 12TH, 1963...**

...TODAY.

SHRRAAAOM! KOOM!

FOUR OF THE MIGHTIEST MORTALS IN THE UNIVERSE COLLIDE ABOVE THE FROZEN TUNDRA, ALL THEIR TERRIBLE POWER RELEASED IN A BLIND INSTANT.

THE ENIGMATIC ALIEN KNOWN AS **WARPSMITH** TOUCHES A STUD AND THE SHOCKWAVES ARE INSTANTLY STILLED, THE SOUND OF COLLISION CUT OFF DEAD...

OUR TASK HERE IS **COMPLETED**, MIRACLEMAN. I HAVE WARPED THE ENERGIES INTO **NULL-SPACE,** READY TO RETRIEVE WHEN WE RETURN TO OUR **OWN TIME.**

WH-WHAT ABOUT THE **MIRACLEMAN FAMILY?** THEY'LL REMEMBER...

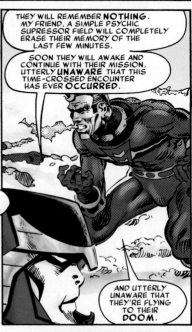

THEY WILL REMEMBER **NOTHING,** MY FRIEND. A SIMPLE PSYCHIC SUPPRESSOR FIELD WILL COMPLETELY ERASE THEIR MEMORY OF THE LAST FEW MINUTES.

SOON THEY WILL AWAKE AND CONTINUE WITH THEIR MISSION, UTTERLY **UNAWARE** THAT THIS TIME-CROSSED ENCOUNTER HAS EVER **OCCURRED.**

AND UTTERLY UNAWARE THAT THEY'RE FLYING TO THEIR **DOOM.**

THAT SKY-FORTRESS THEY'RE INVESTIGATING IS BOOBY-TRAPPED WITH AN **A-BOMB.** IT PUT ME OUT OF ACTION FOR **TWO DECADES,** YOUNG MIRACLE-MAN WAS **KILLED** AND...

...AND I GUESS WE **ALL** KNOW WHAT HAPPENED TO **KID MIRACLEMAN.** CAN'T WE STOP THEM, WARPSMITH? CAN'T WE PREVENT THIS WHOLE **CHAIN OF TRAGEDY** TAKING PLACE?

DON'T BE **NAIVE,** MIRACLEMAN. YOU **KNOW** THAT IS NOT POSSIBLE WITHIN THE INFLEXIBLE STRUCTURE OF TIME.

COME...WE STILL HAVE ONE **TIME PERIOD** LEFT TO VISIT. WHICH WILL IT **BE?**

I'VE JUST WITNESSED THE DAY OF MY **DEATH,** WARPSMITH. I SUPPOSE IT'S ONLY FITTING I VISIT THE DAY OF MY **REBIRTH.** IT HAPPENED ON **FEBRUARY 4TH, 1982.**

WARPSMITH NODS, ONE CIRCUIT-LADEN HAND ALREADY DESCRIBING A CIRCLE IN THE ARCTIC AIR. FOR AN INSTANT THE SNOWSCAPE IS BATHED IN A HARSH ALIEN BRILLIANCE...

...AND THEN THEY **VANISH,** TIME HEALING ITS OWN WOUNDS IN THEIR WAKE.

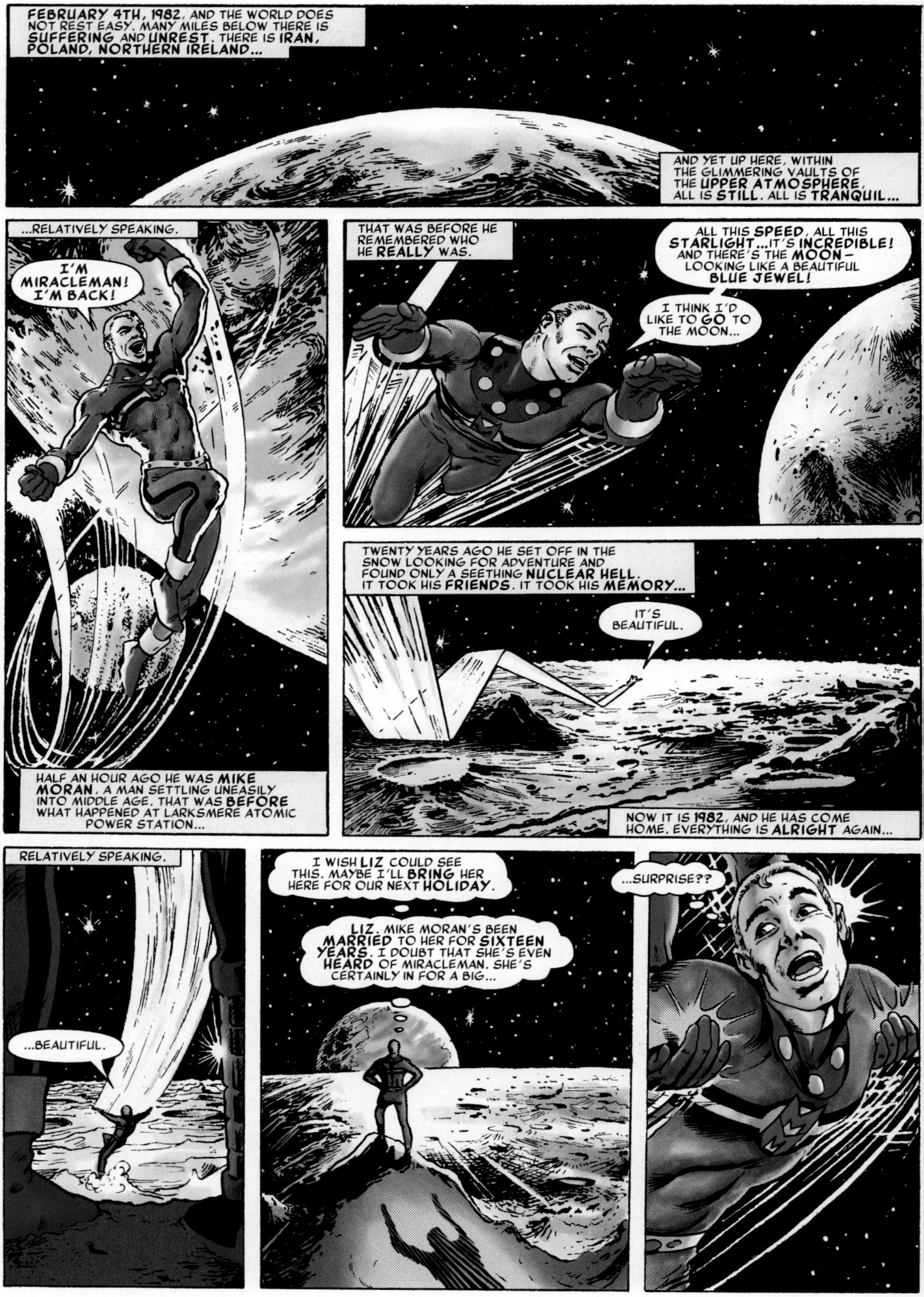
FEBRUARY 4TH, 1982, AND THE WORLD DOES NOT REST EASY. MANY MILES BELOW THERE IS SUFFERING AND UNREST. THERE IS IRAN, POLAND, NORTHERN IRELAND...
AND YET UP HERE, WITHIN THE GLIMMERING VAULTS OF THE UPPER ATMOSPHERE, ALL IS STILL. ALL IS TRANQUIL...
...RELATIVELY SPEAKING.
I'M MIRACLEMAN! I'M BACK!
HALF AN HOUR AGO HE WAS MIKE MORAN, A MAN SETTLING UNEASILY INTO MIDDLE AGE. THAT WAS BEFORE WHAT HAPPENED AT LARKSMERE ATOMIC POWER STATION...
THAT WAS BEFORE HE REMEMBERED WHO HE REALLY WAS.
ALL THIS SPEED, ALL THIS STARLIGHT...IT'S INCREDIBLE! AND THERE'S THE MOON— LOOKING LIKE A BEAUTIFUL BLUE JEWEL!
I THINK I'D LIKE TO GO TO THE MOON...
TWENTY YEARS AGO HE SET OFF IN THE SNOW LOOKING FOR ADVENTURE AND FOUND ONLY A SEETHING NUCLEAR HELL. IT TOOK HIS FRIENDS. IT TOOK HIS MEMORY...
IT'S BEAUTIFUL.
NOW IT IS 1982, AND HE HAS COME HOME. EVERYTHING IS ALRIGHT AGAIN...
RELATIVELY SPEAKING.
...BEAUTIFUL.
I WISH LIZ COULD SEE THIS. MAYBE I'LL BRING HER HERE FOR OUR NEXT HOLIDAY.
LIZ. MIKE MORAN'S BEEN MARRIED TO HER FOR SIXTEEN YEARS. I DOUBT THAT SHE'S EVEN HEARD OF MIRACLEMAN. SHE'S CERTAINLY IN FOR A BIG...
...SURPRISE??

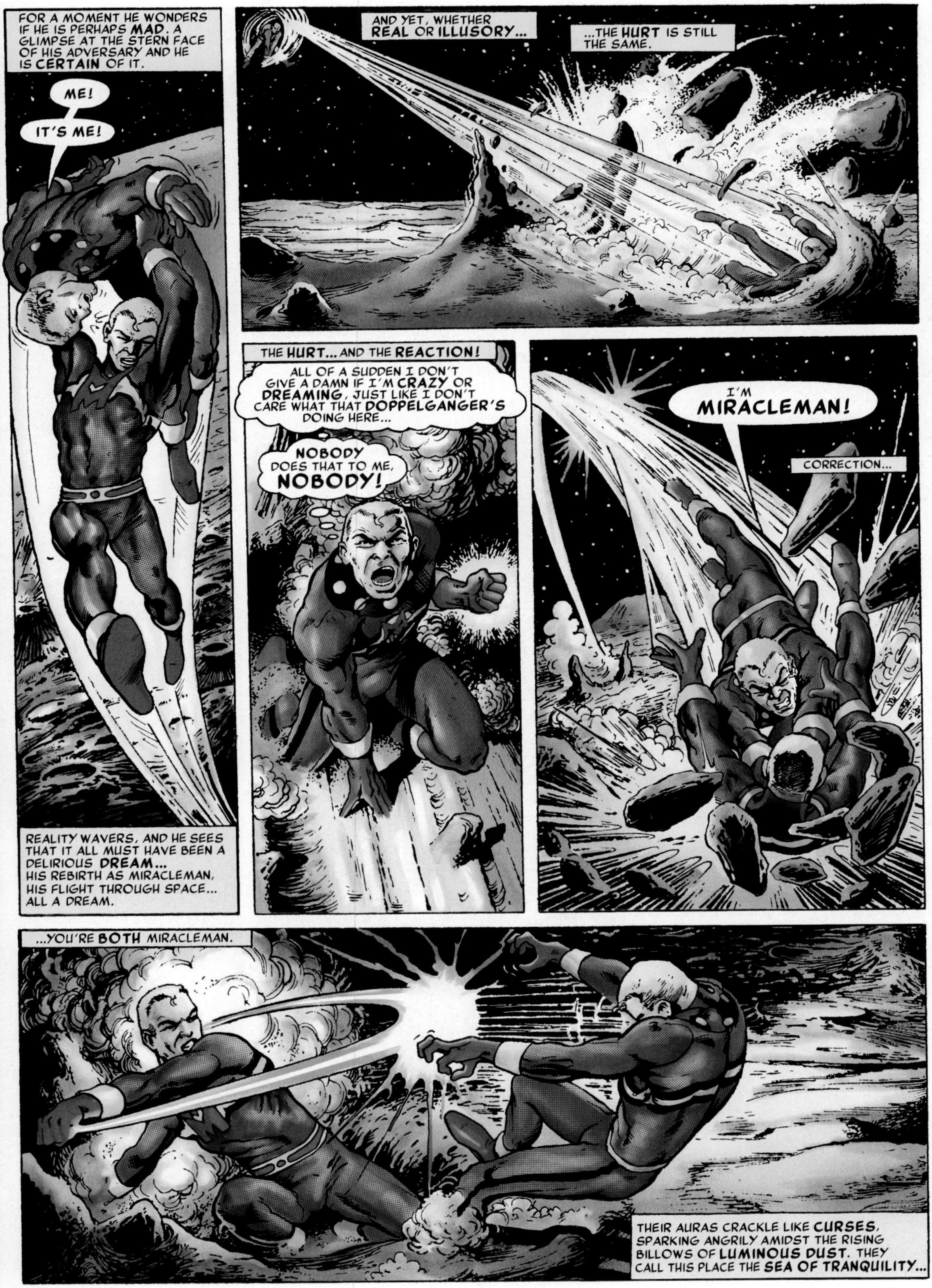
FOR A MOMENT HE WONDERS IF HE IS PERHAPS MAD. A GLIMPSE AT THE STERN FACE OF HIS ADVERSARY AND HE IS CERTAIN OF IT.
ME!
IT'S ME!
REALITY WAVERS, AND HE SEES THAT IT ALL MUST HAVE BEEN A DELIRIOUS DREAM... HIS REBIRTH AS MIRACLEMAN, HIS FLIGHT THROUGH SPACE... ALL A DREAM.
AND YET, WHETHER REAL OR ILLUSORY...
...THE HURT IS STILL THE SAME.
THE HURT... AND THE REACTION!
ALL OF A SUDDEN I DON'T GIVE A DAMN IF I'M CRAZY OR DREAMING, JUST LIKE I DON'T CARE WHAT THAT DOPPELGANGER'S DOING HERE...
NOBODY DOES THAT TO ME, NOBODY!
I'M MIRACLEMAN!
CORRECTION...
...YOU'RE BOTH MIRACLEMAN.
THEIR AURAS CRACKLE LIKE CURSES, SPARKING ANGRILY AMIDST THE RISING BILLOWS OF LUMINOUS DUST. THEY CALL THIS PLACE THE SEA OF TRANQUILITY...

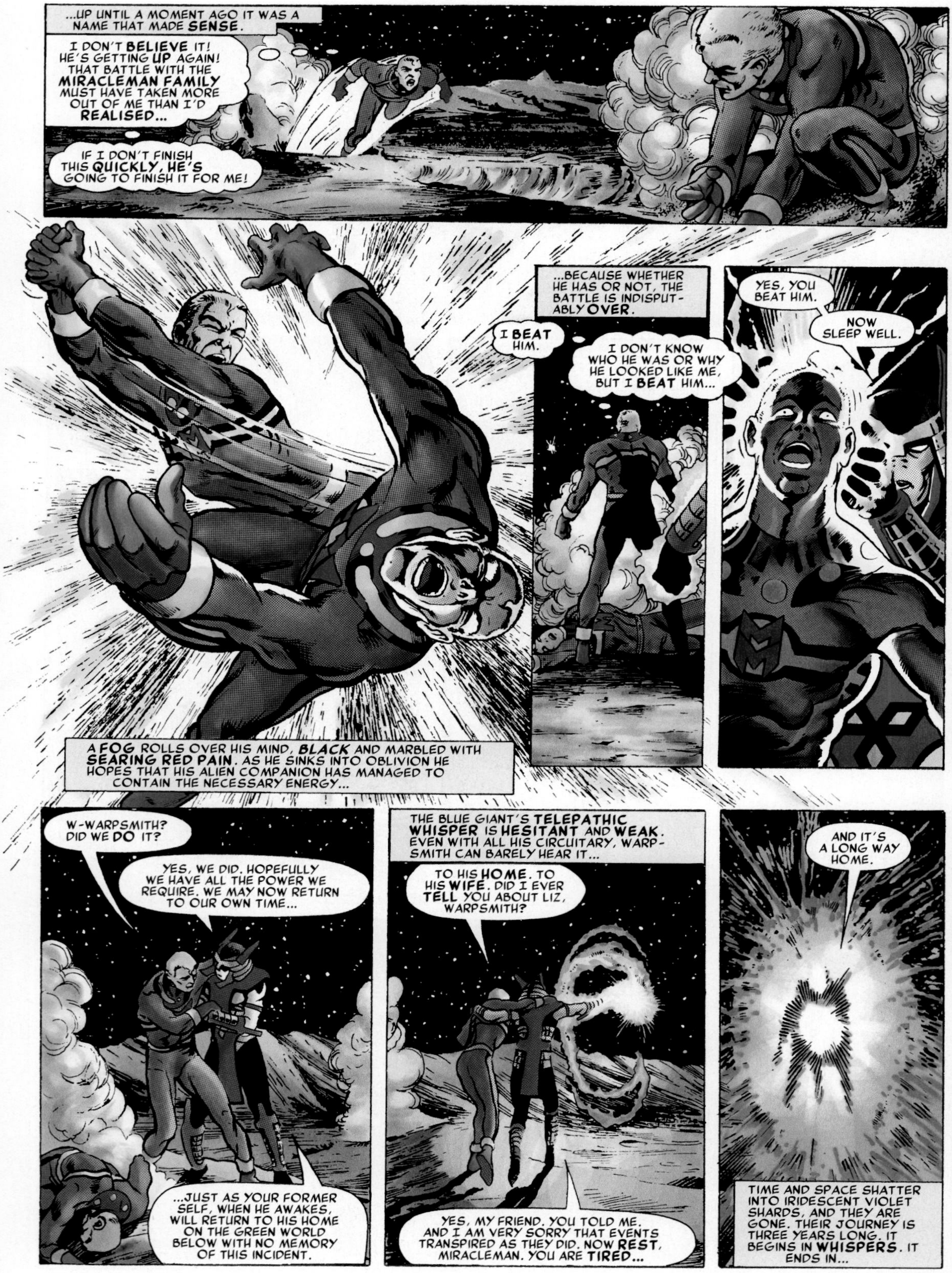

...UP UNTIL A MOMENT AGO IT WAS A NAME THAT MADE SENSE.
I DON'T BELIEVE IT! HE'S GETTING UP AGAIN! THAT BATTLE WITH THE MIRACLEMAN FAMILY MUST HAVE TAKEN MORE OUT OF ME THAN I'D REALISED...
IF I DON'T FINISH THIS QUICKLY, HE'S GOING TO FINISH IT FOR ME!
A FOG ROLLS OVER HIS MIND, BLACK AND MARBLED WITH SEARING RED PAIN. AS HE SINKS INTO OBLIVION HE HOPES THAT HIS ALIEN COMPANION HAS MANAGED TO CONTAIN THE NECESSARY ENERGY...
...BECAUSE WHETHER HE HAS OR NOT, THE BATTLE IS INDISPUTABLY OVER.
I BEAT HIM.
I DON'T KNOW WHO HE WAS OR WHY HE LOOKED LIKE ME, BUT I BEAT HIM...
YES, YOU BEAT HIM.
NOW SLEEP WELL.
W-WARPSMITH? DID WE DO IT?
YES, WE DID. HOPEFULLY WE HAVE ALL THE POWER WE REQUIRE. WE MAY NOW RETURN TO OUR OWN TIME...
...JUST AS YOUR FORMER SELF, WHEN HE AWAKES, WILL RETURN TO HIS HOME ON THE GREEN WORLD BELOW WITH NO MEMORY OF THIS INCIDENT.
THE BLUE GIANT'S TELEPATHIC WHISPER IS HESITANT AND WEAK. EVEN WITH ALL HIS CIRCUITARY, WARPSMITH CAN BARELY HEAR IT...
TO HIS HOME. TO HIS WIFE. DID I EVER TELL YOU ABOUT LIZ, WARPSMITH?
YES, MY FRIEND. YOU TOLD ME. AND I AM VERY SORRY THAT EVENTS TRANSPIRED AS THEY DID. NOW REST, MIRACLEMAN. YOU ARE TIRED...
AND IT'S A LONG WAY HOME.
TIME AND SPACE SHATTER INTO IRIDESCENT VIOLET SHARDS, AND THEY ARE GONE. THEIR JOURNEY IS THREE YEARS LONG. IT BEGINS IN WHISPERS. IT ENDS IN...

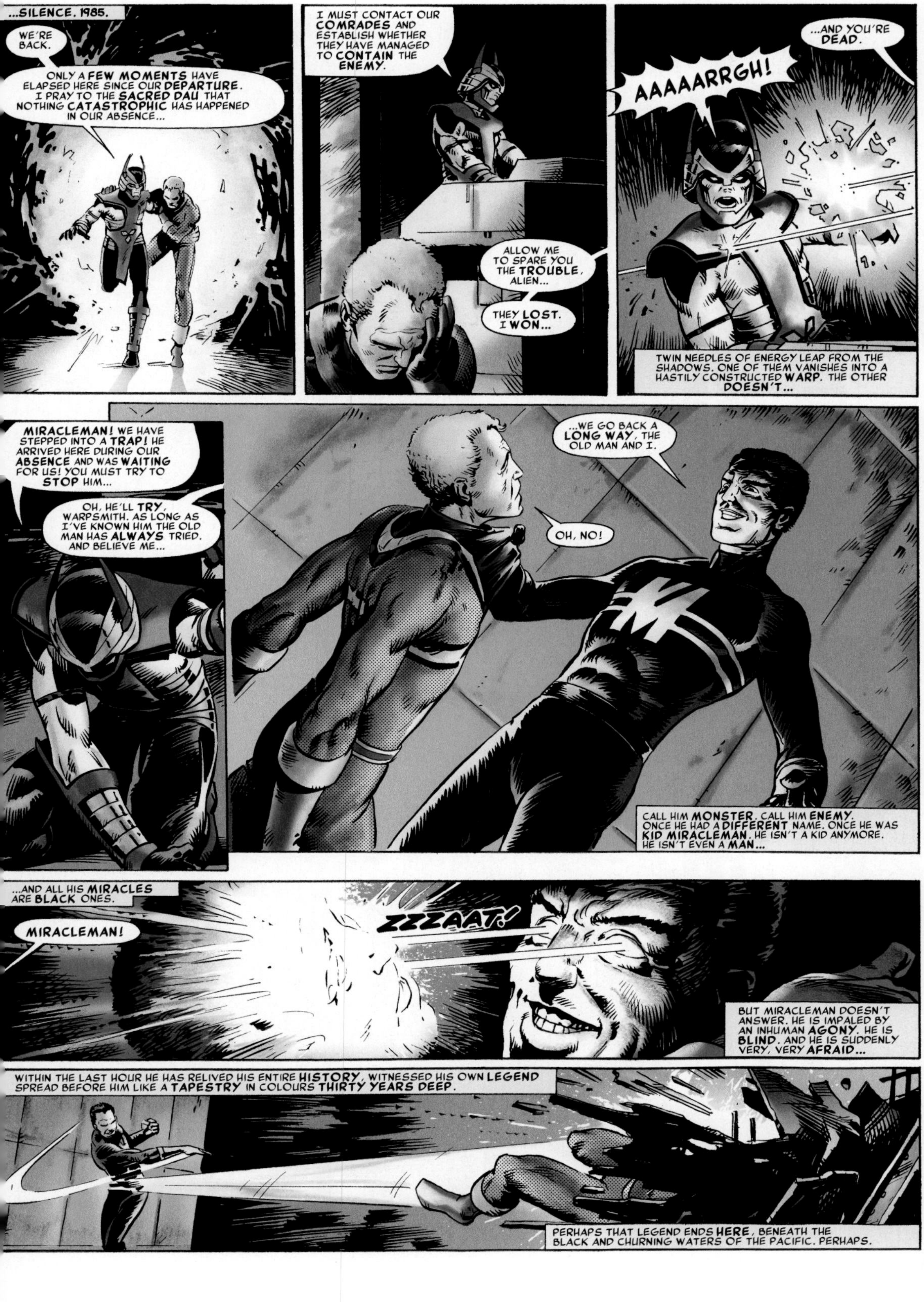
...SILENCE. 1985.
WE'RE BACK.
ONLY A FEW MOMENTS HAVE ELAPSED HERE SINCE OUR DEPARTURE. I PRAY TO THE SACRED DAU THAT NOTHING CATASTROPHIC HAS HAPPENED IN OUR ABSENCE...
I MUST CONTACT OUR COMRADES AND ESTABLISH WHETHER THEY HAVE MANAGED TO CONTAIN THE ENEMY.
ALLOW ME TO SPARE YOU THE TROUBLE, ALIEN...
THEY LOST. I WON...
...AND YOU'RE DEAD.
AAAAARRGH!
TWIN NEEDLES OF ENERGY LEAP FROM THE SHADOWS. ONE OF THEM VANISHES INTO A HASTILY CONSTRUCTED WARP. THE OTHER DOESN'T...
MIRACLEMAN! WE HAVE STEPPED INTO A TRAP! HE ARRIVED HERE DURING OUR ABSENCE AND WAS WAITING FOR US! YOU MUST TRY TO STOP HIM...
OH, HE'LL TRY, WARPSMITH. AS LONG AS I'VE KNOWN HIM THE OLD MAN HAS ALWAYS TRIED. AND BELIEVE ME...
...WE GO BACK A LONG WAY, THE OLD MAN AND I.
OH, NO!
CALL HIM MONSTER. CALL HIM ENEMY. ONCE HE HAD A DIFFERENT NAME. ONCE HE WAS KID MIRACLEMAN. HE ISN'T A KID ANYMORE. HE ISN'T EVEN A MAN...
...AND ALL HIS MIRACLES ARE BLACK ONES.
MIRACLEMAN!
ZZZAAT!
BUT MIRACLEMAN DOESN'T ANSWER. HE IS IMPALED BY AN INHUMAN AGONY. HE IS BLIND. AND HE IS SUDDENLY VERY, VERY AFRAID...
WITHIN THE LAST HOUR HE HAS RELIVED HIS ENTIRE HISTORY, WITNESSED HIS OWN LEGEND SPREAD BEFORE HIM LIKE A TAPESTRY IN COLOURS THIRTY YEARS DEEP.
PERHAPS THAT LEGEND ENDS HERE, BENEATH THE BLACK AND CHURNING WATERS OF THE PACIFIC. PERHAPS.

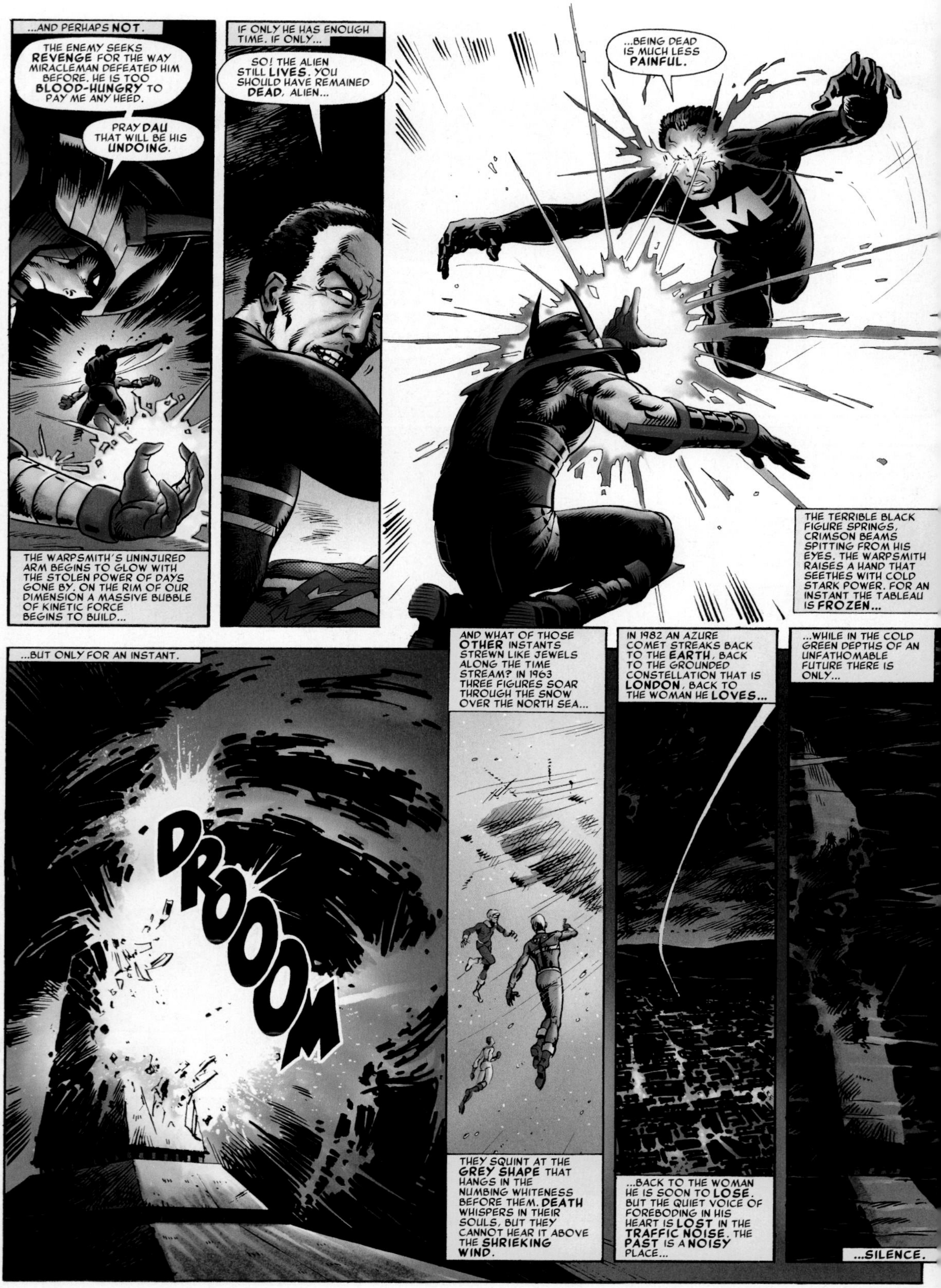

...AND PERHAPS NOT.
THE ENEMY SEEKS REVENGE FOR THE WAY MIRACLEMAN DEFEATED HIM BEFORE. HE IS TOO BLOOD-HUNGRY TO PAY ME ANY HEED.
PRAY DAU THAT WILL BE HIS UNDOING.
THE WARPSMITH'S UNINJURED ARM BEGINS TO GLOW WITH THE STOLEN POWER OF DAYS GONE BY. ON THE RIM OF OUR DIMENSION A MASSIVE BUBBLE OF KINETIC FORCE BEGINS TO BUILD...
IF ONLY HE HAS ENOUGH TIME. IF ONLY...
SO! THE ALIEN STILL LIVES. YOU SHOULD HAVE REMAINED DEAD, ALIEN...
...BEING DEAD IS MUCH LESS PAINFUL.
THE TERRIBLE BLACK FIGURE SPRINGS, CRIMSON BEAMS SPITTING FROM HIS EYES. THE WARPSMITH RAISES A HAND THAT SEETHES WITH COLD STARK POWER. FOR AN INSTANT THE TABLEAU IS FROZEN...
...BUT ONLY FOR AN INSTANT.
DROOOOM
AND WHAT OF THOSE OTHER INSTANTS STREWN LIKE JEWELS ALONG THE TIME STREAM? IN 1963 THREE FIGURES SOAR THROUGH THE SNOW OVER THE NORTH SEA...
THEY SQUINT AT THE GREY SHAPE THAT HANGS IN THE NUMBING WHITENESS BEFORE THEM. DEATH WHISPERS IN THEIR SOULS, BUT THEY CANNOT HEAR IT ABOVE THE SHRIEKING WIND.
IN 1982 AN AZURE COMET STREAKS BACK TO THE EARTH, BACK TO THE GROUNDED CONSTELLATION THAT IS LONDON, BACK TO THE WOMAN HE LOVES...
...BACK TO THE WOMAN HE IS SOON TO LOSE. BUT THE QUIET VOICE OF FOREBODING IN HIS HEART IS LOST IN THE TRAFFIC NOISE. THE PAST IS A NOISY PLACE...
...WHILE IN THE COLD GREEN DEPTHS OF AN UNFATHOMABLE FUTURE THERE IS ONLY...
...SILENCE.

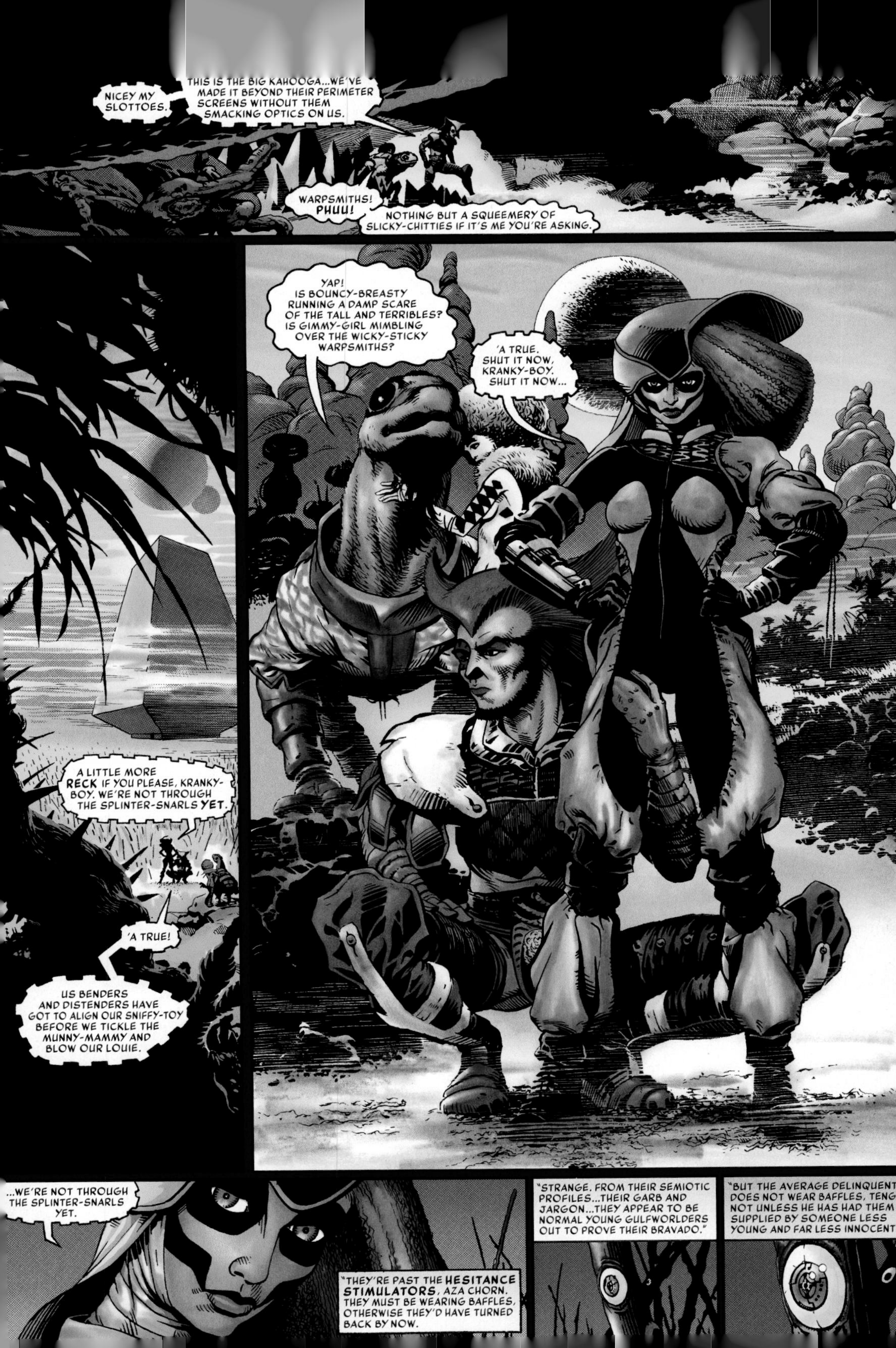

NICEY MY SLOTTOES.
THIS IS THE BIG KAHOOGA...WE'VE MADE IT BEYOND THEIR PERIMETER SCREENS WITHOUT THEM SMACKING OPTICS ON US.
WARPSMITHS! PHUU!
NOTHING BUT A SQUEEMERY OF SLICKY-CHITTIES IF IT'S ME YOU'RE ASKING.
YAP! IS BOUNCY-BREASTY RUNNING A DAMP SCARE OF THE TALL AND TERRIBLES? IS GIMMY-GIRL MIMBLING OVER THE WICKY-STICKY WARPSMITHS?
'A TRUE. SHUT IT NOW, KRANKY-BOY. SHUT IT NOW...
A LITTLE MORE RECK IF YOU PLEASE, KRANKY-BOY. WE'RE NOT THROUGH THE SPLINTER-SNARLS YET.
'A TRUE!
US BENDERS AND DISTENDERS HAVE GOT TO ALIGN OUR SNIFFY-TOY BEFORE WE TICKLE THE MUNNY-MAMMY AND BLOW OUR LOUIE.
...WE'RE NOT THROUGH THE SPLINTER-SNARLS YET.
"THEY'RE PAST THE HESITANCE STIMULATORS, AZA CHORN. THEY MUST BE WEARING BAFFLES, OTHERWISE THEY'D HAVE TURNED BACK BY NOW.
"STRANGE. FROM THEIR SEMIOTIC PROFILES...THEIR GARB AND JARGON...THEY APPEAR TO BE NORMAL YOUNG GULFWORLDERS OUT TO PROVE THEIR BRAVADO."
"BUT THE AVERAGE DELINQUENT DOES NOT WEAR BAFFLES, TENGA NOT UNLESS HE HAS HAD THEM SUPPLIED BY SOMEONE LESS YOUNG AND FAR LESS INNOCENT."

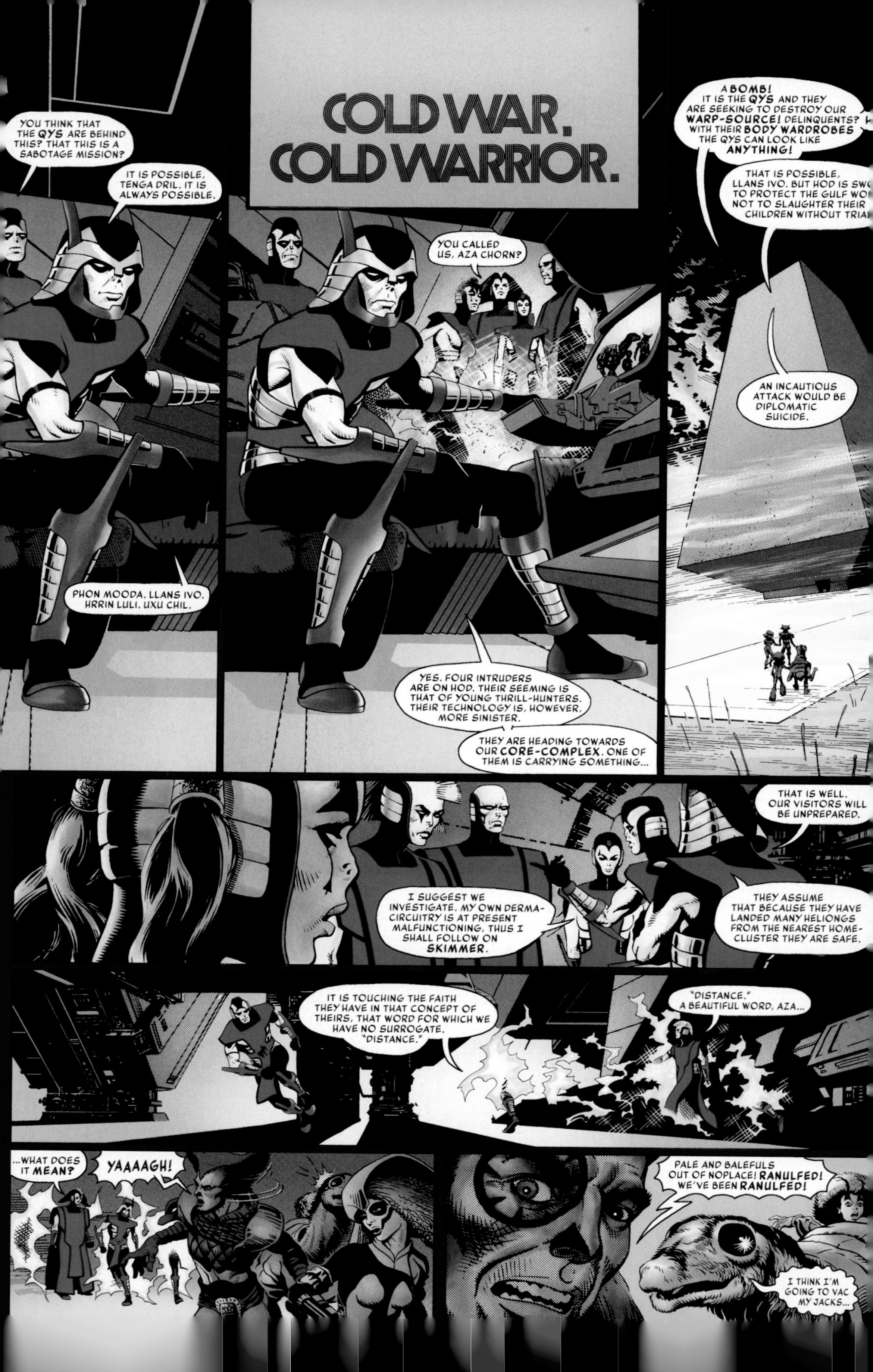

COLD WAR, COLD WARRIOR.
YOU THINK THAT THE QYS ARE BEHIND THIS? THAT THIS IS A SABOTAGE MISSION?
IT IS POSSIBLE, TENGA DRIL. IT IS ALWAYS POSSIBLE.
PHON MOODA. LLANS IVO. HRRIN LULI. UXU CHIL.
YOU CALLED US, AZA CHORN?
YES. FOUR INTRUDERS ARE ON HOD. THEIR SEEMING IS THAT OF YOUNG THRILL-HUNTERS. THEIR TECHNOLOGY IS, HOWEVER, MORE SINISTER.
THEY ARE HEADING TOWARDS OUR CORE-COMPLEX. ONE OF THEM IS CARRYING SOMETHING...
A BOMB! IT IS THE QYS AND THEY ARE SEEKING TO DESTROY OUR WARP-SOURCE! DELINQUENTS? WITH THEIR BODY WARDROBES THE QYS CAN LOOK LIKE ANYTHING!
THAT IS POSSIBLE, LLANS IVO. BUT HOD IS SWO TO PROTECT THE GULF WO NOT TO SLAUGHTER THEIR CHILDREN WITHOUT TRIA
AN INCAUTIOUS ATTACK WOULD BE DIPLOMATIC SUICIDE.
THAT IS WELL. OUR VISITORS WILL BE UNPREPARED.
I SUGGEST WE INVESTIGATE. MY OWN DERMA-CIRCUITRY IS AT PRESENT MALFUNCTIONING, THUS I SHALL FOLLOW ON SKIMMER.
THEY ASSUME THAT BECAUSE THEY HAVE LANDED MANY HELIONGS FROM THE NEAREST HOME-CLUSTER THEY ARE SAFE.
IT IS TOUCHING THE FAITH THEY HAVE IN THAT CONCEPT OF THEIRS, THAT WORD FOR WHICH WE HAVE NO SURROGATE. "DISTANCE."
"DISTANCE." A BEAUTIFUL WORD, AZA...
...WHAT DOES IT MEAN?
YAAAAGH!
PALE AND BALEFULS OUT OF NOPLACE! RANULFED! WE'VE BEEN RANULFED!
I THINK I'M GOING TO VAC MY JACKS...

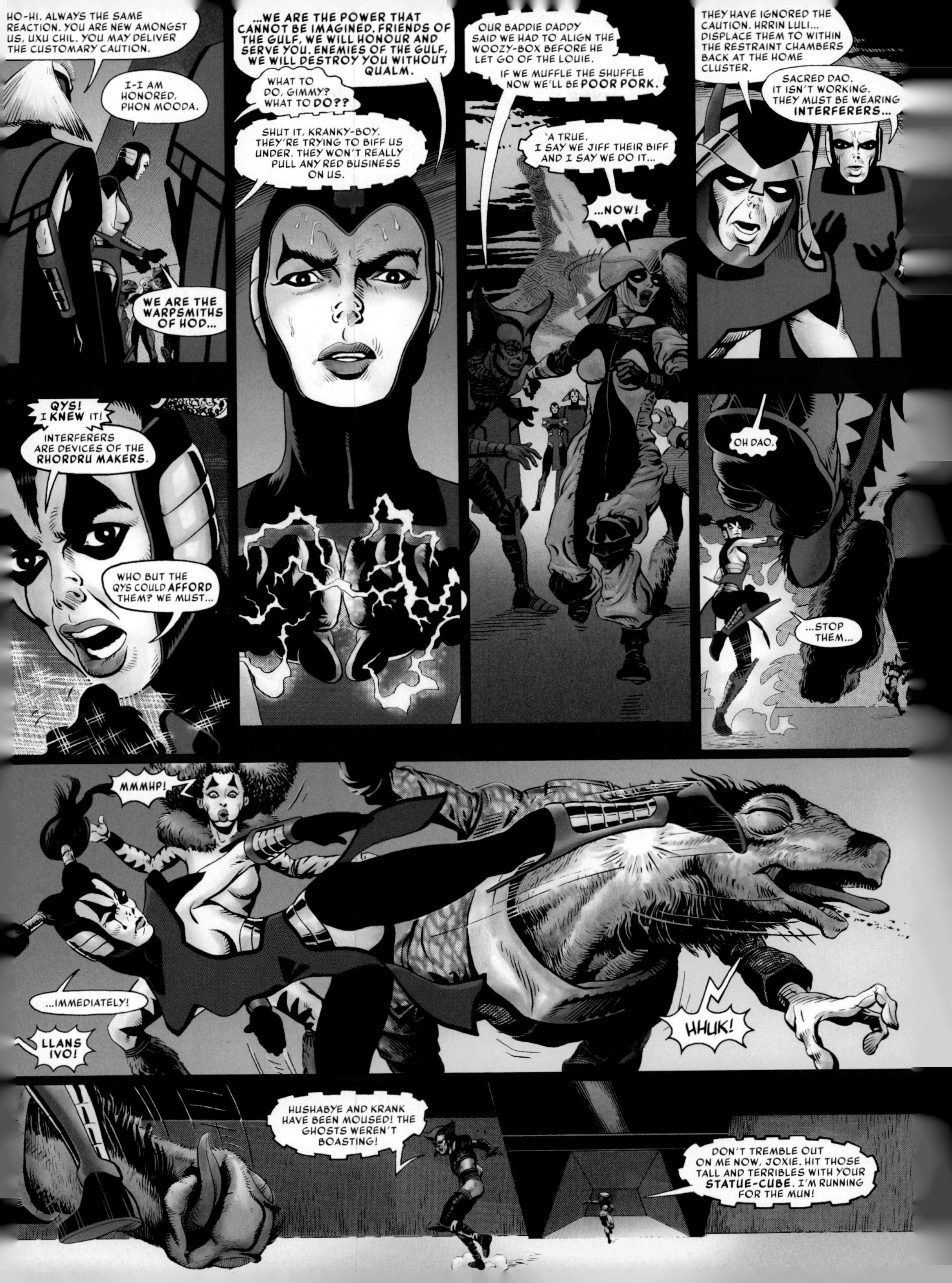
HO-HI. ALWAYS THE SAME REACTION. YOU ARE NEW AMONGST US, UXU CHIL. YOU MAY DELIVER THE CUSTOMARY CAUTION.
I-I AM HONORED, PHON MOODA.
WE ARE THE WARPSMITHS OF HOD...
...WE ARE THE POWER THAT CANNOT BE IMAGINED. FRIENDS OF THE GULF, WE WILL HONOUR AND SERVE YOU. ENEMIES OF THE GULF, WE WILL DESTROY YOU WITHOUT QUALM.
WHAT TO DO, GIMMY? WHAT TO DO??
SHUT IT, KRANKY-BOY. THEY'RE TRYING TO BIFF US UNDER. THEY WON'T REALLY PULL ANY RED BUSINESS ON US.
OUR BADDIE DADDY SAID WE HAD TO ALIGN THE WOOZY-BOX BEFORE HE LET GO OF THE LOUIE.
IF WE MUFFLE THE SHUFFLE NOW WE'LL BE POOR PORK.
'A TRUE. I SAY WE JIFF THEIR BIFF AND I SAY WE DO IT...
...NOW!
THEY HAVE IGNORED THE CAUTION. HRRIN LULI... DISPLACE THEM TO WITHIN THE RESTRAINT CHAMBERS BACK AT THE HOME CLUSTER.
SACRED DAO. IT ISN'T WORKING. THEY MUST BE WEARING INTERFERERS...
QYS! I KNEW IT!
INTERFERERS ARE DEVICES OF THE RHORDRU MAKERS.
WHO BUT THE QYS COULD AFFORD THEM? WE MUST...
OH DAO.
...STOP THEM...
MMMHP!
...IMMEDIATELY!
LLANS IVO!
HHUK!
HUSHABYE AND KRANK HAVE BEEN MOUSED! THE GHOSTS WEREN'T BOASTING!
DON'T TREMBLE OUT ON ME NOW, JOXIE. HIT THOSE TALL AND TERRIBLES WITH YOUR STATUE-CUBE. I'M RUNNING FOR THE MUN!

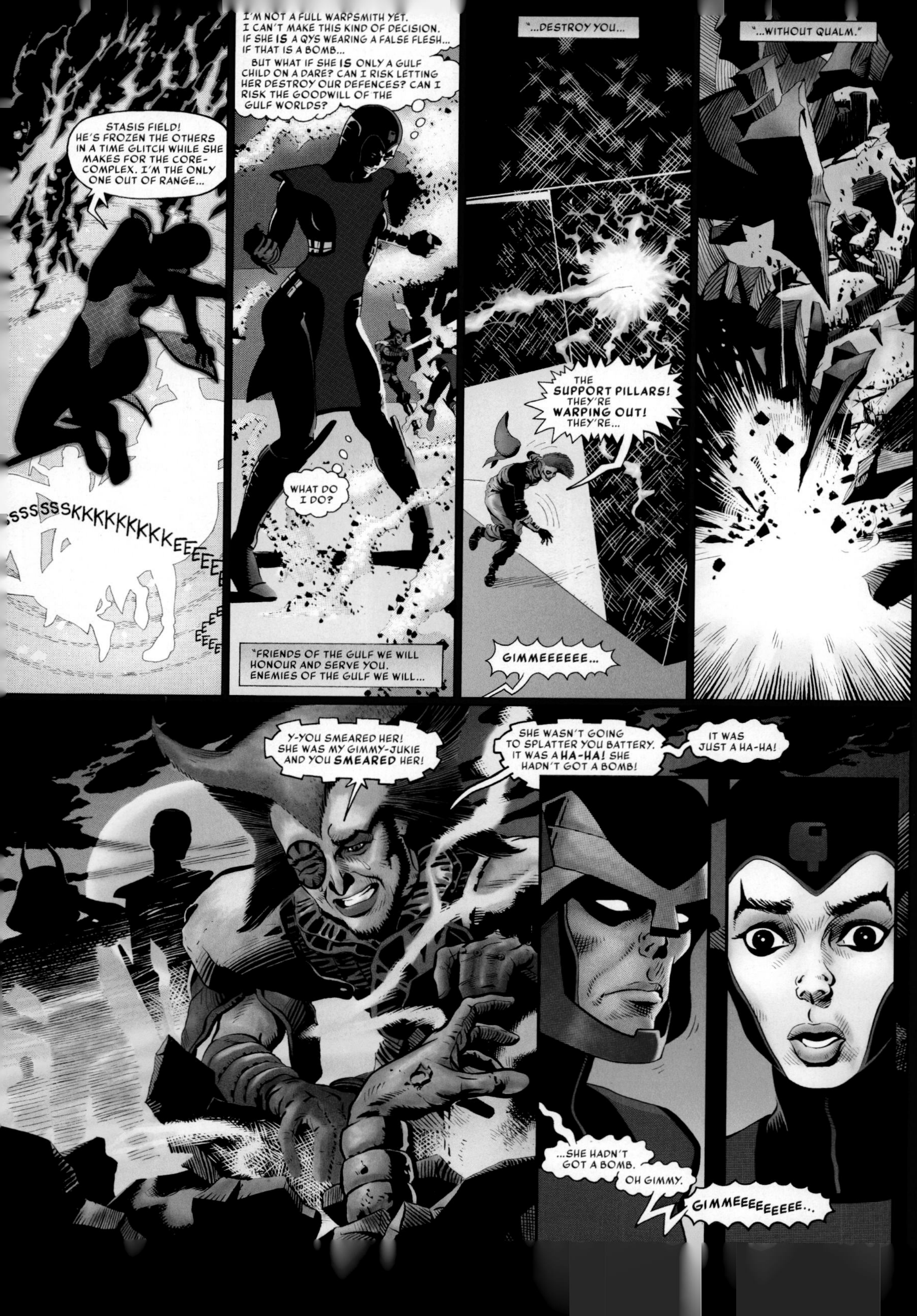
STASIS FIELD! HE'S FROZEN THE OTHERS IN A TIME GLITCH WHILE SHE MAKES FOR THE CORE-COMPLEX. I'M THE ONLY ONE OUT OF RANGE...
SSSSSSKKKKKKKKKEEEEEEEEEE
I'M NOT A FULL WARPSMITH YET. I CAN'T MAKE THIS KIND OF DECISION. IF SHE IS A QYS WEARING A FALSE FLESH... IF THAT IS A BOMB...
BUT WHAT IF SHE IS ONLY A GULF CHILD ON A DARE? CAN I RISK LETTING HER DESTROY OUR DEFENCES? CAN I RISK THE GOODWILL OF THE GULF WORLDS?
WHAT DO I DO?
"FRIENDS OF THE GULF WE WILL HONOUR AND SERVE YOU. ENEMIES OF THE GULF WE WILL...
"...DESTROY YOU...
THE SUPPORT PILLARS! THEY'RE WARPING OUT! THEY'RE...
GIMMEEEEEE...
"...WITHOUT QUALM."
Y-YOU SMEARED HER! SHE WAS MY GIMMY-JUKIE AND YOU SMEARED HER!
SHE WASN'T GOING TO SPLATTER YOU BATTERY. IT WAS A HA-HA! SHE HADN'T GOT A BOMB!
IT WAS JUST A HA-HA!
...SHE HADN'T GOT A BOMB.
OH GIMMY.
GIMMEEEEEEEEE...

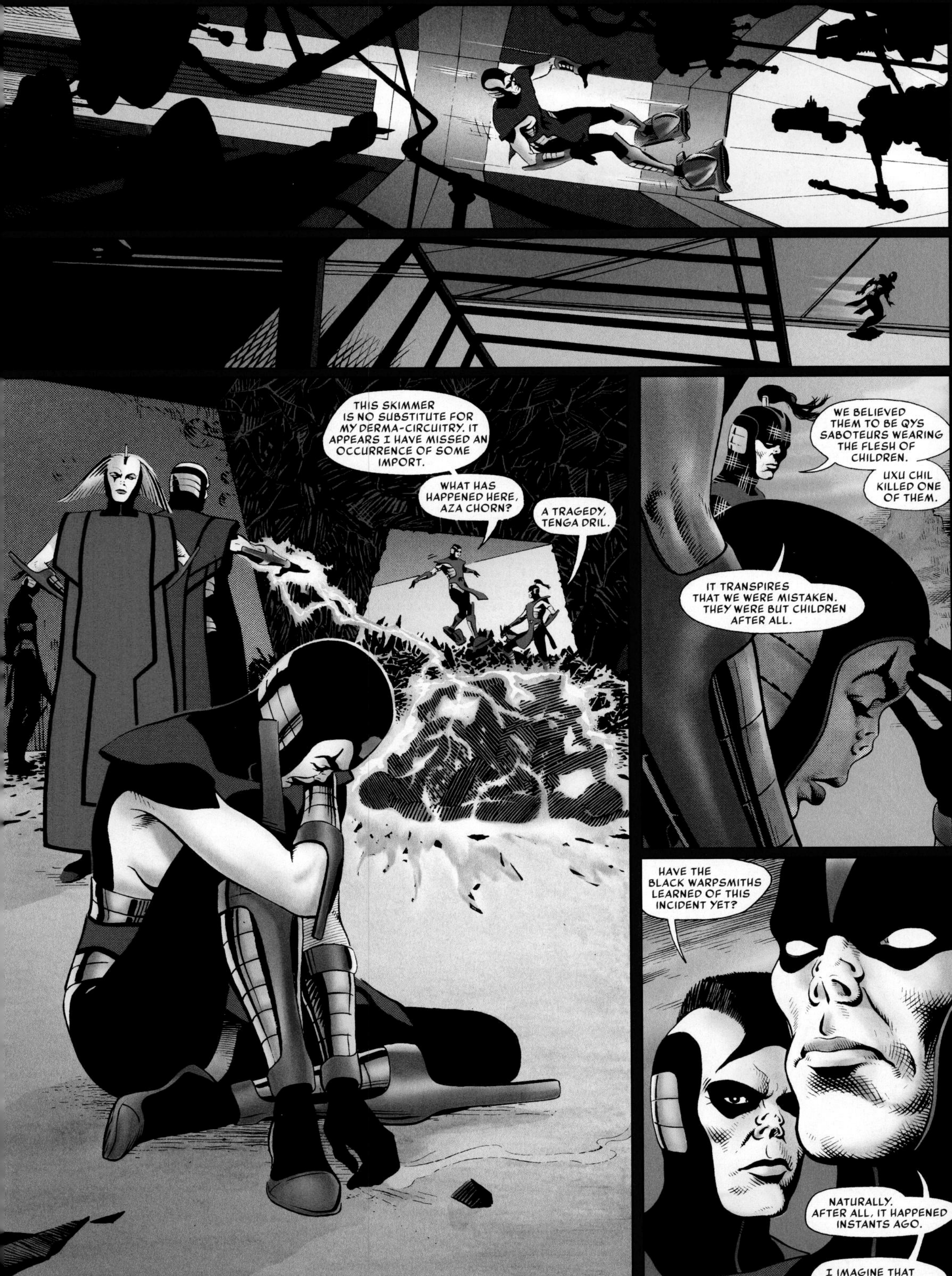
THIS SKIMMER IS NO SUBSTITUTE FOR MY DERMA-CIRCUITRY. IT APPEARS I HAVE MISSED AN OCCURRENCE OF SOME IMPORT.
WHAT HAS HAPPENED HERE, AZA CHORN?
A TRAGEDY, TENGA DRIL.
WE BELIEVED THEM TO BE QYS SABOTEURS WEARING THE FLESH OF CHILDREN.
UXU CHIL KILLED ONE OF THEM.
IT TRANSPIRES THAT WE WERE MISTAKEN. THEY WERE BUT CHILDREN AFTER ALL.
HAVE THE BLACK WARPSMITHS LEARNED OF THIS INCIDENT YET?
NATURALLY. AFTER ALL, IT HAPPENED INSTANTS AGO.
I IMAGINE THAT THEY WILL SHORTLY BE SUMMONING US INTO THEIR...

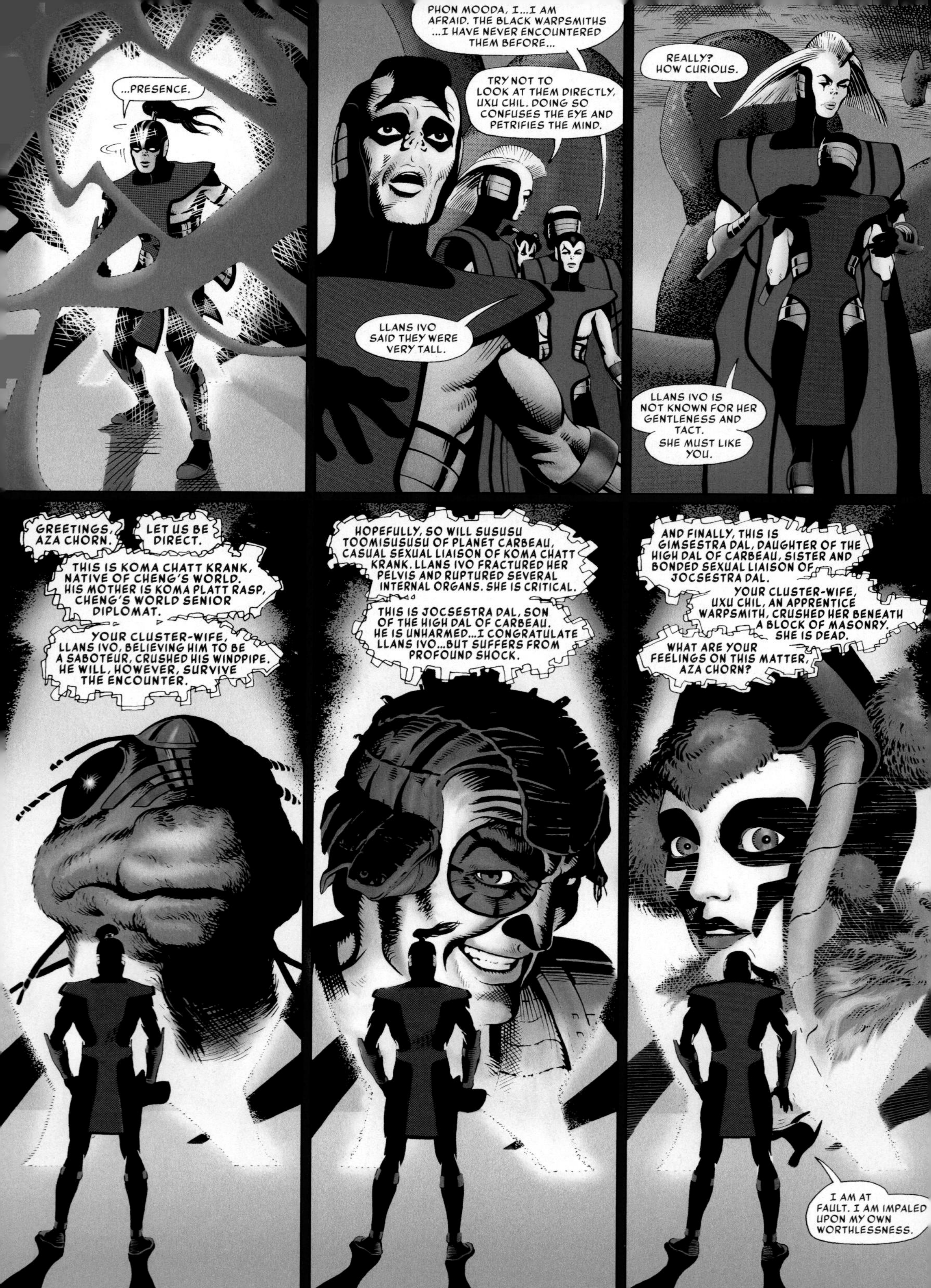
...PRESENCE.
PHON MOODA, I...I AM AFRAID. THE BLACK WARPSMITHS ...I HAVE NEVER ENCOUNTERED THEM BEFORE...
TRY NOT TO LOOK AT THEM DIRECTLY, UXU CHIL. DOING SO CONFUSES THE EYE AND PETRIFIES THE MIND.
LLANS IVO SAID THEY WERE VERY TALL.
REALLY? HOW CURIOUS.
LLANS IVO IS NOT KNOWN FOR HER GENTLENESS AND TACT.
SHE MUST LIKE YOU.
GREETINGS, AZA CHORN.
LET US BE DIRECT.
THIS IS KOMA CHATT KRANK, NATIVE OF CHENG'S WORLD. HIS MOTHER IS KOMA PLATT RASP, CHENG'S WORLD SENIOR DIPLOMAT.
YOUR CLUSTER-WIFE, LLANS IVO, BELIEVING HIM TO BE A SABOTEUR, CRUSHED HIS WINDPIPE. HE WILL, HOWEVER, SURVIVE THE ENCOUNTER.
HOPEFULLY, SO WILL SUSUSU TOOMISUSUSU OF PLANET CARBEAU, CASUAL SEXUAL LIAISON OF KOMA CHATT KRANK. LLANS IVO FRACTURED HER PELVIS AND RUPTURED SEVERAL INTERNAL ORGANS. SHE IS CRITICAL.
THIS IS JOCSESTRA DAL, SON OF THE HIGH DAL OF CARBEAU. HE IS UNHARMED...I CONGRATULATE LLANS IVO...BUT SUFFERS FROM PROFOUND SHOCK.
AND FINALLY, THIS IS GIMSESTRA DAL, DAUGHTER OF THE HIGH DAL OF CARBEAU, SISTER AND BONDED SEXUAL LIAISON OF JOCSESTRA DAL.
YOUR CLUSTER-WIFE, UXU CHIL, AN APPRENTICE WARPSMITH, CRUSHED HER BENEATH A BLOCK OF MASONRY. SHE IS DEAD.
WHAT ARE YOUR FEELINGS ON THIS MATTER, AZA CHORN?
I AM AT FAULT. I AM IMPALED UPON MY OWN WORTHLESSNESS.

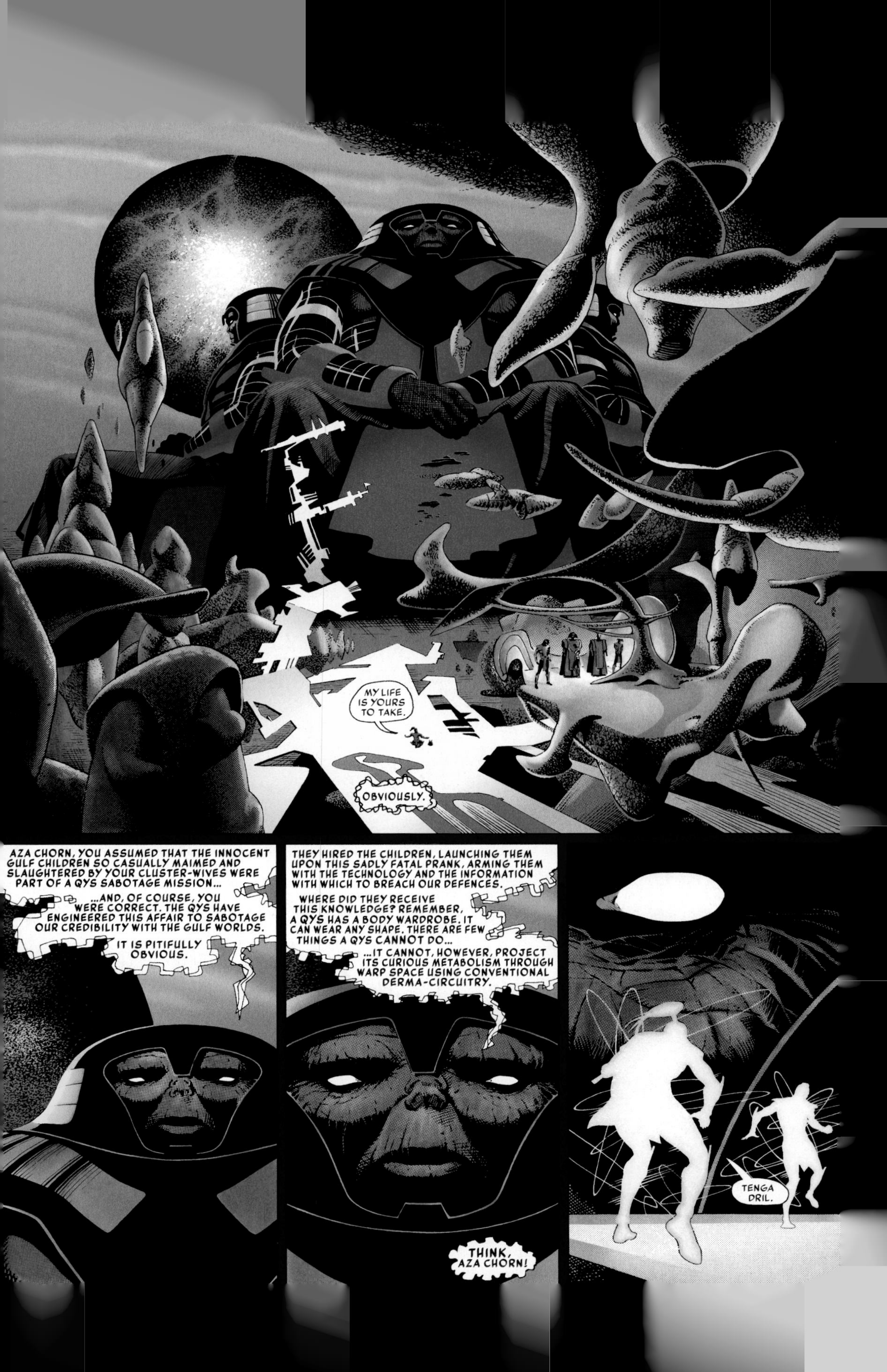
MY LIFE IS YOURS TO TAKE.
OBVIOUSLY.
AZA CHORN, YOU ASSUMED THAT THE INNOCENT GULF CHILDREN SO CASUALLY MAIMED AND SLAUGHTERED BY YOUR CLUSTER-WIVES WERE PART OF A QYS SABOTAGE MISSION...
...AND, OF COURSE, YOU WERE CORRECT. THE QYS HAVE ENGINEERED THIS AFFAIR TO SABOTAGE OUR CREDIBILITY WITH THE GULF WORLDS.
IT IS PITIFULLY OBVIOUS.
THEY HIRED THE CHILDREN, LAUNCHING THEM UPON THIS SADLY FATAL PRANK, ARMING THEM WITH THE TECHNOLOGY AND THE INFORMATION WITH WHICH TO BREACH OUR DEFENCES.
WHERE DID THEY RECEIVE THIS KNOWLEDGE? REMEMBER, A QYS HAS A BODY WARDROBE. IT CAN WEAR ANY SHAPE. THERE ARE FEW THINGS A QYS CANNOT DO...
...IT CANNOT, HOWEVER, PROJECT ITS CURIOUS METABOLISM THROUGH WARP SPACE USING CONVENTIONAL DERMA-CIRCUITRY.
THINK, AZA CHORN!
TENGA DRIL.

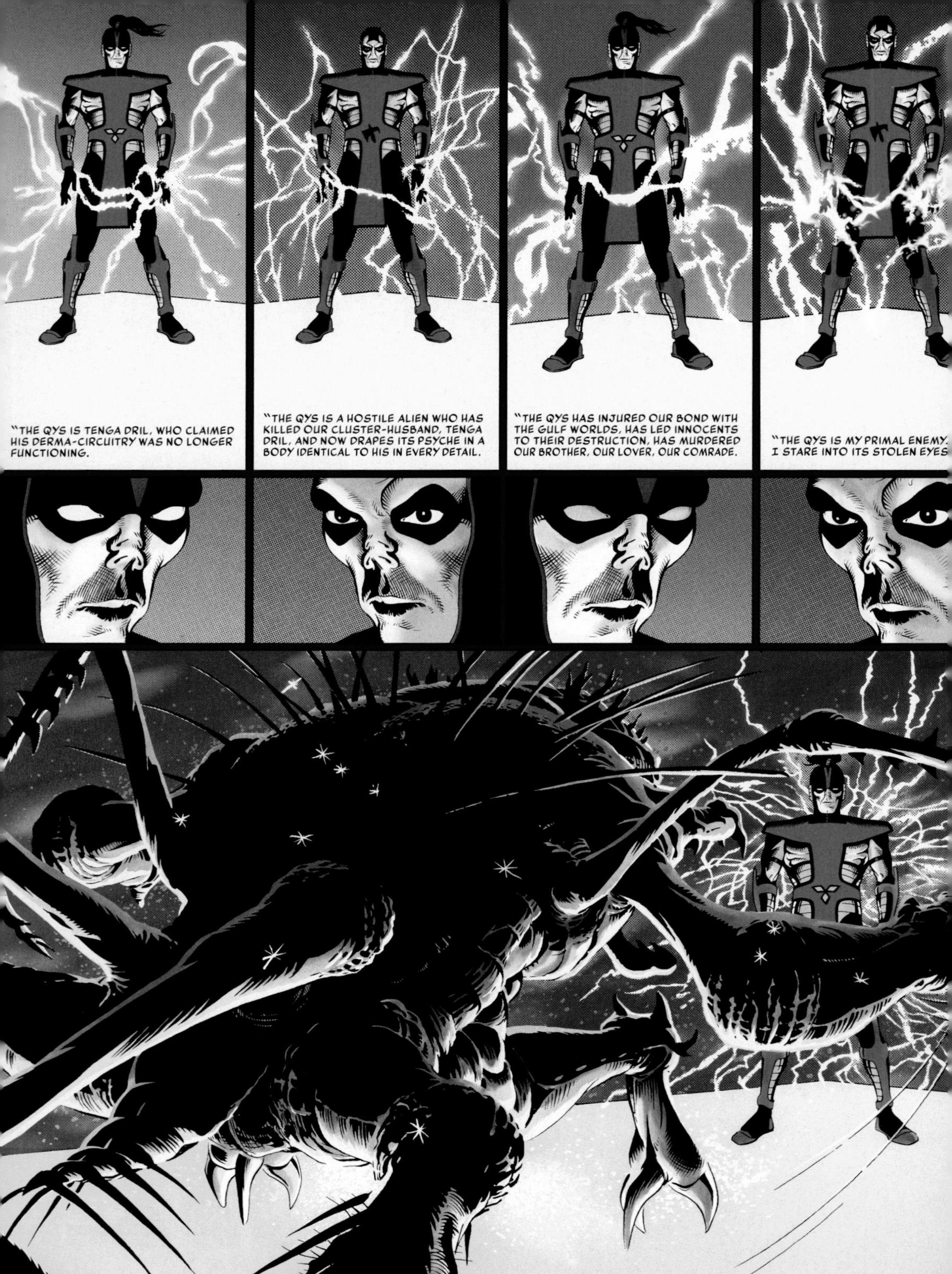
"THE QYS IS TENGA DRIL, WHO CLAIMED HIS DERMA-CIRCUITRY WAS NO LONGER FUNCTIONING.
"THE QYS IS A HOSTILE ALIEN WHO HAS KILLED OUR CLUSTER-HUSBAND, TENGA DRIL, AND NOW DRAPES ITS PSYCHE IN A BODY IDENTICAL TO HIS IN EVERY DETAIL.
"THE QYS HAS INJURED OUR BOND WITH THE GULF WORLDS, HAS LED INNOCENTS TO THEIR DESTRUCTION, HAS MURDERED OUR BROTHER, OUR LOVER, OUR COMRADE.
"THE QYS IS MY PRIMAL ENEMY. I STARE INTO ITS STOLEN EYES

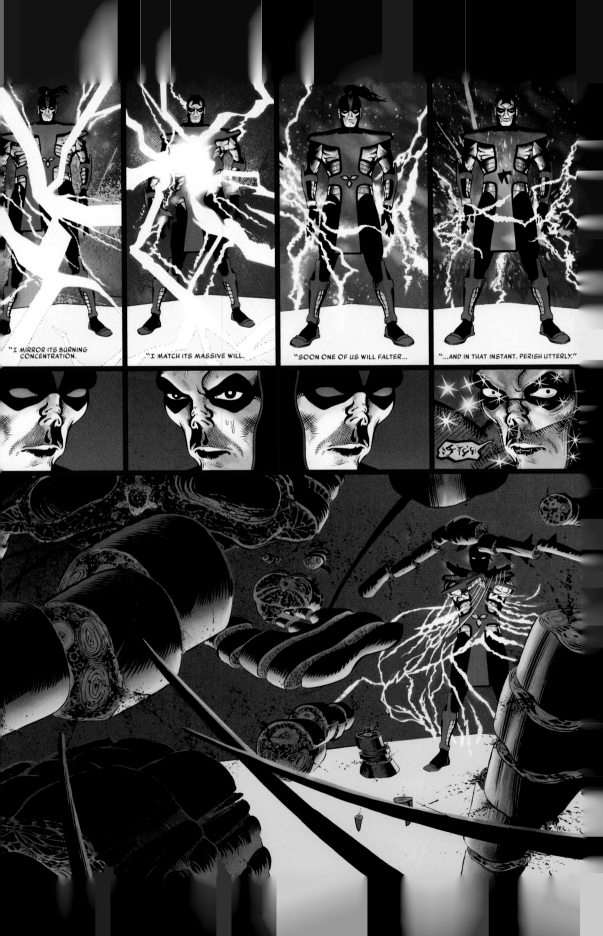

"I MIRROR ITS BURNING CONCENTRATION.

"I MATCH ITS MASSIVE WILL.

"SOON ONE OF US WILL FALTER...

"...AND IN THAT INSTANT, PERISH UTTERLY."

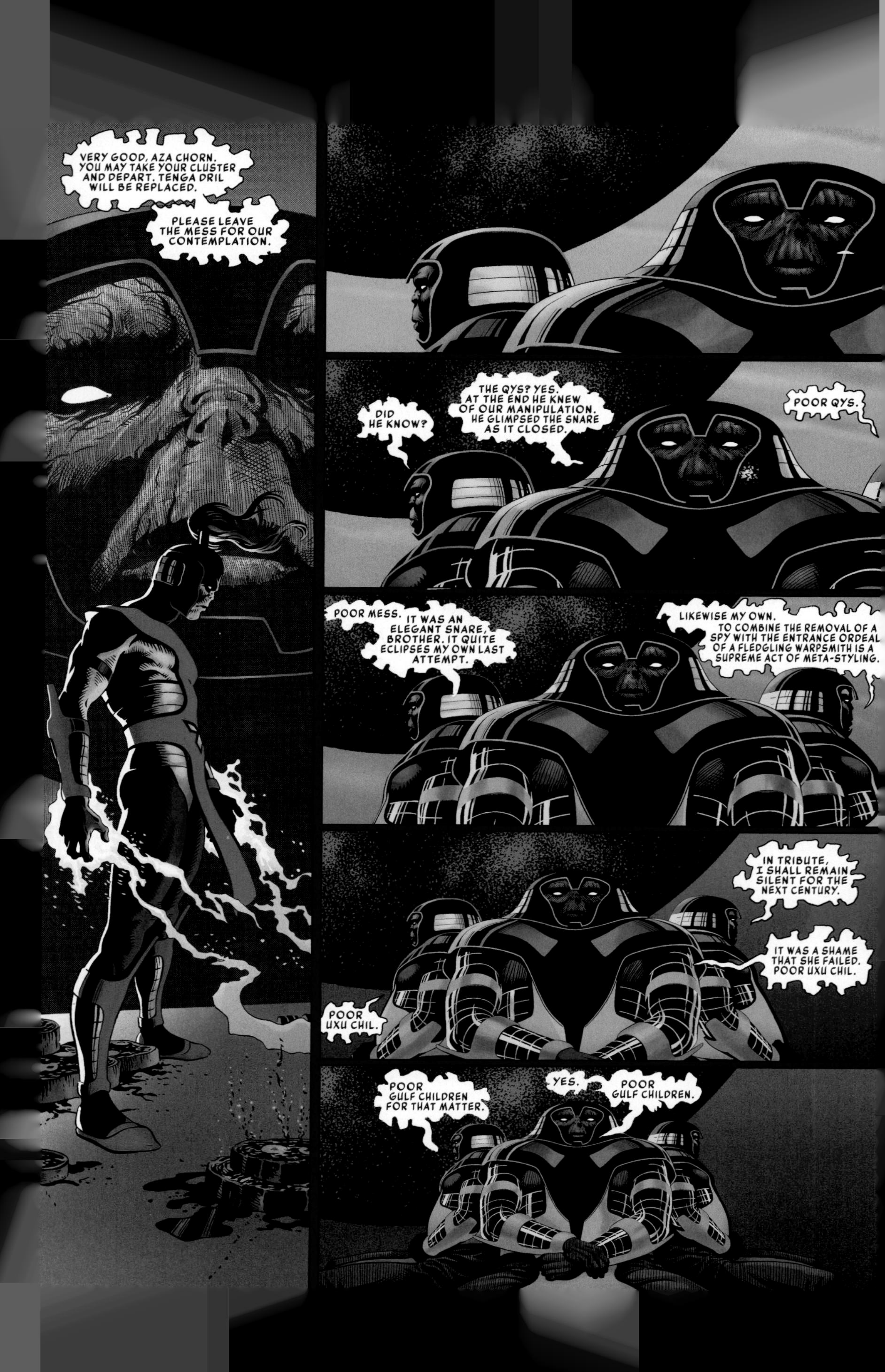
VERY GOOD, AZA CHORN. YOU MAY TAKE YOUR CLUSTER AND DEPART. TENGA DRIL WILL BE REPLACED.
PLEASE LEAVE THE MESS FOR OUR CONTEMPLATION.
DID HE KNOW?
THE QYS? YES. AT THE END HE KNEW OF OUR MANIPULATION. HE GLIMPSED THE SNARE AS IT CLOSED.
POOR QYS.
POOR MESS.
IT WAS AN ELEGANT SNARE, BROTHER. IT QUITE ECLIPSES MY OWN LAST ATTEMPT.
LIKEWISE MY OWN.
TO COMBINE THE REMOVAL OF A SPY WITH THE ENTRANCE ORDEAL OF A FLEDGLING WARPSMITH IS A SUPREME ACT OF META-STYLING.
IN TRIBUTE, I SHALL REMAIN SILENT FOR THE NEXT CENTURY.
IT WAS A SHAME THAT SHE FAILED. POOR UXU CHIL.
POOR UXU CHIL.
POOR GULF CHILDREN FOR THAT MATTER.
YES.
POOR GULF CHILDREN.

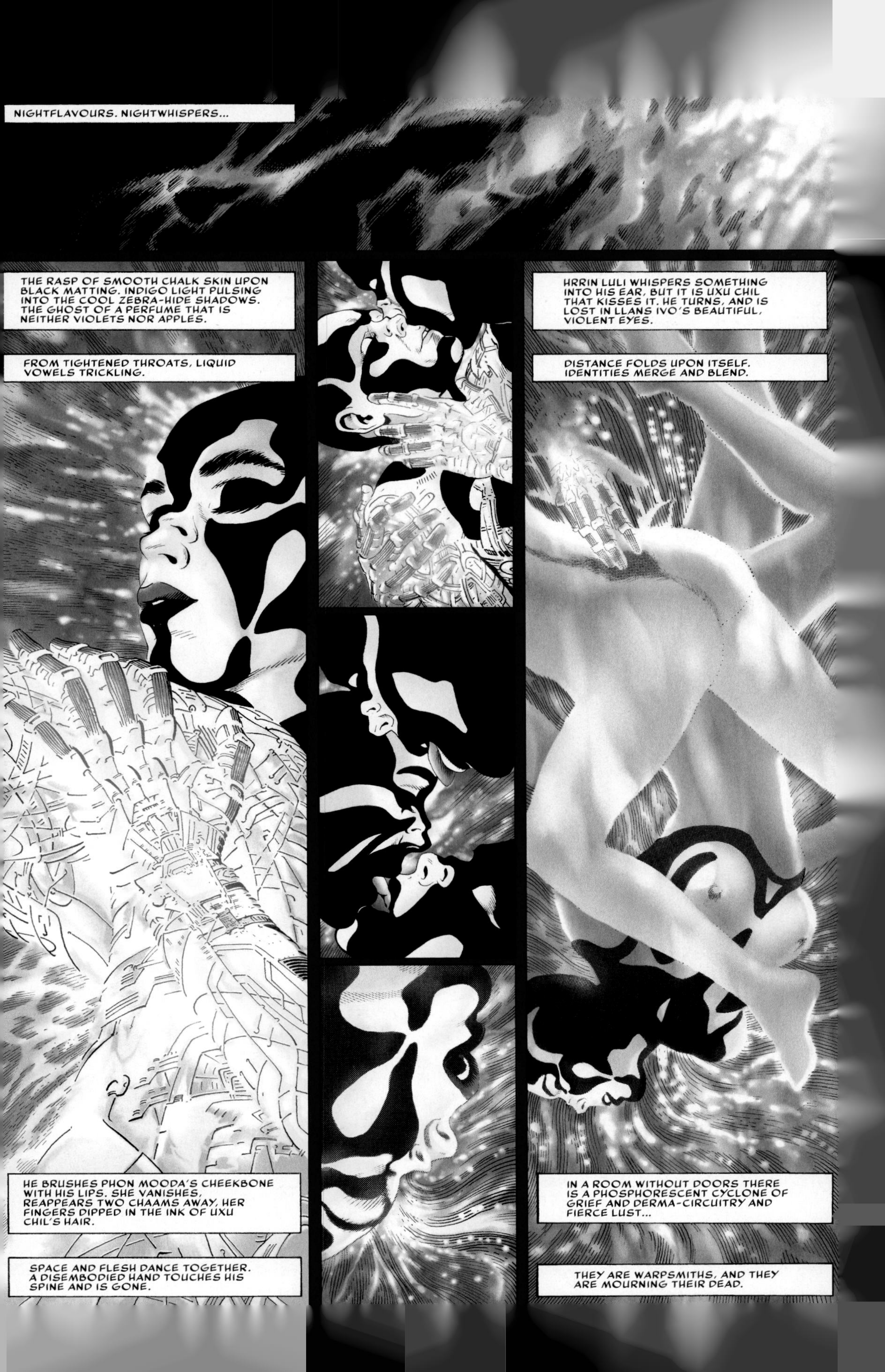
NIGHTFLAVOURS. NIGHTWHISPERS...
THE RASP OF SMOOTH CHALK SKIN UPON BLACK MATTING. INDIGO LIGHT PULSING INTO THE COOL ZEBRA-HIDE SHADOWS. THE GHOST OF A PERFUME THAT IS NEITHER VIOLETS NOR APPLES.
FROM TIGHTENED THROATS, LIQUID VOWELS TRICKLING.
HE BRUSHES PHON MOODA'S CHEEKBONE WITH HIS LIPS. SHE VANISHES, REAPPEARS TWO CHAAMS AWAY, HER FINGERS DIPPED IN THE INK OF UXU CHIL'S HAIR.
SPACE AND FLESH DANCE TOGETHER. A DISEMBODIED HAND TOUCHES HIS SPINE AND IS GONE.
HRRIN LULI WHISPERS SOMETHING INTO HIS EAR, BUT IT IS UXU CHIL THAT KISSES IT. HE TURNS, AND IS LOST IN LLANS IVO'S BEAUTIFUL, VIOLENT EYES.
DISTANCE FOLDS UPON ITSELF. IDENTITIES MERGE AND BLEND.
IN A ROOM WITHOUT DOORS THERE IS A PHOSPHORESCENT CYCLONE OF GRIEF AND DERMA-CIRCUITRY AND FIERCE LUST...
THEY ARE WARPSMITHS, AND THEY ARE MOURNING THEIR DEAD.

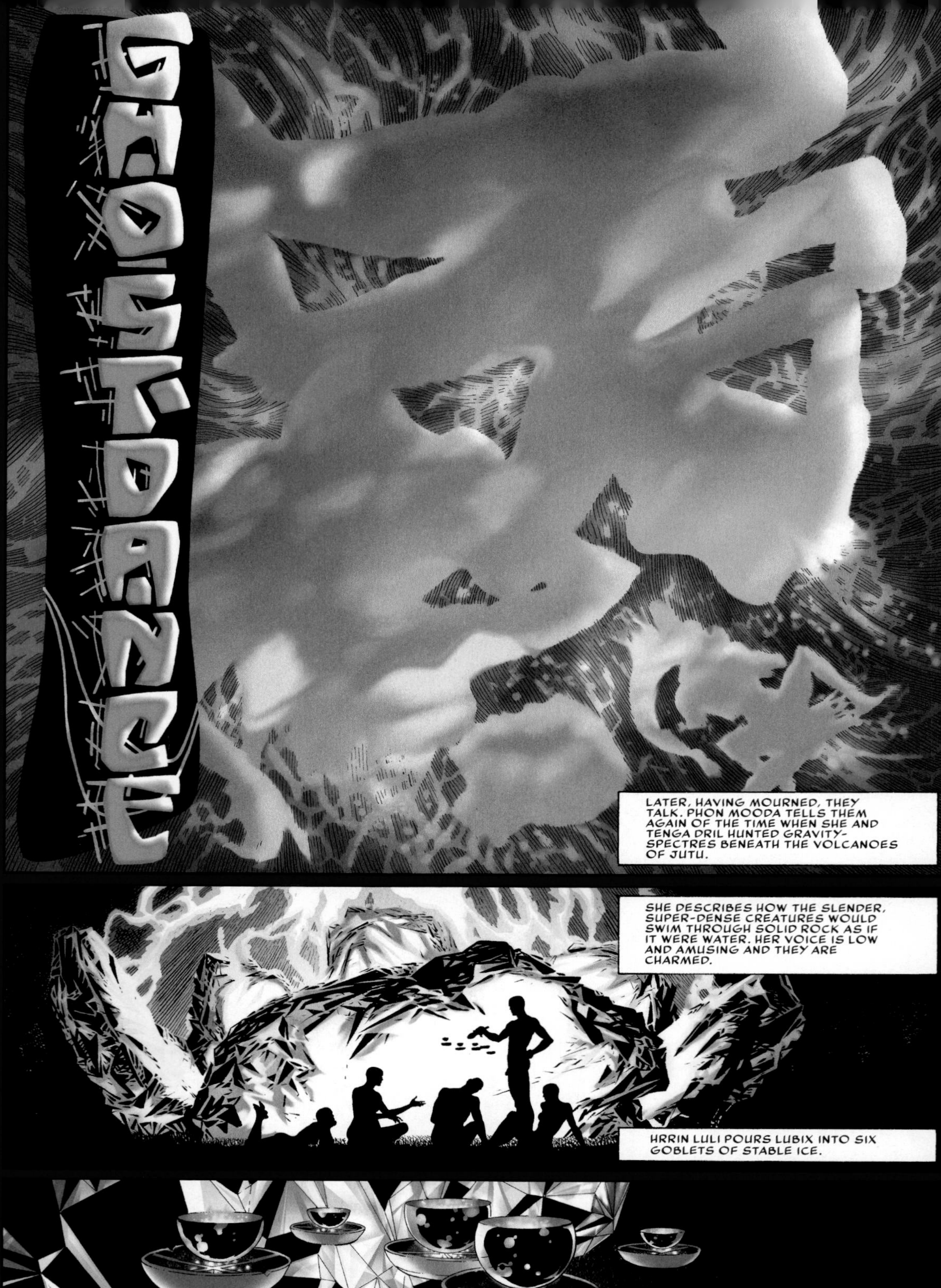
GHOST DANCE
LATER, HAVING MOURNED, THEY TALK. PHON MOODA TELLS THEM AGAIN OF THE TIME WHEN SHE AND TENGA DRIL HUNTED GRAVITY-SPECTRES BENEATH THE VOLCANOES OF JUTU.
SHE DESCRIBES HOW THE SLENDER, SUPER-DENSE CREATURES WOULD SWIM THROUGH SOLID ROCK AS IF IT WERE WATER. HER VOICE IS LOW AND AMUSING AND THEY ARE CHARMED.
HRRIN LULI POURS LUBIX INTO SIX GOBLETS OF STABLE ICE.
AND THEN THEY RETURN TO WORK.

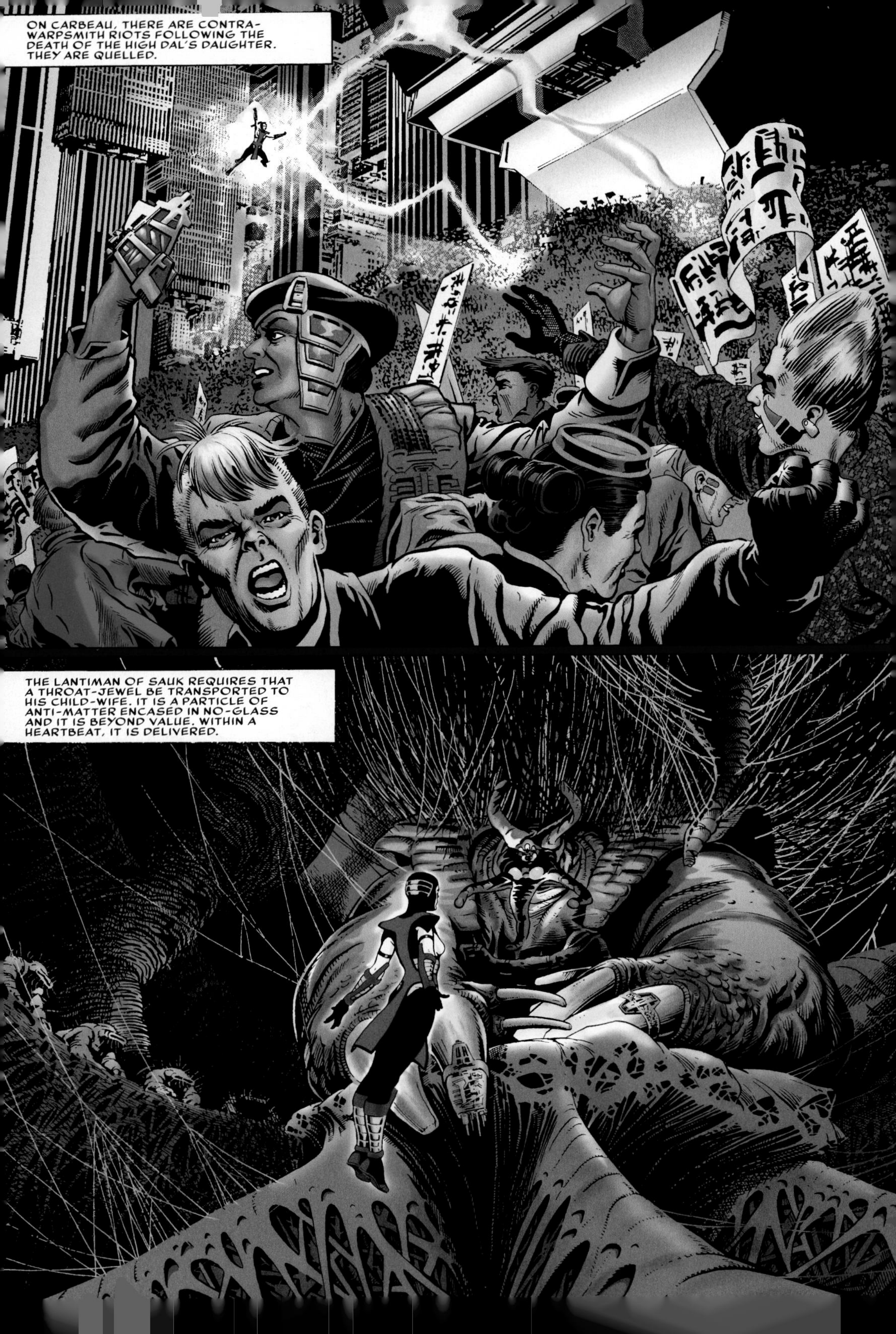
ON CARBEAU, THERE ARE CONTRA-WARPSMITH RIOTS FOLLOWING THE DEATH OF THE HIGH DAL'S DAUGHTER. THEY ARE QUELLED.
THE LANTIMAN OF SAUK REQUIRES THAT A THROAT-JEWEL BE TRANSPORTED TO HIS CHILD-WIFE. IT IS A PARTICLE OF ANTI-MATTER ENCASED IN NO-GLASS AND IT IS BEYOND VALUE. WITHIN A HEARTBEAT, IT IS DELIVERED.

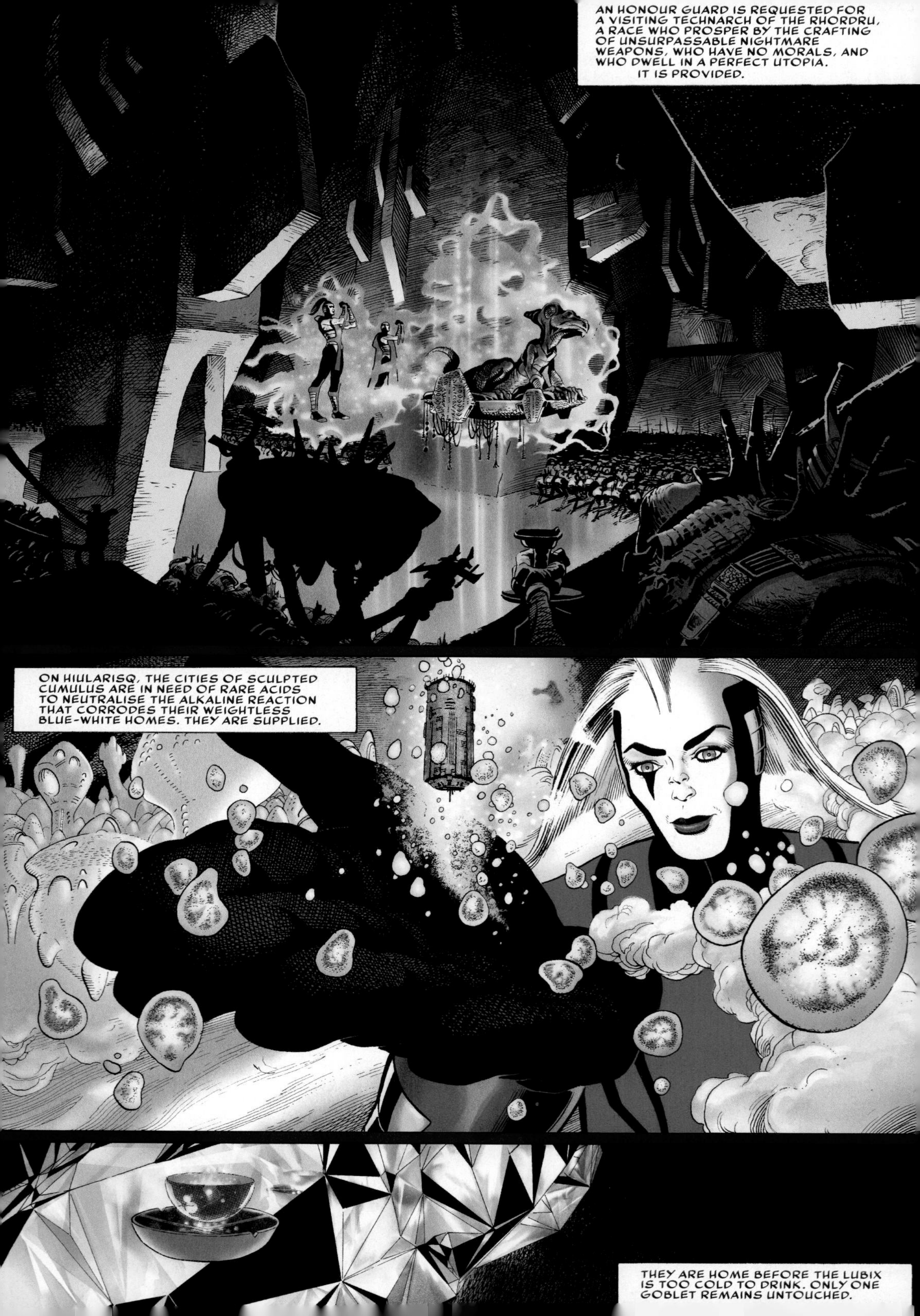
AN HONOUR GUARD IS REQUESTED FOR A VISITING TECHNARCH OF THE RHORDRU, A RACE WHO PROSPER BY THE CRAFTING OF UNSURPASSABLE NIGHTMARE WEAPONS, WHO HAVE NO MORALS, AND WHO DWELL IN A PERFECT UTOPIA.
IT IS PROVIDED.
ON HIULARISQ, THE CITIES OF SCULPTED CUMULUS ARE IN NEED OF RARE ACIDS TO NEUTRALISE THE ALKALINE REACTION THAT CORRODES THEIR WEIGHTLESS BLUE-WHITE HOMES. THEY ARE SUPPLIED.
THEY ARE HOME BEFORE THE LUBIX IS TOO COLD TO DRINK. ONLY ONE GOBLET REMAINS UNTOUCHED.

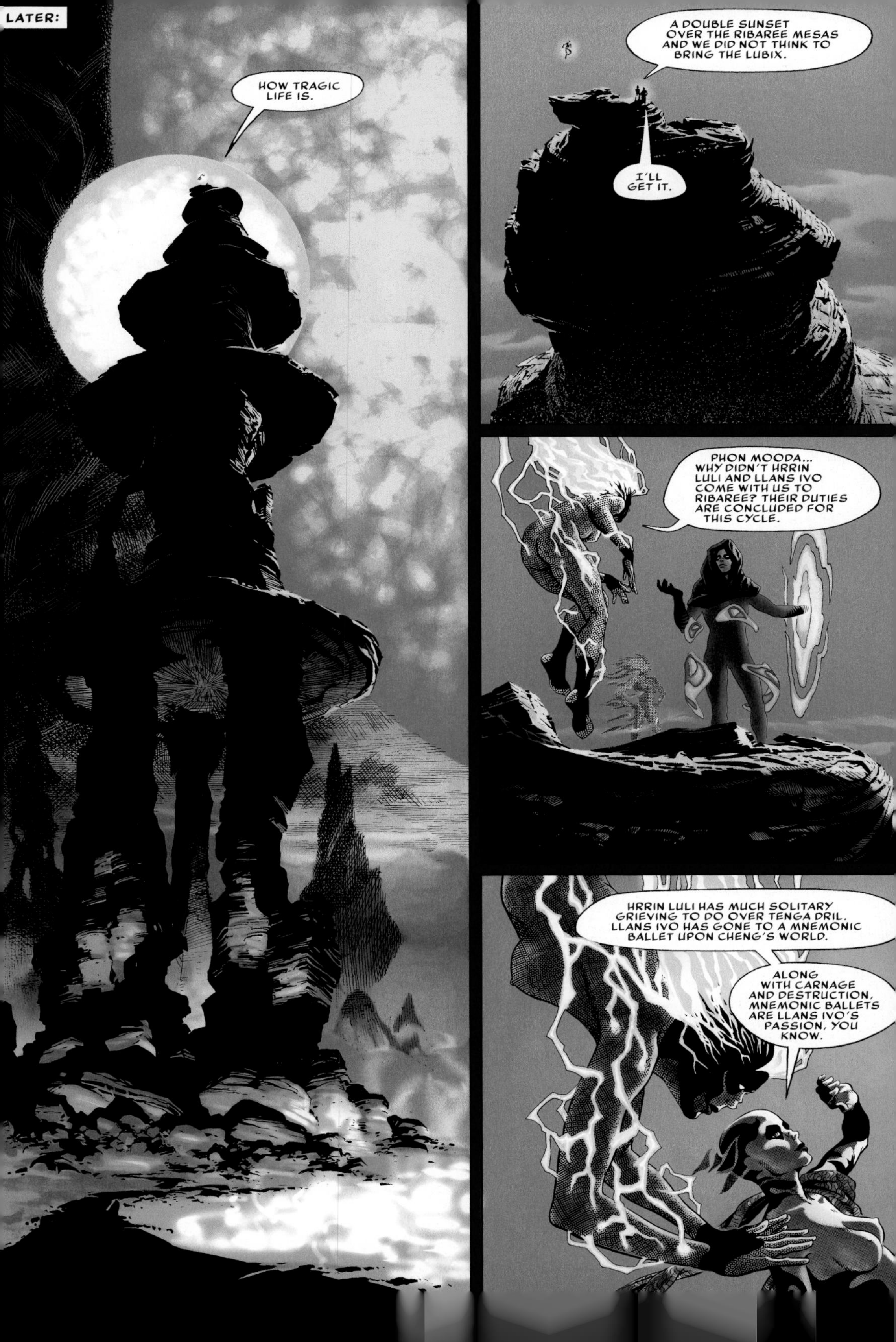
LATER:
HOW TRAGIC LIFE IS.
A DOUBLE SUNSET OVER THE RIBAREE MESAS AND WE DID NOT THINK TO BRING THE LUBIX.
I'LL GET IT.
PHON MOODA... WHY DIDN'T HRRIN LULI AND LLANS IVO COME WITH US TO RIBAREE? THEIR DUTIES ARE CONCLUDED FOR THIS CYCLE.
HRRIN LULI HAS MUCH SOLITARY GRIEVING TO DO OVER TENGA DRIL. LLANS IVO HAS GONE TO A MNEMONIC BALLET UPON CHENG'S WORLD.
ALONG WITH CARNAGE AND DESTRUCTION, MNEMONIC BALLETS ARE LLANS IVO'S PASSION, YOU KNOW.

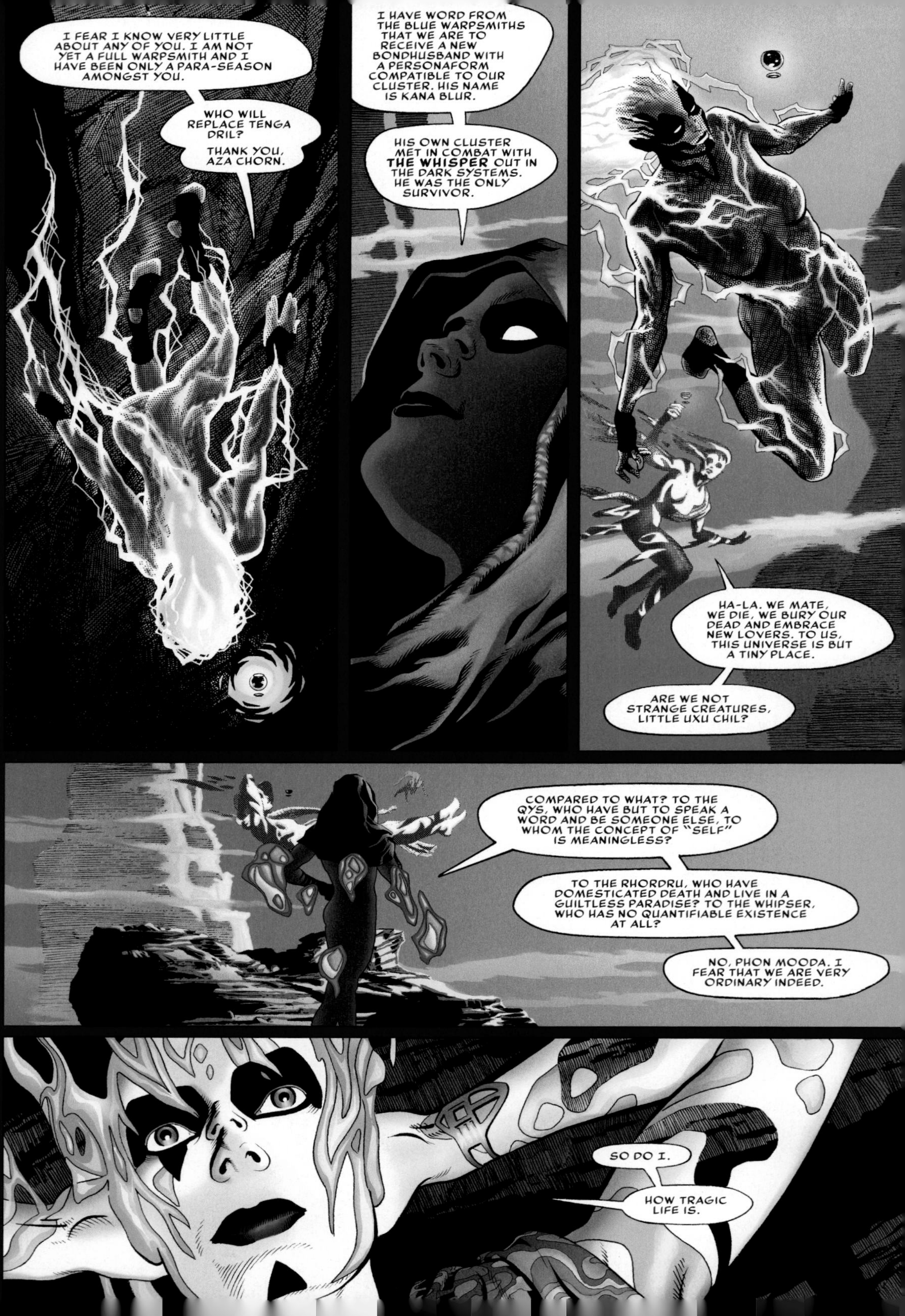

I FEAR I KNOW VERY LITTLE ABOUT ANY OF YOU. I AM NOT YET A FULL WARPSMITH AND I HAVE BEEN ONLY A PARA-SEASON AMONGST YOU.
WHO WILL REPLACE TENGA DRIL?
THANK YOU, AZA CHORN.
I HAVE WORD FROM THE BLUE WARPSMITHS THAT WE ARE TO RECEIVE A NEW BONDHUSBAND WITH A PERSONAFORM COMPATIBLE TO OUR CLUSTER. HIS NAME IS KANA BLUR.
HIS OWN CLUSTER MET IN COMBAT WITH THE WHISPER OUT IN THE DARK SYSTEMS. HE WAS THE ONLY SURVIVOR.
HA-LA. WE MATE, WE DIE, WE BURY OUR DEAD AND EMBRACE NEW LOVERS. TO US, THIS UNIVERSE IS BUT A TINY PLACE.
ARE WE NOT STRANGE CREATURES, LITTLE UXU CHIL?
COMPARED TO WHAT? TO THE QYS, WHO HAVE BUT TO SPEAK A WORD AND BE SOMEONE ELSE, TO WHOM THE CONCEPT OF "SELF" IS MEANINGLESS?
TO THE RHORDRU, WHO HAVE DOMESTICATED DEATH AND LIVE IN A GUILTLESS PARADISE? TO THE WHIPSER, WHO HAS NO QUANTIFIABLE EXISTENCE AT ALL?
NO, PHON MOODA. I FEAR THAT WE ARE VERY ORDINARY INDEED.
SO DO I.
HOW TRAGIC LIFE IS.

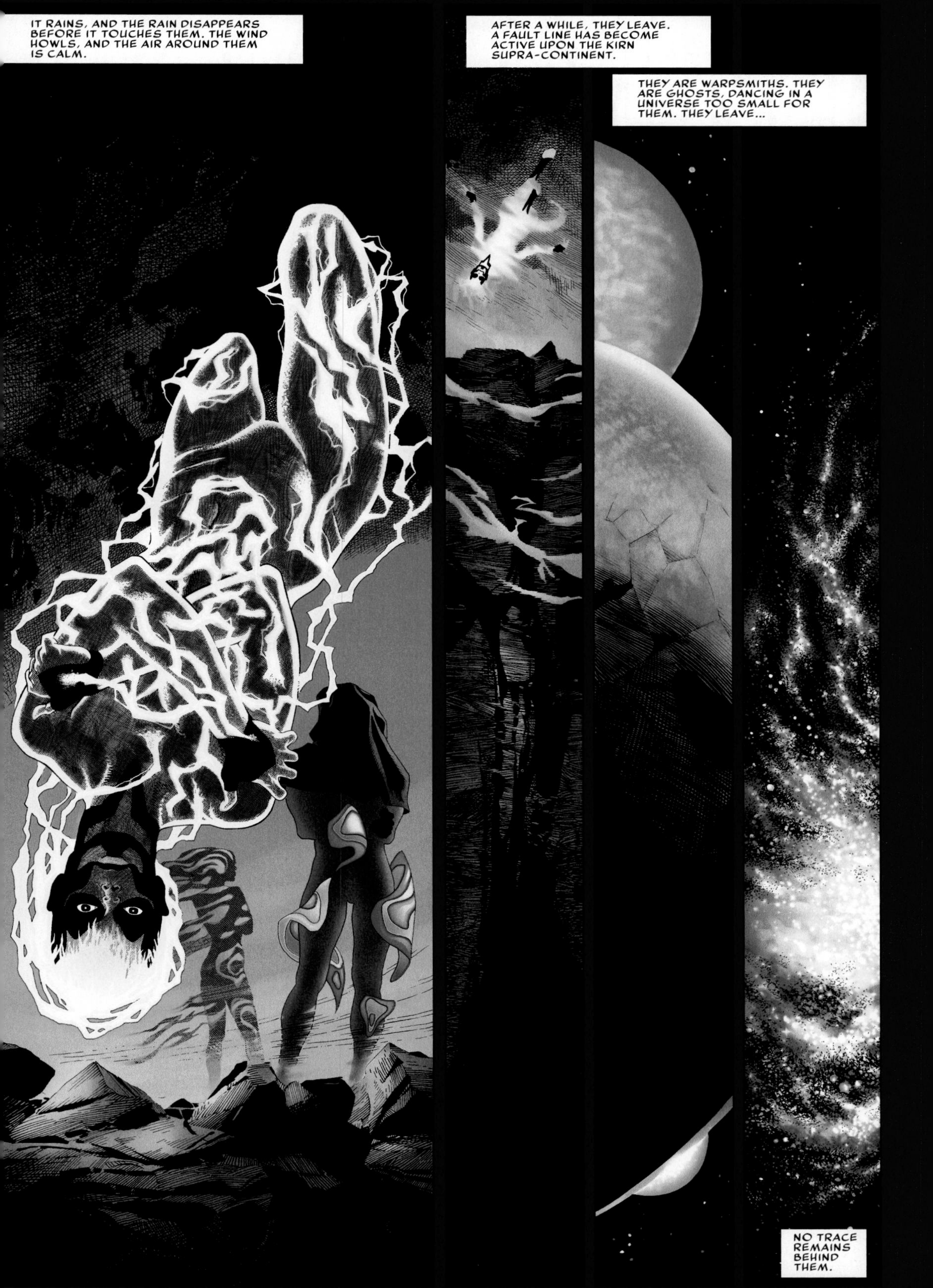
IT RAINS, AND THE RAIN DISAPPEARS BEFORE IT TOUCHES THEM. THE WIND HOWLS, AND THE AIR AROUND THEM IS CALM.
AFTER A WHILE, THEY LEAVE. A FAULT LINE HAS BECOME ACTIVE UPON THE KIRN SUPRA-CONTINENT.
THEY ARE WARPSMITHS. THEY ARE GHOSTS, DANCING IN A UNIVERSE TOO SMALL FOR THEM. THEY LEAVE...
NO TRACE REMAINS BEHIND THEM.

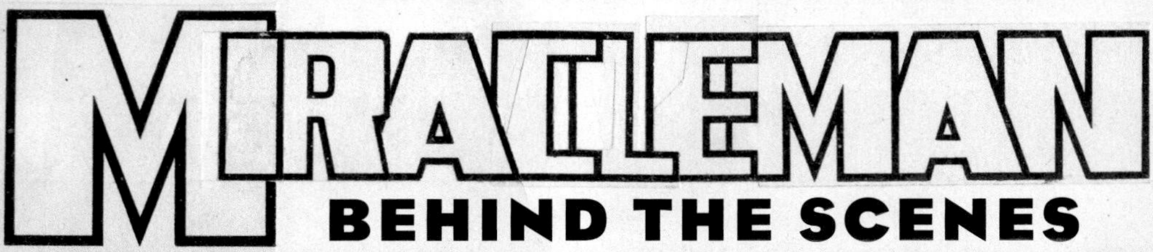

MIRACLEMAN BEHIND THE SCENES

The character that would come to be known as Miracleman originally debuted as "Marvelman" in *Marvelman* #25 (February 3, 1954). British comics pioneer Mick Anglo steered the Marvelman Family's adventures in *Marvelman*, *Young Marvelman* and *Marvelman Family* from 1954-1963 until their series' end.

When Marvelman was revived in 1982, new series artist Garry Leach updated the hero's costume with a modernized chest emblem and collar and a refined color scheme. Although certain the classic "sky blue" colors (top-right) would be the perfect fit, Garry explored a few variations including one that inverted the character's traditional color scheme.

ABOVE: The original production art Garry Leach stitched together to transform the "Marvelman" title logo into "Miracleman."

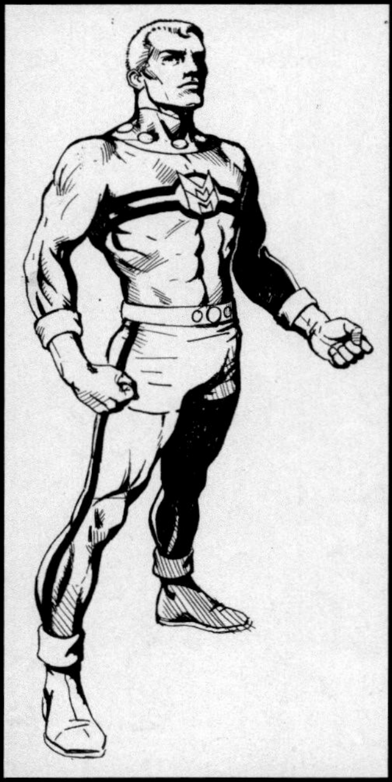

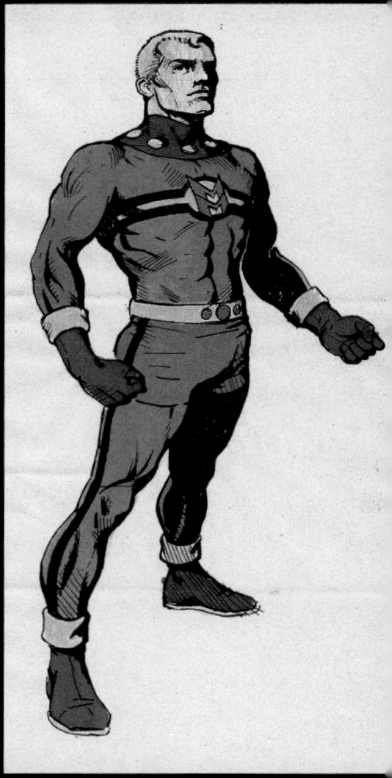

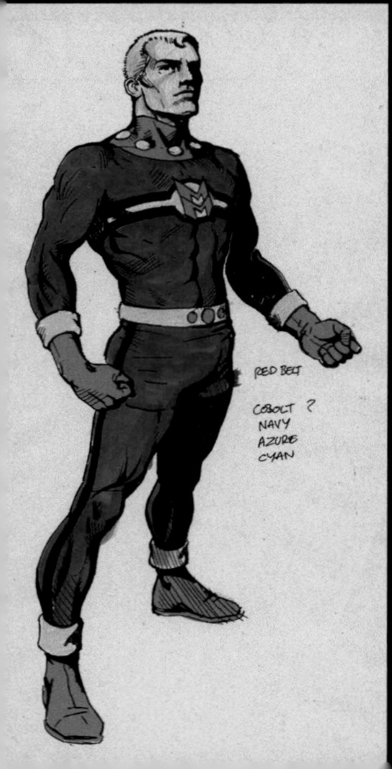
RED BELT
COBOLT ?
NAVY
AZURE
CYAN

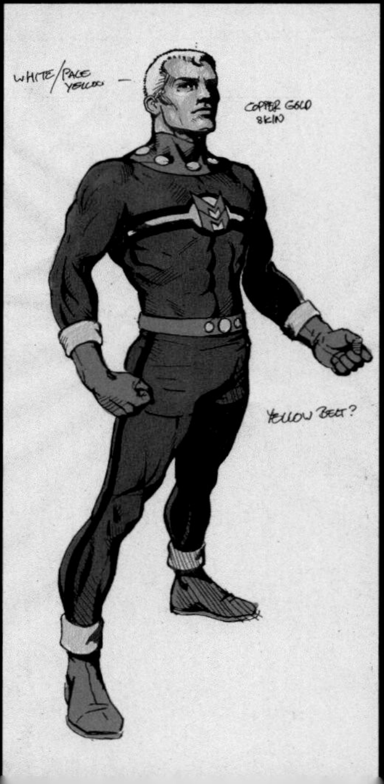
WHITE/PALE YELLOW
COPPER GOLD SKIN
YELLOW BELT?

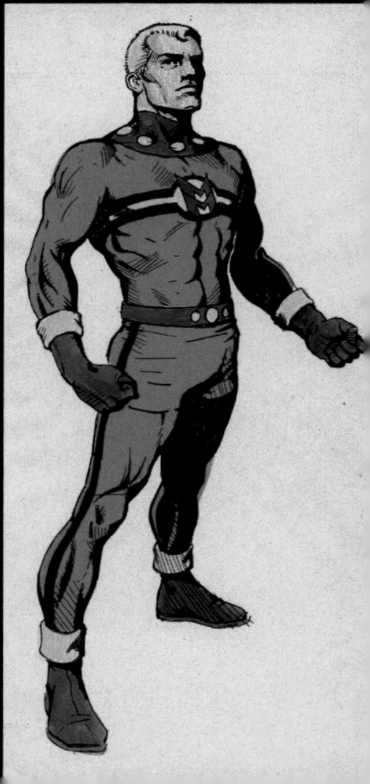

As part of his creative process, Garry produced loose "pencil prelim" sketches to explore pose, composition and design concepts. Once he hit upon an idea he liked, he would reduce or enlarge the prelim to the appropriate size and use it as a basis for the final pencils. This process allowed him to keep the final art boards "clean" for the application of the Letratone halftone screens.

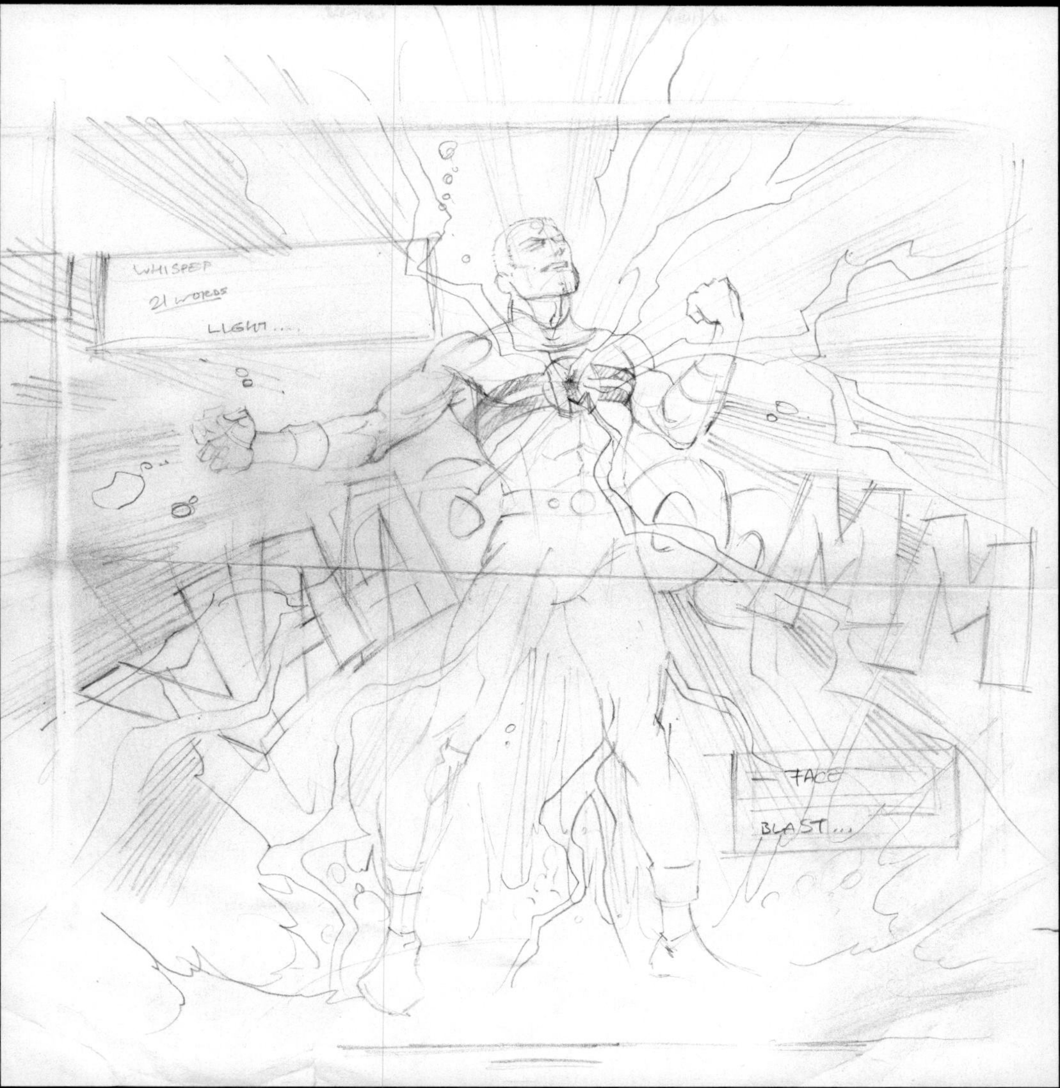
21 WORDS
LIGHT...
FACE
BLAST...

Miracleman reborn from *Warrior* #1, page 6, panel 2.

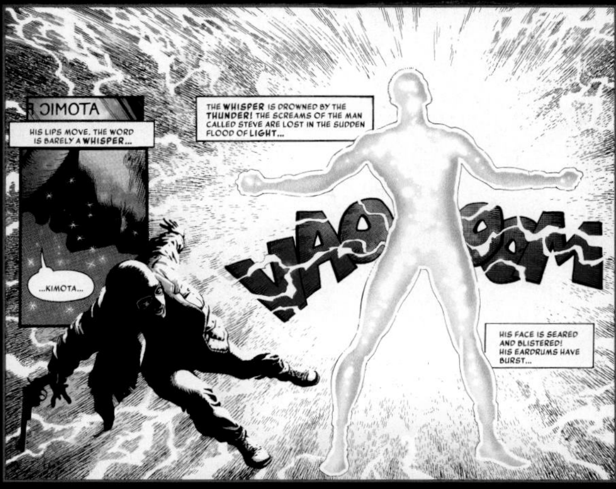
HIS LIPS MOVE. THE WORD IS BARELY A WHISPER...
...KIMOTA...
THE WHISPER IS DROWNED BY THE THUNDER! THE SCREAMS OF THE MAN CALLED STEVE ARE LOST IN THE SUDDEN FLOOD OF LIGHT...
HIS FACE IS SEARED AND BLISTERED! HIS EARDRUMS HAVE BURST...

Headlining his first cover since 1963, Miracleman burst from human "Kimota!" to superhuman in Garry Leach's beautifully rendered cover to *Warrior* #2 (April 1982).

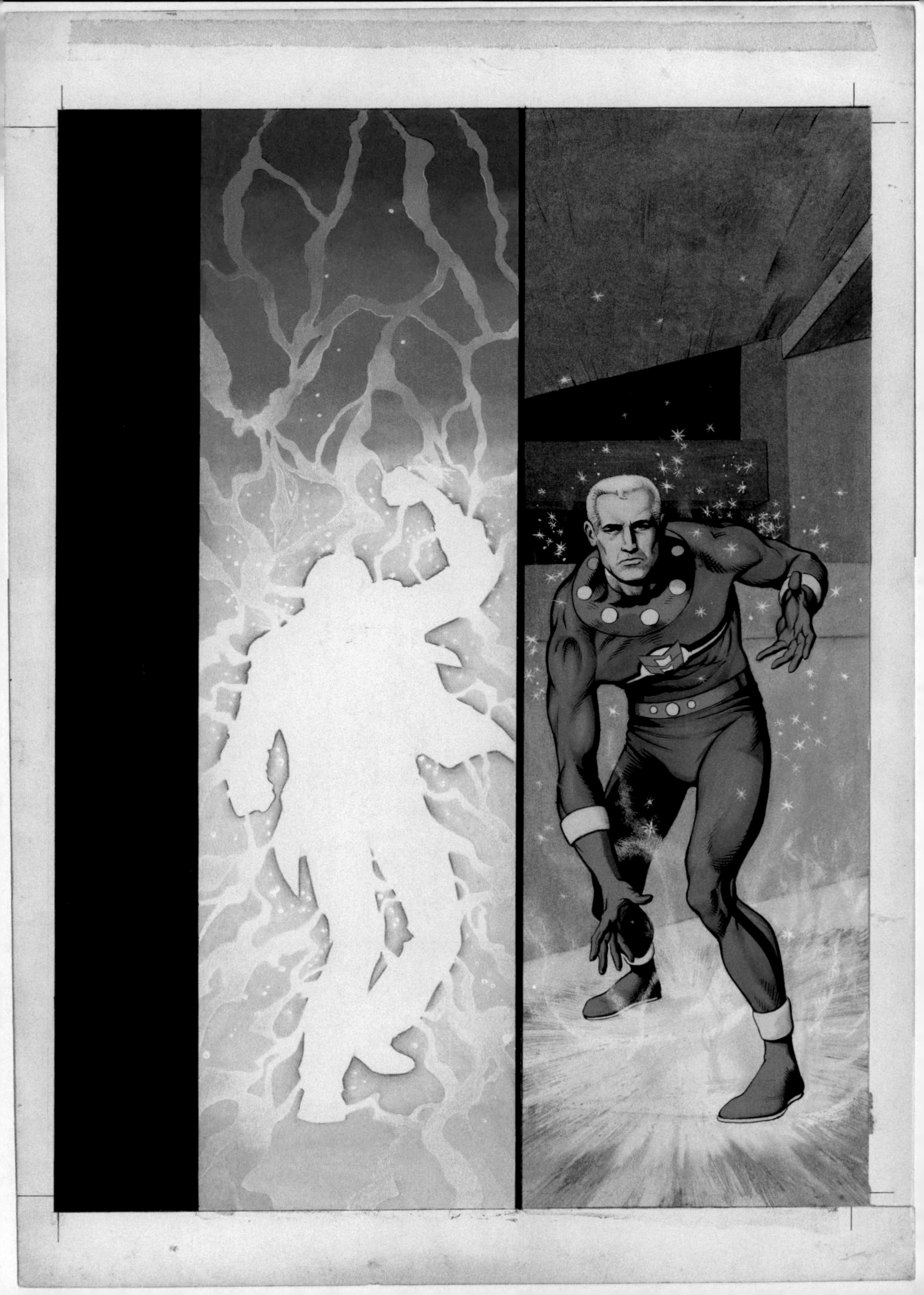

To provide the printer with instruction on how to handle the *Warrior* #2 cover's logos and design, the following vellum overlay was attached to the cover art board.

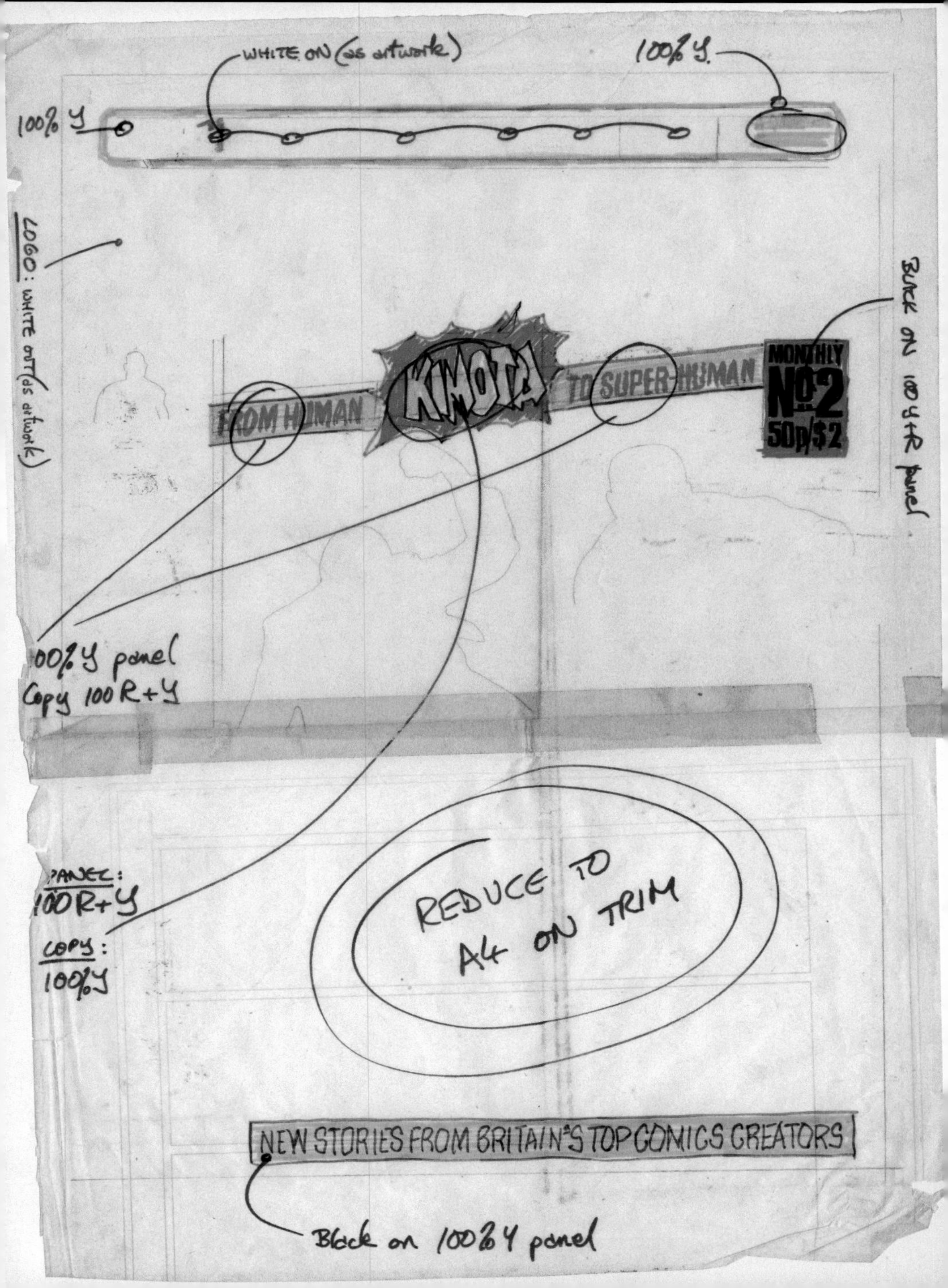

WHITE ON (as artwork)
100% Y.
100% Y
LOGO: WHITE OUT (as artwork)
BLACK ON 100 Y+R panel
FROM HUMAN
KIMOTA
TO SUPER-HUMAN
MONTHLY
No 2
50p/$2
00% Y panel
Copy 100 R+Y
PANEL:
100 R+Y
COPY:
100% Y
REDUCE TO A4 ON TRIM
NEW STORIES FROM BRITAIN'S TOP COMICS CREATORS
Black on 100% Y panel

Miracleman's origin is retold in this *Warrior* #2, page 3, panel 4 preliminary pencil rough by Garry Leach.

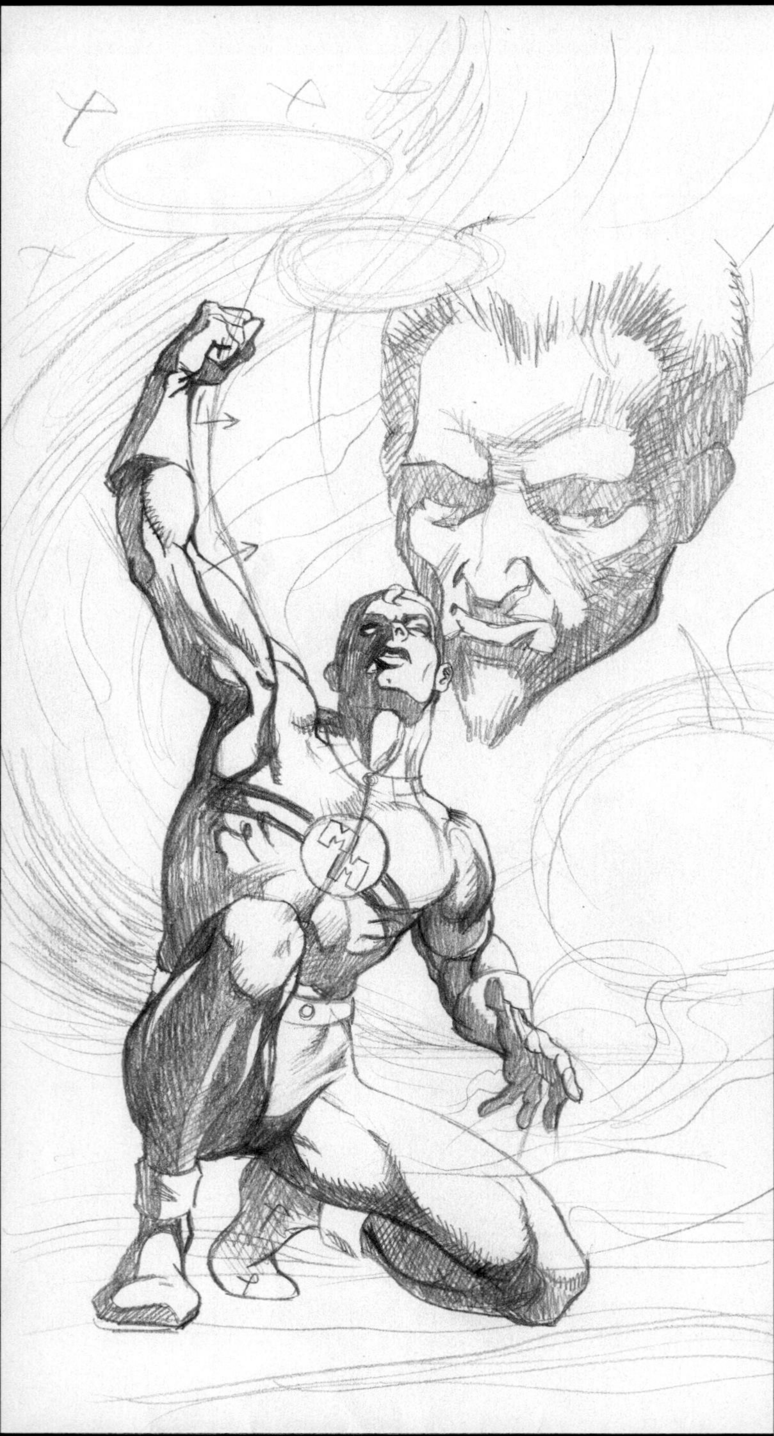

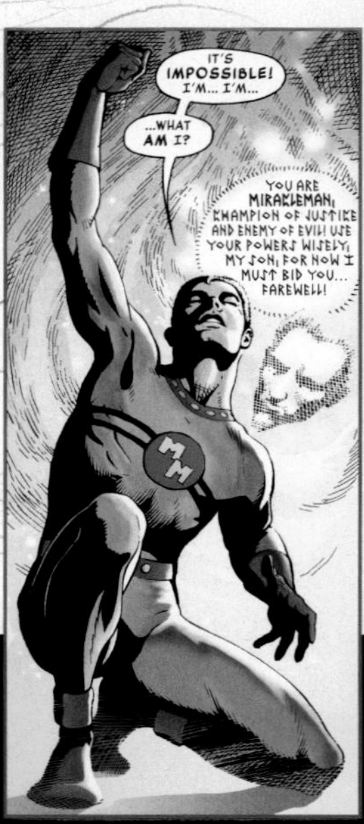
IT'S IMPOSSIBLE! I'M... I'M...
...WHAT AM I?
YOU ARE MIRACLEMAN, CHAMPION OF JUSTICE AND ENEMY OF EVIL! USE YOUR POWERS WISELY, MY SON, FOR NOW I MUST BID YOU... FAREWELL!

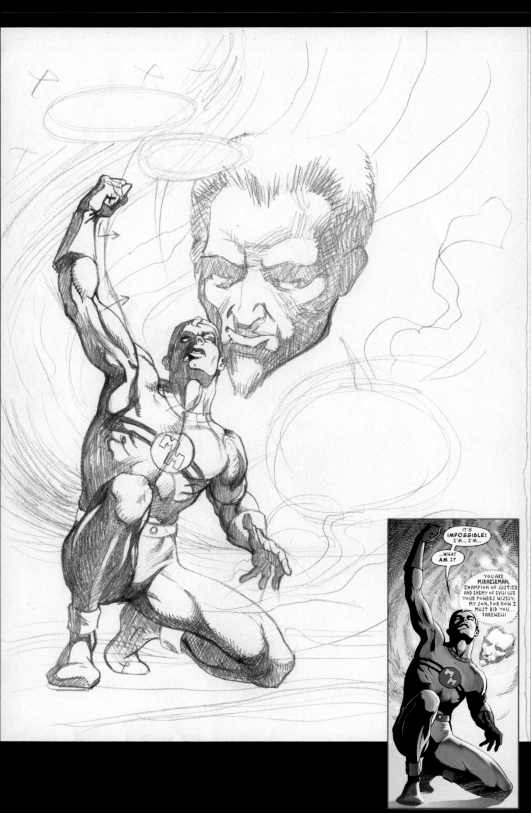

Kid Miracleman attacks the Subterranean from *Warrior* #2, page 4, panel 5. Preliminary pencil rough by Garry Leach.

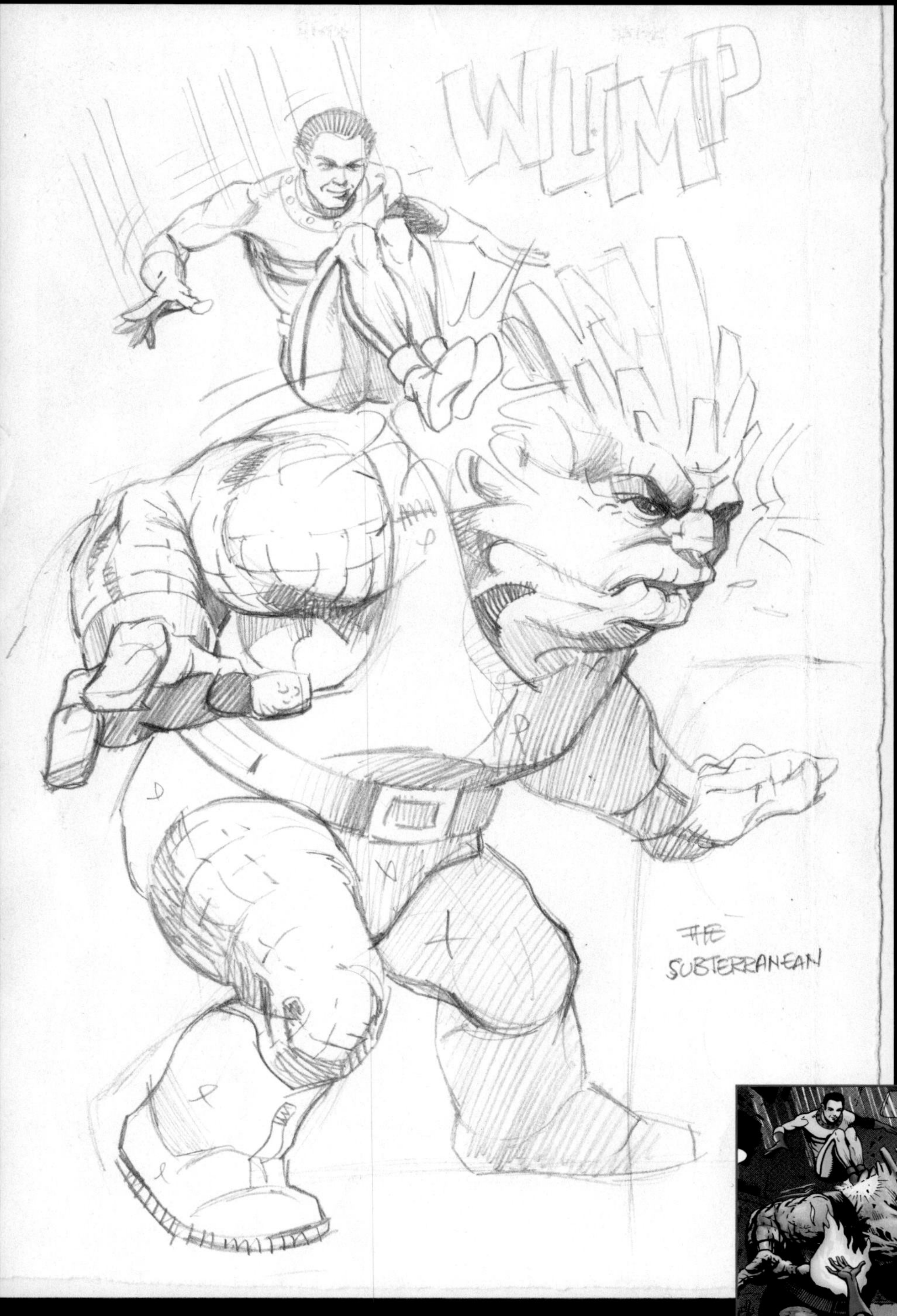
WUMP
THE SUBTERRANEAN

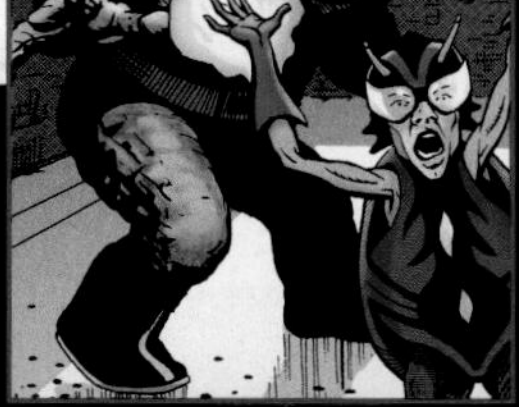

Growing up in the country, Garry was fond of fishing for newts. When it came time to create 1950s-style villains for *Warrior* #2's flashback scenes, he tapped those childhood experiences for "Newtilus." *Warrior* #2, page 4, panel 5 preliminary pencil rough by Garry Leach.

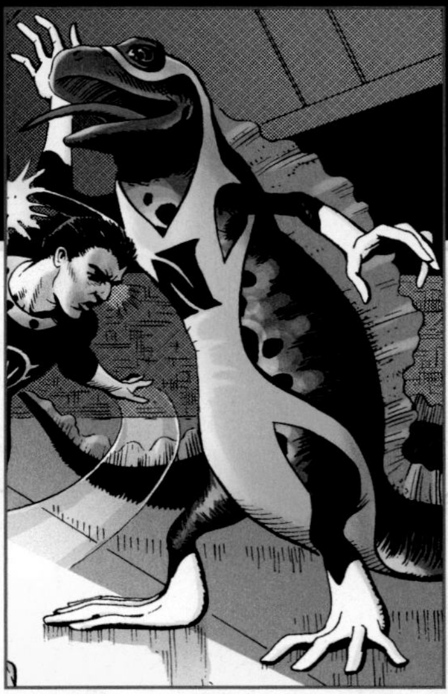

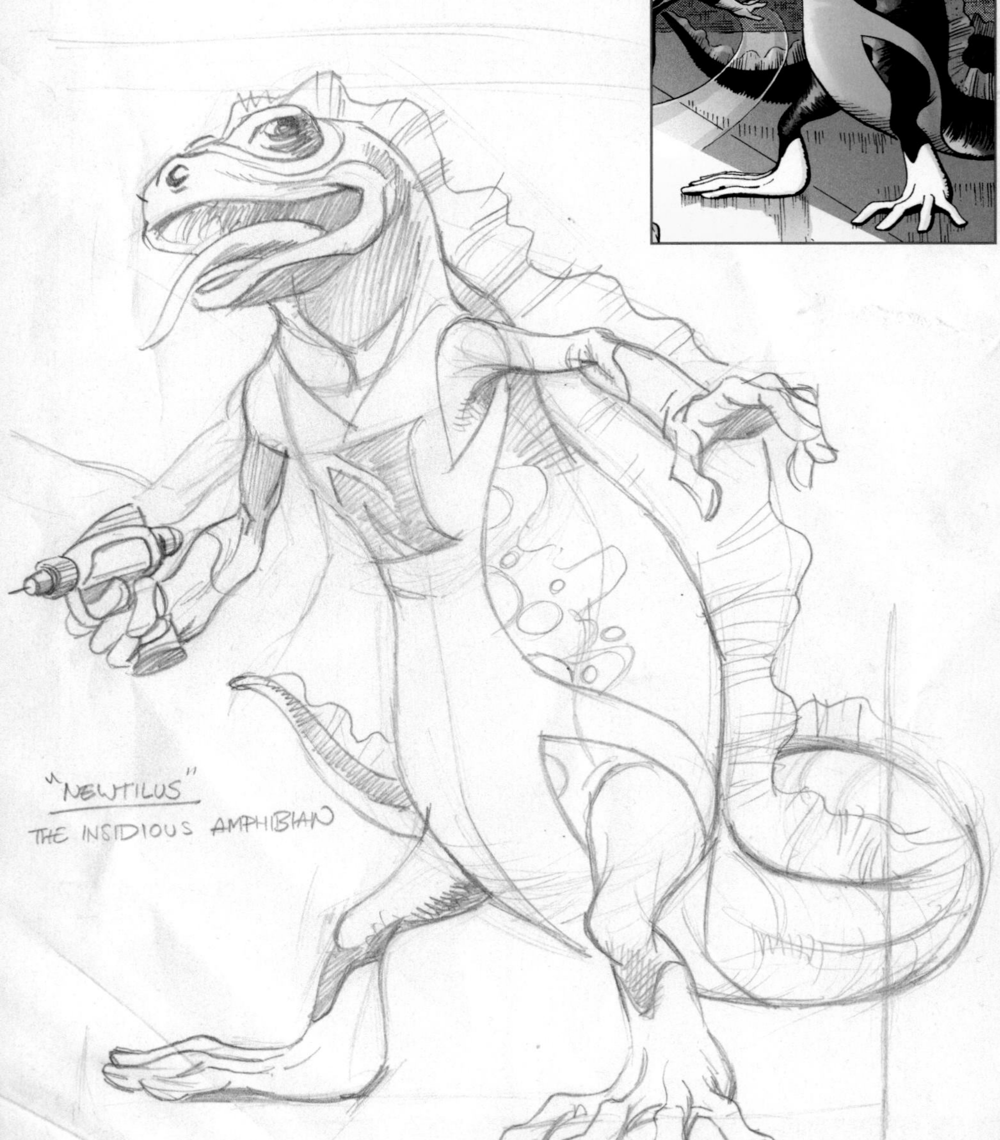
"NEWTILUS"
THE INSIDIOUS AMPHIBIAN

Warrior #3, page 1 original artwork, pencil, India ink and Letratone on illustration board by Garry Leach.

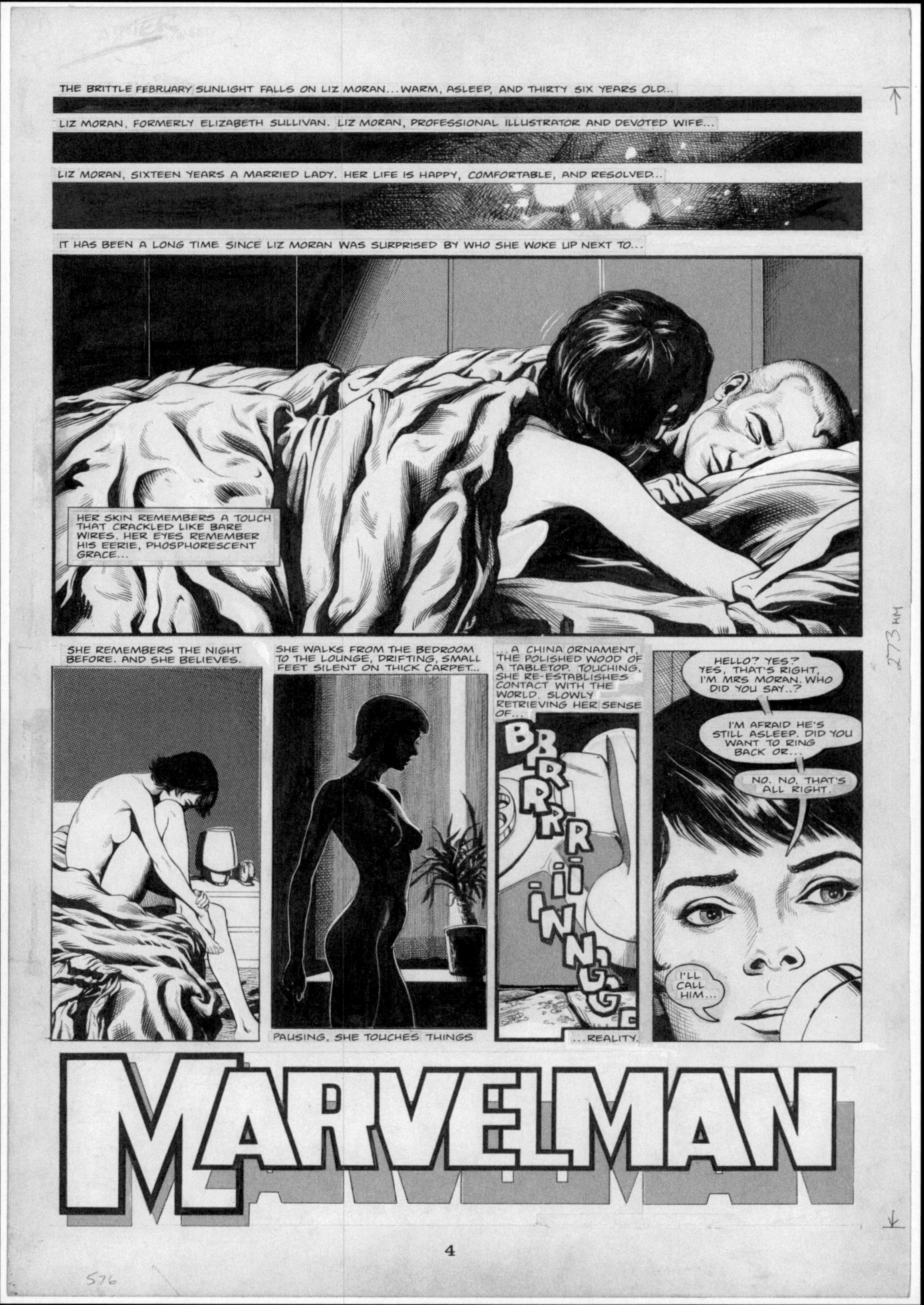
THE BRITTLE FEBRUARY SUNLIGHT FALLS ON LIZ MORAN... WARM, ASLEEP, AND THIRTY SIX YEARS OLD...
LIZ MORAN, FORMERLY ELIZABETH SULLIVAN. LIZ MORAN, PROFESSIONAL ILLUSTRATOR AND DEVOTED WIFE...
LIZ MORAN, SIXTEEN YEARS A MARRIED LADY. HER LIFE IS HAPPY, COMFORTABLE, AND RESOLVED...
IT HAS BEEN A LONG TIME SINCE LIZ MORAN WAS SURPRISED BY WHO SHE WOKE UP NEXT TO...
HER SKIN REMEMBERS A TOUCH THAT CRACKLED LIKE BARE WIRES. HER EYES REMEMBER HIS EERIE, PHOSPHORESCENT GRACE...
SHE REMEMBERS THE NIGHT BEFORE. AND SHE BELIEVES.
SHE WALKS FROM THE BEDROOM TO THE LOUNGE, DRIFTING, SMALL FEET SILENT ON THICK CARPET...
PAUSING, SHE TOUCHES THINGS
...A CHINA ORNAMENT, THE POLISHED WOOD OF A TABLETOP. TOUCHING, SHE RE-ESTABLISHES CONTACT WITH THE WORLD, SLOWLY RETRIEVING HER SENSE OF...
BBRRRRIIINNNGG
...REALITY.
HELLO? YES? YES, THAT'S RIGHT, I'M MRS MORAN. WHO DID YOU SAY..?
I'M AFRAID HE'S STILL ASLEEP. DID YOU WANT TO RING BACK OR...
NO. NO. THAT'S ALL RIGHT.
I'LL CALL HIM...
MARVELMAN
4

Johnny Bates returns in this preliminary pencil rough for *Warrior* #3, page 2, panel 6 by Garry Leach.

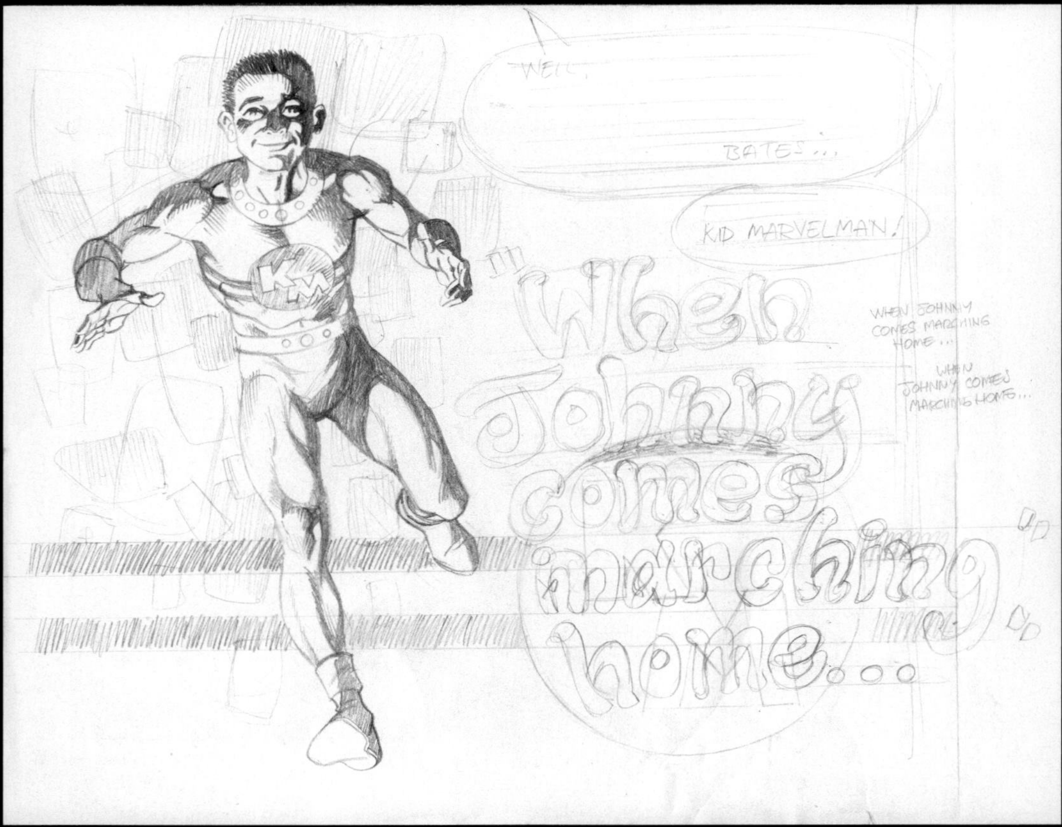
WELL,
BATES...
KID MARVELMAN!
"When Johnny comes marching home..."
WHEN JOHNNY COMES MARCHING HOME...
WHEN JOHNNY COMES MARCHING HOME...

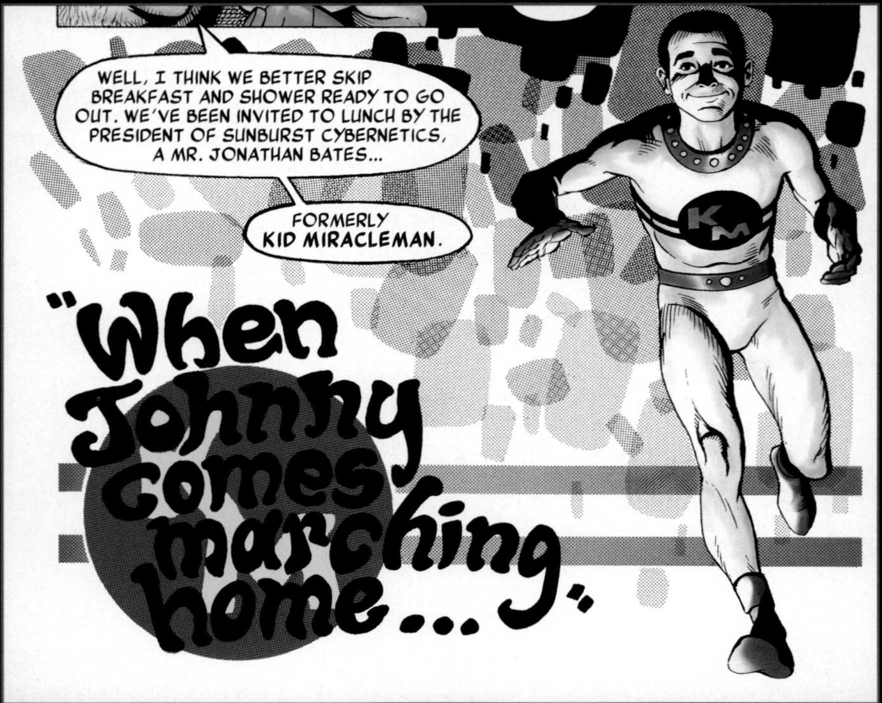
WELL, I THINK WE BETTER SKIP BREAKFAST AND SHOWER READY TO GO OUT. WE'VE BEEN INVITED TO LUNCH BY THE PRESIDENT OF SUNBURST CYBERNETICS, A MR. JONATHAN BATES...
FORMERLY KID MIRACLEMAN.
"When Johnny comes marching home..."

Warrior #3, page 2 original artwork, pencil, India ink and Letratone on illustration board by Garry Leach

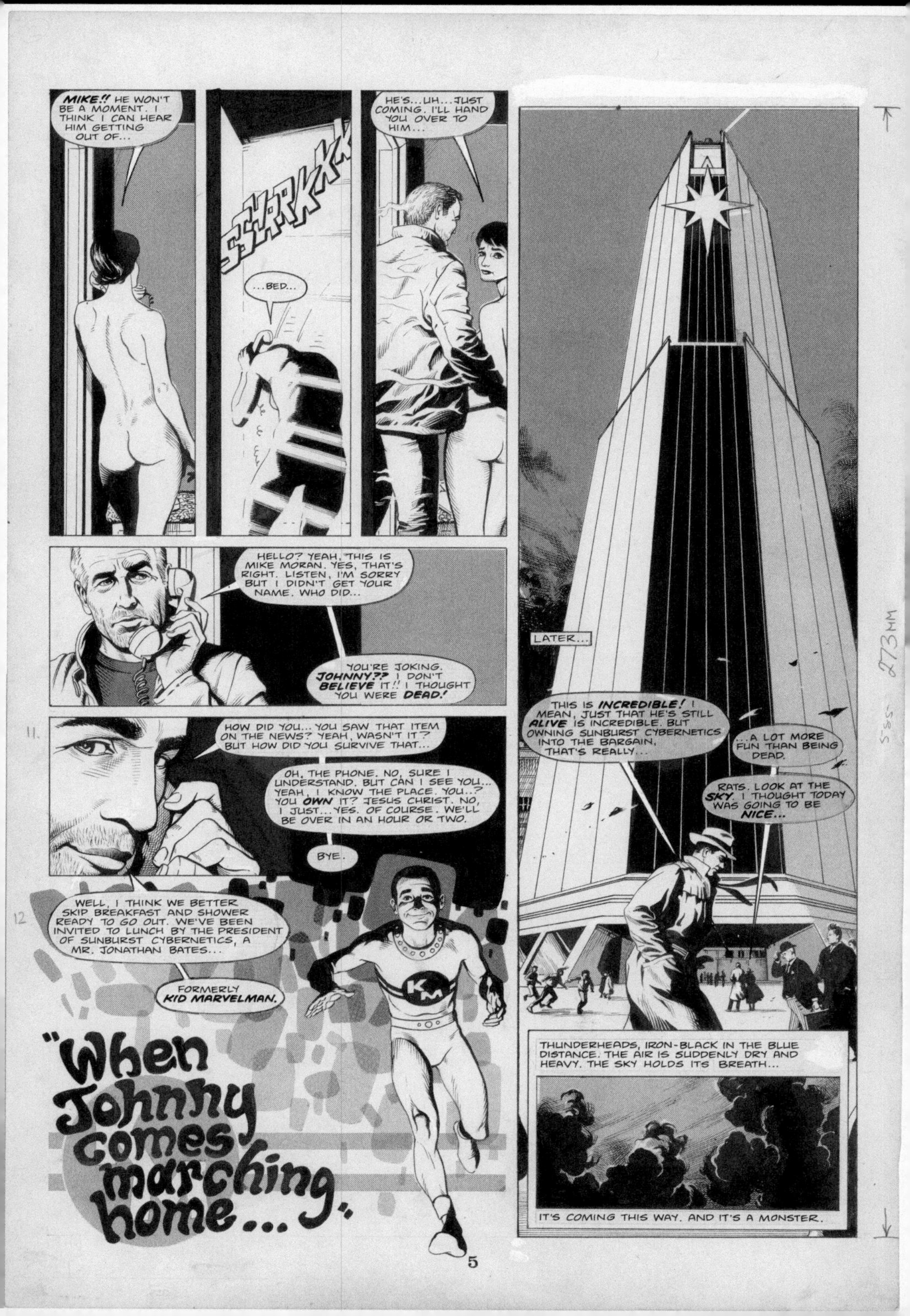

MIKE!! HE WON'T BE A MOMENT. I THINK I CAN HEAR HIM GETTING OUT OF...
SSHRKKK
...BED...
HE'S...UH...JUST COMING. I'LL HAND YOU OVER TO HIM...
HELLO? YEAH, THIS IS MIKE MORAN. YES, THAT'S RIGHT. LISTEN, I'M SORRY BUT I DIDN'T GET YOUR NAME. WHO DID...
YOU'RE JOKING. JOHNNY?? I DON'T BELIEVE IT!! I THOUGHT YOU WERE DEAD!
11.
HOW DID YOU... YOU SAW THAT ITEM ON THE NEWS? YEAH, WASN'T IT? BUT HOW DID YOU SURVIVE THAT...
OH, THE PHONE. NO, SURE I UNDERSTAND. BUT CAN I SEE YOU... YEAH, I KNOW THE PLACE. YOU...? YOU OWN IT? JESUS CHRIST. NO, I JUST... YES. OF COURSE. WE'LL BE OVER IN AN HOUR OR TWO.
BYE.
12
WELL, I THINK WE BETTER SKIP BREAKFAST AND SHOWER READY TO GO OUT. WE'VE BEEN INVITED TO LUNCH BY THE PRESIDENT OF SUNBURST CYBERNETICS, A MR. JONATHAN BATES...
FORMERLY KID MARVELMAN.
KM
"When Johnny Comes marching home..."
LATER...
THIS IS INCREDIBLE! I MEAN, JUST THAT HE'S STILL ALIVE IS INCREDIBLE. BUT OWNING SUNBURST CYBERNETICS INTO THE BARGAIN, THAT'S REALLY...
...A LOT MORE FUN THAN BEING DEAD.
RATS. LOOK AT THE SKY. I THOUGHT TODAY WAS GOING TO BE NICE...
THUNDERHEADS, IRON-BLACK IN THE BLUE DISTANCE. THE AIR IS SUDDENLY DRY AND HEAVY. THE SKY HOLDS ITS BREATH...
IT'S COMING THIS WAY. AND IT'S A MONSTER.
273MM
5

Warrior #3, page 6 original artwork, pencil, India ink and Letratone on illustration board by Garry Leach

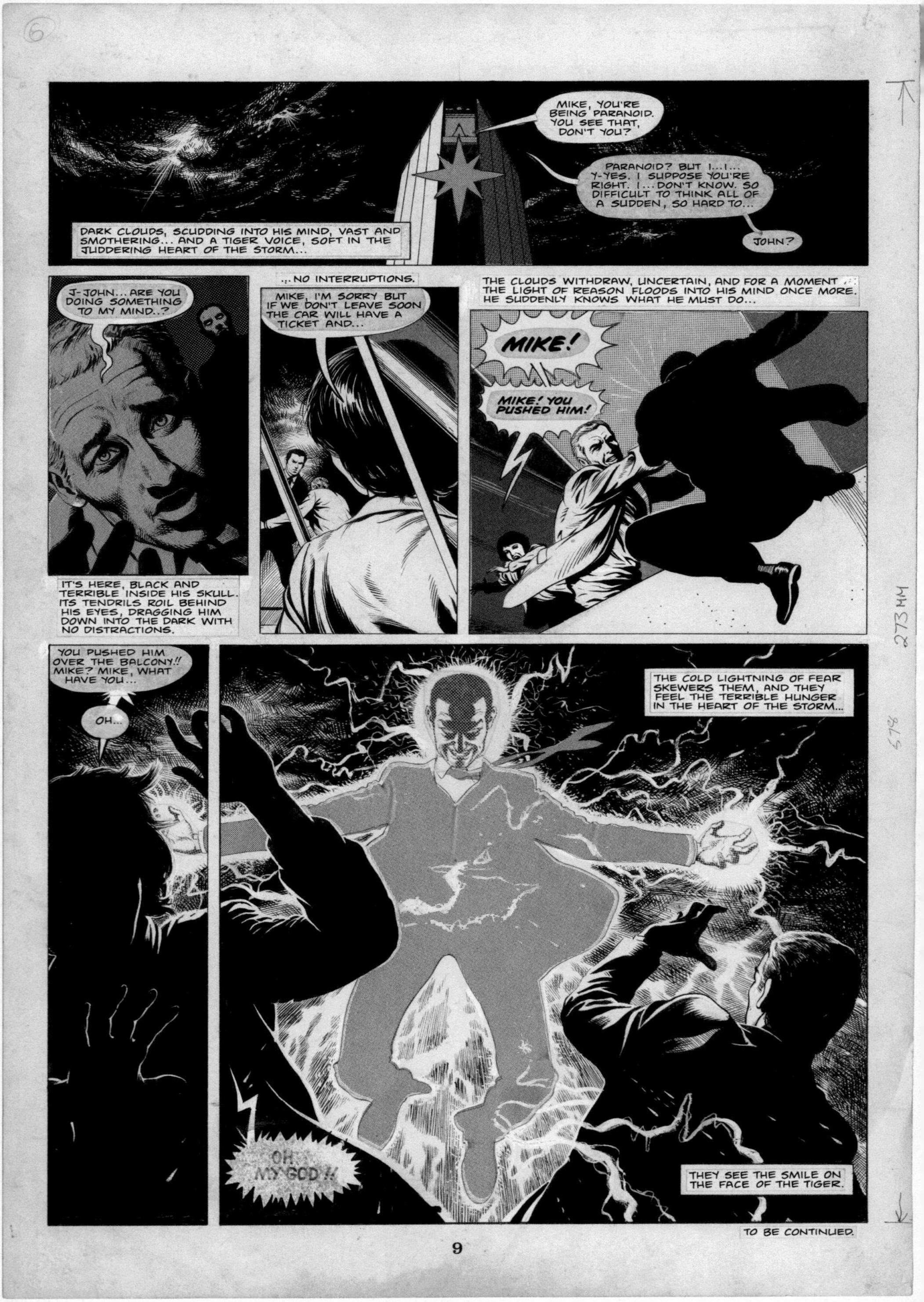
MIKE, YOU'RE BEING PARANOID. YOU SEE THAT, DON'T YOU?
PARANOID? BUT I...I... Y-YES. I SUPPOSE YOU'RE RIGHT. I... DON'T KNOW. SO DIFFICULT TO THINK ALL OF A SUDDEN, SO HARD TO...
JOHN?
DARK CLOUDS, SCUDDING INTO HIS MIND, VAST AND SMOTHERING... AND A TIGER VOICE, SOFT IN THE JUDDERING HEART OF THE STORM...
J-JOHN... ARE YOU DOING SOMETHING TO MY MIND..?
IT'S HERE, BLACK AND TERRIBLE INSIDE HIS SKULL. ITS TENDRILS ROIL BEHIND HIS EYES, DRAGGING HIM DOWN INTO THE DARK WITH NO DISTRACTIONS.
...NO INTERRUPTIONS.
MIKE, I'M SORRY BUT IF WE DON'T LEAVE SOON THE CAR WILL HAVE A TICKET AND...
THE CLOUDS WITHDRAW, UNCERTAIN, AND FOR A MOMENT THE LIGHT OF REASON FLOODS INTO HIS MIND ONCE MORE. HE SUDDENLY KNOWS WHAT HE MUST DO...
MIKE!
MIKE! YOU PUSHED HIM!
YOU PUSHED HIM OVER THE BALCONY!! MIKE? MIKE, WHAT HAVE YOU...
OH...
THE COLD LIGHTNING OF FEAR SKEWERS THEM, AND THEY FEEL THE TERRIBLE HUNGER IN THE HEART OF THE STORM...
OH MY GOD!!
THEY SEE THE SMILE ON THE FACE OF THE TIGER.
TO BE CONTINUED.
9

Kid Miracleman's true nature is revealed in Garry Leach's preliminary rough for *Warrior* #5, page 2, panel 5, red and blue Biro on layout paper.

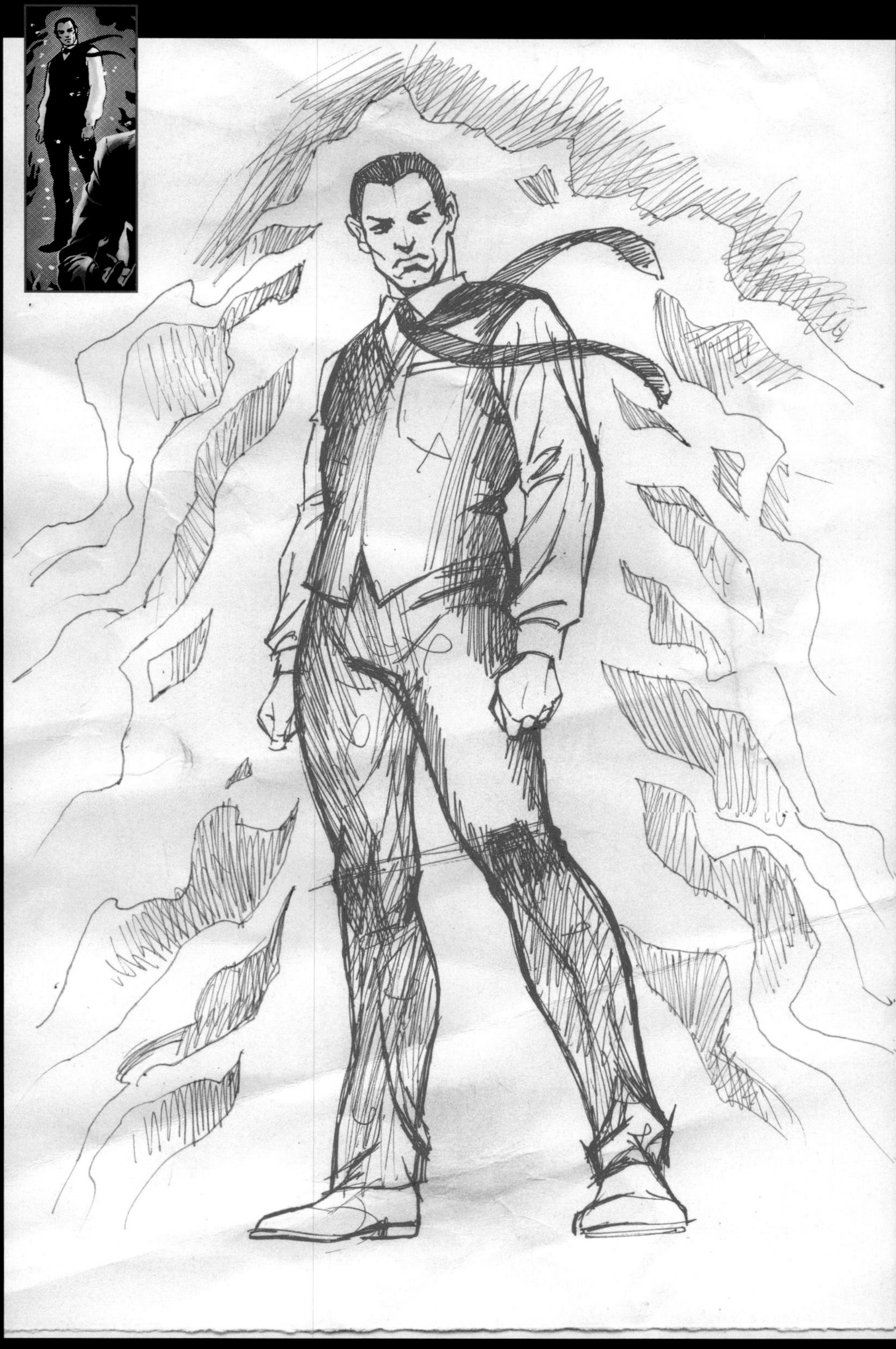

Warrior #5, page 6, panel 7 preliminary pencil rough by Garry Leach. This famous panel was later repurposed as a title page for the story and as the cover to a French reprint album.

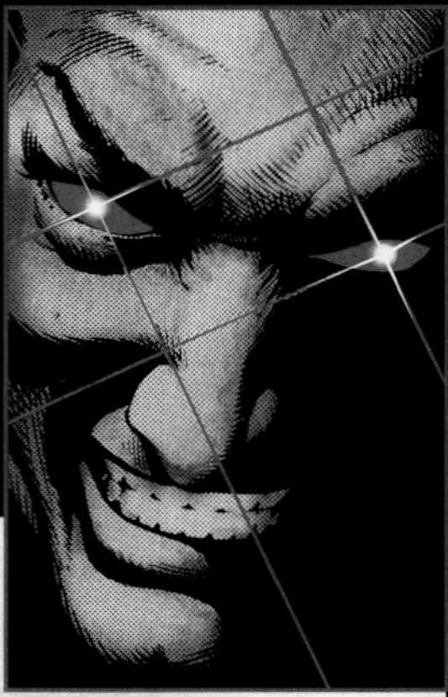

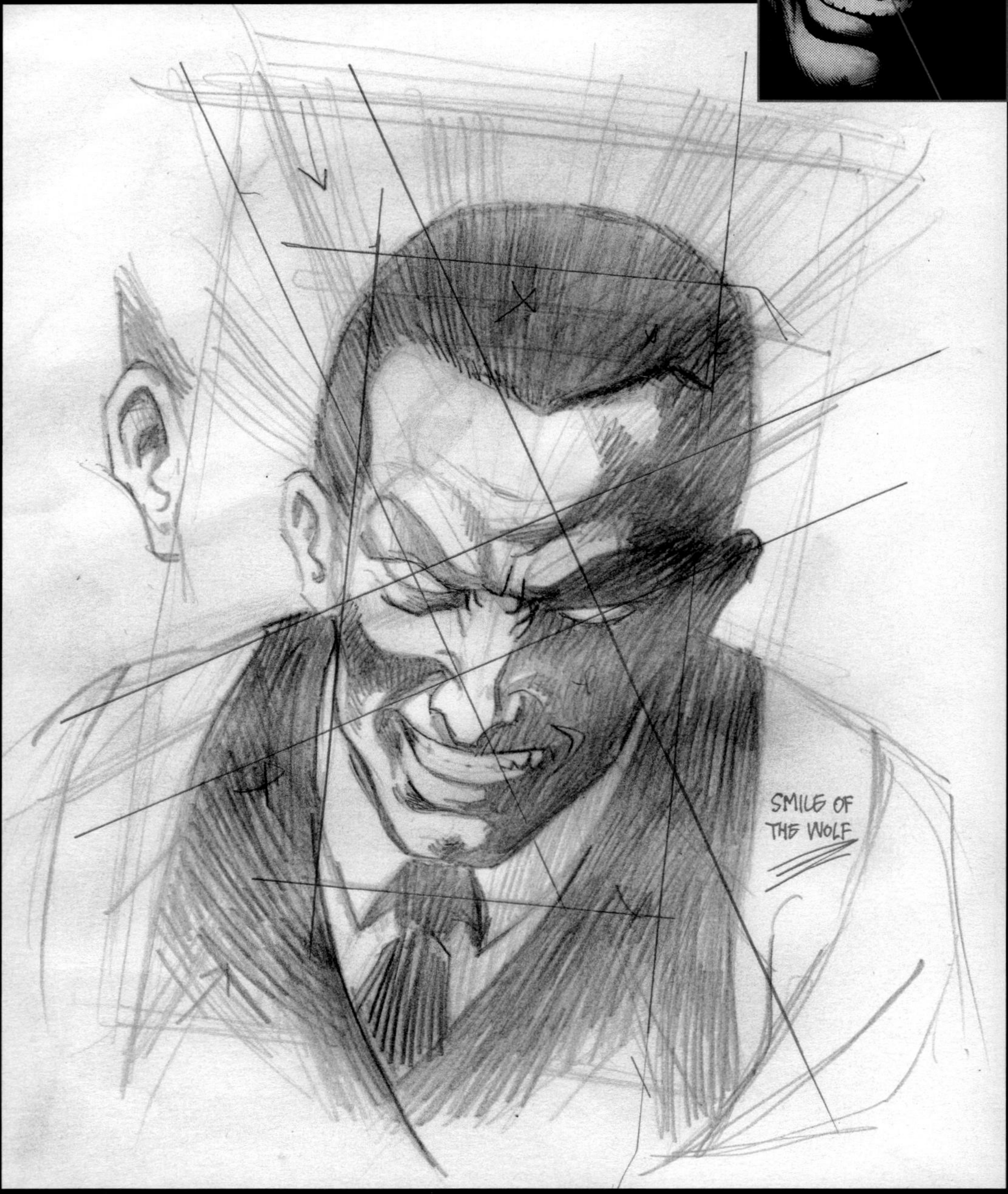
SMILE OF THE WOLF

Original art to Mick Austin's award-winning cover painting for *Warrior* #7 (November 1982).

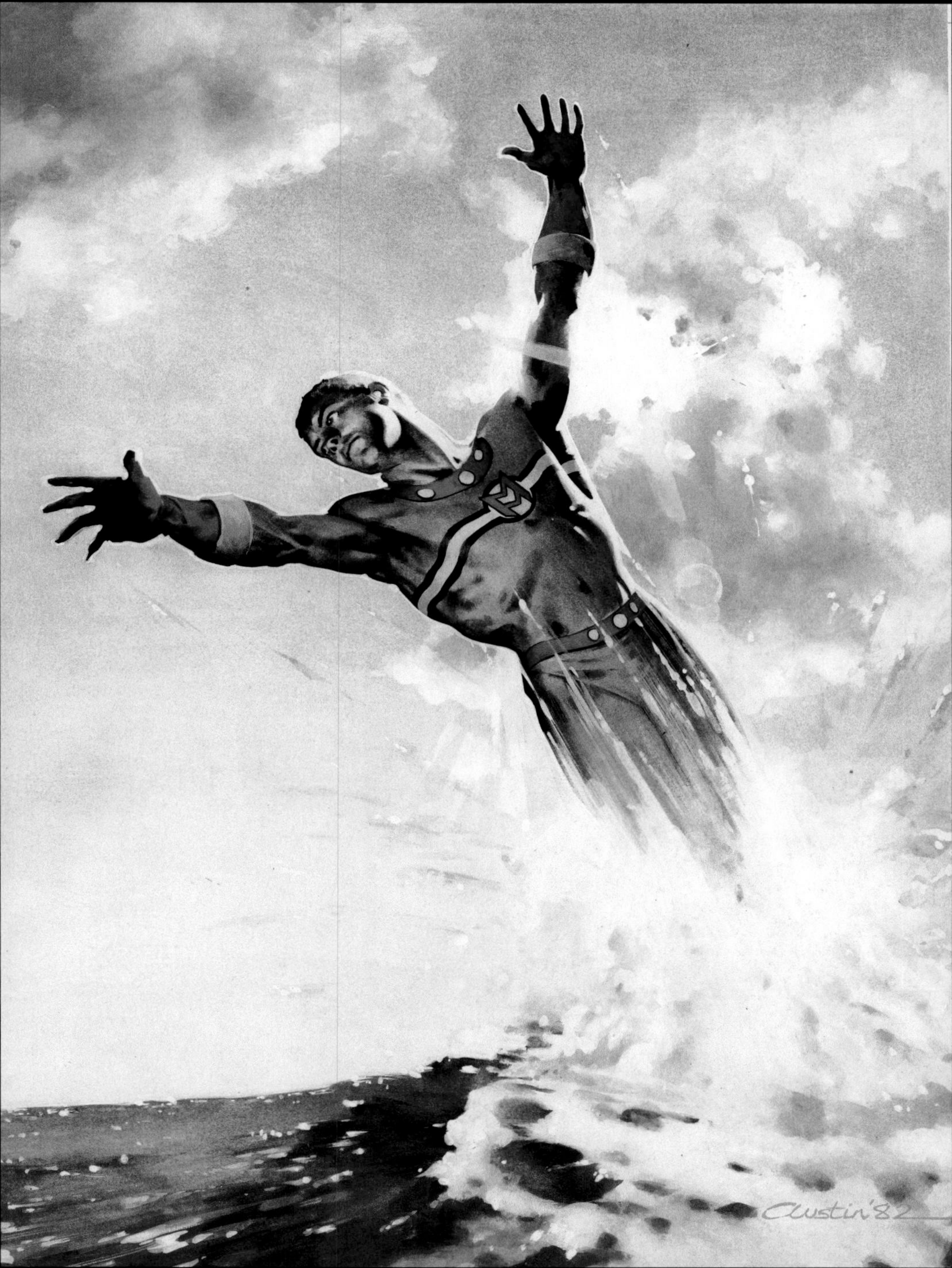
Austin'82

Warrior #7, page 6 original artwork, pencil, India ink and Letratone on illustration board by Alan Davis and Garry Leach.

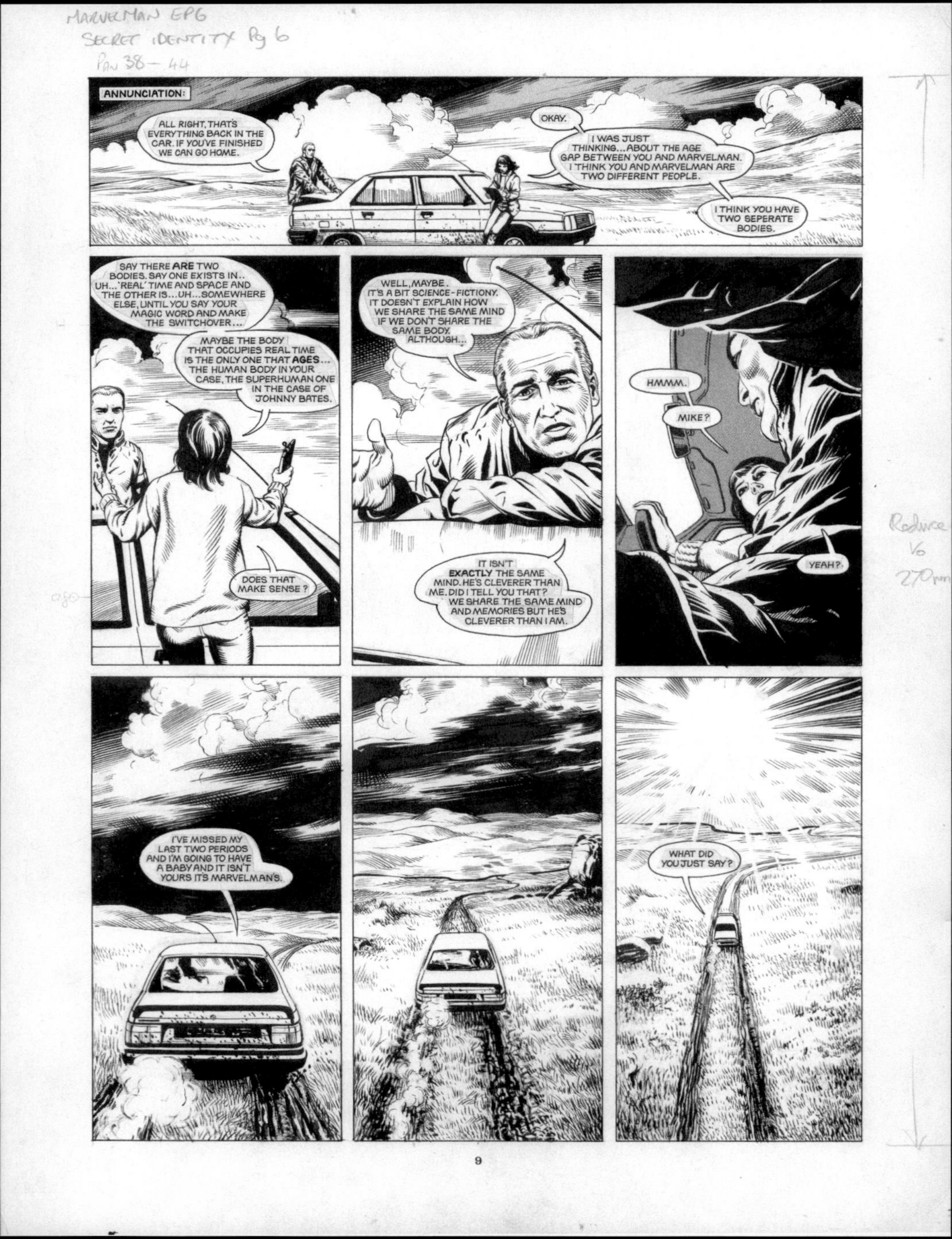
ANNUNCIATION:
ALL RIGHT, THAT'S EVERYTHING BACK IN THE CAR. IF YOU'VE FINISHED WE CAN GO HOME.
OKAY.
I WAS JUST THINKING...ABOUT THE AGE GAP BETWEEN YOU AND MARVELMAN. I THINK YOU AND MARVELMAN ARE TWO DIFFERENT PEOPLE.
I THINK YOU HAVE TWO SEPERATE BODIES.
SAY THERE **ARE** TWO BODIES. SAY ONE EXISTS IN.. UH...'REAL' TIME AND SPACE AND THE OTHER IS...UH...SOMEWHERE ELSE, UNTIL YOU SAY YOUR MAGIC WORD AND MAKE THE SWITCHOVER...
MAYBE THE BODY THAT OCCUPIES REAL TIME IS THE ONLY ONE THAT **AGES**... THE HUMAN BODY IN YOUR CASE, THE SUPERHUMAN ONE IN THE CASE OF JOHNNY BATES.
DOES THAT MAKE SENSE?
WELL, MAYBE. IT'S A BIT SCIENCE-FICTIONY. IT DOESN'T EXPLAIN HOW WE SHARE THE SAME MIND IF WE DON'T SHARE THE SAME BODY. ALTHOUGH...
IT ISN'T **EXACTLY** THE SAME MIND. HE'S CLEVERER THAN ME. DID I TELL YOU THAT? WE SHARE THE SAME MIND AND MEMORIES BUT HE'S CLEVERER THAN I AM.
HMMM.
MIKE?
YEAH?
I'VE MISSED MY LAST TWO PERIODS AND I'M GOING TO HAVE A BABY AND IT ISN'T YOURS IT'S MARVELMAN'S.
WHAT DID YOU JUST SAY?
9

Warrior #8, page 7 original artwork, pencil, India ink and Letratone on illustration board by Alan Davis

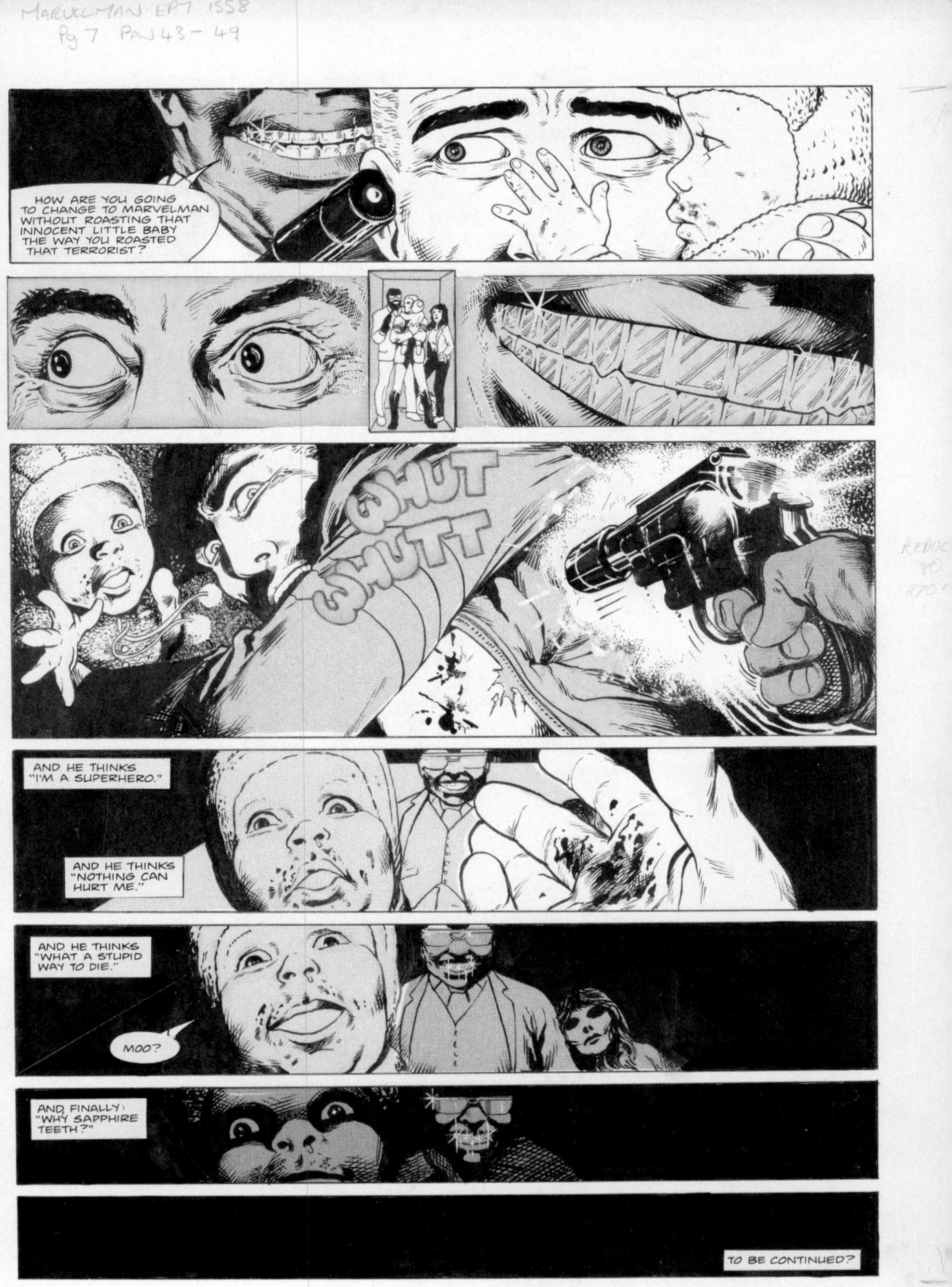

MARVELMAN EP7 1558
Pg 7 PAN 43-49
HOW ARE YOU GOING TO CHANGE TO MARVELMAN WITHOUT ROASTING THAT INNOCENT LITTLE BABY THE WAY YOU ROASTED THAT TERRORIST?
WHUT
WHUTT
AND HE THINKS "I'M A SUPERHERO."
AND HE THINKS "NOTHING CAN HURT ME."
AND HE THINKS "WHAT A STUPID WAY TO DIE."
MOO?
AND, FINALLY: "WHY SAPPHIRE TEETH?"
TO BE CONTINUED?

Warrior #9, page 7 original artwork, pencil, India ink and Letratone on illustration board by Alan Davis.

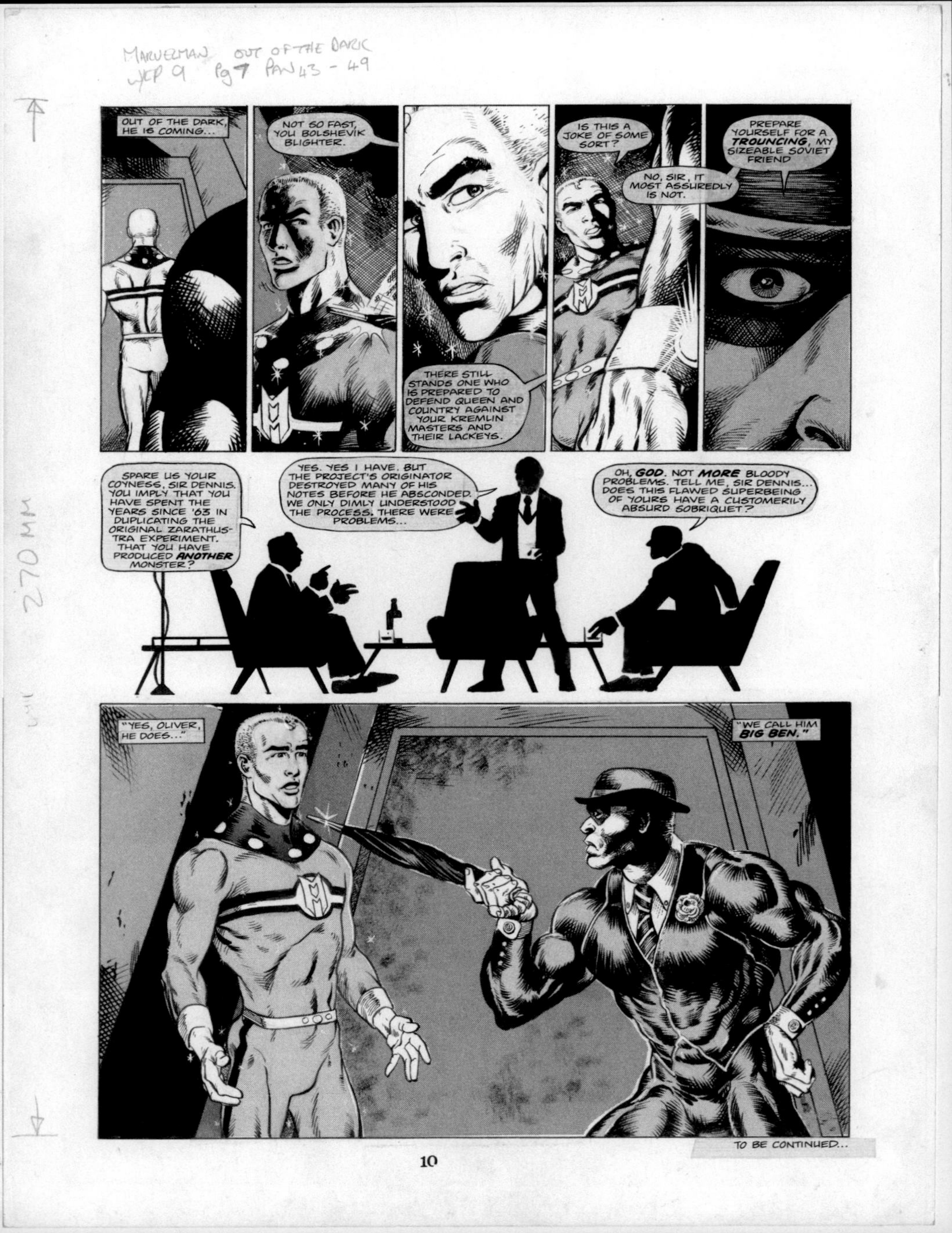
MARVELMAN OUT OF THE DARK
WAR 9 Pg 7 PAN 43 - 49
OUT OF THE DARK, HE IS COMING...
NOT SO FAST, YOU BOLSHEVIK BLIGHTER.
THERE STILL STANDS ONE WHO IS PREPARED TO DEFEND QUEEN AND COUNTRY AGAINST YOUR KREMLIN MASTERS AND THEIR LACKEYS.
IS THIS A JOKE OF SOME SORT?
NO, SIR, IT MOST ASSUREDLY IS NOT.
PREPARE YOURSELF FOR A **TROUNCING**, MY SIZEABLE SOVIET FRIEND
SPARE US YOUR COYNESS, SIR DENNIS. YOU IMPLY THAT YOU HAVE SPENT THE YEARS SINCE '63 IN DUPLICATING THE ORIGINAL ZARATHUSTRA EXPERIMENT. THAT YOU HAVE PRODUCED **ANOTHER** MONSTER?
YES. YES I HAVE. BUT THE PROJECT'S ORIGINATOR DESTROYED MANY OF HIS NOTES BEFORE HE ABSCONDED. WE ONLY DIMLY UNDERSTOOD THE PROCESS. THERE WERE PROBLEMS...
OH, **GOD**. NOT **MORE** BLOODY PROBLEMS. TELL ME, SIR DENNIS... DOES THIS FLAWED SUPERBEING OF YOURS HAVE A CUSTOMERILY ABSURD SOBRIQUET?
"YES, OLIVER, HE DOES..."
"WE CALL HIM **BIG BEN**."
TO BE CONTINUED...
270 MM
10

Warrior #11, page 2 original artwork, pencil, India ink and Letratone on illustration board by Alan Davis.

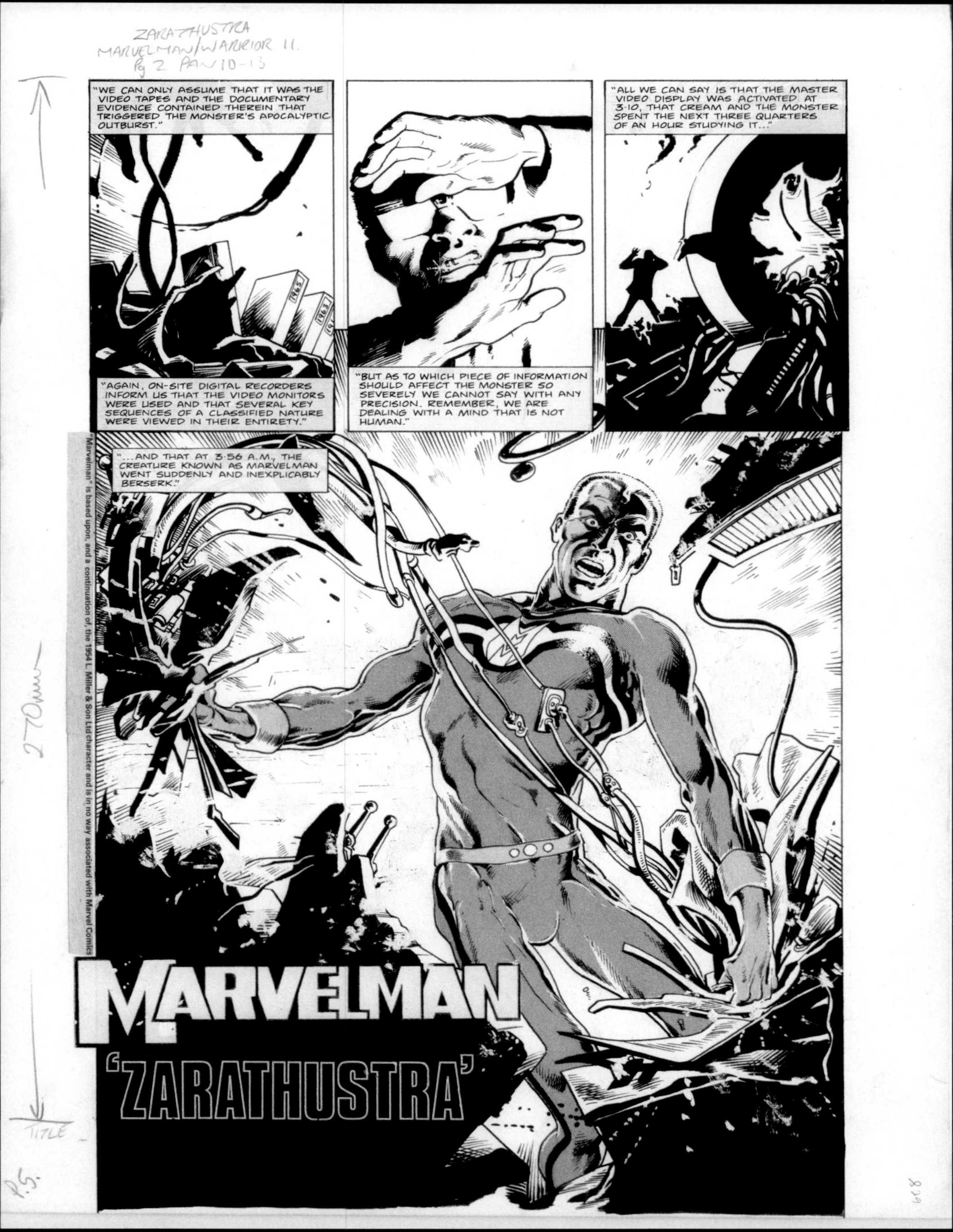
ZARATHUSTRA
MARVELMAN/WARRIOR 11.
Pg 2 PAN 10-13
"WE CAN ONLY ASSUME THAT IT WAS THE VIDEO TAPES AND THE DOCUMENTARY EVIDENCE CONTAINED THEREIN THAT TRIGGERED THE MONSTER'S APOCALYPTIC OUTBURST."
1965
1963
"AGAIN, ON-SITE DIGITAL RECORDERS INFORM US THAT THE VIDEO MONITORS WERE USED AND THAT SEVERAL KEY SEQUENCES OF A CLASSIFIED NATURE WERE VIEWED IN THEIR ENTIRETY."
"BUT AS TO WHICH PIECE OF INFORMATION SHOULD AFFECT THE MONSTER SO SEVERELY WE CANNOT SAY WITH ANY PRECISION. REMEMBER, WE ARE DEALING WITH A MIND THAT IS NOT HUMAN."
"ALL WE CAN SAY IS THAT THE MASTER VIDEO DISPLAY WAS ACTIVATED AT 3·10, THAT CREAM AND THE MONSTER SPENT THE NEXT THREE QUARTERS OF AN HOUR STUDYING IT..."
"...AND THAT AT 3·56 A.M., THE CREATURE KNOWN AS MARVELMAN WENT SUDDENLY AND INEXPLICABLY BERSERK."
"Marvelman" is based upon, and a continuation of, the 1954 L. Miller & Son Ltd character and is in no way associated with Marvel Comics
MARVELMAN
'ZARATHUSTRA'
TITLE

Warrior #11, page 7 original artwork, pencil, India ink and Letratone on illustration board by Alan Davis

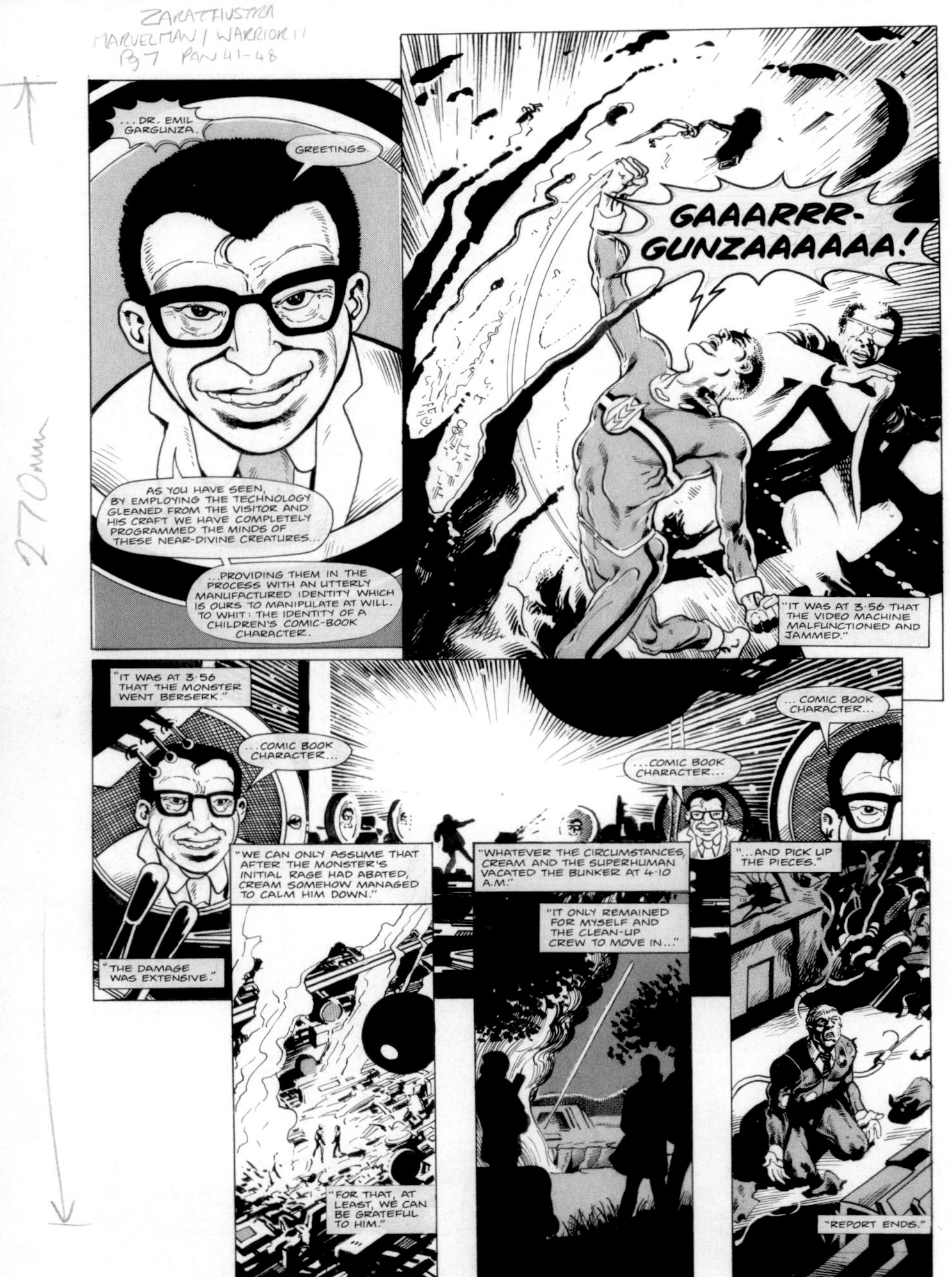
ZARATHUSTRA
MARVELMAN / WARRIOR 11
PG 7 PAN 41-48
... DR. EMIL GARGUNZA.
GREETINGS.
AS YOU HAVE SEEN, BY EMPLOYING THE TECHNOLOGY GLEANED FROM THE VISITOR AND HIS CRAFT WE HAVE COMPLETELY PROGRAMMED THE MINDS OF THESE NEAR-DIVINE CREATURES...
...PROVIDING THEM IN THE PROCESS WITH AN UTTERLY MANUFACTURED IDENTITY WHICH IS OURS TO MANIPULATE AT WILL. TO WHIT: THE IDENTITY OF A CHILDREN'S COMIC-BOOK CHARACTER.
GAAARRR-GUNZAAAAAAA!
"IT WAS AT 3·56 THAT THE VIDEO MACHINE MALFUNCTIONED AND JAMMED."
"IT WAS AT 3·56 THAT THE MONSTER WENT BERSERK."
...COMIC BOOK CHARACTER...
...COMIC BOOK CHARACTER...
...COMIC BOOK CHARACTER...
"THE DAMAGE WAS EXTENSIVE."
"WE CAN ONLY ASSUME THAT AFTER THE MONSTER'S INITIAL RAGE HAD ABATED, CREAM SOMEHOW MANAGED TO CALM HIM DOWN."
"FOR THAT, AT LEAST, WE CAN BE GRATEFUL TO HIM."
"WHATEVER THE CIRCUMSTANCES, CREAM AND THE SUPERHUMAN VACATED THE BUNKER AT 4·10 A.M."
"IT ONLY REMAINED FOR MYSELF AND THE CLEAN-UP CREW TO MOVE IN..."
"...AND PICK UP THE PIECES."
"REPORT ENDS."
270mm

Marvelman Special #1, page 1 original artwork, pencil, India ink and Letratone on illustration board by Alan Davis.

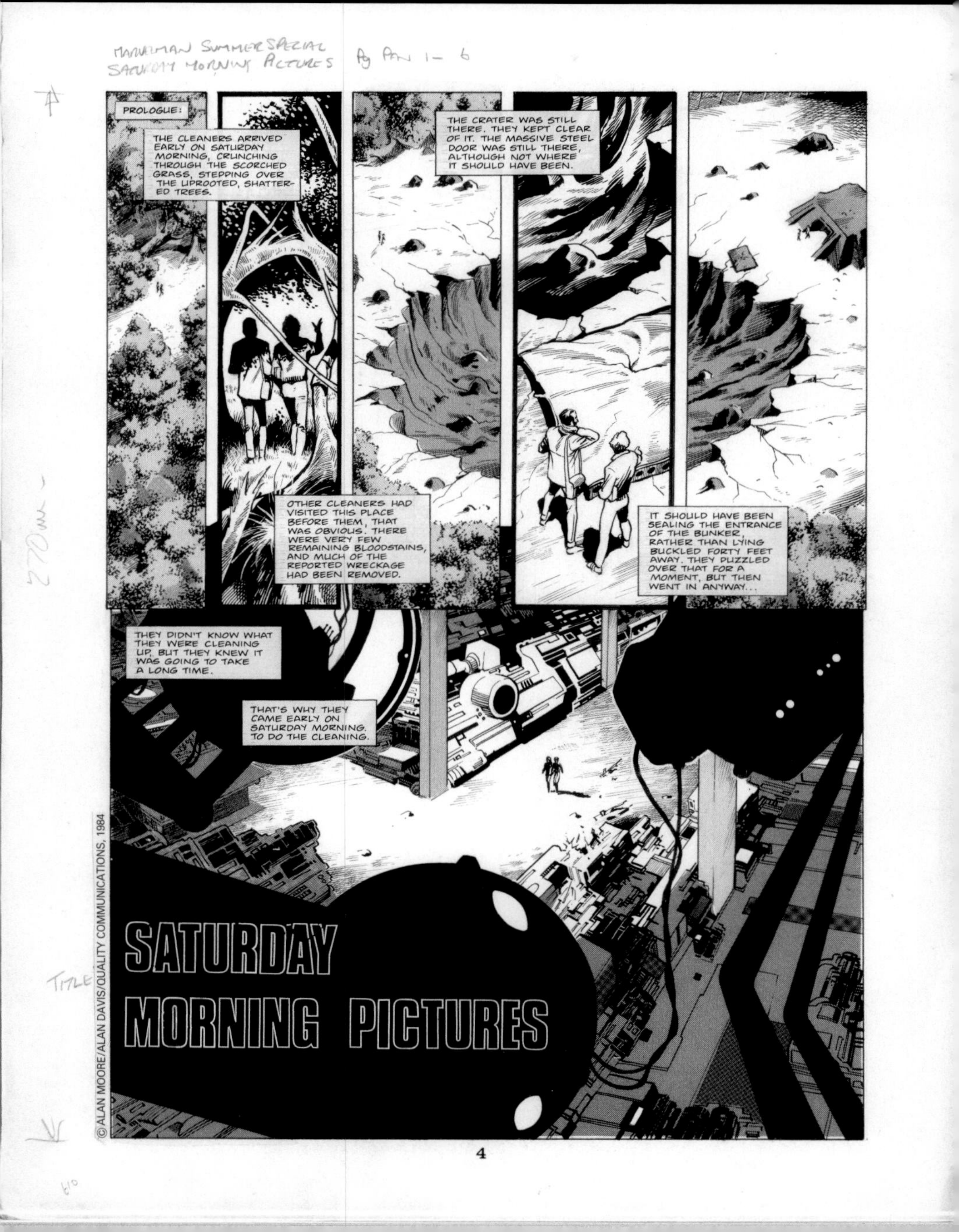
MARVELMAN SUMMER SPECIAL
SATURDAY MORNING PICTURES
Pg PAN 1 – 6
PROLOGUE:
THE CLEANERS ARRIVED EARLY ON SATURDAY MORNING, CRUNCHING THROUGH THE SCORCHED GRASS, STEPPING OVER THE UPROOTED, SHATTERED TREES.
OTHER CLEANERS HAD VISITED THIS PLACE BEFORE THEM, THAT WAS OBVIOUS. THERE WERE VERY FEW REMAINING BLOODSTAINS, AND MUCH OF THE REPORTED WRECKAGE HAD BEEN REMOVED.
THE CRATER WAS STILL THERE. THEY KEPT CLEAR OF IT. THE MASSIVE STEEL DOOR WAS STILL THERE, ALTHOUGH NOT WHERE IT SHOULD HAVE BEEN.
IT SHOULD HAVE BEEN SEALING THE ENTRANCE OF THE BUNKER, RATHER THAN LYING BUCKLED FORTY FEET AWAY. THEY PUZZLED OVER THAT FOR A MOMENT, BUT THEN WENT IN ANYWAY...
THEY DIDN'T KNOW WHAT THEY WERE CLEANING UP, BUT THEY KNEW IT WAS GOING TO TAKE A LONG TIME.
THAT'S WHY THEY CAME EARLY ON SATURDAY MORNING. TO DO THE CLEANING.
SATURDAY MORNING PICTURES
TITLE
© ALAN MOORE/ALAN DAVIS/QUALITY COMMUNICATIONS, 1984
4

Garry Leach adapted his illustration for the *Warrior* cover sidebar into this piece that he recalls as being intended as either a pinup or a back cover ad. It likely went unused in lieu of a *Warrior* back issue or merchandise house ad.

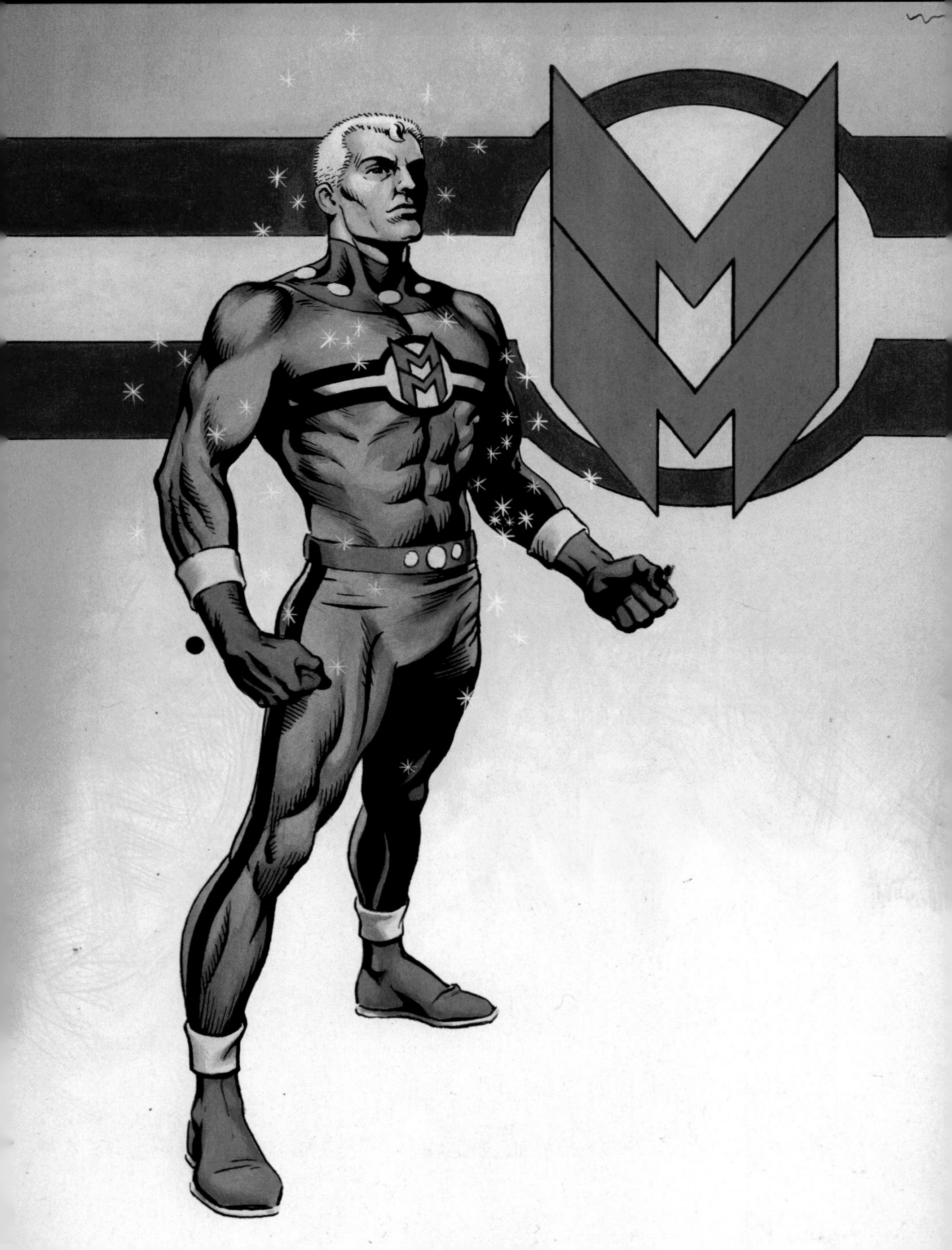

Mick Austin's cover painting to *Marvelman Special* #1 (1984).

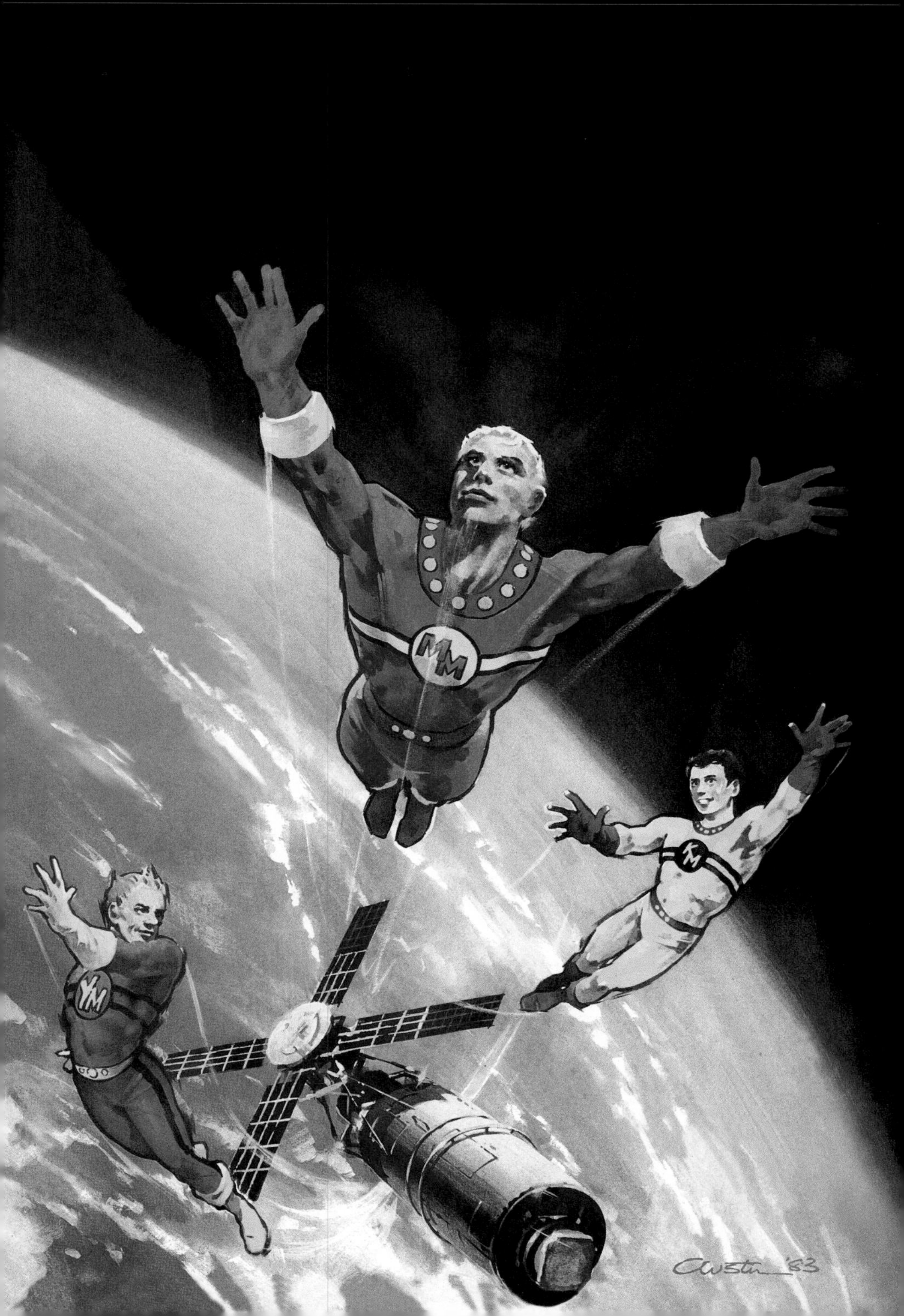
MM
KM
YM
Austin '83

ouse ad from *Warrior* #11 (July 1983). The artwork
vaders from the Future" splash page by Don Lawre
ch Garry Leach adapted for *Miracleman* #1's splash

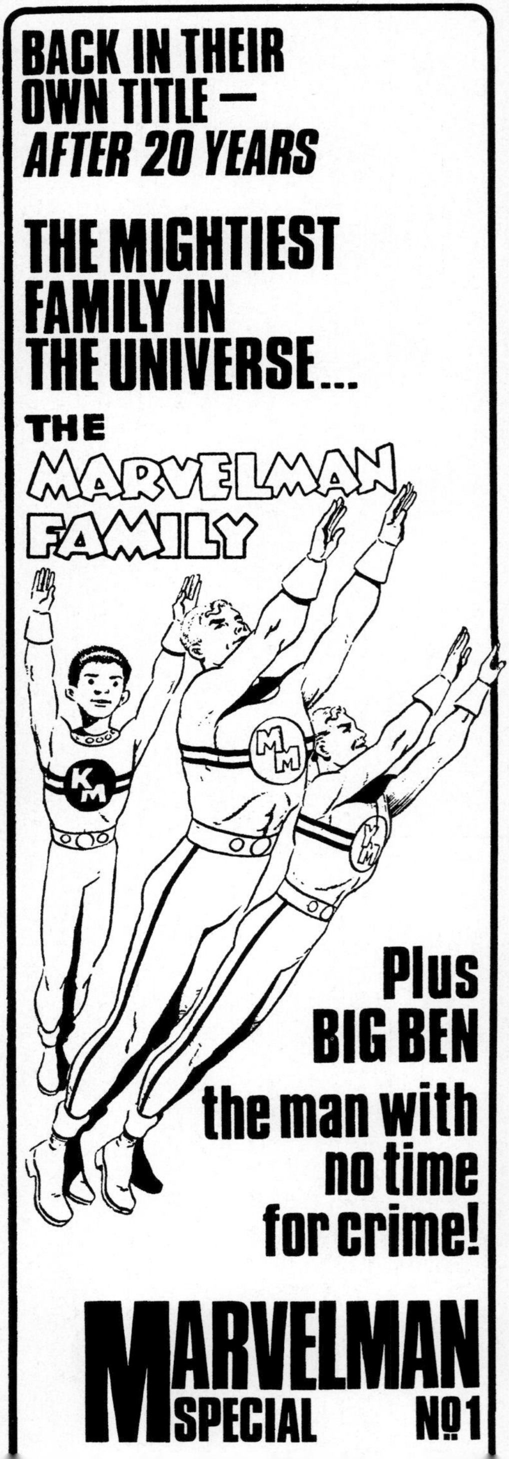
BACK IN THEIR OWN TITLE — *AFTER 20 YEARS*
THE MIGHTIEST FAMILY IN THE UNIVERSE...
THE MARVELMAN FAMILY
KM
MM
YM
Plus BIG BEN the man with no time for crime!
MARVELMAN SPECIAL No1

ZARATHUSTRA BUNKER · JULY 10th 1982

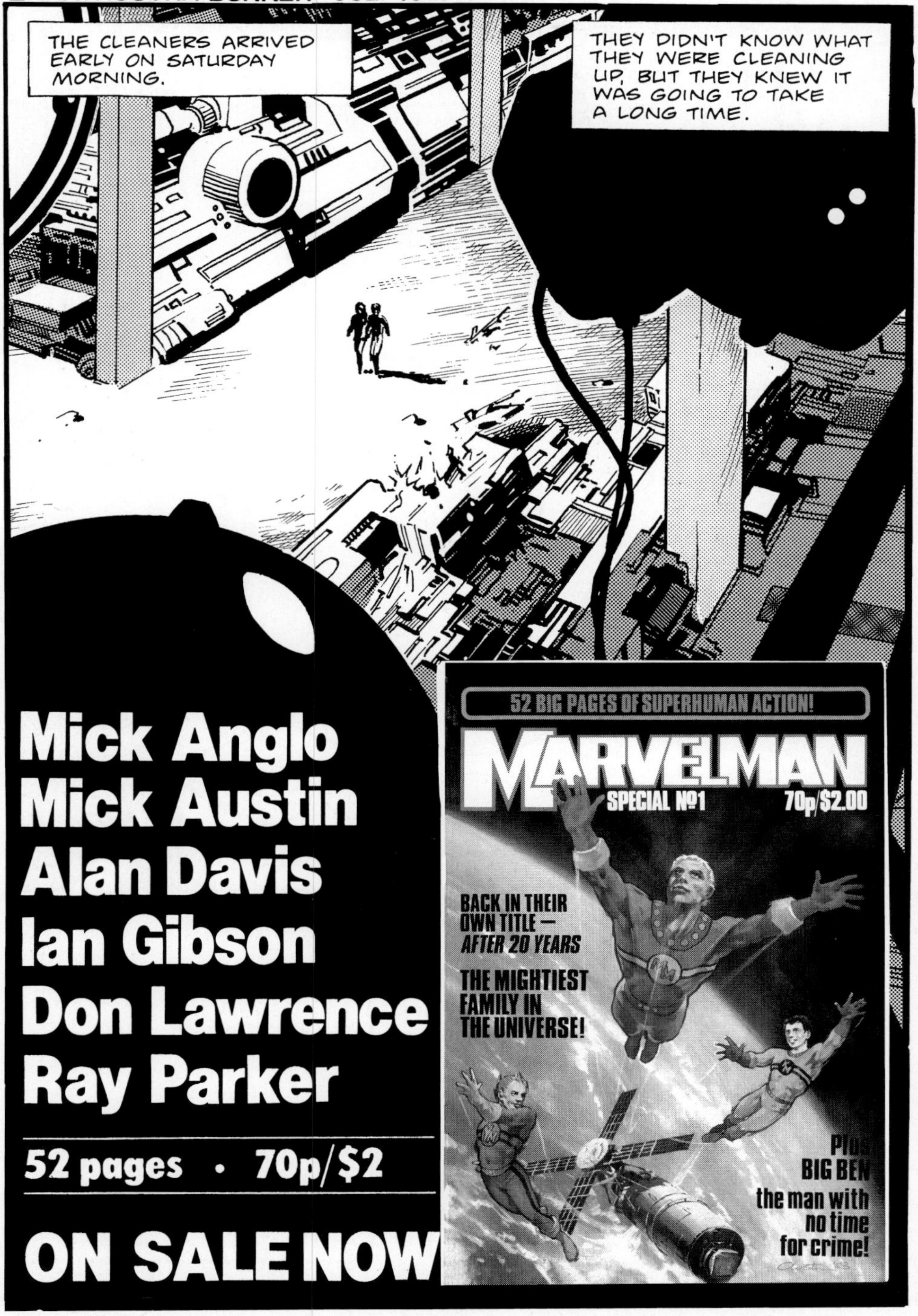
THE CLEANERS ARRIVED EARLY ON SATURDAY MORNING.
THEY DIDN'T KNOW WHAT THEY WERE CLEANING UP, BUT THEY KNEW IT WAS GOING TO TAKE A LONG TIME.
Mick Anglo
Mick Austin
Alan Davis
Ian Gibson
Don Lawrence
Ray Parker
52 pages · 70p/$2
ON SALE NOW
52 BIG PAGES OF SUPERHUMAN ACTION!
MARVELMAN
SPECIAL №1
70p/$2.00
BACK IN THEIR OWN TITLE — AFTER 20 YEARS
THE MIGHTIEST FAMILY IN THE UNIVERSE!
Plus BIG BEN the man with no time for crime!

Garry Leach repurposed this panel from the Nietzschean closing page of *Miracleman* #1's prologue as a promotional flyer for comic shops and conventions.

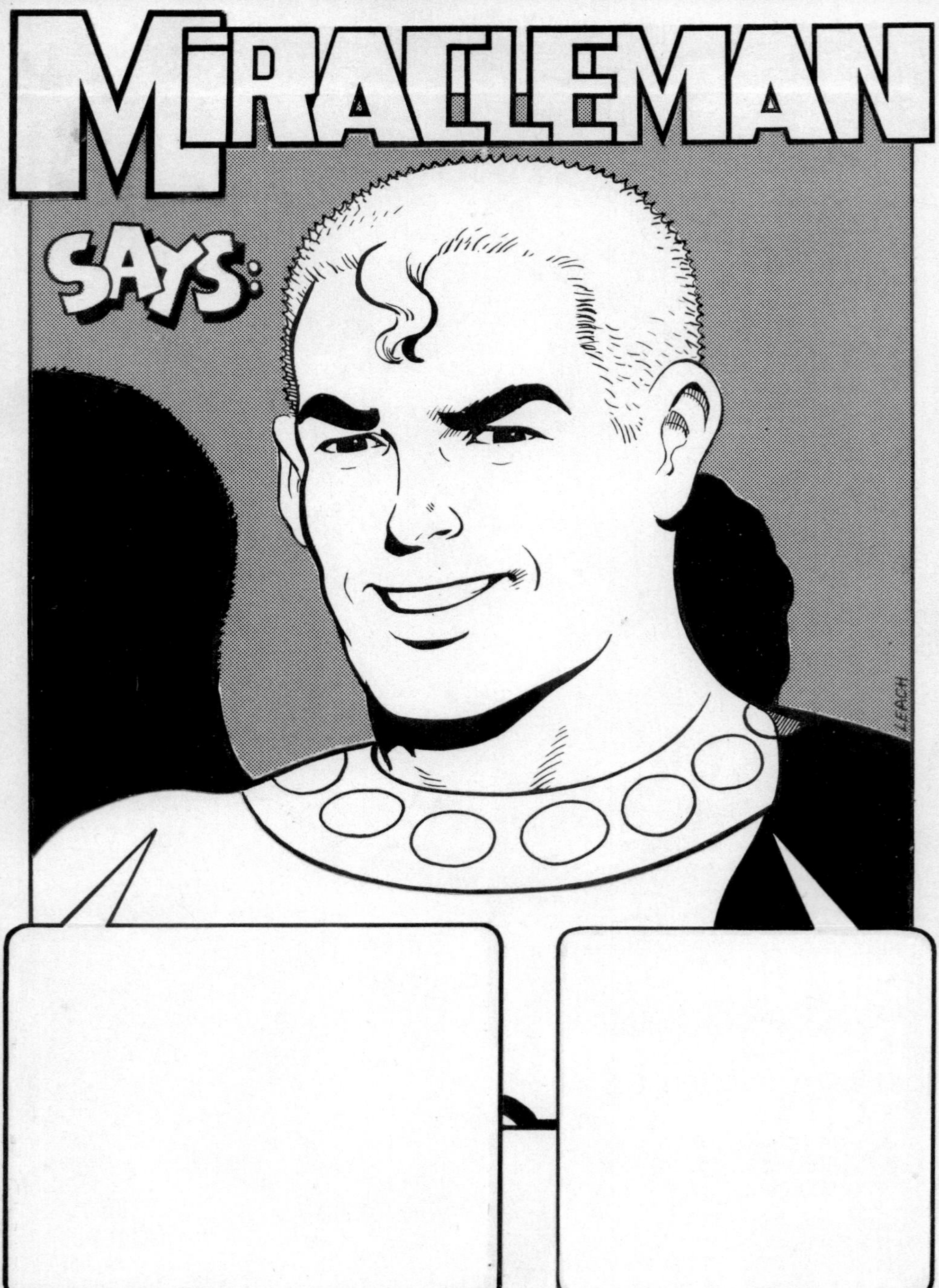
MIRACLEMAN
SAYS:
LEACH

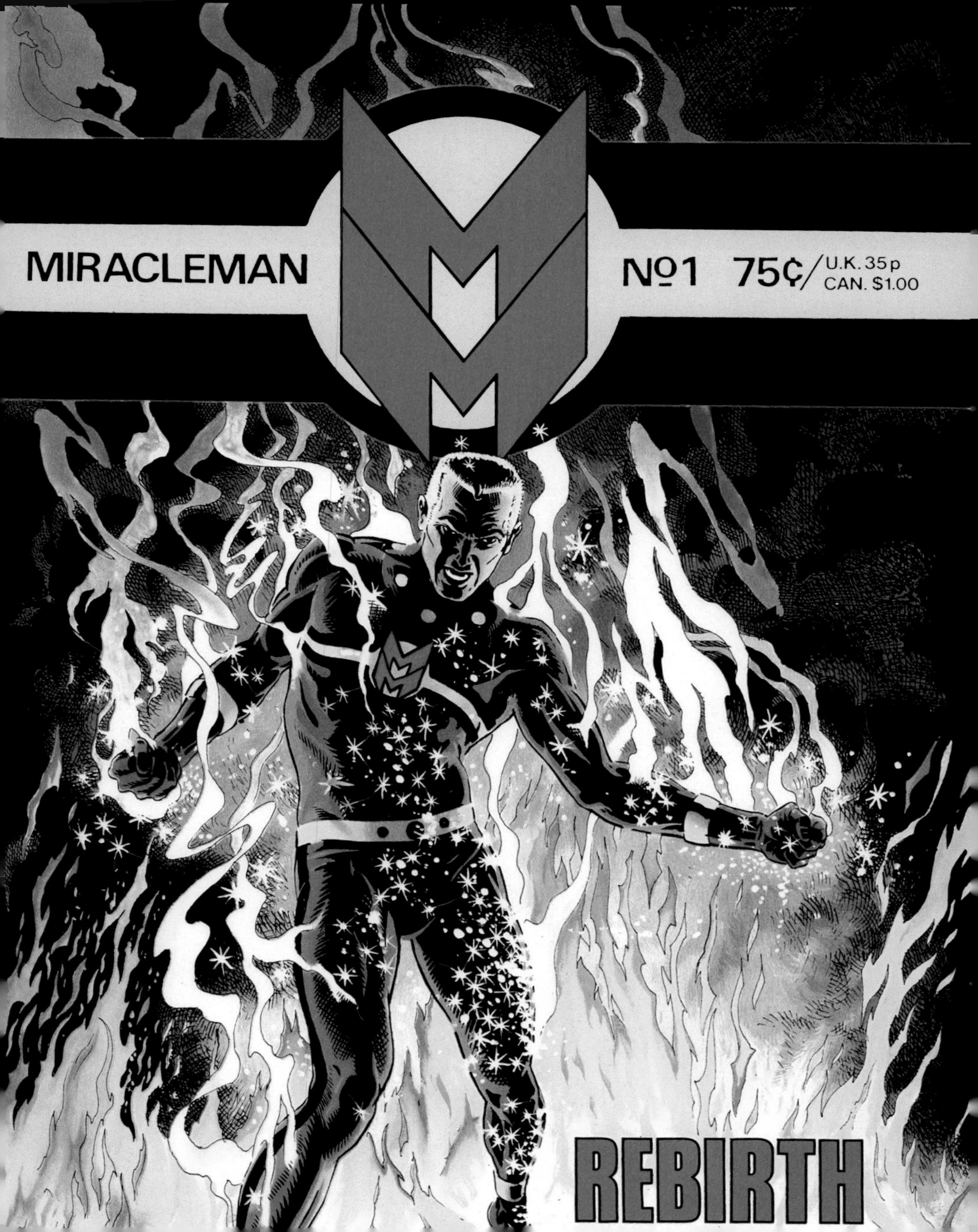
MIRACLEMAN
№1 75¢/U.K. 35p
CAN. $1.00
REBIRTH

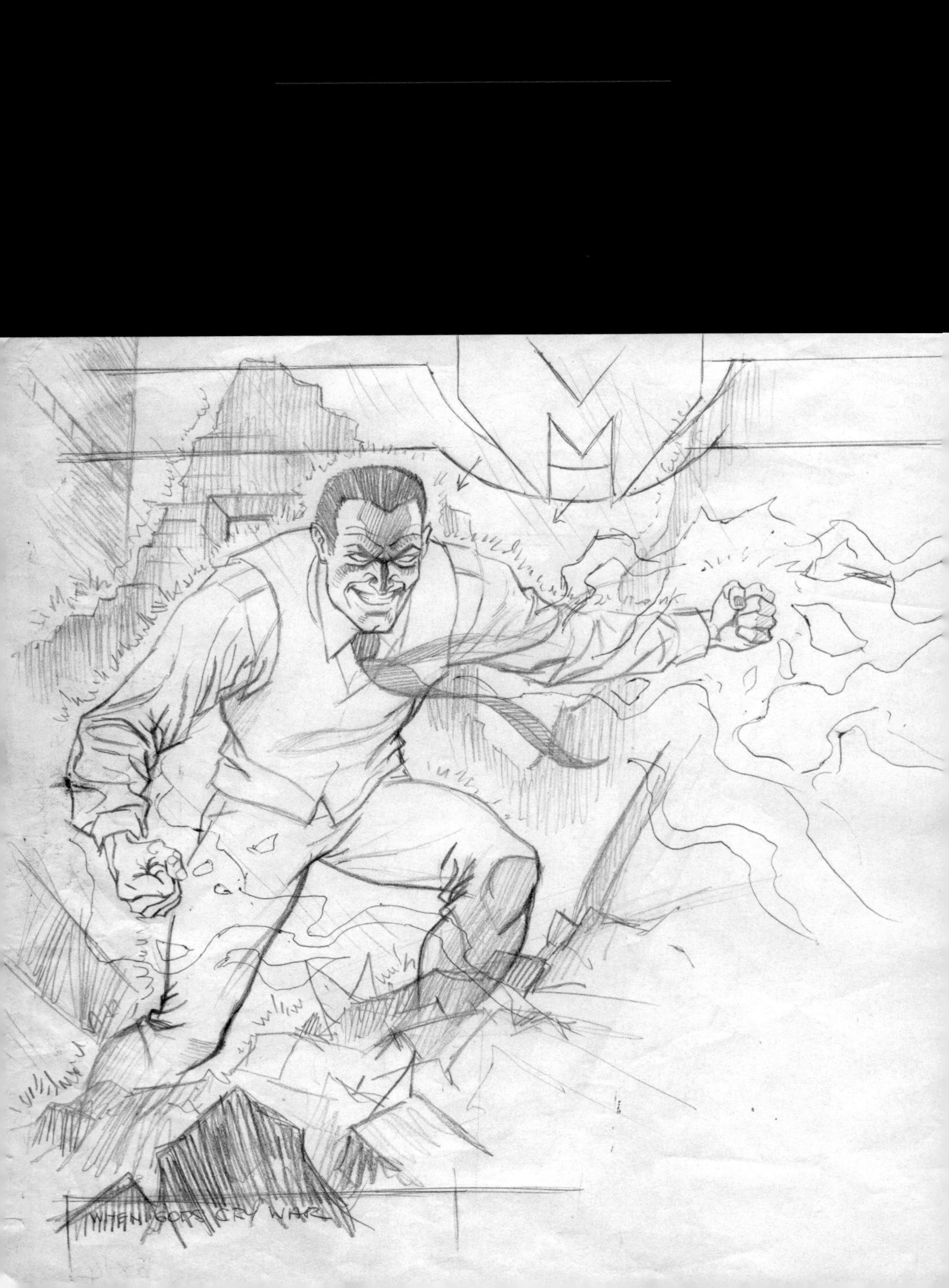
WHEN GODS CRY WAR

Garry Leach's cover to *Miracleman* #2 (October 1985).

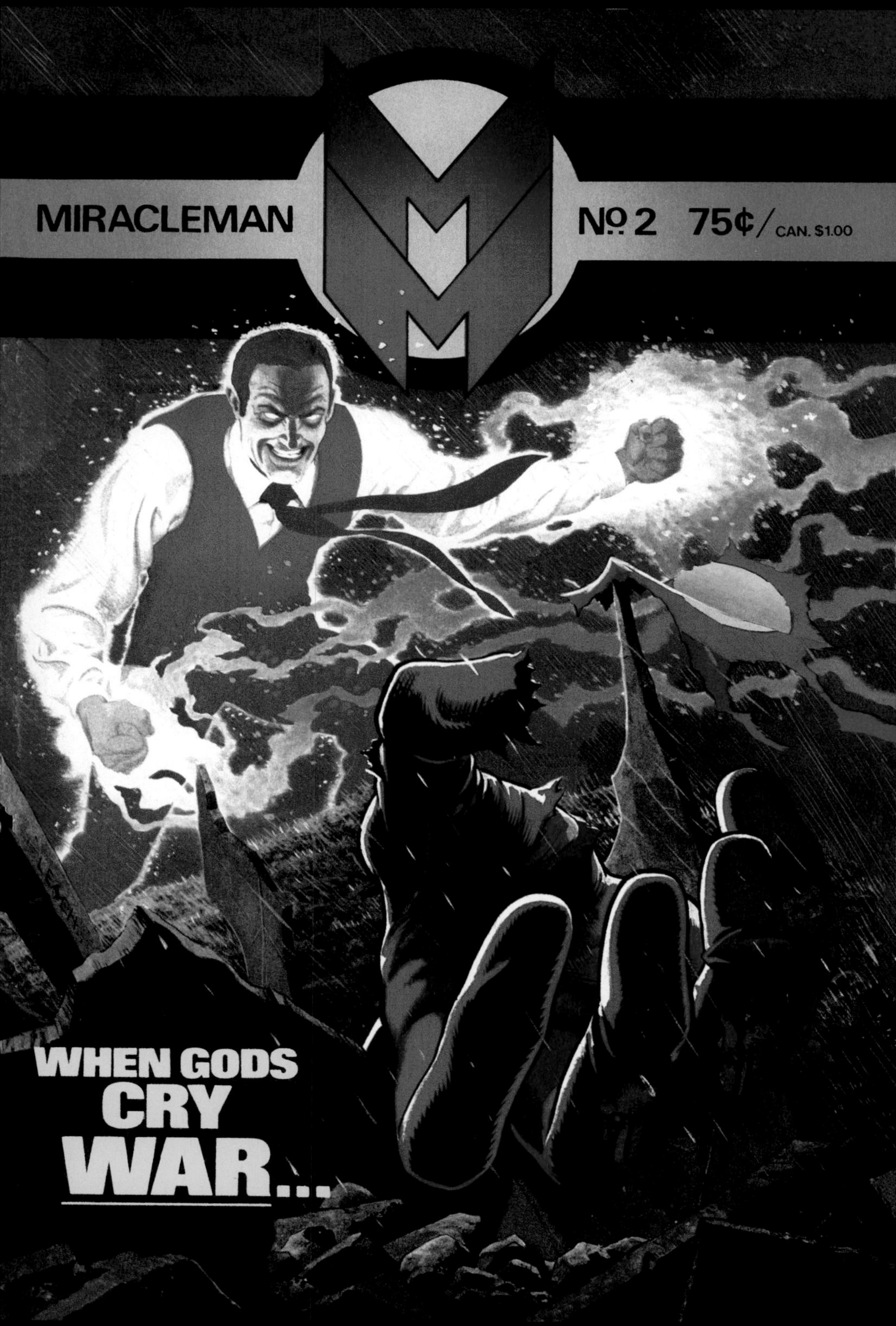
MIRACLEMAN
№ 2 75¢/ CAN. $1.00
WHEN GODS
CRY
WAR...

Original art to Garry Leach's cover painting for *Miracleman Book One: A Dream of Flying* (1988).

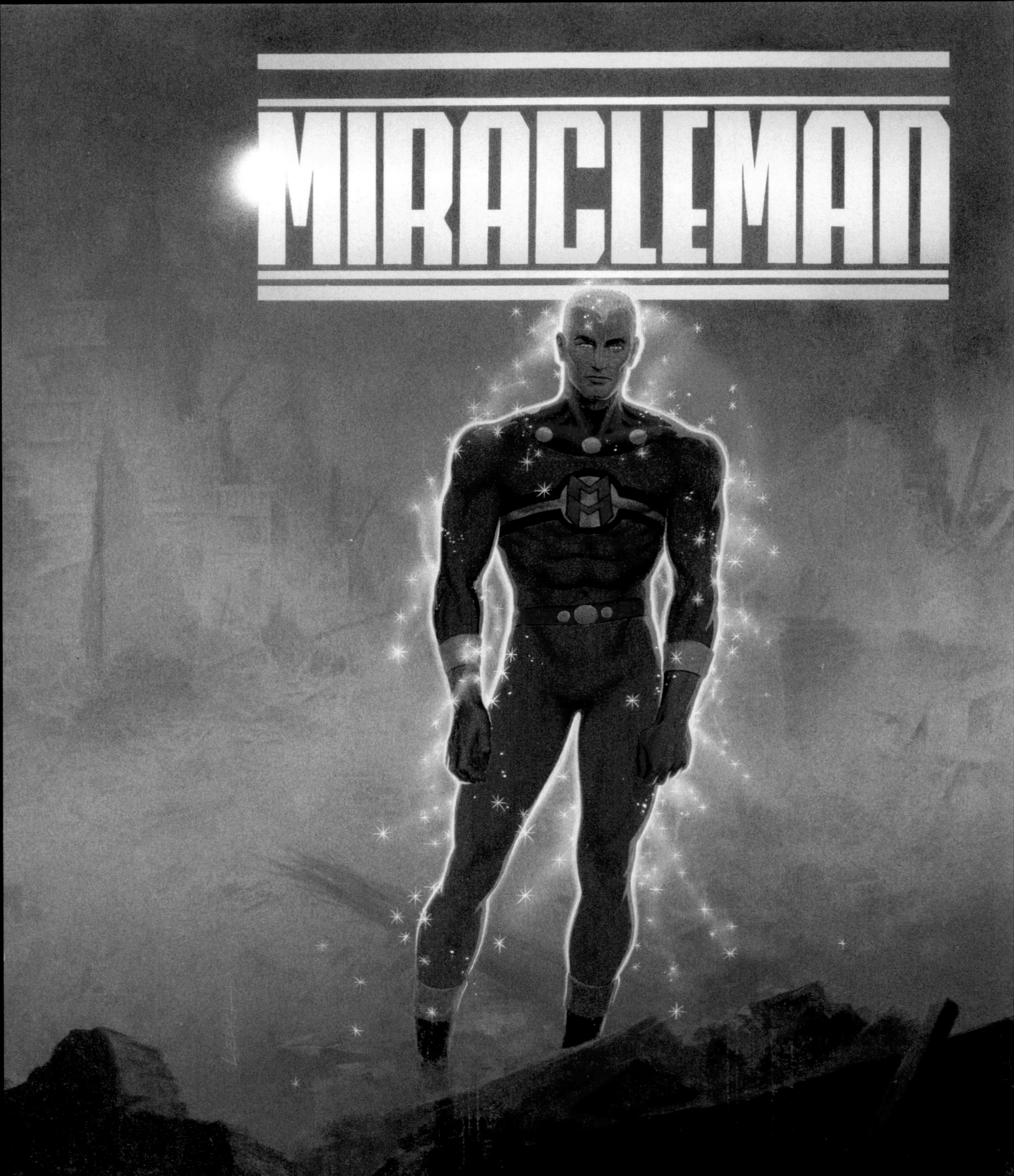
MIRACLEMAN

Garry Leach sketches from *AT Sketchbook* (2004). Clockwise from top-left: Miracleman profile sketch pencils; final inks; Kid Miracleman sketch; and a "transitional Miracleman" blending Mick Anglo and Garry's versions of the hero.

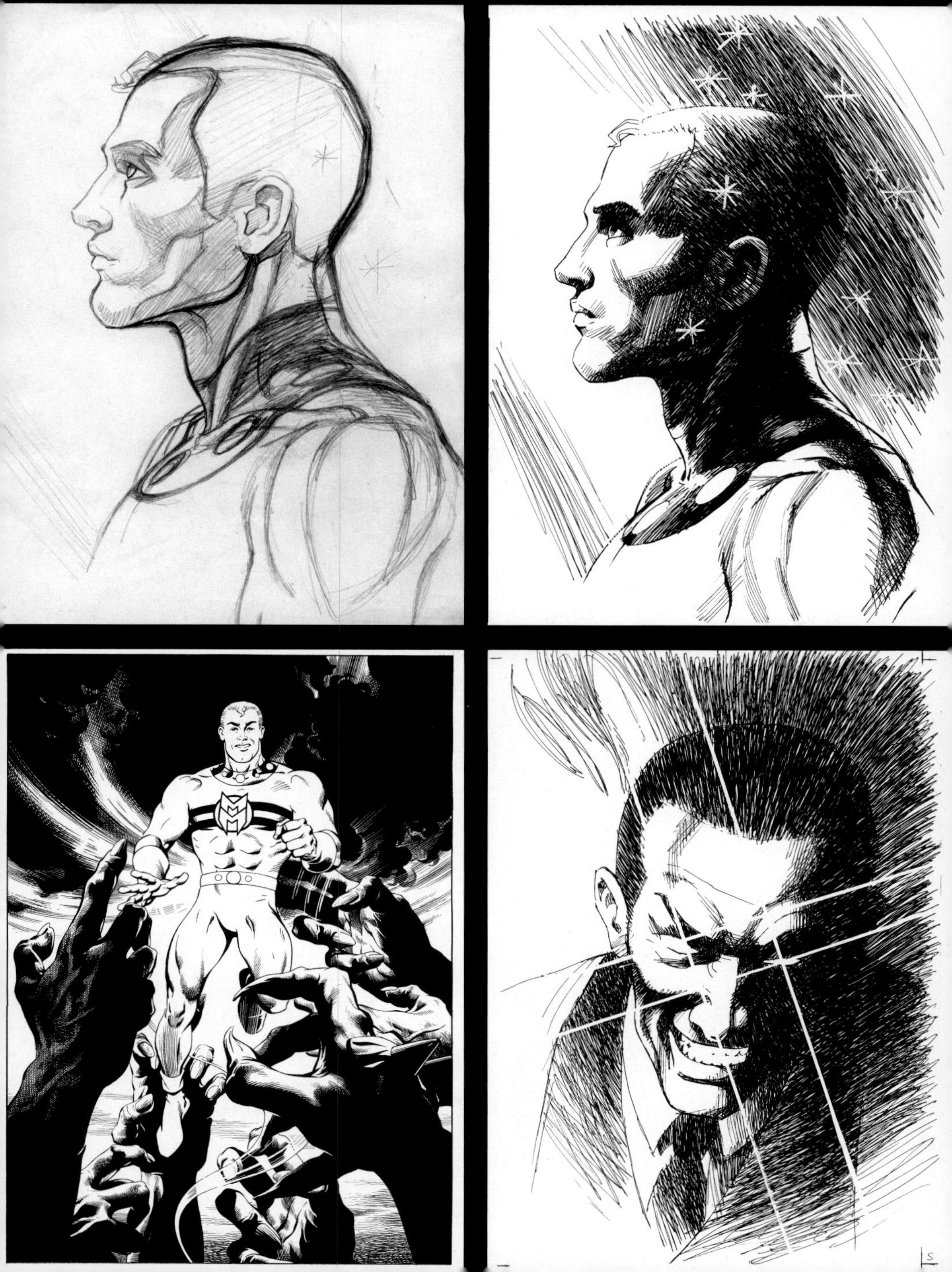

Warpsmith rough concept sketch, red biro on graph paper, by Garry Leach. Garry jettisoned this approach feeling it skewed too strongly toward science fiction and adapted it into the final, more super-hero-style design.

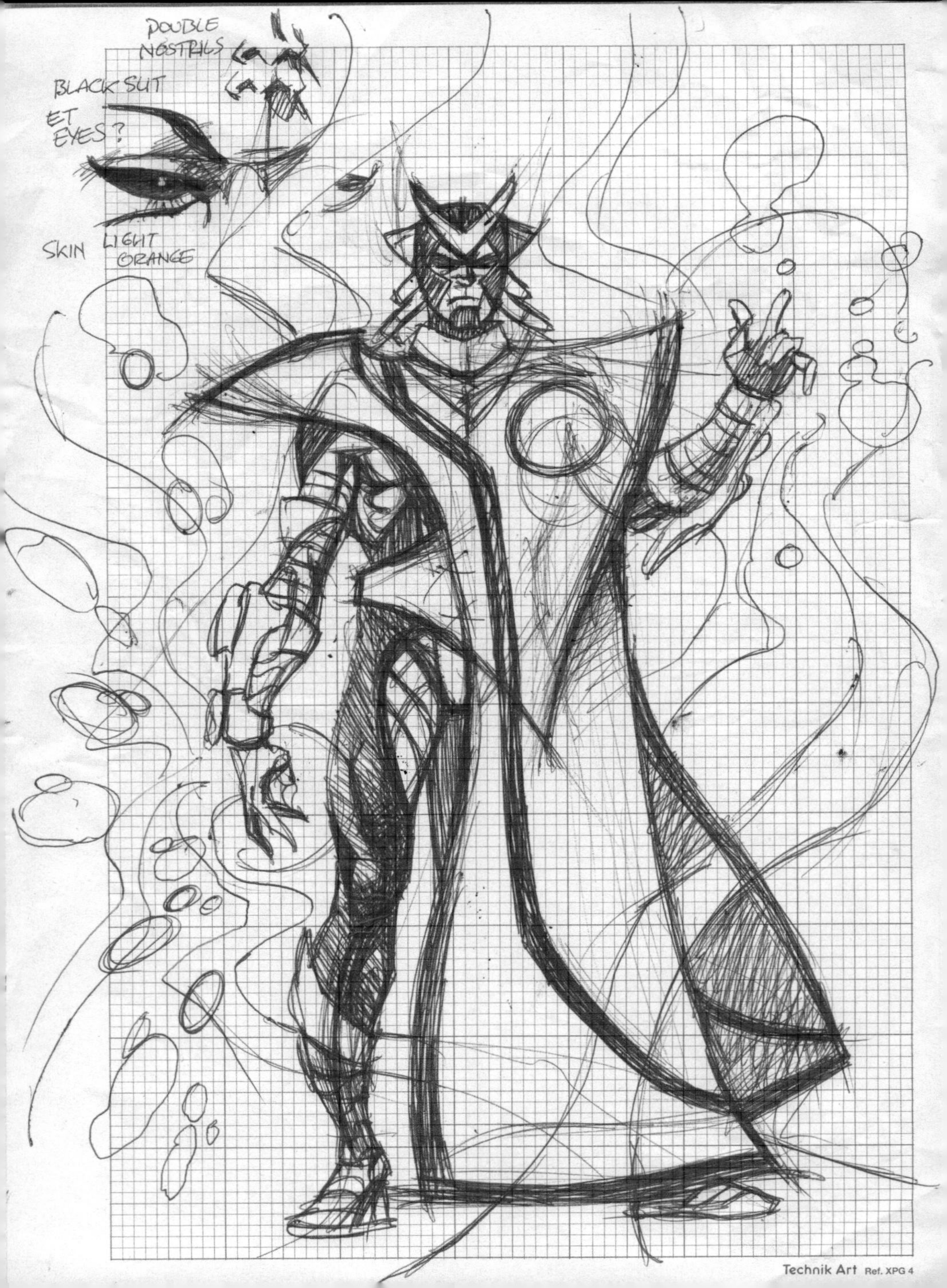
DOUBLE NOSTRILS
BLACK SUIT
ET EYES?
SKIN LIGHT ORANGE
Technik Art Ref. XPG 4

Aza Chorn model sheet, felt tip pen on layout paper, by Garry Leach. Garry drew this style guide for Steve Dillon, Paul Neary and Alan Davis to follow for the character's appearance in *Warrior* #4's 'The Yesterday Gambit." He further streamlined the Warpsmith's look from this piece, amending the helmet so that its "tusks" wouldn't interfere with the view of Aza Chorn's face.

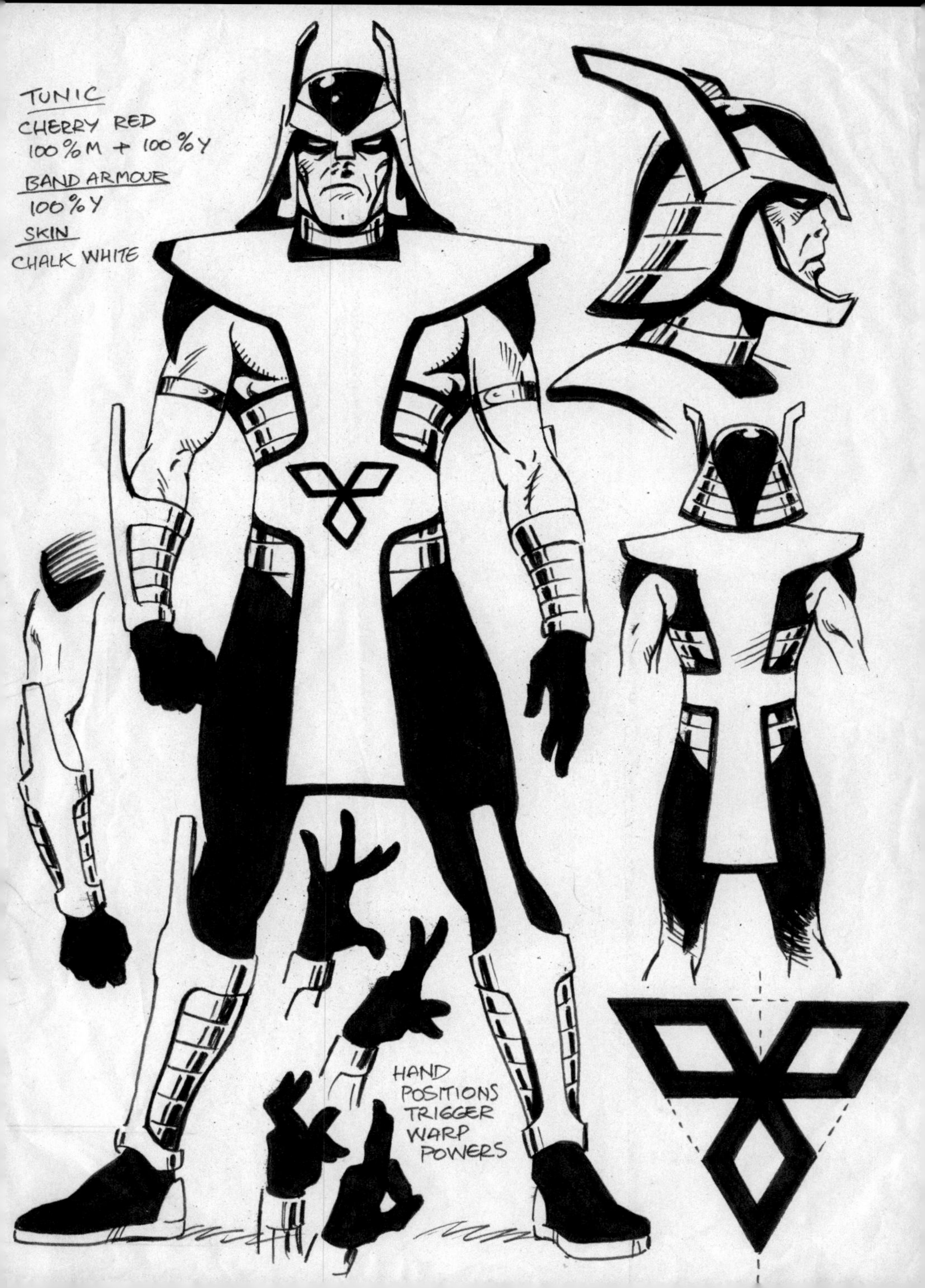

TUNIC
CHERRY RED
100%M + 100%Y
BAND ARMOUR
100%Y
SKIN
CHALK WHITE
HAND POSITIONS TRIGGER WARP POWERS

Original art to Garry Leach's cover painting for *Warrior* #10 (April-May 1983).

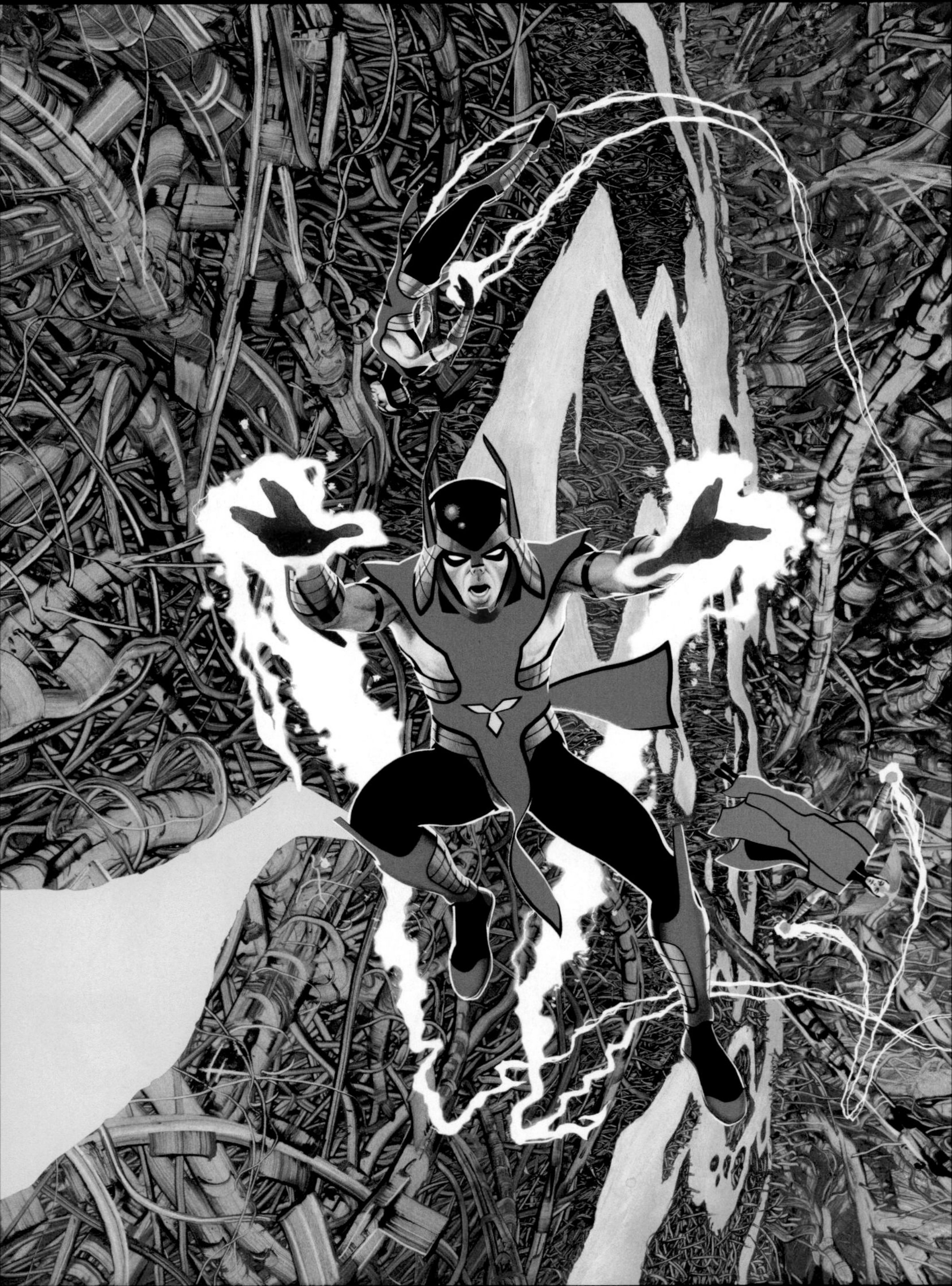

In 1984, Garry Leach remastered his artwork, stripping out much of the original Letratone, and hand-painted the coloring for the first color edition of "Cold War, Cold Warrior." A selection of his color originals, which were used as the basis for this edition's coloring, are presented below.

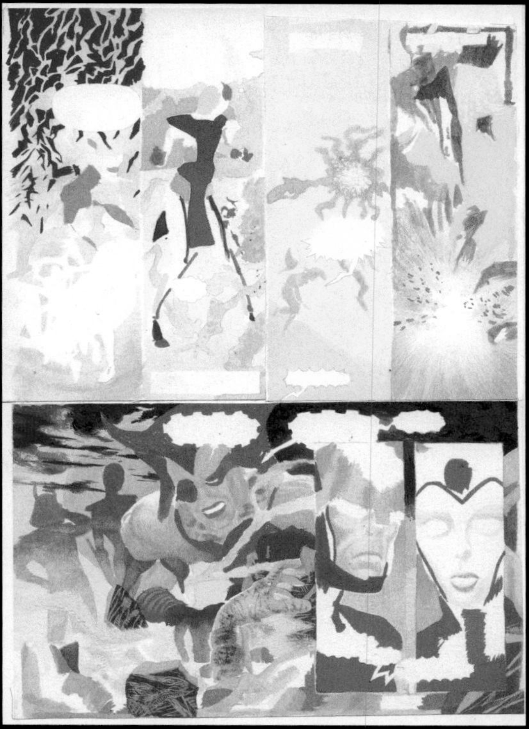

Page 4, hand-painted color

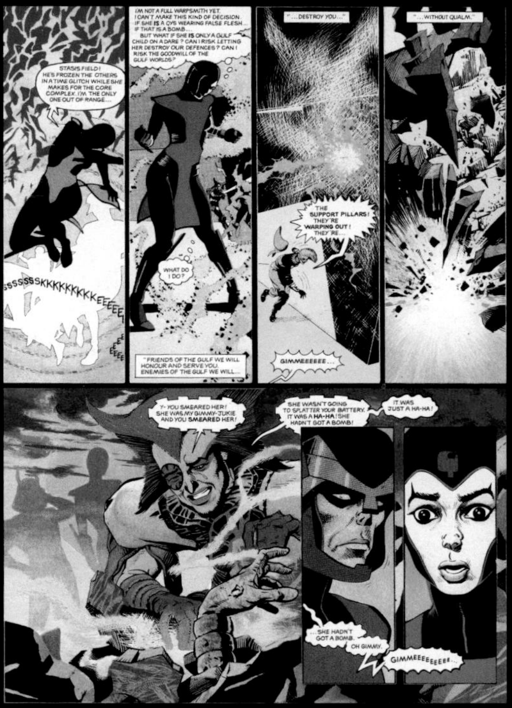
STASIS FIELD! HE'S FROZEN THE OTHERS IN A TIME GLITCH WHILE SHE MAKES FOR THE CORE COMPLEX. I'M THE ONLY ONE OUT OF RANGE...
SSSSSSSKKKKKKKKKKEEEEEE
I'M NOT A FULL WARPSMITH YET. I CAN'T MAKE THIS KIND OF DECISION. IF SHE IS A CYS WEARING FALSE FLESH... IF THAT IS A BOMB... BUT WHAT IF SHE IS ONLY A GULF CHILD ON A DARE? CAN I RISK LETTING HER DESTROY OUR DEFENCES? CAN I RISK THE GOODWILL OF THE GULF WORLDS?
WHAT DO I DO?
"FRIENDS OF THE GULF WE WILL HONOUR AND SERVE YOU. ENEMIES OF THE GULF WE WILL...
"...DESTROY YOU..."
THE SUPPORT PILLARS! THEY'RE WARPING OUT! THEY'RE...
GIMMEEEEEEE...
"...WITHOUT QUALM."
Y- YOU SMEARED HER! SHE WAS MY GIMMY-JUKIE AND YOU SMEARED HER!
SHE WASN'T GOING TO SPLATTER YOUR BATTERY. IT WAS A HA-HA! SHE HADN'T GOT A BOMB!
IT WAS JUST A HA-HA!
...SHE HADN'T GOT A BOMB.
OH GIMMY.
GIMMEEEEEEEEEE...

Page 4, hand-painted color and film overlay

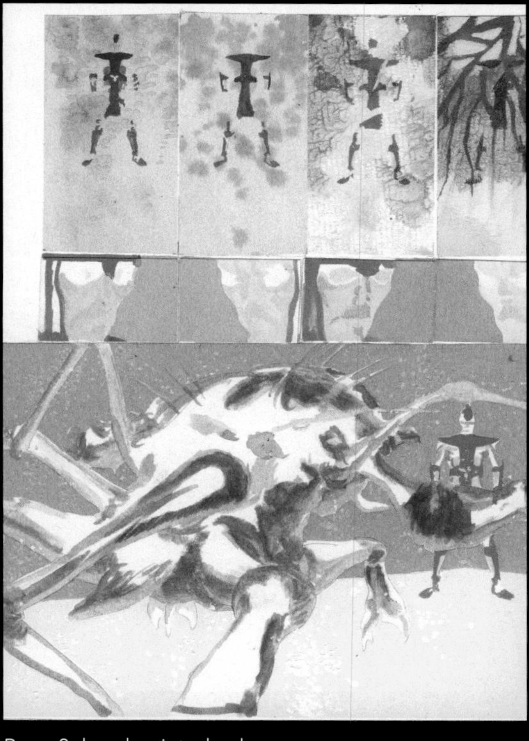

Page 8, hand-painted color

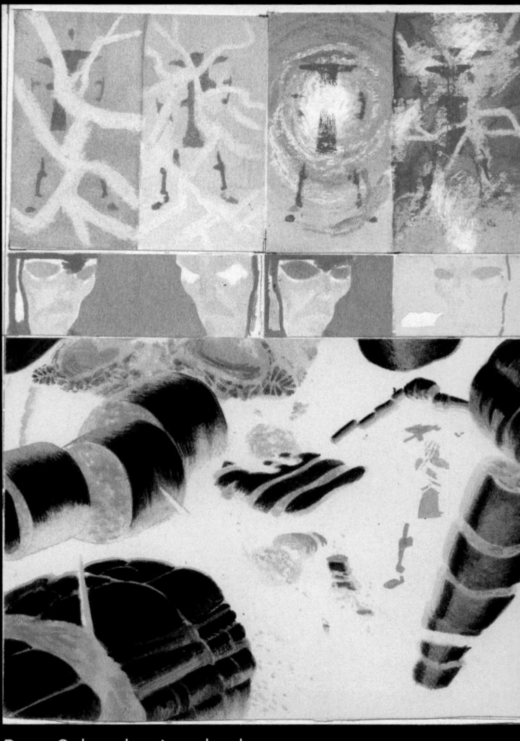

Page 9, hand-painted color

Warrior #9, "Cold War, Cold Warrior." page 2, panel 1 Aza Chorn preliminary rough, red Biro on cartridge paper by Garry Leach.

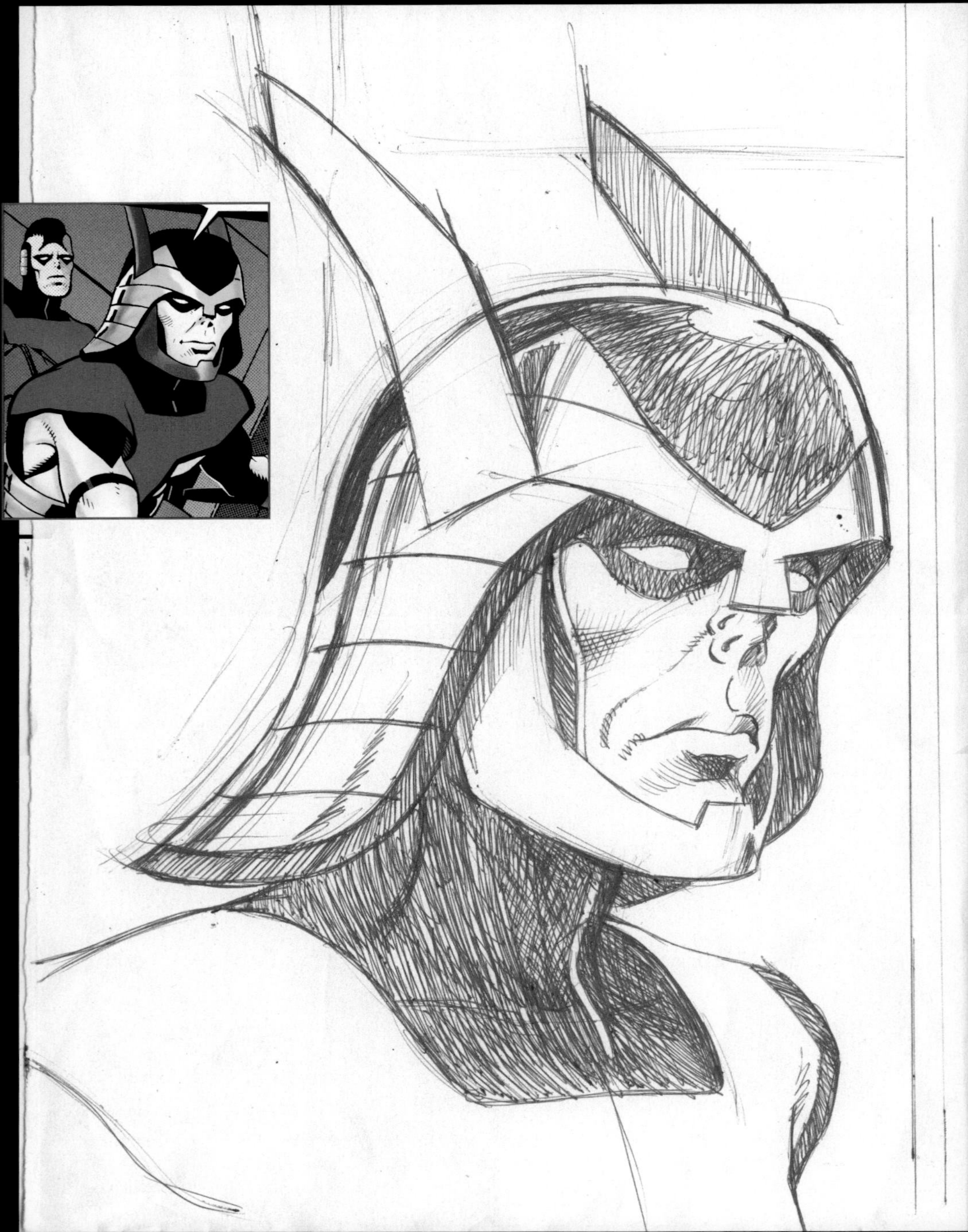

Warrior #9, "Cold War, Cold Warrior." page 3 Uxu Chil preliminary pencil rough, pencil on cartridge paper by Garry Leach.

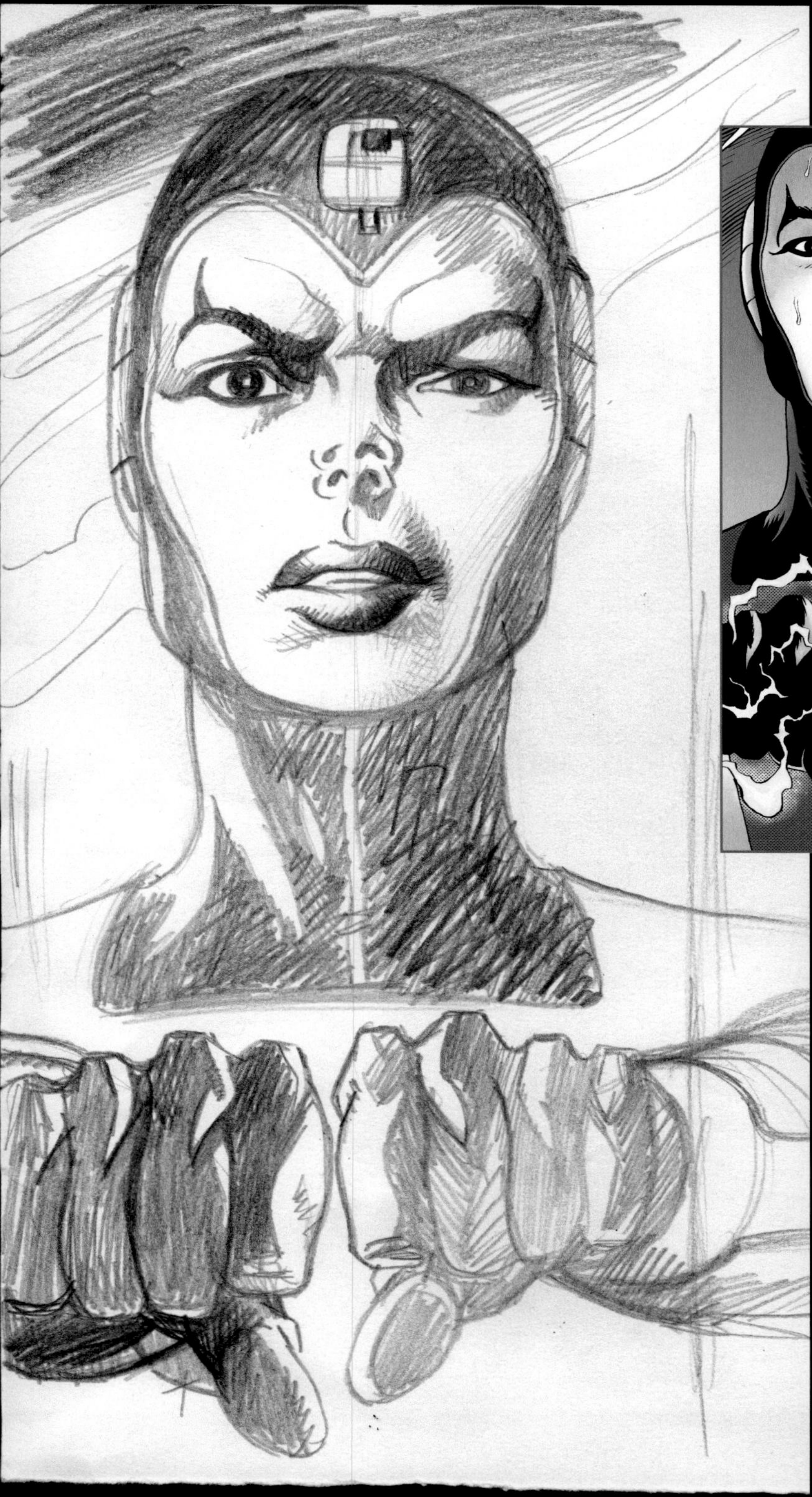

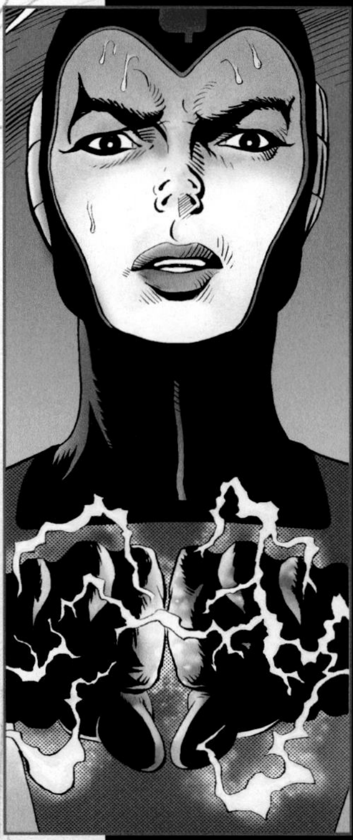

Warrior #9, "Cold War, Cold Warrior." page 3 original art, pencil, India ink and Letratone on CS
board by Garry Leach.

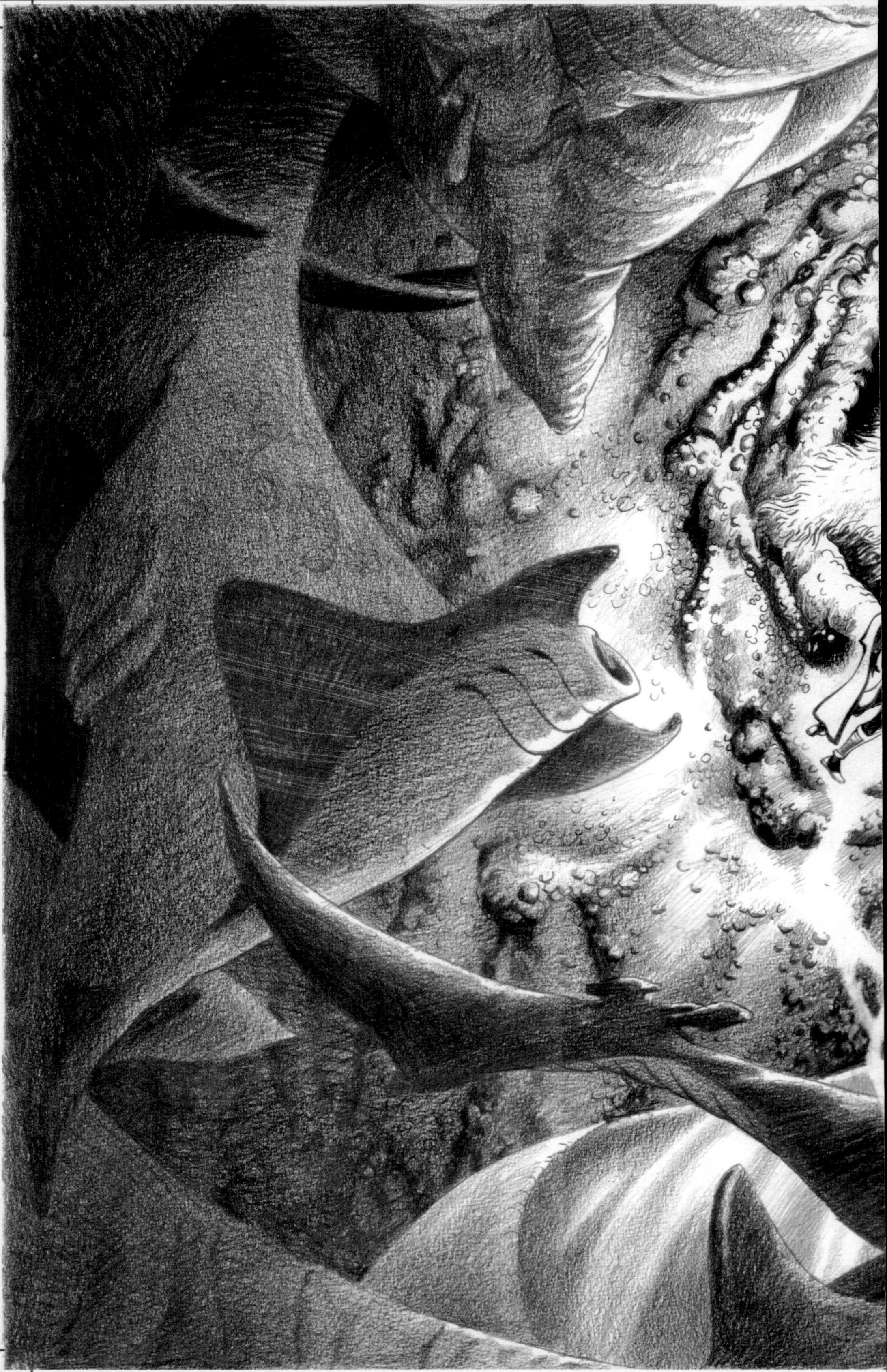

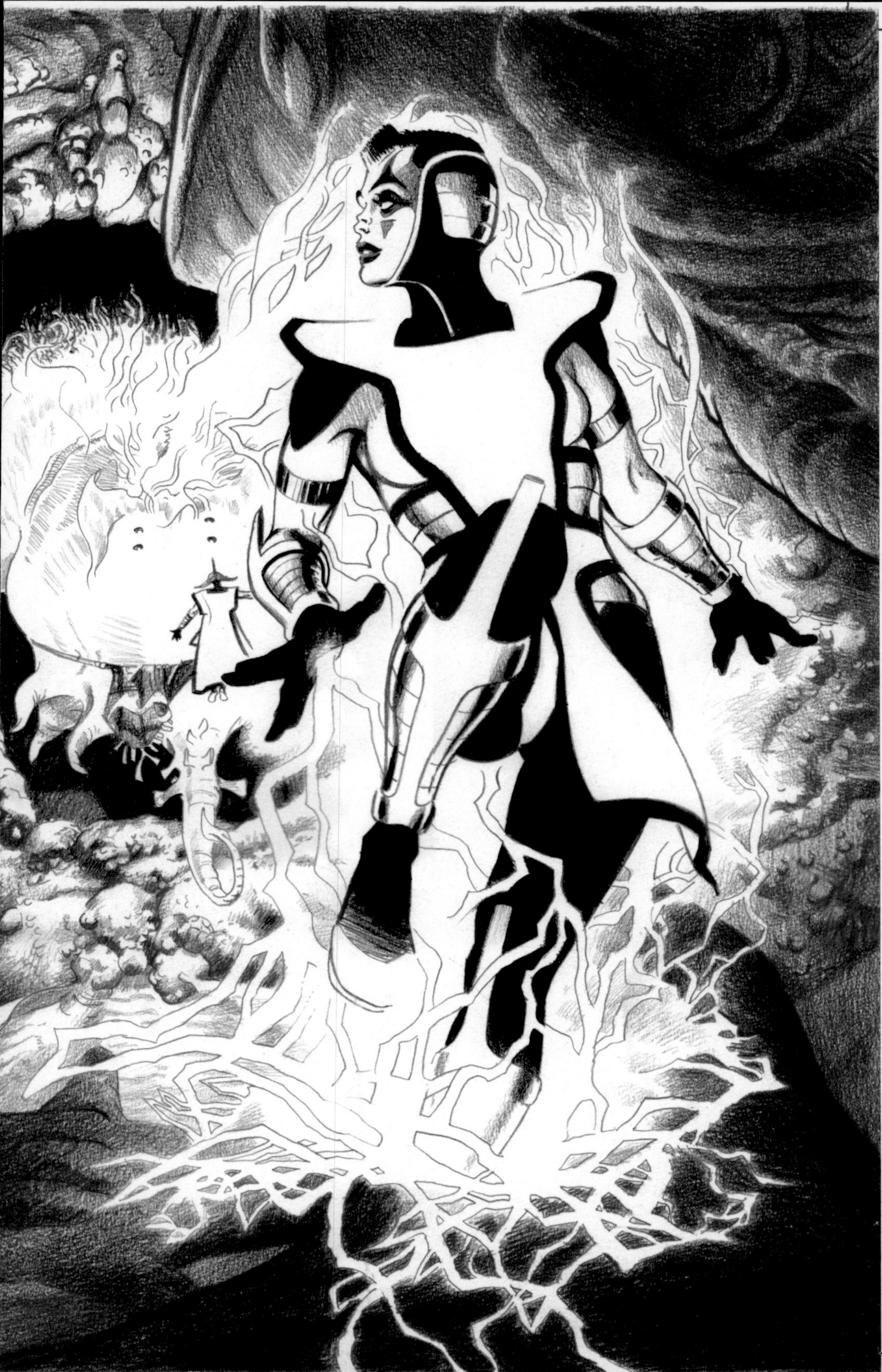

PREVIOUS PAGE: Pencil underdrawing to Garry Leach's *A1* #1 (1989) cover.
THIS PAGE: Final *A1* #1 cover painting.

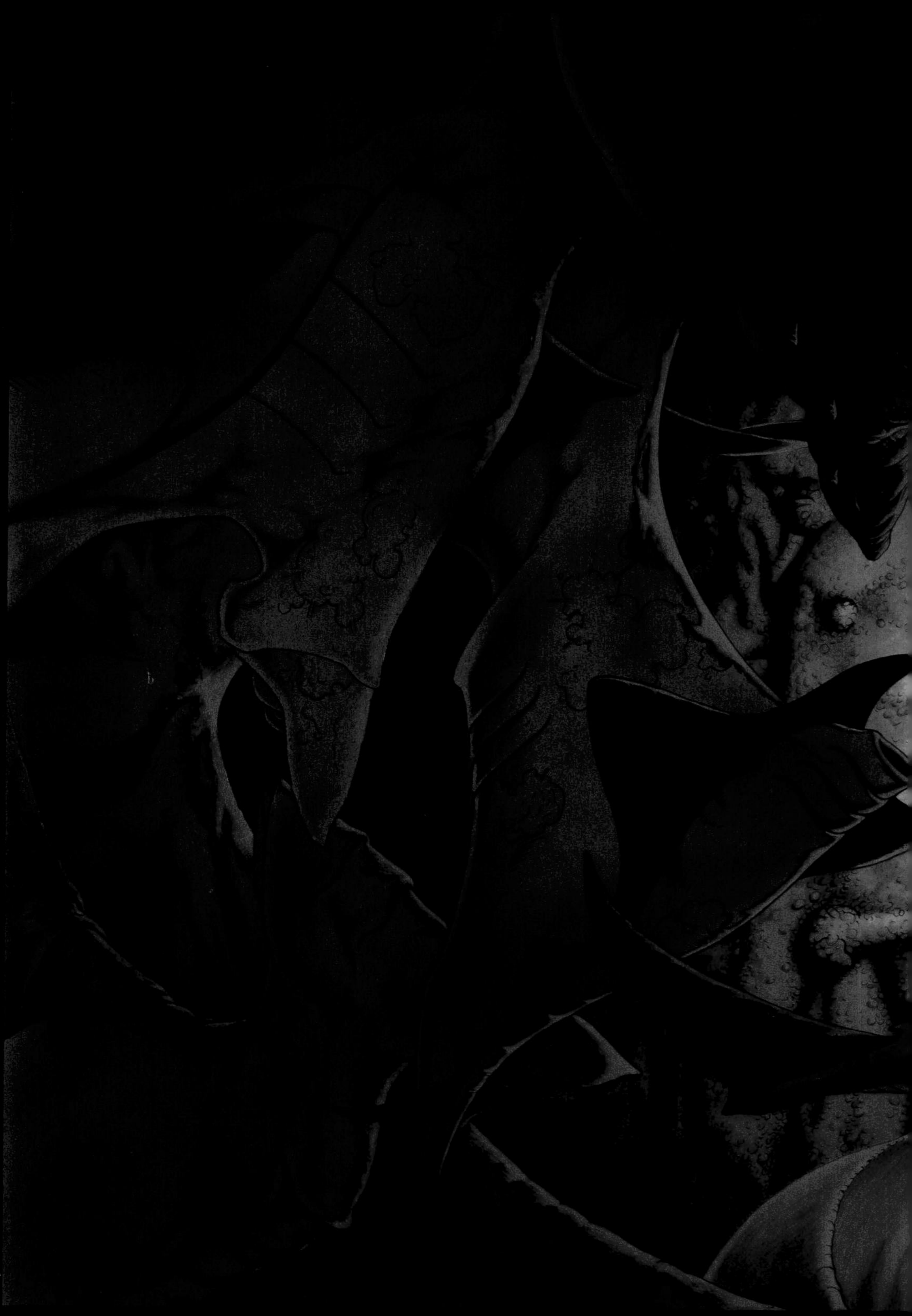

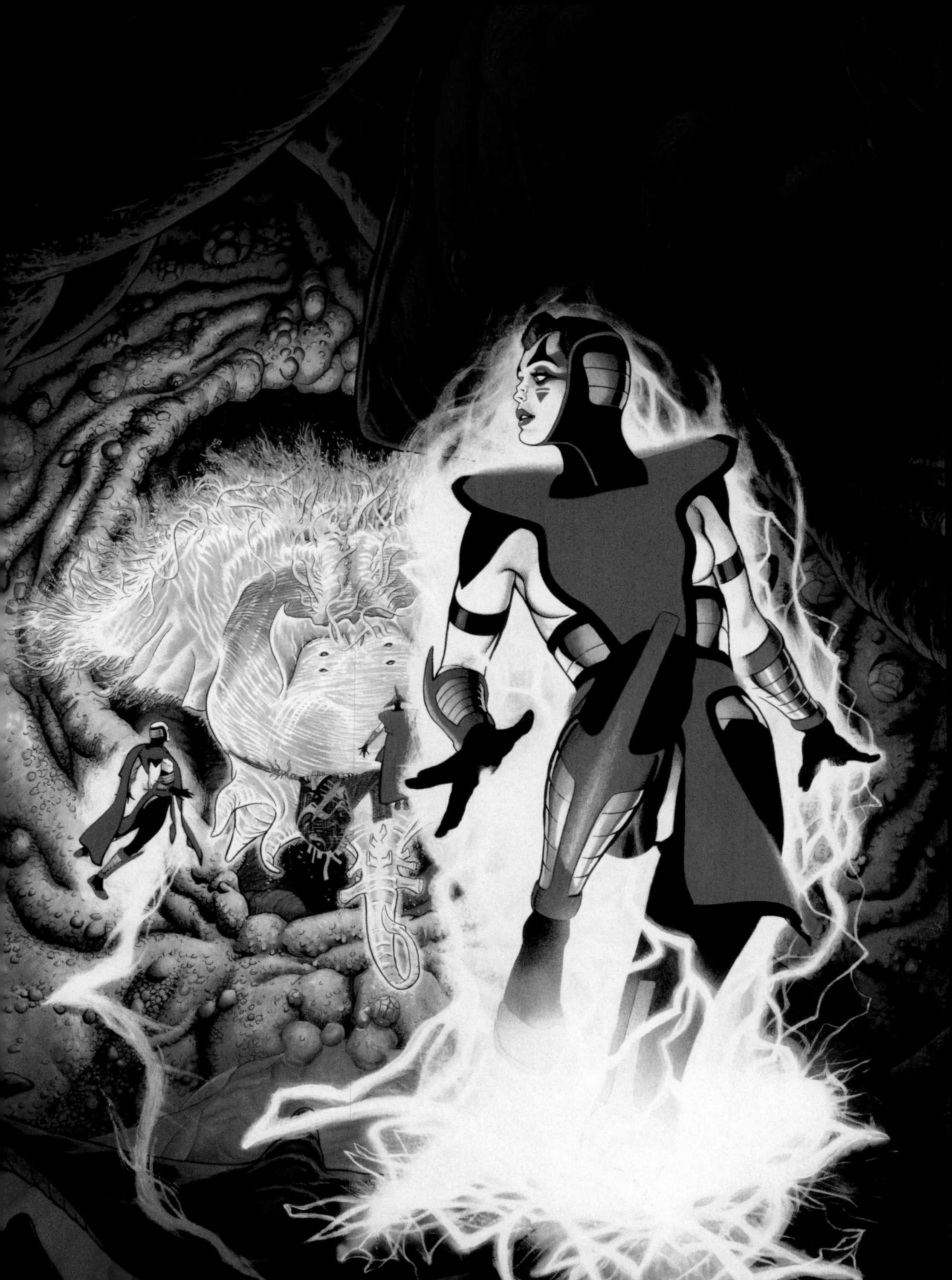

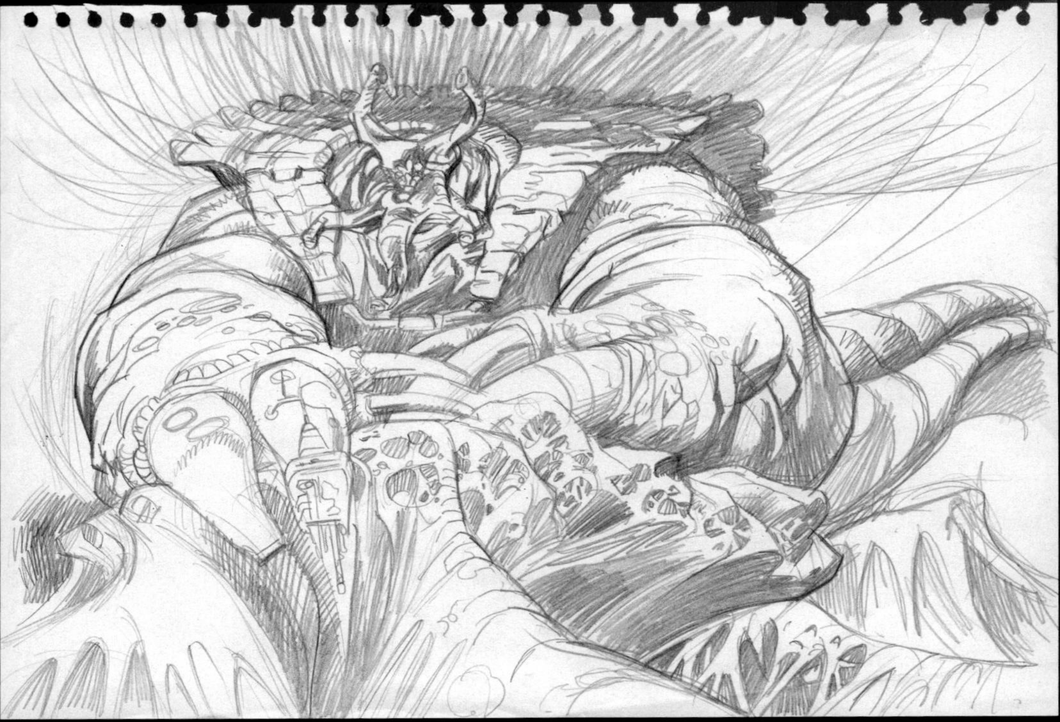

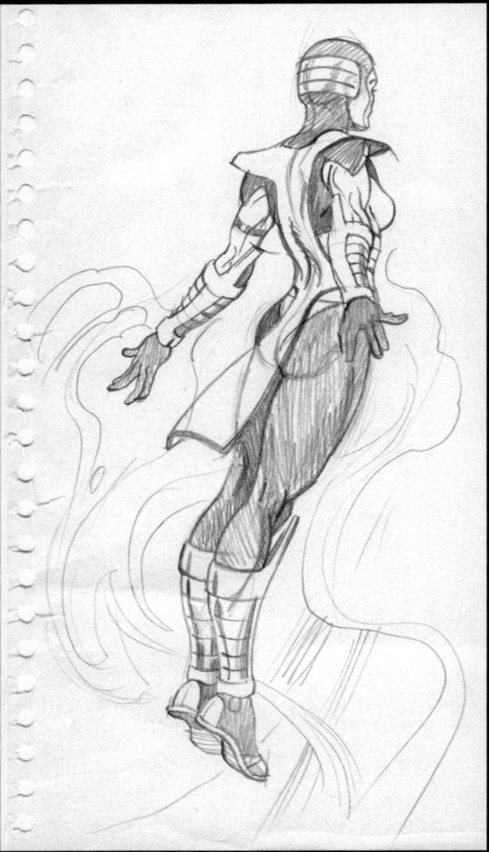

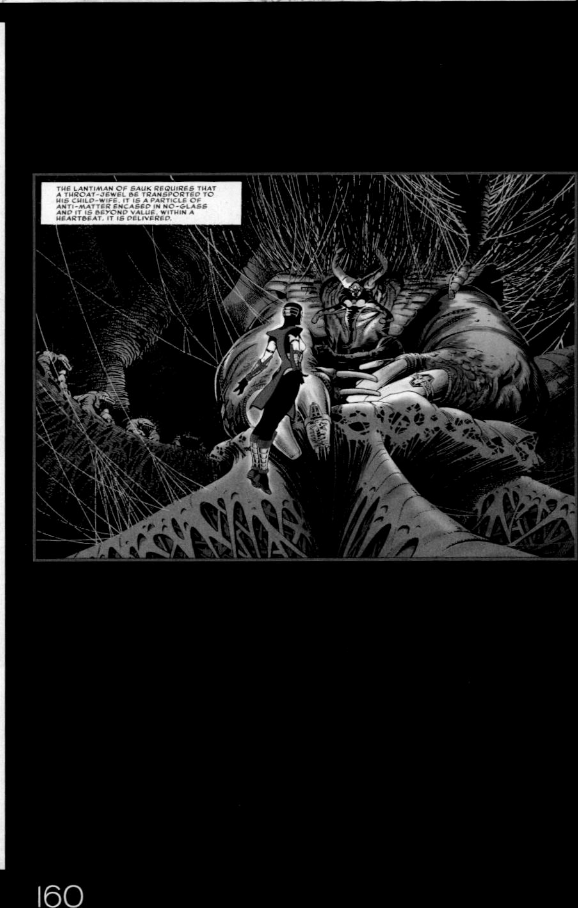
THE LANTIMAN OF SAUK REQUIRES THAT A THROAT-JEWEL BE TRANSPORTED TO HIS CHILD-WIFE. IT IS A PARTICLE OF ANTI-MATTER ENCASED IN NO-GLASS AND IT IS BEYOND VALUE. WITHIN A HEARTBEAT, IT IS DELIVERED.

A+X #1, page 8, panel 1 Oxu Chil preliminary pencil rough by Garry Leach.

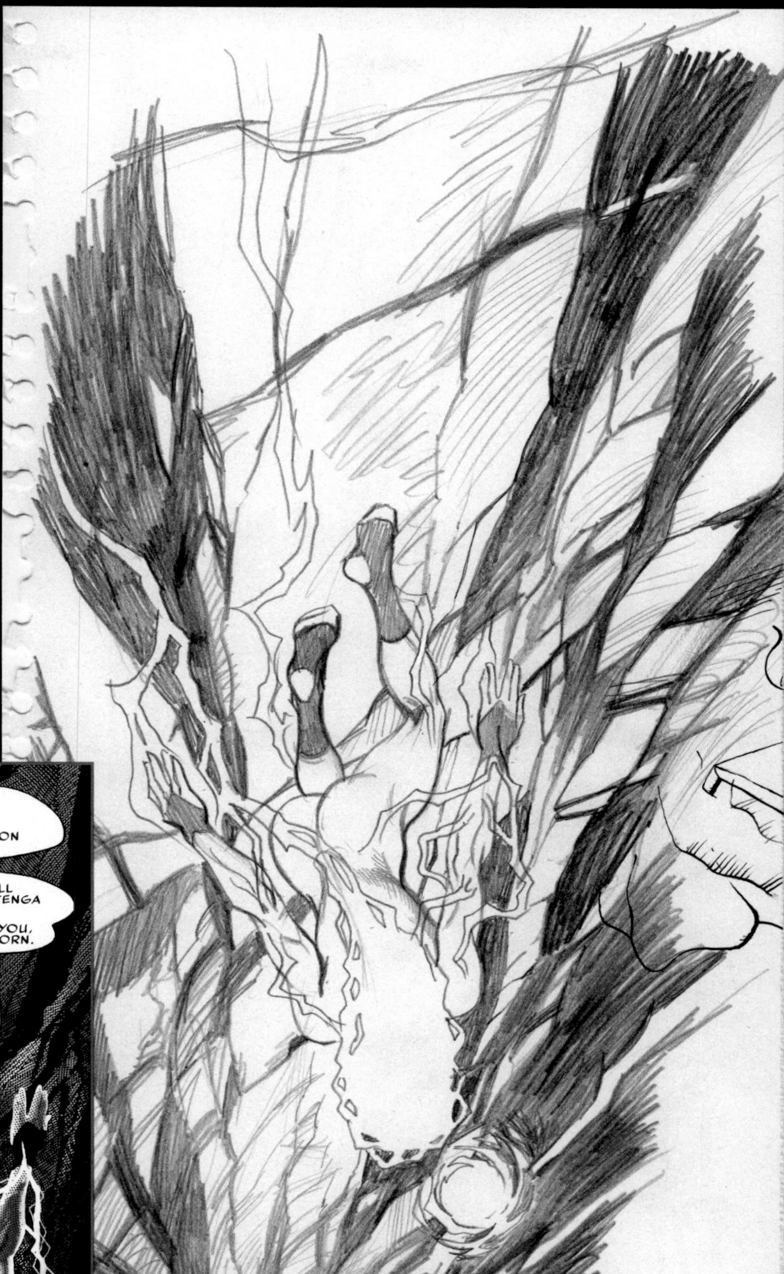

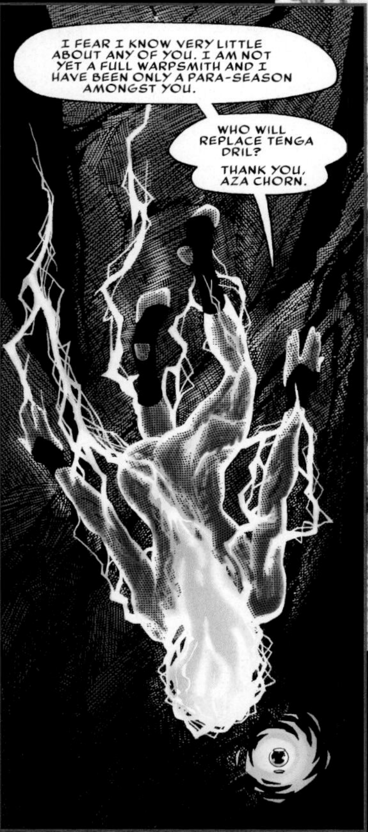

I FEAR I KNOW VERY LITTLE ABOUT ANY OF YOU. I AM NOT YET A FULL WARPSMITH AND I HAVE BEEN ONLY A PARA-SEASON AMONGST YOU.
WHO WILL REPLACE TENGA DRIL?
THANK YOU, AZA CHORN.

trilogy ("Ghostdance" had originally been planned for *Warrior* #14),

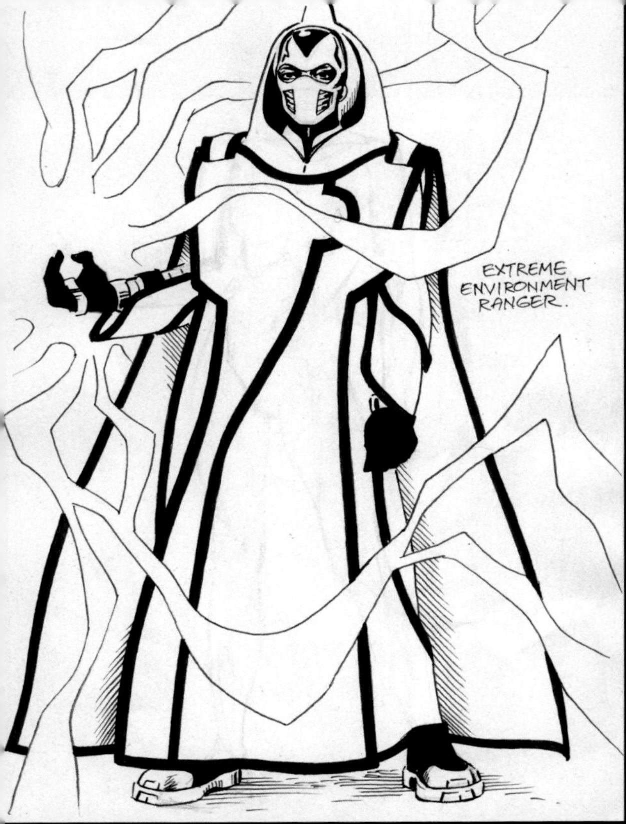
EXTREME
ENVIRONMENT
RANGER.

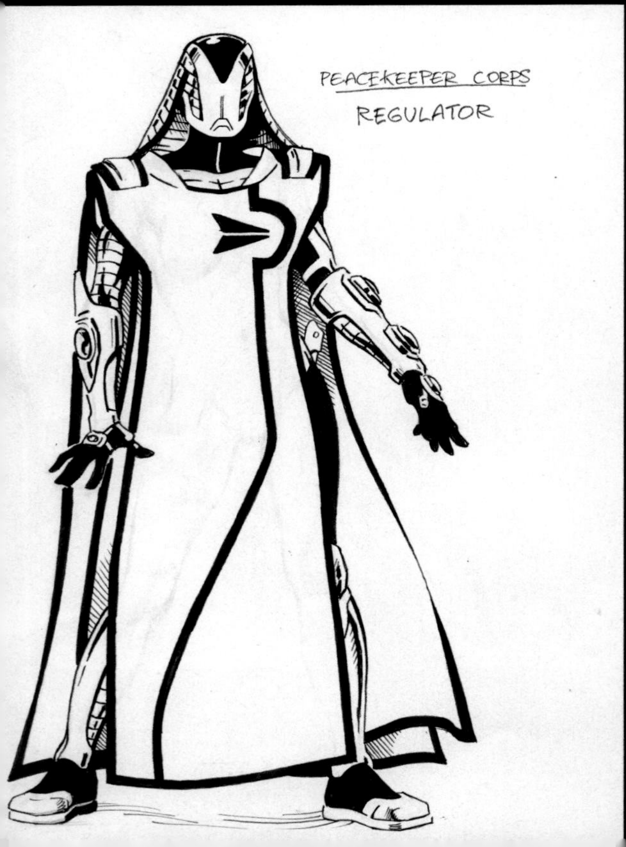
PEACEKEEPER CORPS
REGULATOR

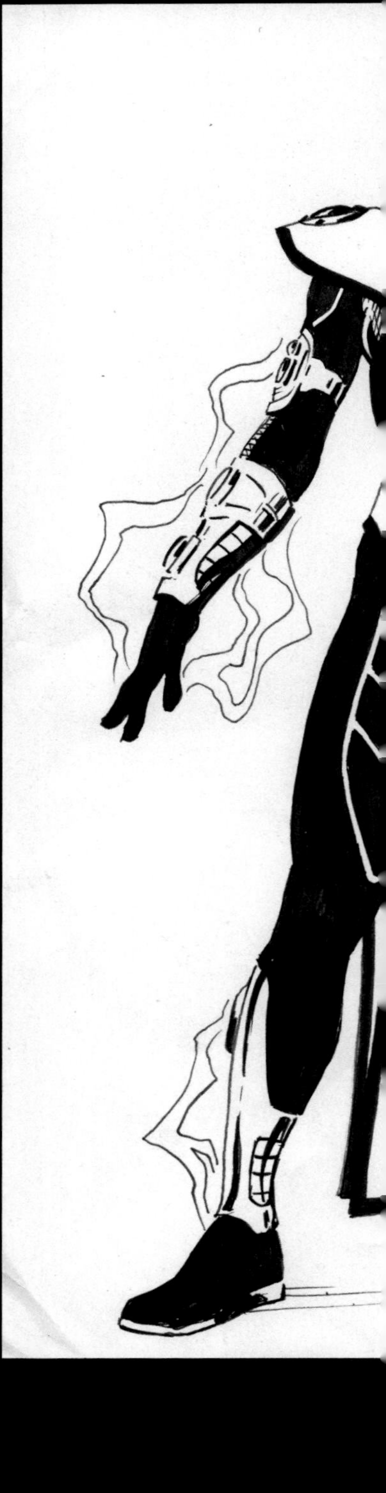

Garry Leach created designs for an unrealized expansion of the characters and their universe.

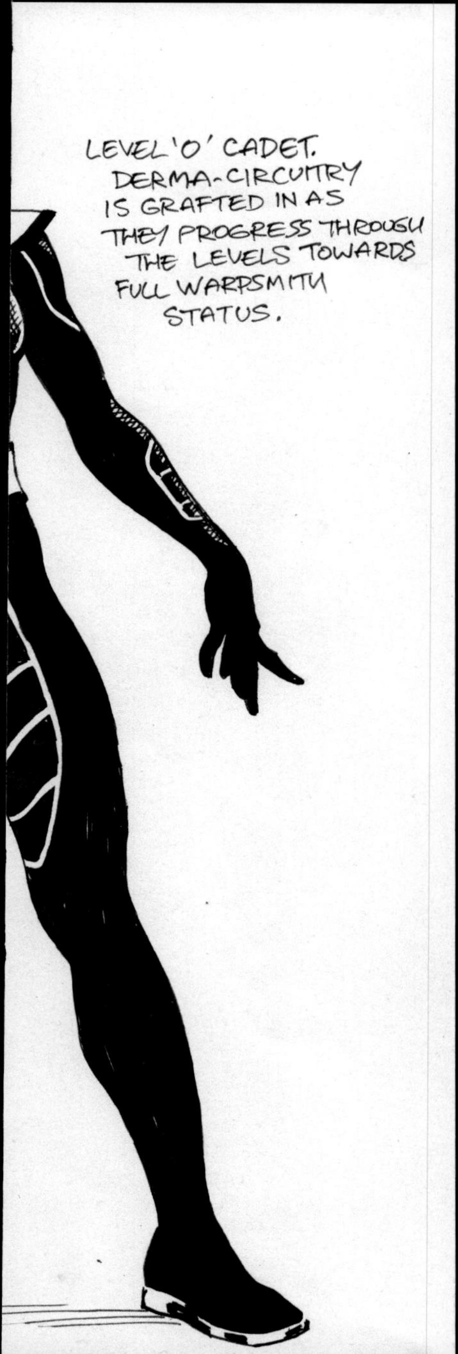
LEVEL 'O' CADET.
DERMA-CIRCUITRY
IS GRAFTED IN AS
THEY PROGRESS THROUGH
THE LEVELS TOWARDS
FULL WARPSMITH
STATUS.

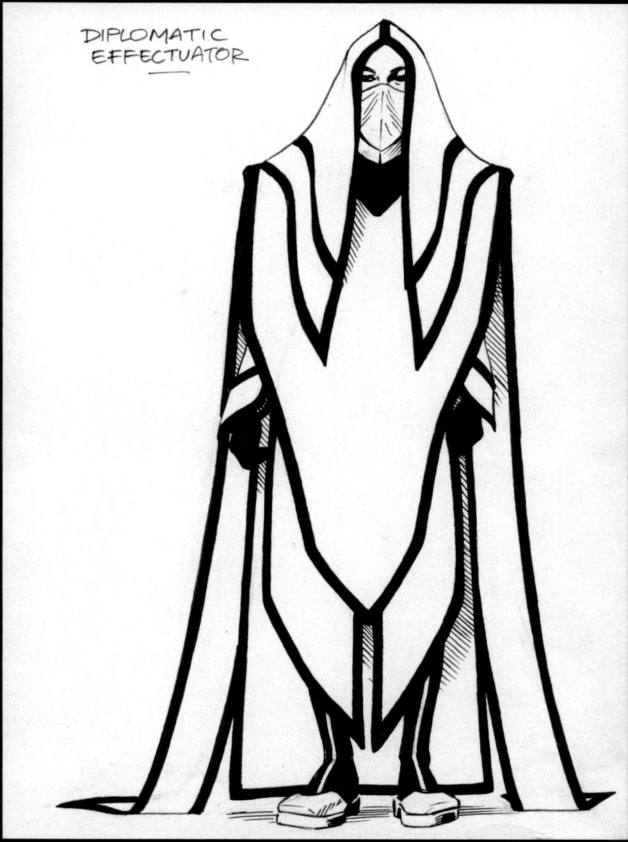
DIPLOMATIC
EFFECTUATOR

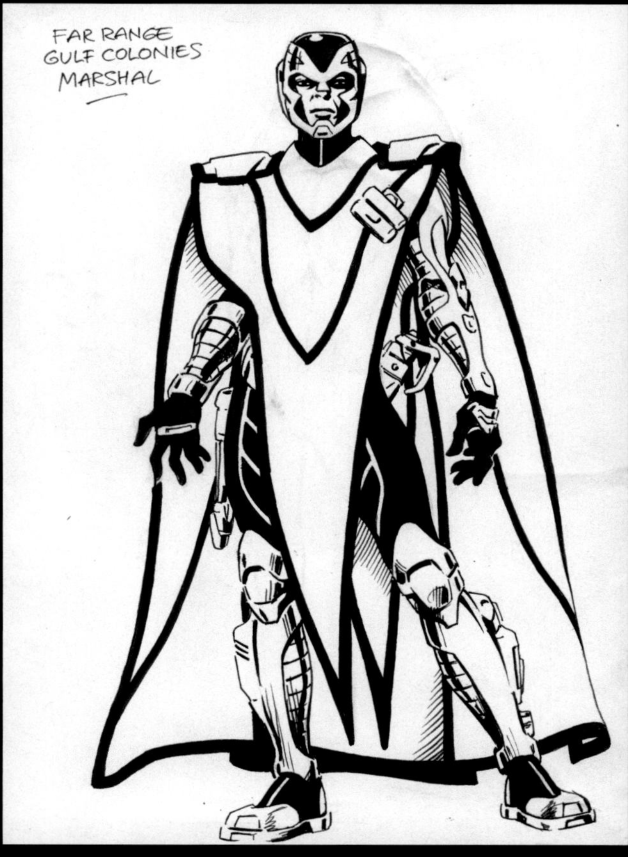
FAR RANGE
GULF COLONIES
MARSHAL

A1 Sketchbook (2004) Aza Chorn pinup adapted from the cover to *Warrior* #10 by Garry Leach.

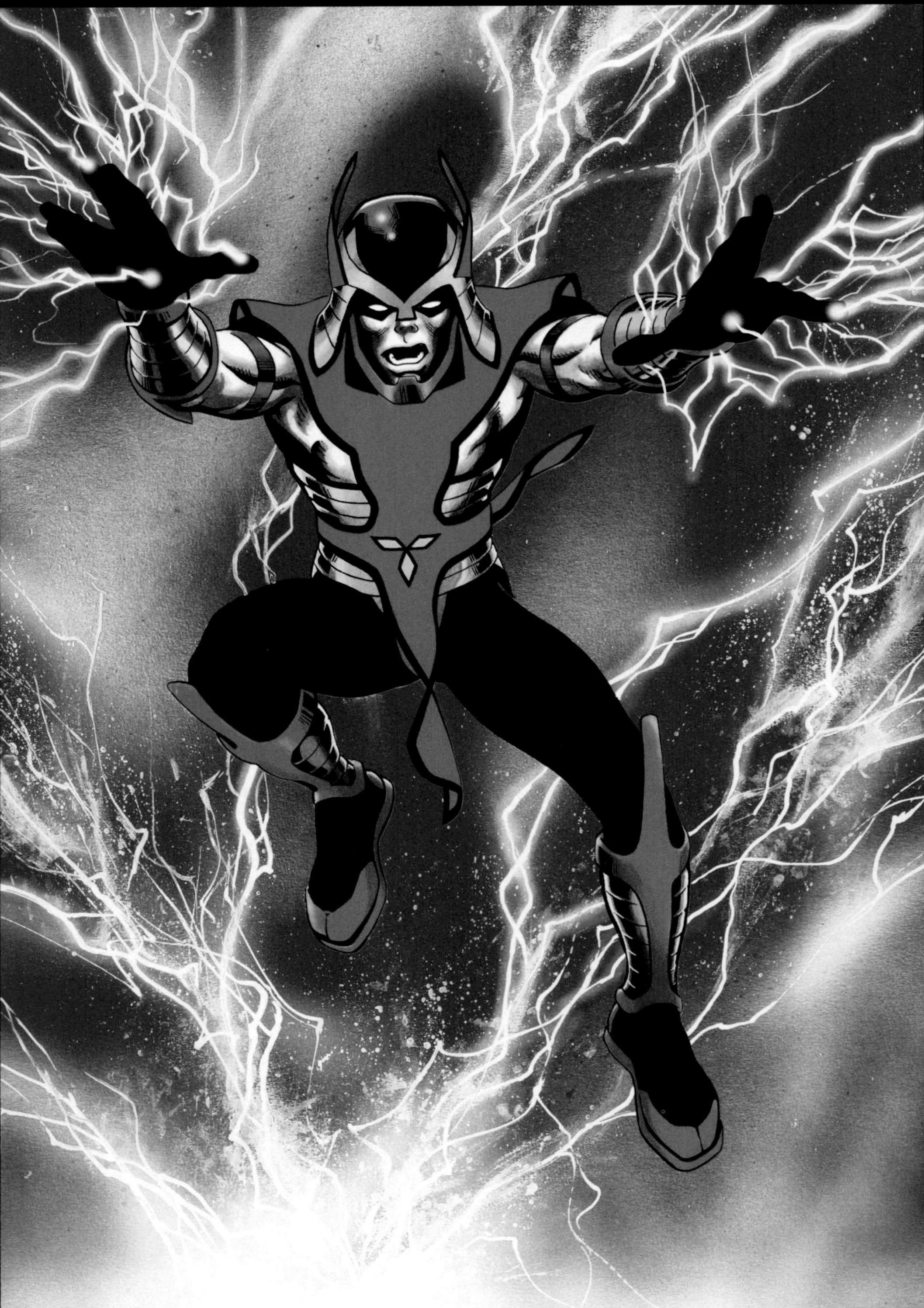

A1 Sketchbook (2004) Phon Mooda pinup by Garry Leach.

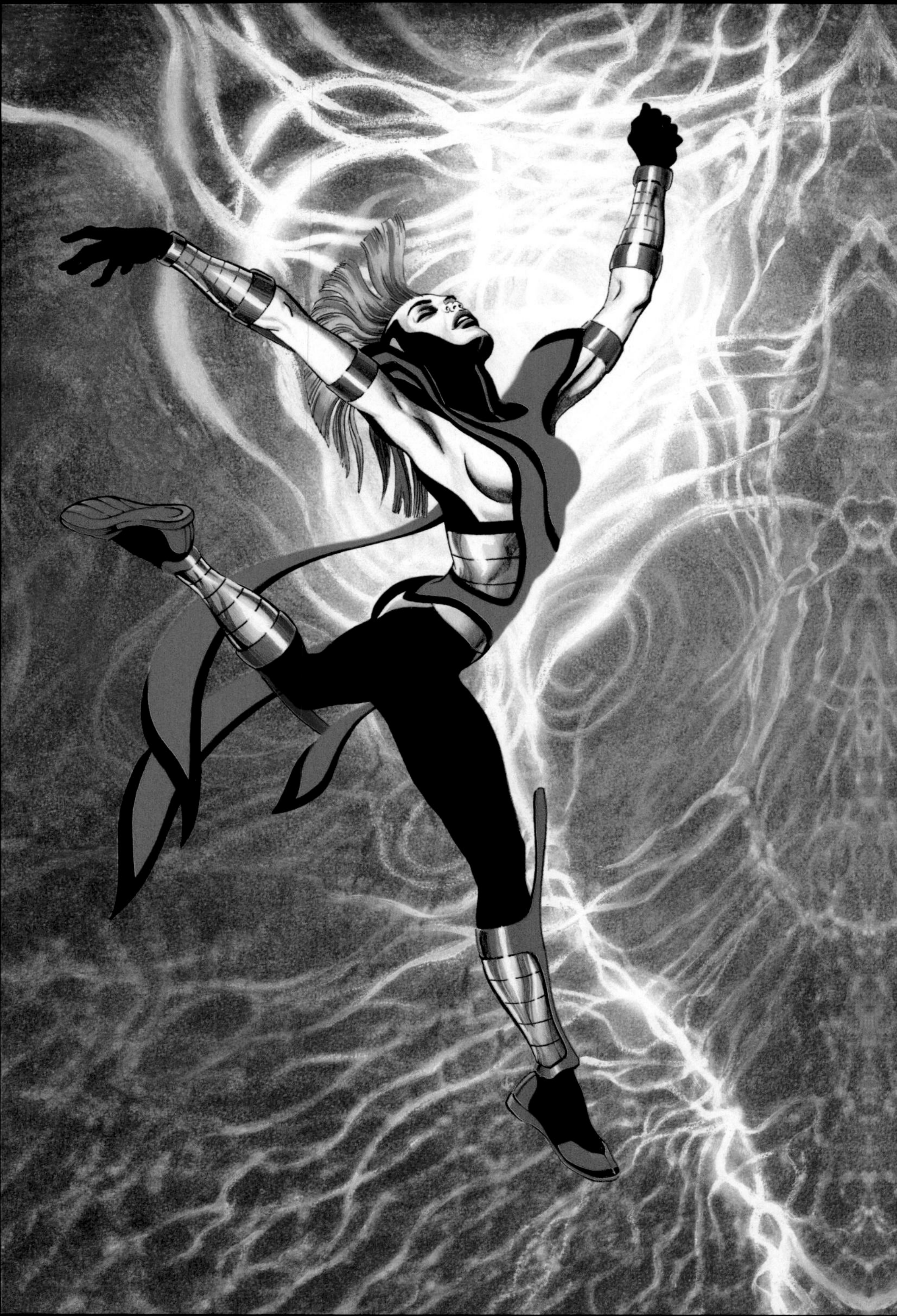

Miracleman #1 (2014) cover art by Joe Quesada, Danny Miki & Richard Isanove.

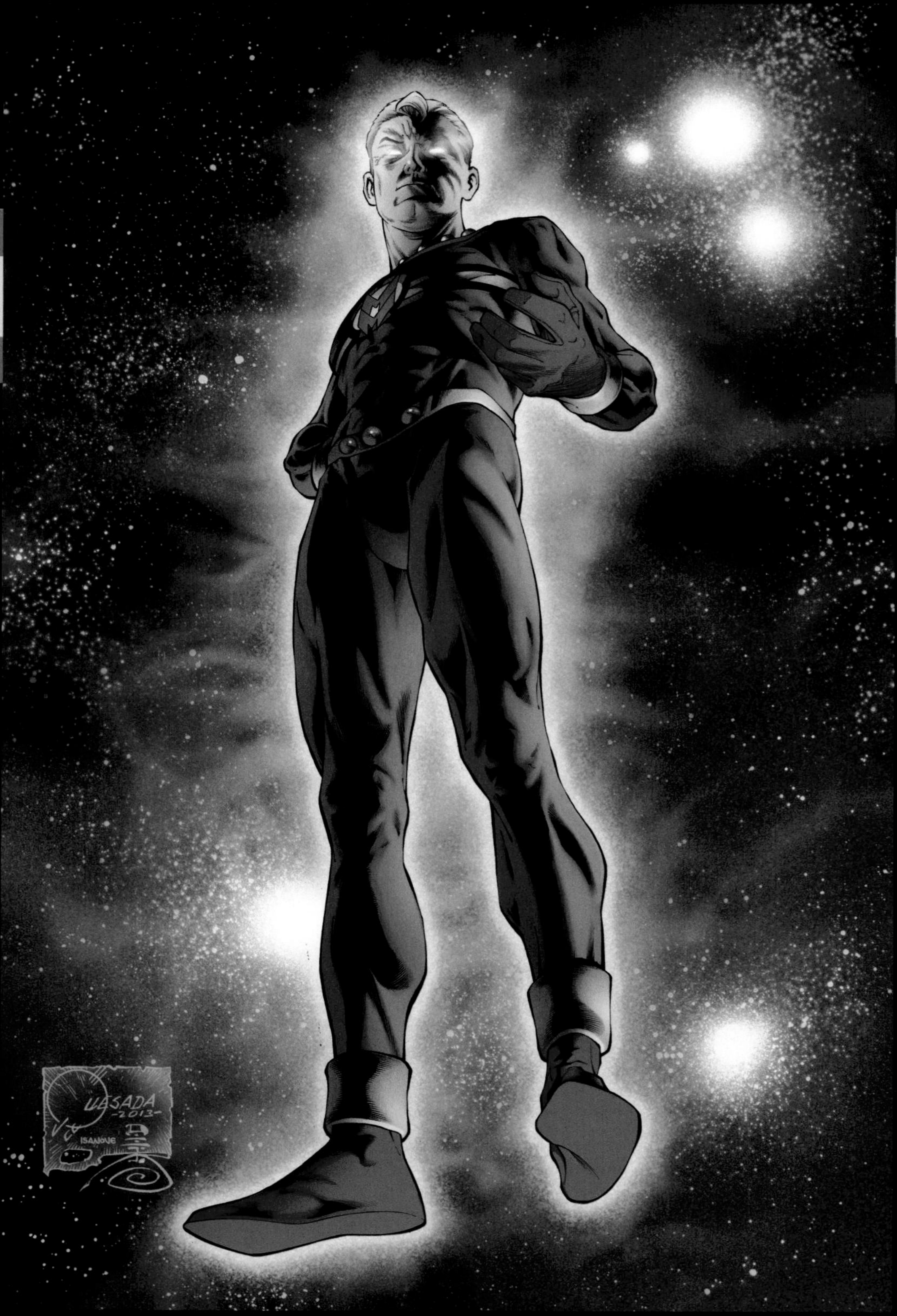
QUESADA
-2013-
ISANOVE

Miracleman #1 (2014) variant cover art (clockwise from top left) by John Cassaday & Paul Mounts, Leinil Yu, Gerry Alanguilan & Laura Martin; Skottie Young; and Mark Buckingham & D'Israeli.

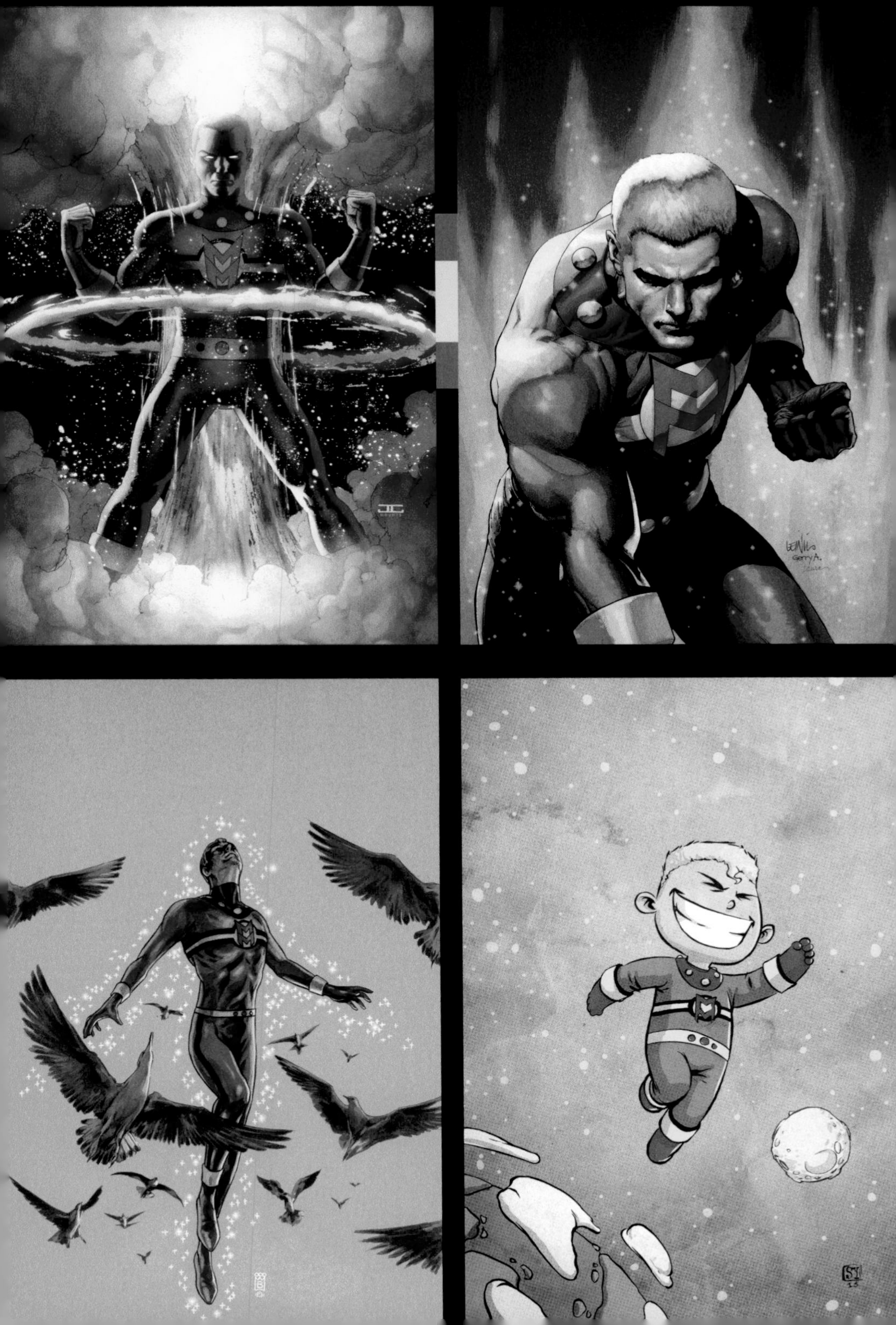

Miracleman #1 (2014) variant cover art (counter-clockwise from top-left) by Jerome Opeña & Dean White; Garry Leach & Steve Oliff; and Joe Quesada & Danny Miki.

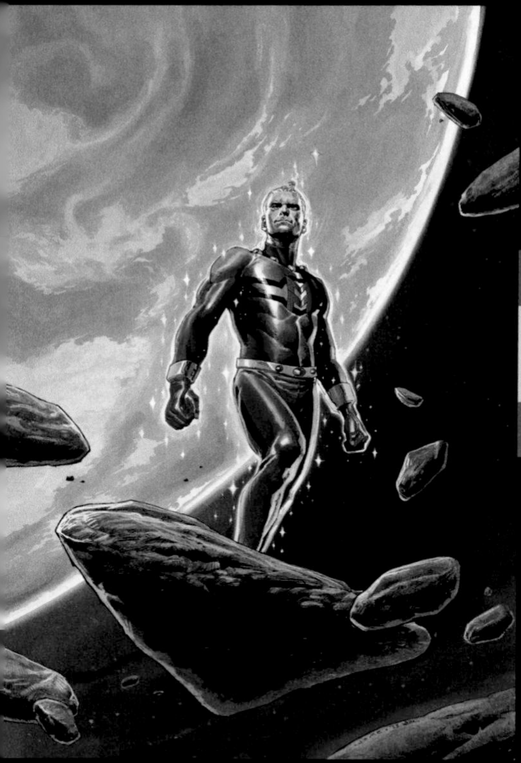

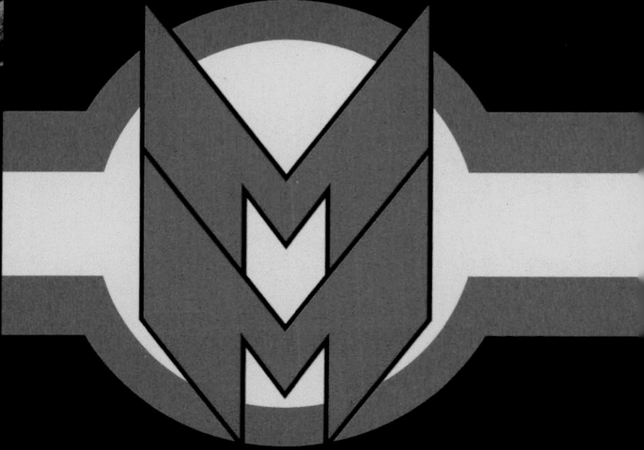

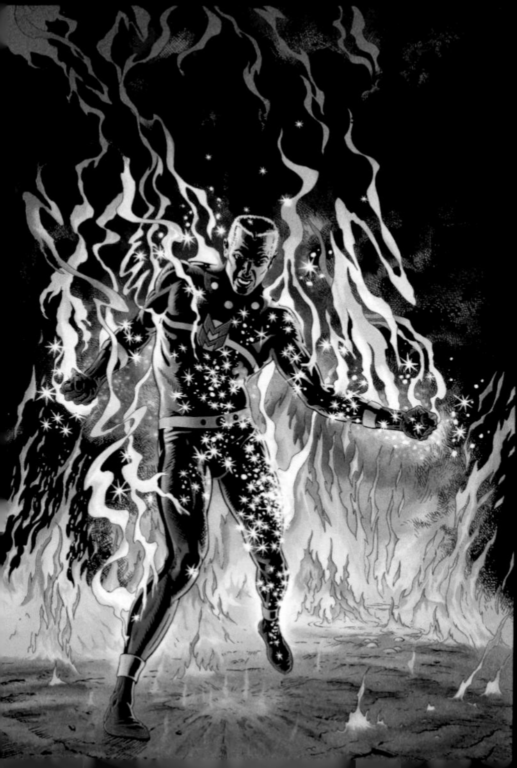

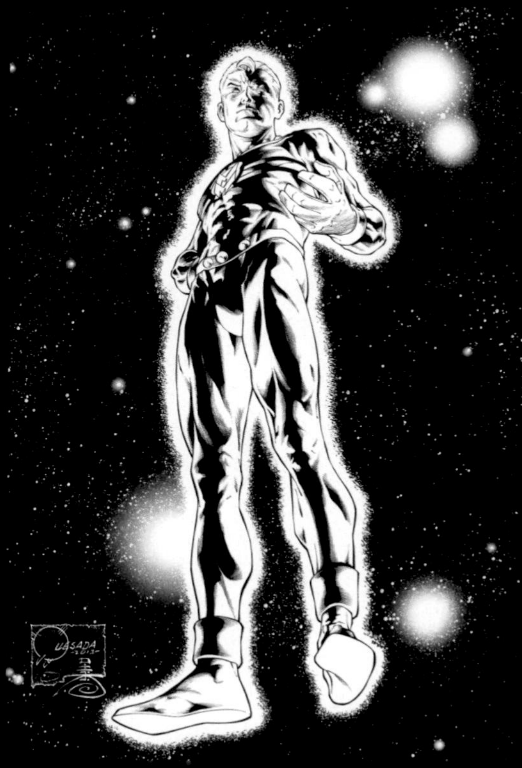

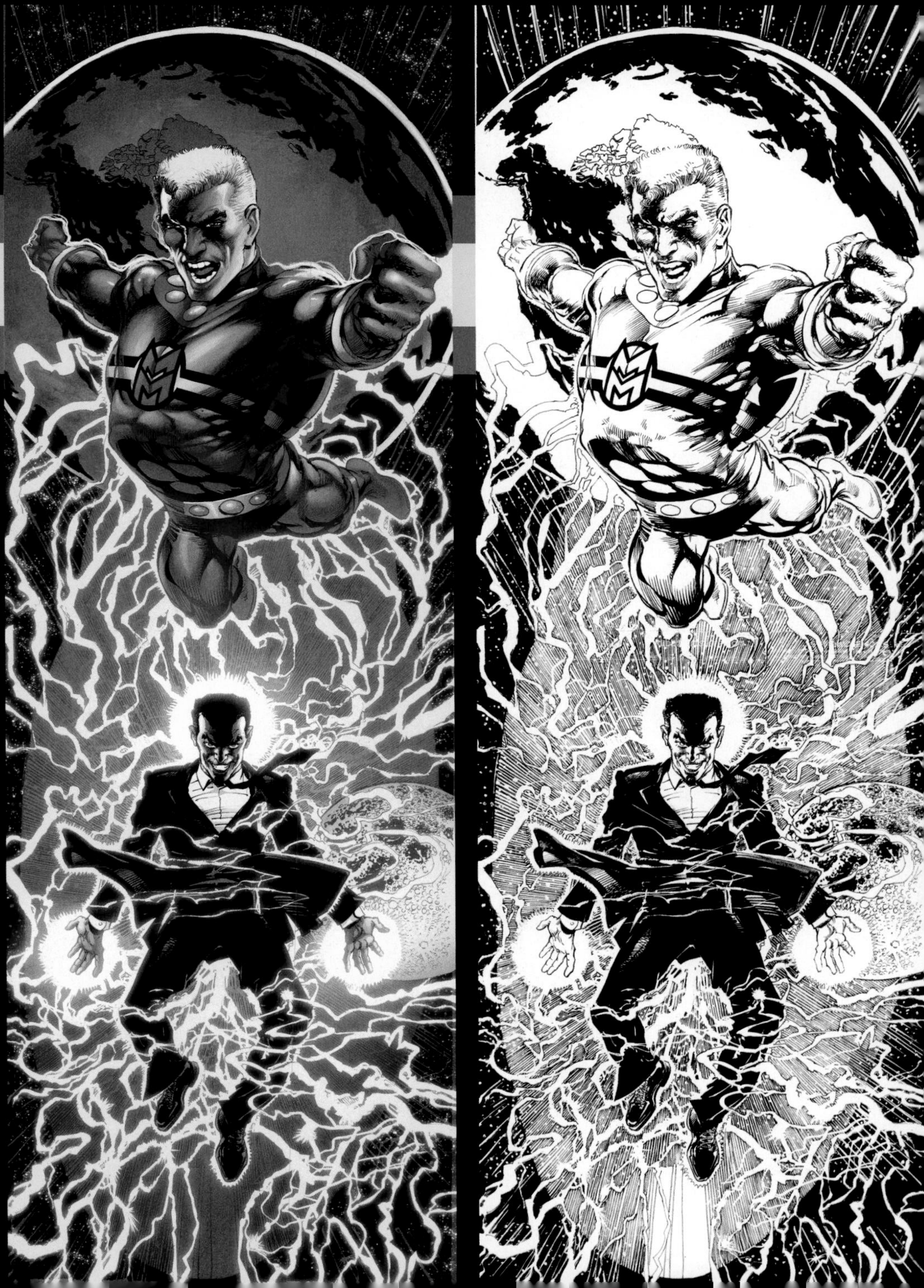

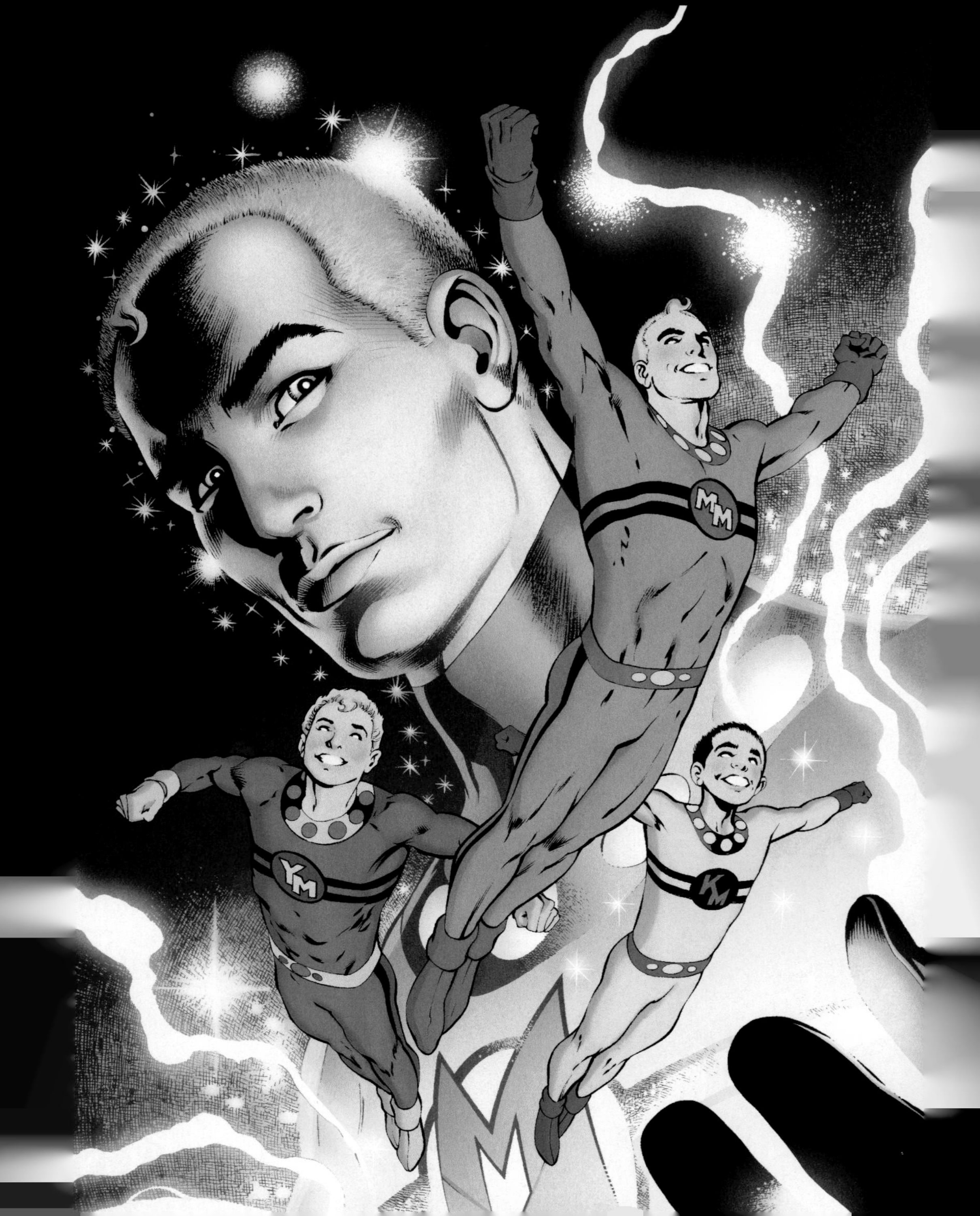
MM
YM
KM

Miracleman #2 (2014) variant cover art (clockwise from top left) by Arthur Adams & Peter Steigerwald; Mike Perkins & Andy Troy; Alan Davis & Mark Farmer; and Mike McKone & Frank Martin.

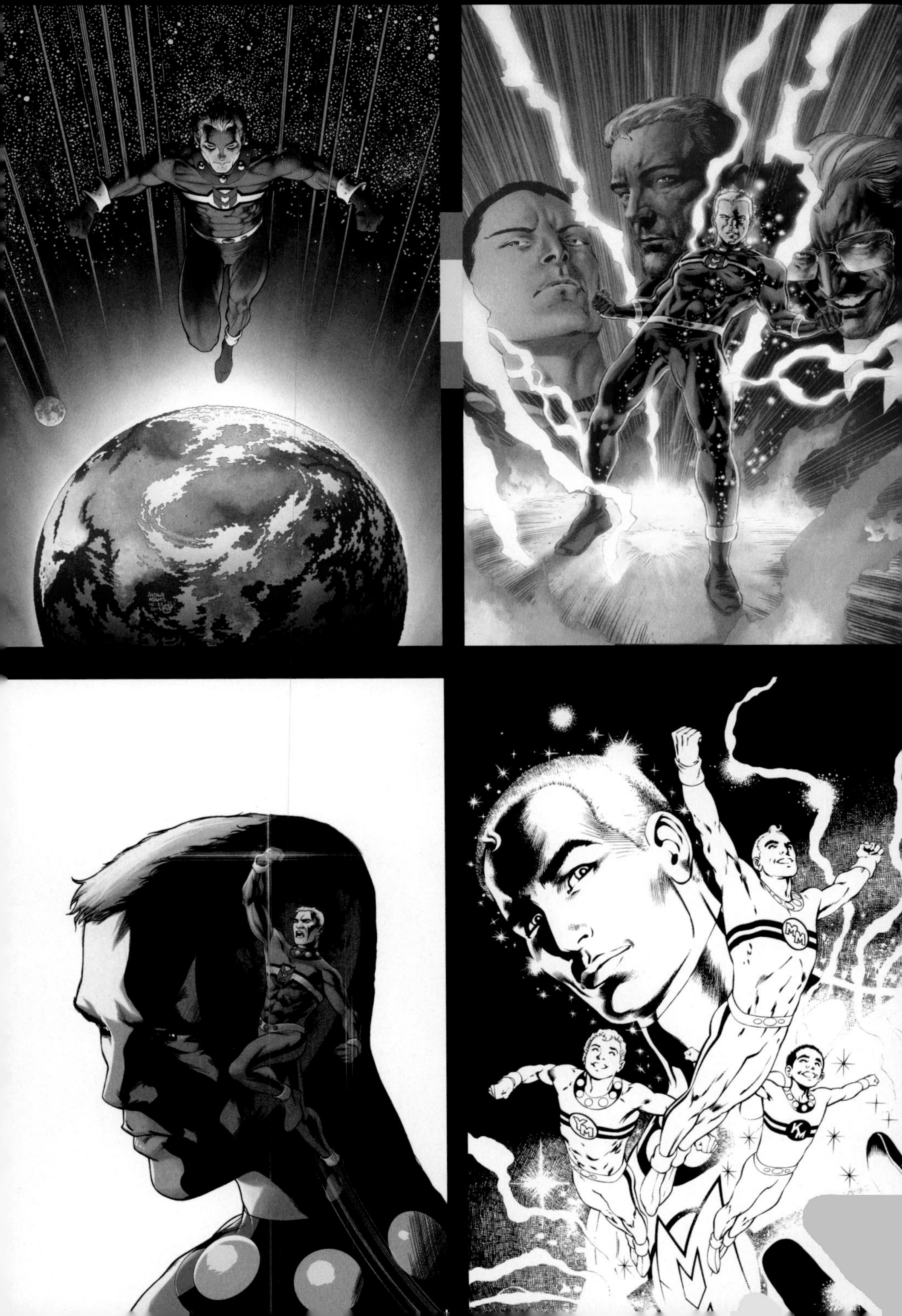
MM
YM
KM

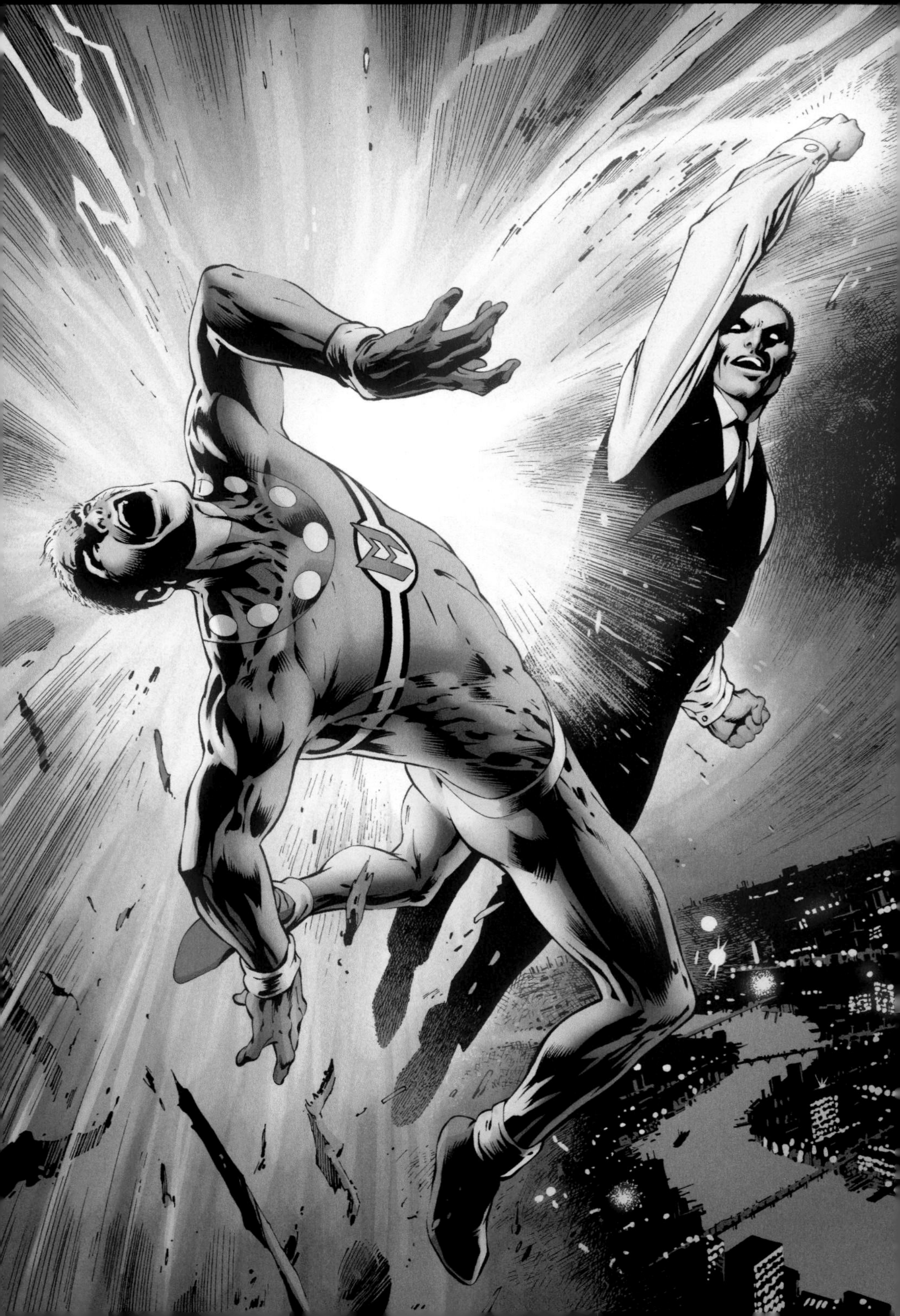

Miracleman #3 (2014) variant cover art (clockwise from top-right) by Pablo Rivera; Mike Deodato & Rain Beredo; and J.G. Jones & Laura Martin.

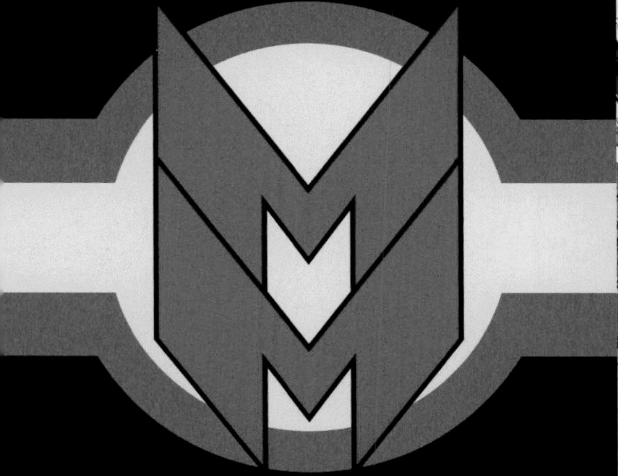

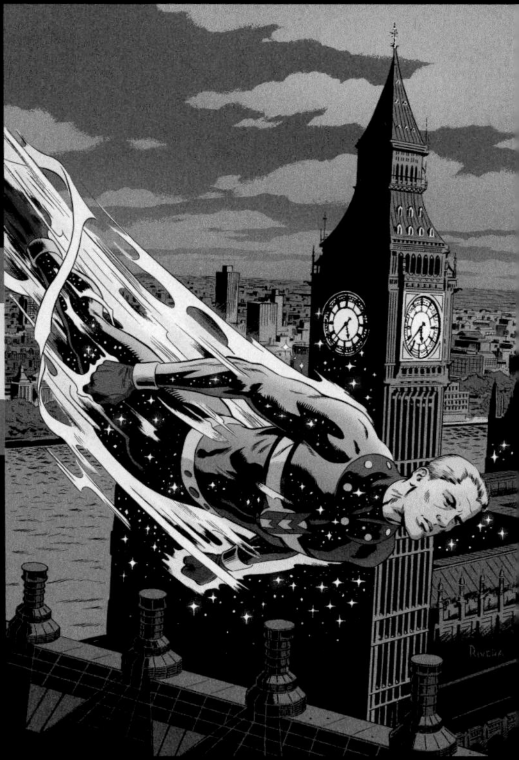

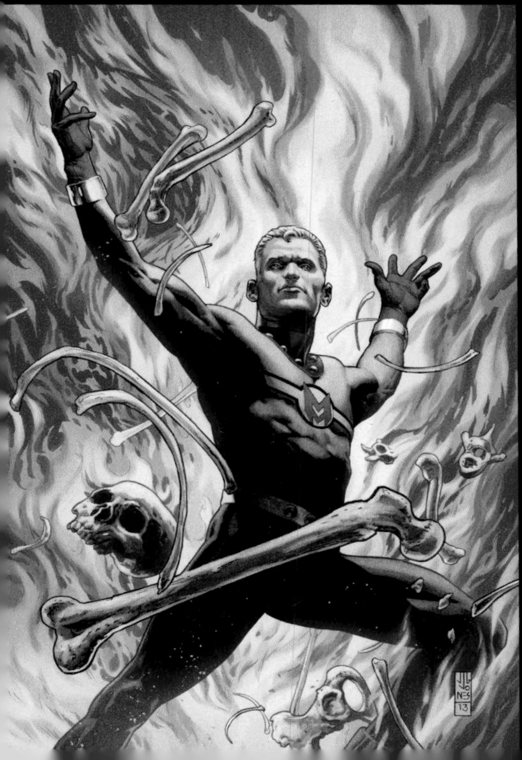

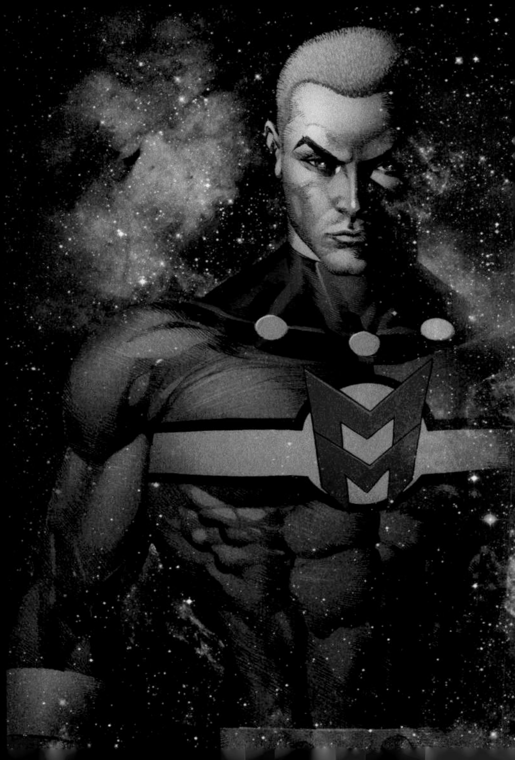

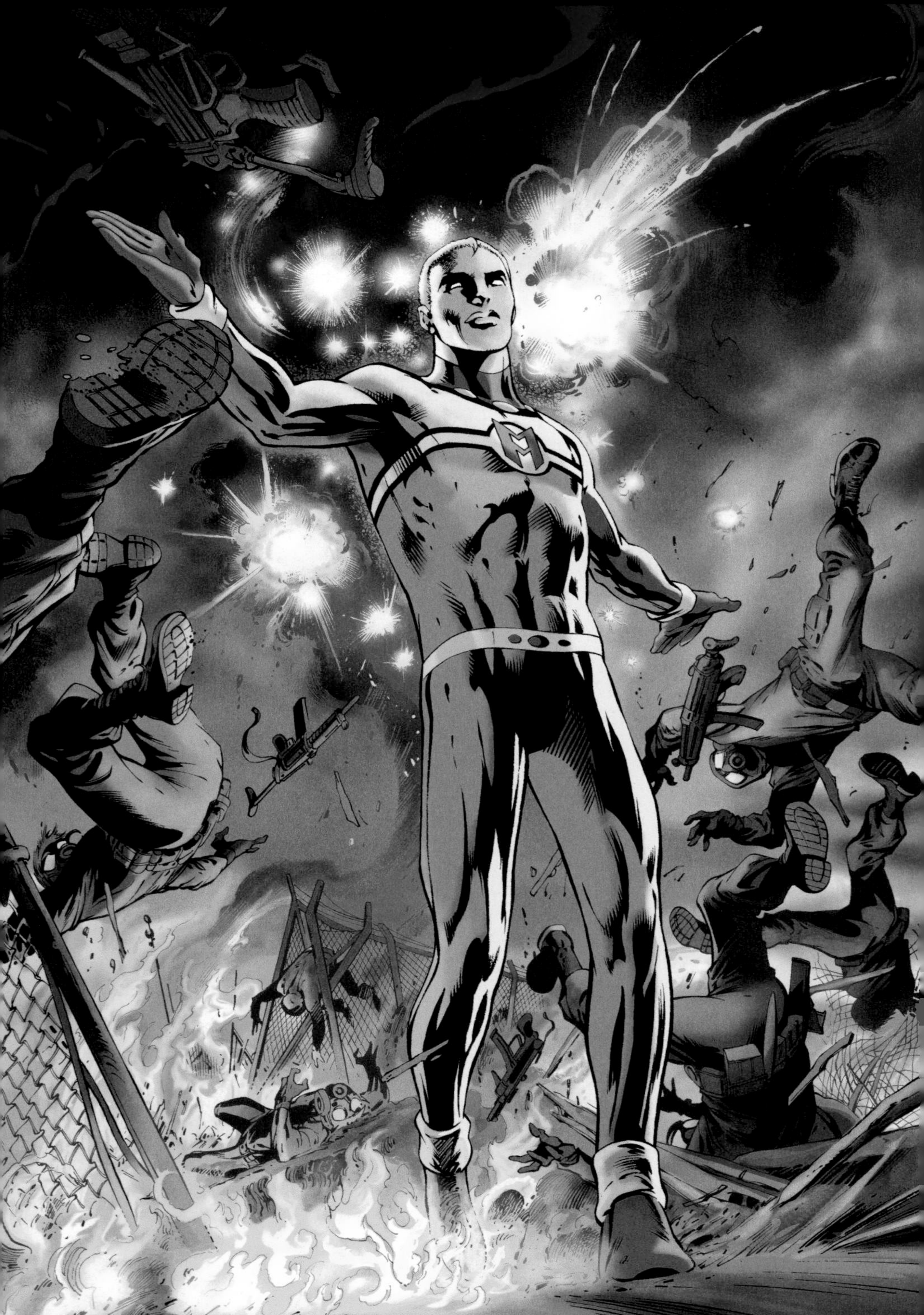

Miracleman #4 (2014) variant cover art (clockwise from top-right) by John Tyler Christopher; Gerald Parel; and Bryan Hitch & Dean White.

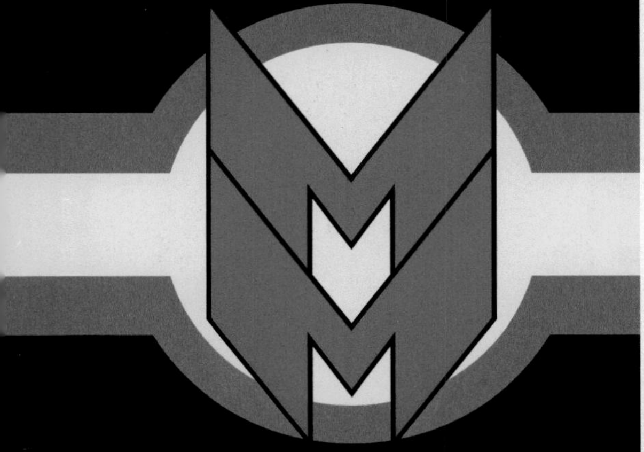

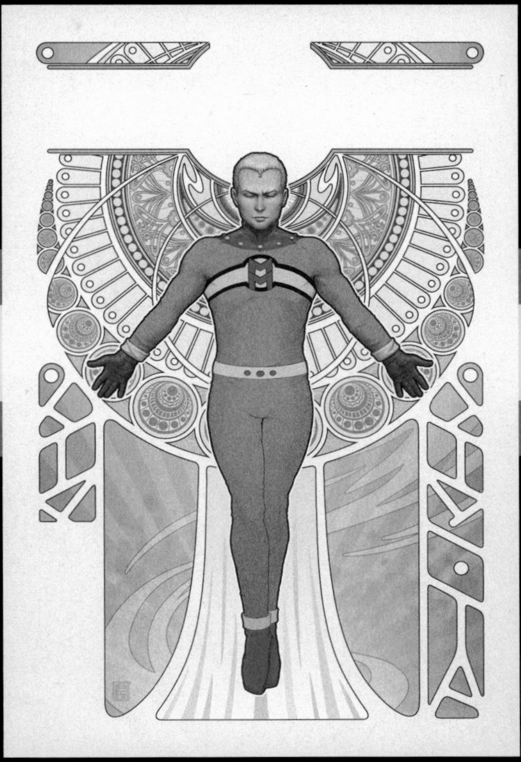

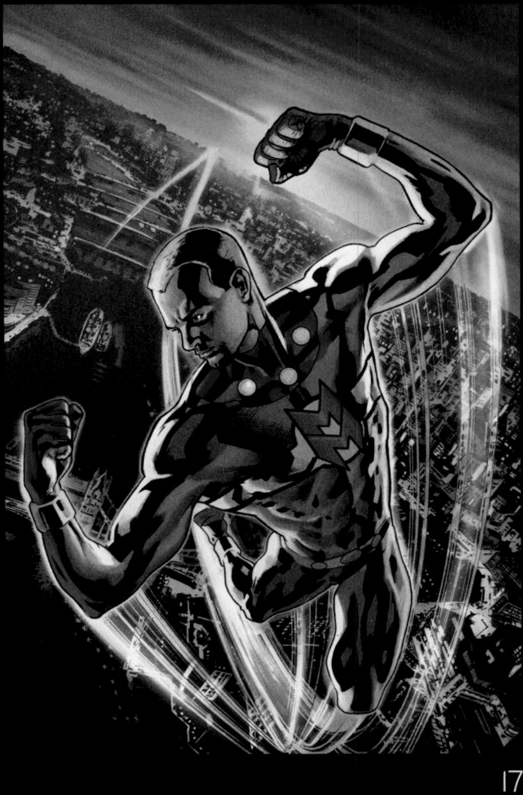

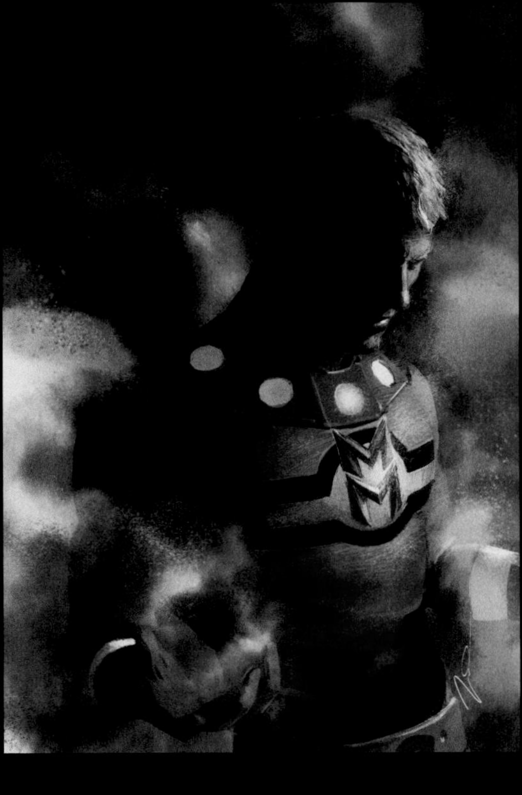

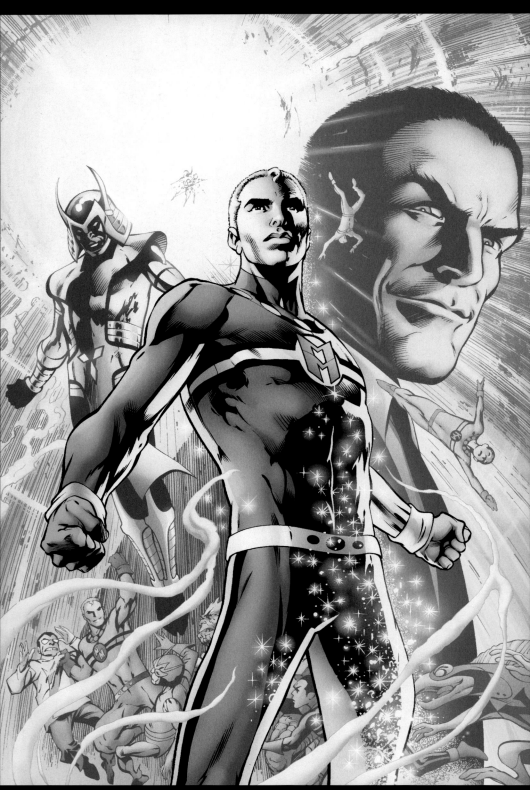

Miracleman Book One: A Dream of Flying (2014) cover art by Alan Davis & Laura Martin.